# Java Graphics for Games 1:
# **JavaFX Line, Shape and Color**

Recipes and techniques for creating 2D images using JavaFX

**Mike Ohlson de Fine**

# Java Graphics for Games 1:

# **JavaFX Line, Shape and Color**

Mike Ohlson de Fine



First published: July, 2017

Published by Mike Ohlson de Fine.

Mike.ohlsondefine@gmail.com

ISBN 978-0-620-76434-6

# DEDICATION

I humbly dedicate this book to my wife Suzy.
Suzy for love, forbearance and patience. I love you Suzanne.

Also to all the warriors of the Open Source Ideals.

# PREFACE

This book is a collection of working Java programs that give us the ability to create two-dimensional images and drawings on our computer screen.

We start with the simplest possible programs and basic, clear explanations. We systematically build up a set of software techniques that allow us to draw and color practically any shape on a computer screen.

JavaFX is the best Java graphics library. A library in the context of computer languages is a collection of programs that make the language useful – they are the tools that allow us to create useful and beautiful things. Although it has been around for a good few years, JavaFX is badly documented on the internet. Java is a complex language that necessarily carries a lot of historical baggage with it. For the novice teaching themselves Java by using the internet is a mild nightmare – it is not unlike trying to build a fast sports car using components from a large scrap yard.

The internet is full of technical blogs containing examples of Java and JavaFX code examples. A lot of them are rubbish – of you try to run them they will not compile. Many of the official "java docs" pages have errors and are sometimes misleading. They also have numerous spelling and grammatical errors. One exception is the "java2s.com" website. It is rather excellent.

Much of its syntax or rules, of grammar, are derived from C and C++. However this is only a surface impression because constructing Java programs is very, very different because it is designed to run on any computer platform. A computer platform is the combination of motherboard hardware together with the software operating system that controls the hardware. In order to do this Java needs to make all computers look the same. It does this by running on a virtual machine, called the "Java Virtual Machine" or JVM. So there is a JVM for each different type of computer or architecture.

Another complicating factor is Java's legacy, its inherited attributes from the past. It was intended to be able to run on any device connected to the internet. So from around 1995 thousands of engineering man-hours were dedicated to writing Java programs all over the world. Today, in 2017, there are an estimated 9 million Java developers on Earth. Java would lose its popularity and fade into obscurity if it did anything that stopped all the old code from working. Java also has to introduce new features in order to remain popular and useful. Therefore it has to somehow match up old and new code instructions – this is what makes Java so difficult to learn. The old legacy features are mixed in with more modern techniques in a way that makes the code seem overly complicated and tangled in design. It is extremely difficult to understand a large program easily just by reading the source code.

In this book we accept this harsh reality. We try to clarify key concepts by using visual analogies and metaphors. However this is not a primer on the Java language as such. Our aim is to put Java code for working graphics into the hands of the reader as easily as possible. So you dear reader are invited and urged to take the code and hack it into different forms for your own fun and edification. It is free and open source. If you want to make money from it, do that, with the author's blessing. Allow others to do the same.

So firstly this is a cookbook of recipes of Java programs that enable the reader to do all kinds of interesting things with drawings and images . We assume the readers are not experienced programmers – this book is written for the novice who is impatient to do visually interesting things on their computer screens. This foundation, together with the other books in this series are designed in the end to allow the reader to become a competent creator of games and simulations.

The Java programs are designed to be self contained. Simply copy-pasting them into an editor and then executing them should result in immediate execution.

The plan of this book is as follows:

Chapter 1 **Getting Started with Java**

The central design concept of Java is that it would be a language that could run on any computing device. A Java with JavaFX source code program is cleaner and more logical than Java programs that used the outdated AWT and Swing graphics libraries.

The structure of a typical JavaFX graphics application is explained with reference to a circus show with stages, scenes and performers.

Chapter 2 **JavaFX Graphics Primitives**

Primitives are the fundamental drawn shapes like lines, curves, circles. ellipses, rectangles, polygons. A reference example of each primitive is given as a back-to-basics handbook.

Chapter 3 **Lines and Polylines**

Lines can be styled by width, dash patterns, end cap styles, color. Shapes enclosed by straight line segments can also be filled with various colors, a chosen degree of transparency, fill patterns and shading variations. These same attributes apply to all the other graphic primitives.

Chapter 4 **Rectangles**

Examples of the outline and fill style possibilities are given, including gradient fill patterns. The different ways of packaging different Java classes together to make an a single applications are given.

Chapter 5 **Color**

The complexities of color description and specification are dealt with in detail. Color terminology like brightness, hue and saturation are explained. The simplest and most consistent way of specifying color is suggested. Ways of mixing colors and transforming one color into another are shown.

Chapter 6 **Circles, Ellipses**

Use of the various constructor for circles and ellipses are explained. Using Java arrays to construct families of similar shapes are demonstrated.

Chapter 7 **Polygons**

Polygons composed of many straight line segments are the most obvious way of drawing complex shapes. In chapters 9, 10, and 11 we see there are better ways to draw complex shapes but a polygon is a good place to begin. The methods of deriving sub-shapes by getting the intersection, the subtraction or the union of two shapes is demonstrated.

Chapter 8 **Arcs**

The basic principles of arc drawing are demonstrated. Arcs are used a lot in constructing the much used pie charts in the business world.

Chapter 9 **Quadratic Curves**

The construction and behavior of quadratic bezier curves is demonstrated. Quadratic curves may be thought of as the younger brother of Cubic Bezier curves, the subject of the next chapter.

Chapter 10 **Cubic Curves**

Cubic Bezier curves are the most important and useful graphic primitive available. Using only cubic curves absolutely any two dimensional drawn shape can be made. In the next chapter on paths we see how this can be done with relative ease.

Chapter 11 **Paths**

The key to creating absolutely any known shape is the JavaFX path. With a view to being able to capture and reproduce drawings created in a vector drawing editor like Inkscape, the techniques for manipulating Java arrays are explained.

The refinement of using multiple randomized copies of a drawing that more closely resembles the results of drawing with pencils on paper are shown.

Chapter 12 **SVG**

In this chapter we deal firstly with how to capture a drawing in a Vector Graphics editor such as Inkscape. The same principles will apply to any other vector graphics editing package. We see how to convert the resulting captured SVG file into Java arrays. SVG or Scaled Vector Graphics, is the XML standard in web design.

Chapter 13 **Text Control**

Text is a special type of graphic image that has its own unique properties and attributes that are governed by their universal use in written communication.

The control of fonts (typefaces), size, style, alignment color and layout are demonstrated.

Chapter 14 **Image**

The JavaFX Image class deals with raster images – photos, paintings or any image that is not in a vector format. Essentially this chapter deals with jpg, png and gif images – how to retrieve them and how to display them.

Chapter 15 **Layout**

Layout is concerned with how to present graphic objects on a surface. The choices are many: absolute, flow, tile, stack, grid, anchor, border, horizontal, vertical and dialog. There are short examples of each.

Chapter 16 **Visual Effects**

Visual effects are a range enhancements that can be added to graphics: shadows, glows, blurring, reflections, displacement mapping, tones and filters, blending and color filtering.

Chapter 17 **Mouse Control**

When working with graphics the computer mouse is the main user control device rather than the keyboard. This chapter deals with the detail of mouse event handling.

Chapter 18 **User Interface Controls – Part 1**

User interface control covers a large library of classes. Each one offers complex usage options. Learning to use them effectively requires us to experiment with them extensively. In this chapter the following are covered: Button, RadioButton, ToggleButton, CheckBox, ChoiceBox, Slider, ProgressBar, Progress Indicator, ScrollBar, ScrollPane , ComboBox, ListView.

Brief examples of each are given to get us started.

Chapter 19 **User Interface Controls – Part 2**

This chapter is a continuation of the previous one and covers:

TextField, PasswordField, Hyperlink, DatePicker, FileChooser, Menu, Tooltip, Separator, HTMLEditor, Pagination, TableView, TreeView, TreeTableView

Chapter 20 **Geometry Transforms: Rotation, Scaling, Translation and Shear**

JavaFX has standard classes for altering the geometry of shapes which are presented here. Methods of achieving identical results using more fundamental Java code are given.

# Table of Contents

# CHAPTER 1

## GETTING STARTED WITH JAVA

In this chapter we will cover:

1. Where to find Java
2. How to install Java
3. How to verify that Java is working
4. How to write and compile simple Java programs
5. How to run or execute Java programs
6. A brief introduction to JavaFX and reasons for using it

**Introduction: Why Java. Why JavaFX.**

Java was invented in 1991 at Sun Microsystems, a company that no longer exists. Originally it was designed to control set-top boxes for the TV manufacturers and not for the internet at all. The central design concept of Java is that it would be a language that could run on any computing device. The trick is to create a virtual machine in software that appears exactly the same to any compiled Java program. So every different type of computing platform will need its own specially written software Java machine. This software is called the Java Virtual Machine or JVM. This design scheme has been largely successful. Most of the Applications ("Apps") and games that run on Android smart-phones are written in Java. Up until a few years ago writing graphic applications in Java was a nightmare. Fortunately JavaFX changed that. JavaFX is the most recent, modern collection of graphics and user-interface libraries for Java. It will replace Swing. JavaFX goes a long way to simplifying the writing of graphic and user interface code.

There are three major graphics libraries in Java: AWT, Swing and JavaFX. The older AWT and Swing libraries were a nightmare for anyone trying to learn Java for the first time. One had to use a lot of very complex, awkward and seemingly redundant code to achieve basic results. The animation was terrible – jerky and slow.

So thanks to the designers of JavaFX, writing Java with graphics is quicker, simpler and more logical. The programs can be made to look cleaner and more understandable.

Nearly all the programs in this book use JavaFX classes and terminology. For this reason a brief introduction to JavaFX is included so that we have a general idea of the architecture behind Java and JavaFX. We do not need a perfect understanding of every line of code in these examples. Rather we need a general picture, a high altitude view of the ideas of Application, Stage, Scene, Groups and Nodes so that when we come across them we know what they are and where they fit in.

## *The Simplest Old Program that does nothing*

Using pure Java, without any classes from the large library of JavaFX classes, we have this minimalist program below. The terms *application* and *program* mean the same thing. A program or application is a self-contained sequence of Java code that can be compiled and run as a unit.

Here is possibly the shortest Java program we can write. The main thing to note is that every traditional Java application must have this **public static void main(String[] args)** method.

Using JavaFX we do NOT need this method.
*class Nada{    public static void main(String[] args) {    }    }*
However modern applications using JavaFX do not need a main(..) method
Although the available Java Development Systems (JDS) insert this redundant code no doubt to preserve backward compatibility of some kind..

In this book we do not use JDS or any other programming crutches. Rather we try to use logically laid out, clean looking code. It is the ideal to strive for.

## The Simplest Old-style Program that does something

*HellooWorld.java ×

```
// The classic Hello World program!
class HellooWorld {

    public static void main(String[] args) {
       //Write Hello World to the terminal window.
       System.out.println("Hello World!") ;
    }
}
```

This program is a single class with only one method, the **main(...) { }** method. It used to be that every Java program had to have a main method and execution would always start with the main method. Note that with JavaFX the main(...) method is redundant.

**Step 1**

Type the above HelooWorld program into an editor. Editors like gedit automatically use different colors for different types of Java instruction. For example green is used for class, method and variable declarations, blue for comments, pink for strings and grey for the rest. This helps a lot when reading programs.

**Step 2.**

Save the program in your home folder, giving it the name HelooWorld.java. IMPORTANT: Our java program file MUST have the same name as the *class name* inside the file.

**Step 3.**

Compile the program using the following command in the command terminal interface:

***javac HellooWorld.java***

The *javac* command runs the Java compiler that converts our java instructions into intermediate code that has the extension .class. The HellooWorld.class is the code that will run on the virtual machine.

This resulting HellooWorld.class is in a form that the Java Virtual Machine or JVM can interpret and execute.

**Step 4.**

Execute/run the compiled class using the following command:

***Java HellooWorld***

We will know if we have succeeded when we see the following terminal output.

The first line is the compilation step that creates the OldJava_HelloWorld .class that should be able to execute or run on the Java Virtual Machine in your computer.

The second line that results in a "Hello World from old Java!" message being shown on the system terminal is the product of the Java Virtual Machine operating on the OldJava_HelloWorld.class.

Question: How can we be absolutely sure everything worked as it should?
Answer: We received no error messages.

## *Then came JavaFX*

Around 2007 JavaFX was first announced and then introduced in 2008. Version 2 came out in 2011. Version 8 came out in 2014. The examples in this book were all developed and tested on version 8.

Why JavaFX? Trying to learn how to use graphics in applications for a novice is like trying to construct an aircraft using the unlimited resources of the biggest motor car scrapyard in the world – it is neither simple nor logical. The hardest thing to find is the beginning. The end is nowhere in sight. We find that much of the information on the internet is downright misleading. Treat all code examples written before about 2010 with some scepticism. The language has been evolving very quickly and so code much older than six or seven years is likely to be inefficient, hard to understand and even flawed. Because Java has been evolving quite rapidly there is a lot of junk "DNA" of Java around.

There are three major graphics libraries in Java: AWT, Swing and JavaFX. AWT and Swing are yesterday's children and not recommended for modern Java graphics. We will concentrate of JavaFX in this book.

What is different about JavaFX? JavaFX is intended to be the first and final resource for graphics, user interfaces, event handling and media presentation. First we explore the architecture of JavaFX as it applies to programs we will write. There are new concepts and terminology to understand.

As an aid to erecting a mental scaffold we will use the entertainment world and circuses as a metaphor to hold our knowledge together.

**The Circus Analogy: A stage, a scene and a group of performers.**

The Stage is where a performance will take place. The *Group* is the particular collection of performers or actors who will perform in a particular act or scene on the stage. There cannot be more than one group in a scene.

The circus tent is the Application. It is a portable structure made of canvas held up by long poles and ropes. It only becomes real when there are stages, lights and groups of performers inside.

In our analogy we will construct the JavaFX equivalent of the famous three-ring circus from the golden age of circuses. So the JavaFX application we construct will have three stages analogous to the three separate ring-stages shown below.

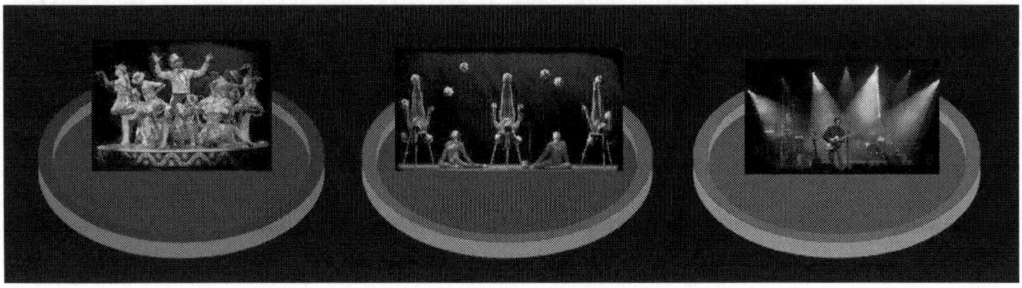

In each ring or stage there are a different *group* of performers: a song-and-dance troupe, five acrobat-jugglers and finally a rock band. Each performer and their equipment needs to be placed on the appropriate stage-ring and then the performance can begin.

In terms of JavaFX software the relationships are illustrated in the code examples below.

## First Make a Stage:

## The Simplest Modern (JavaFX) Program that does nothing

```
import javafx.application.Application;
import javafx.stage.Stage;

public class nothingStage extends Application
{
    public void start(Stage stage)
    { }
}
```

This program will compile and run – it does not have errors. The java instructions have made a Stage object from the Application class. However we will never see it the stage because we have not **shown** it with: *stage.show();*

Note: There is no

```
public static void main(String[] args)
    { Application.launch(args); }
```

It is not needed if we are compiling using "java-8-oracle". Applications churned out by the automatic code writing packages like Java SDK, include the above two redundant lines probably to preserve backward compatibility to older compilers.

So our first JavaFX application does nothing visible and can only be stopped by shutting the terminal from which it was launched. That is not a good way to make programs.

Now we make a stage and show it:

If we go to the circus we want to see some action lights, music, running and jumping. This book does not deal with music or movement (animation). Those are in the next volume. Here and now something visible must happen on our computer screen.

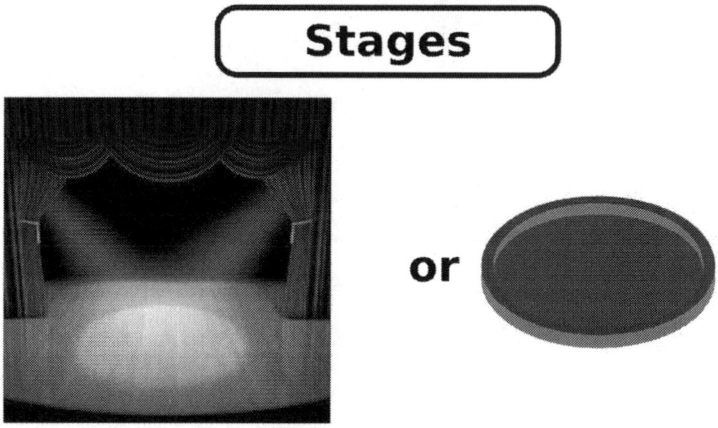

Using the Circus metaphor we create a stage, where performers can later display their entertainments.

The JavaFX stage is produced by the code below.

## *The Simplest Modern (JavaFX) Program*

### (which launches a stage or "window").

```
import javafx.application.Application;
import javafx.stage.Stage;
public class openStage extends Application
{
    public void start(Stage stage)
    { stage.show(); } // Without this instruction no window appears.
};
```

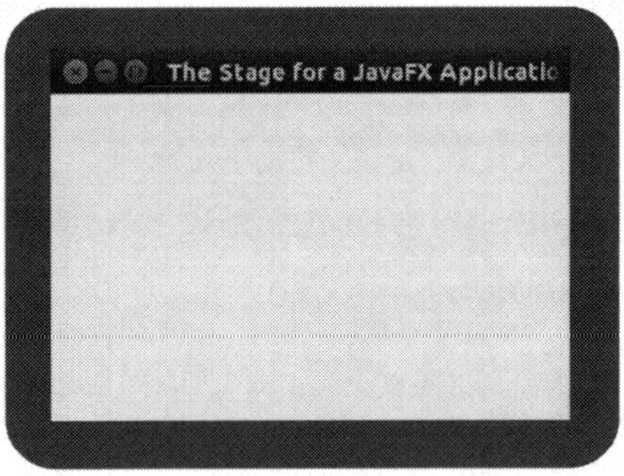


This program will compile and run successfully. And this time we actually created a visible stage or window on the computer screen. Just to remind ourselves what a stage is: the JavaFX stage is analogous to the stage in a theater. A stage in a theater is a raised platform where entertaining performances can take place. Similarly a Stage in JavaFX is an area on a computer display where scenes can be created and graphic objects (the entertainers) can be displayed.

**Remember this about JavaFX – we do not need a main method - despite what many articles and tutorials on the internet say.**

Just to prove a point about how useless (and misleading) information from the internet can be, here is some authentic gobbledegook from Oracle Docs that explains nothing:

"The main() method is not required for JavaFX applications when the JAR file for the application is created with the JavaFX Packager tool, which embeds the JavaFX Launcher in the JAR file. However, it is *useful to include* the main() method so you can run JAR files that were created without the JavaFX Launcher, such as when using an IDE in which the JavaFX tools are not fully integrated. Also, Swing applications that embed JavaFX code require the main() method."

[http://docs.oracle.com/javafx/2/get_started/hello_world.htm].

This is a typical opaque and unhelpful explanation that we encounter when Googling for enlightenment about Java. Experiment yourself. At the end of the day we need to find ways of experimentally discovering how Java works under various circumstances.

This book tries to develop simple code examples that allow us to discover, understand and extend our knowledge. The key to learning is to Hack. Hacking is taking a product and changing the way it behaves by modifying it. Hacking is learning and learning is hacking. You are encouraged to hack the code into different forms. The copyright police are out of this.

## *Display a Graphic Object on a Stage*

To display graphic objects on a stage we have to introduce the JavaFX things called Scenes and Groups.

This is where the circus analogy starts to be useful. On the stage the circus company create a scene. The scene consists of backdrops (scenery), lights, props and spaces where the entertainers can perform. The performers are usually managed in groups. A  bunch of performers are assigned as members of a group. The group is assigned to be a root node and the performers are the children of the root. A caveat to this is that a single graphic object like an image or an action button can be assigned as root nodes by themselves. A root nod is the leader and its children must follow it.

In our circus analogy, high-wire acrobats always perform together as a group and usually have a leader, the principal acrobat. Clowns would be a completely separate group with their own leader, the principal clown.  Similarly in a rock band the principal musician is typically the lead singer.

We will look at a couple of JavaFX examples where we show some graphic objects on a stage. The first graphic object we will show will be some text and in subsequent examples we will add some more objects to the same group. Later we will try more than one group on a stage and then more than one stage in an application. It is easy to get lost so we will proceed in small steps.

Here is the program structure:

1. The program (application) is for display of graphics and is therefore establishes a *Stage*, called primaryStage.

2. We have a single graphic node or object which is  a *label*, called label1.

3. label1 is the child of a root node which is a *Group*, called rootGroup1.

4. A *Scene* is created, called scene1

5. scene1 is set up to appear on primaryStage.

The curtains open with the execution of  *primaryStage.show();* and the spotlight shines on label1.

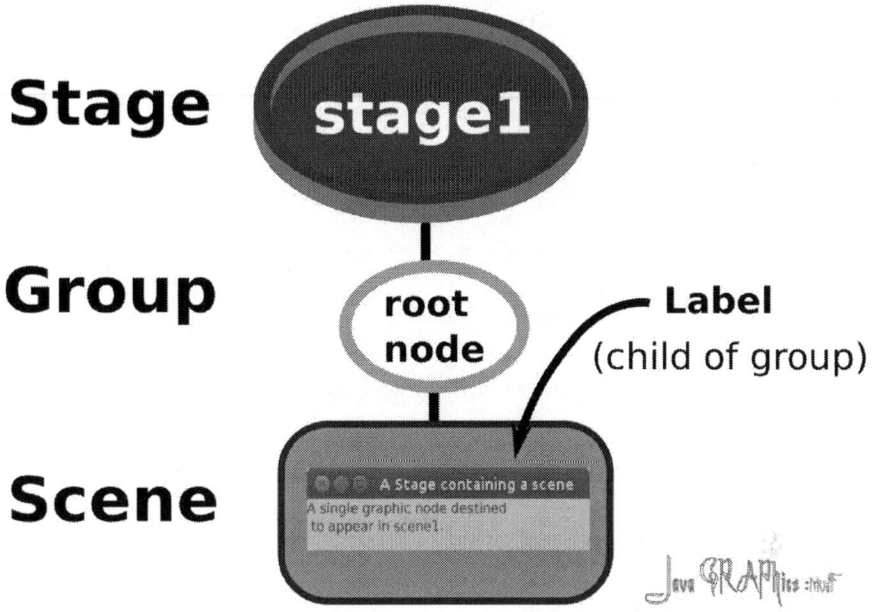


```
// groupSceneStages1.java
/*
Group
A Group node contains the list of visible graphic children.
They are rendered in sequence (as written in the java code) whenever this parent node is
rendered.

Program structure:
1. The program (application) is for display of graphics and is therefore establishes a
Stage, called primaryStage.
2. We have a single graphic node or object which is  a label, called label1.
3. label1 is the child of a root node which is a Group, called rootGroup1.
4. A Scene is created, called scene1
5. scene1 is set up to appear on primaryStage.

The curtains open with the execution of  primaryStage.show(); and the spotlight shines
on label1.
The application must specify the root node for the group.

Stage.
The JavaFX Stage class is the top level JavaFX container.
The primary Stage is constructed by the platform.
Additional Stage objects may be constructed by the application.
```

```
Tested on: java version "java-8-oracle"
Author: Mike Ohlson de Fine
*/
import javafx.application.Application;
import javafx.stage.Stage;
import javafx.scene.Scene;
import javafx.scene.Group;
import javafx.scene.control.Label;
import javafx.scene.paint.*;

public class groupSceneStage1 extends Application {

   public void start(Stage primaryStage) // 1. A Stage is needed for a graphic display.
     {
      primaryStage.setTitle("A Stage containing a scene");
      Group rootGroup1 = new Group(); // 2. Make a root node, the parent of children
nodes.

      Label label1 = new Label("A single graphic node destined\n to appear in scene1.");
      rootGroup1.getChildren().add(label1);

      Scene scene1 = new Scene(rootGroup1, 300, 60, Color.LIGHTBLUE);
      primaryStage.setScene(scene1);
      primaryStage.show();  // Lights, open curtain, action.
      }
}
```

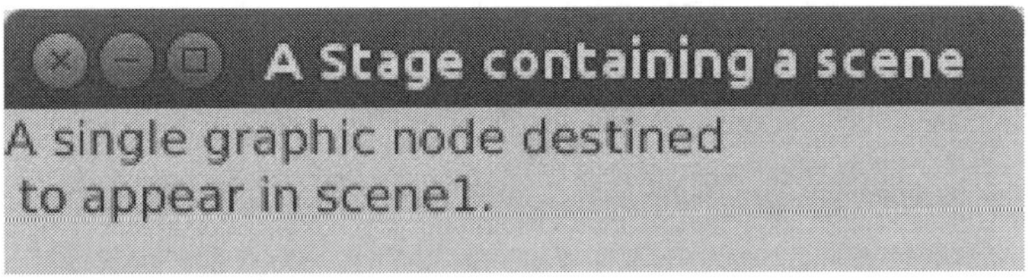


Do nodes always need to be children of a Group? No they do not. A node can be it's own root node if there are no other nodes to be displayed with it.

The following code could be substituted for the “start(...)” method above:

```
public void start(Stage primaryStage) // 1. A Stage is needed for a graphic
display.
```

```
{
primaryStage.setTitle("A Stage containing a scene");
//Group rootGroup1 = new Group();

Label root_label1 = new Label("A single graphic node destined\n to
appear in scene1.");
//rootGroup1.getChildren().add(label1);
Scene scene1 = new Scene(root_label1, 300, 60, Color.LIGHTBLUE);
primaryStage.setScene(scene1);
primaryStage.show();
}
```

The structure if this program is:

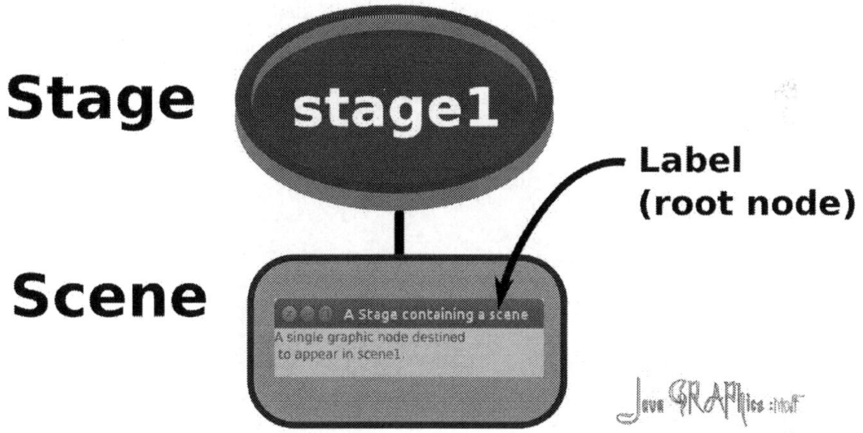


## *Groups of Graphic Objects*

Now we are going to look at how a collection of graphic objects can be parceled out into groups and how those groups can be managed.

To keep the code simple we are only going to use text labels and circles as our graphic objects. Later we will introduce other geometric shapes as well.

### Illustrating this using the Circus Metaphor

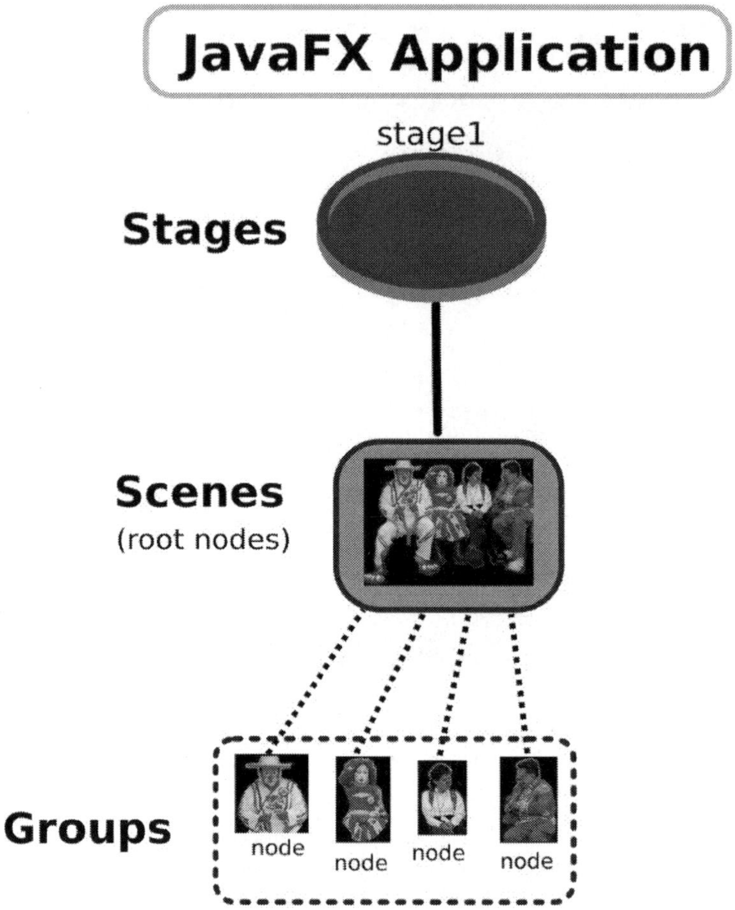


Question: Can we display more than one scene on the same stage? The answer is a qualified NO. Each scene actually DOES get displayed on the stage but not for very long. This is because the Java instructions are executed in strict sequence. We attempt this below and discover only the last *primaryStage.setScene(scene1);* statement stays visible long enough for us to see it.

Compile and run the code below in two different ways. First run it exactly as printed. The second time remove the comment "//" symbol at the beginning of the line

//primaryStage.setScene(scene1); // Try un-commenting this.

The first time we run it the display is:

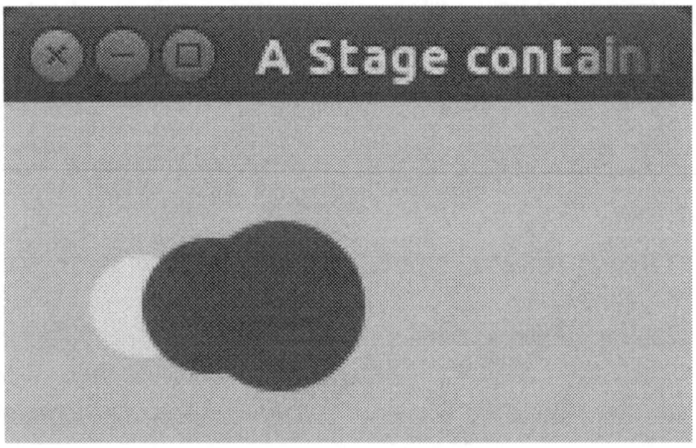


And the second time the display is:

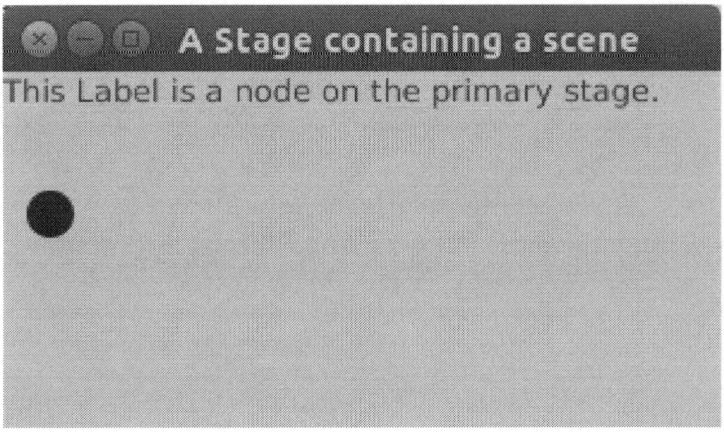


Later in the book we work on a way around this using separate panes (like panes of glass stacked on top of each other.). Note also if some kind of time delay instruction were executed between the two instructions then we would see the first scene for the duration of the delay then the second scene would take over.

```
// groupSceneStage3.java
/*
Group 5 graphic objects together.
A Group node contains the list of visible graphic children.
They are rendered in sequence (as written in the java code) whenever this
parent node is rendered.

Tested on: java version "java-8-oracle"
Author: Mike Ohlson de Fine
*/
```

```
import javafx.application.Application;
import javafx.stage.Stage;
import javafx.scene.Scene;
import javafx.scene.Group;
import javafx.scene.control.Label;
import javafx.scene.paint.*;
import javafx.scene.shape.*;

public class groupSceneStage3 extends Application {

  public void start(Stage primaryStage)
    {
    primaryStage.setTitle("A Stage containing a scene");

    Group rootGroup1 = new Group(); // A root node.
    Group rootGroup2 = new Group(); // Another root node.

    Label label1 = new Label("This Label is a node on the primary stage.");
    Circle circ1 = new Circle(20, 60, 10, Color.BLUE);
    Circle circ2 = new Circle(40, 60, 15, Color.YELLOW);
    Circle circ3 = new Circle(60, 60, 20, Color.GREEN);
    Circle circ4 = new Circle(80, 60, 25, Color.RED);

    rootGroup1.getChildren().add(label1);
    rootGroup1.getChildren().add(circ1);

    rootGroup2.getChildren().add(circ2);
    rootGroup2.getChildren().add(circ3);
    rootGroup2.getChildren().add(circ4);

    Scene scene1 = new Scene(rootGroup1, 400, 150, Color.LIGHTBLUE);
    Scene scene2 = new Scene(rootGroup2, 300, 100, Color.LIGHTGREEN);
    primaryStage.setScene(scene2);
    //primaryStage.setScene(scene1);  // Try un-commenting this.

    primaryStage.show();
    }
}
```

To see Separate Groups we need Separate Stages.

With reference to our three-ring circus analogy this makes sense. In a real circus you cannot mix the clowns with precision jugglers. The crazy antics of the clowns will interfere with the concentration of the jugglers and the combined act will be a failure.

In the example below we create two stages each with a separate scene being displayed.

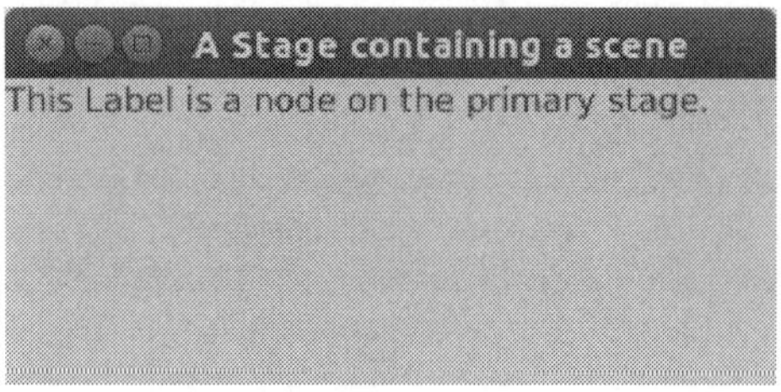


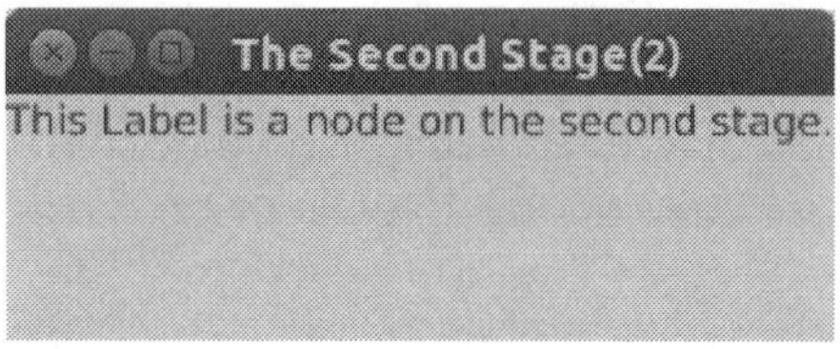


```
// scenes2Stages2.java
/*
Show two stages, each with its separate group.

Tested on: java version "java-8-oracle"
Author: Mike Ohlson de Fine
*/
import javafx.application.Application;
import javafx.stage.Stage;
import javafx.scene.Scene;
import javafx.scene.Group;

import javafx.scene.control.Label;
import javafx.scene.paint.Color;
import javafx.scene.shape.*;

public class scenes2Stages2 extends Application {

  public void start(Stage primaryStage)
    {
     /* The primary stage is instantiated (constructed) automatically
       when the "start()" method executes.
     */
     primaryStage.setTitle("The first Stage containing a scene");

     Group rootGroup1 = new Group();
```

```
        Label label1 = new Label("This Label is a node on the primary stage.");
        rootGroup1.getChildren().add(label1);
        Scene scene1 = new Scene(rootGroup1, 300, 120, Color.LIGHTBLUE)
        primaryStage.setScene(scene1);
        primaryStage.show();

        new SecondStage(); // This constructs the second stage.
        }

    public class SecondStage extends Stage
    {
        SecondStage()
        {
            Group rootGroup2 = new Group();
            setTitle("The Second Stage(2)");
            Label label2 = new Label("This Label is a node on the second stage.");
            rootGroup2.getChildren().add(label2);
            Scene scene2 = new Scene(rootGroup2, 270, 80, Color.PINK);
            setScene(scene2);
            show();
        }
    }
}
```

## How many stages can be added?

Who knows? It is probably limited by the amount of memory available on whatever computing hardware platform we are using.

We can add extra stages by making more classes similar to:

```
public class UmpteenthStage extends Stage
  {
      UmpteenthStage()
      {
          Group rootGroup_umpteen = new Group();
          setTitle("The Umpteenth Stage(N)");
          Label labelN= new Label("This Label is a node on the umpteenth
stage.");
          rootGroup_umpteen.getChildren().add(labelN);
          Scene sceneN = new Scene(rootGroup_umpteen, 270, 80, Color.GREY);
```

```
            setScene(sceneN);
            show();
        }
    }
}
```

We would have to remember to make instances of the extra stages using ***new*** keywords in the start method:

```
public void start(Stage primaryStage)

    {
     primaryStage.setTitle("A Stage containing a scene");

     Group rootGroup1 = new Group();
     Label label1 = new Label("This Label is a node on the primary stage.");
     rootGroup1.getChildren().add(label1);
     Scene scene1 = new Scene(rootGroup1, 300, 120, Color.LIGHTBLUE);
     primaryStage.setScene(scene1);
     primaryStage.show();

     new SecondStage();  // Make instances of extra stages here. Add as many as desired.
     new ThirdStage();
    etc.
    etc.
    etc.
     new UmpteenthStage();
     }
```

The output for three stages would be similar to:

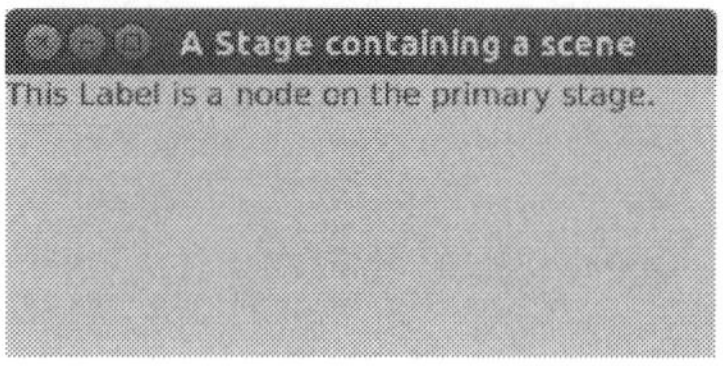


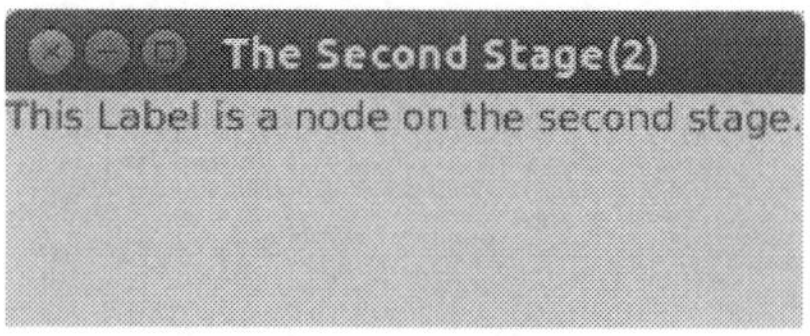


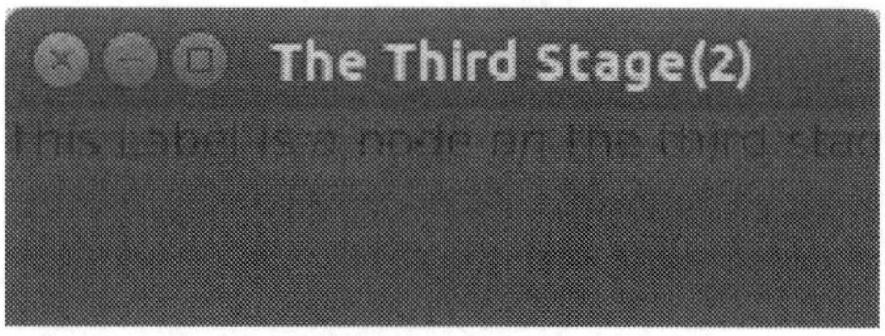

## Using the Circus Metaphor

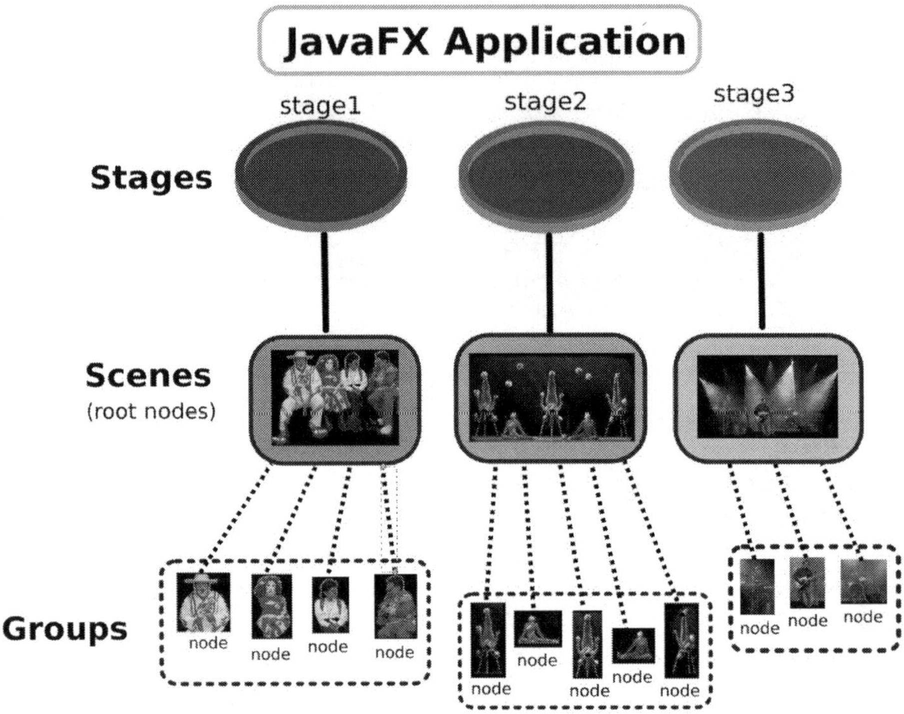


### *Panes can be used instead of Groups*

In our endeavor to keep things simple we have collected our graphic bits and pieces, called nodes, into JavaFX *Groups.* For the moment we can use Pane and Group interchangeably.

A Group node contains a list of children that are rendered in order whenever this node is rendered.

A Group will take on the collective bounds of its children and cannot change this collective size.

Any transform, effect, or state applied to a Group will be applied to all children of that group.

# A footnote on confusion – old Java graphics and JavaFX.

Creating graphics in old Java can very, very confusing because there are so many different ways of doing things. Googling our questions and hoping for clear answers is a nightmare because a lot of the information is outdated and much advice is plain misleading. Many of the ways that do actually work are old, unnecessarily complicated and awkward to use. When you google a question like "How do you draw a line" you get hundreds or even thousands of answers and many of them incorrect.

There are three completely different class libraries that we have to choose between when we want to draw a simple line:

- the AWT library,
- the Swing library
- or the JavaFX library.

They all seem to do very similar jobs until we try to animate graphics, which is essential if we are eventually going to write video game programs.

Through bitter experience I have discovered that trying to animate graphic *objects* (what java documentation calls *nodes*) using AWT or Swing is a waste of time because we can only produce very jerky, un-smooth animated motion.
The only way to get smooth motion is to use the JavaFX class libraries. So in this book we will stick to using JavaFX classes and their methods, knowing that eventually we are going to be creating video games that can be played on desktops, laptops, tablets, smartphones, car dashboards and Rasberry Pi's. A Rasberry Pi is an ultra small computer that can fit in small cigarette packet!

So, as previously mentioned, the metaphor for the structural architecture used in creating animated graphics using JavaFX is the old fashioned theater of entertainment where we sit in the audience and watch the performers on a stage. The terms *stage, scene, group* are part of the Java code we have been writing. Conceptually the stage is the frame or 2D space where the action will take place. The scene is where the performers such as actors, singers, dancers, musicians perform their acts. Groups are the collections of performing individuals whose actions are coordinated with each other – like a troupe of jugglers.

Just a cautionary note here. This book is how to create graphic objects that do not move. This book is not about animation. That is the focus of the next book in this series. If you like hacking code I encourage you wholeheartedly to take the code apart and put it back together differently to do new, different and surprising things.

## What is JavaFX and why use it?

JavaFX is intended eventually to replace Swing as the standard Graphic-User-Interface (GUI) library for Java. JavaFX works on desktop computers and web browsers on Microsoft Windows, Linux, and Apple's iOS as well as Android. The Oracle company, who purchased Java, do not try to support all the hardware existing but the Open Source community of volunteers are developing support for many popular hardware/operating system platforms.

JavaFX is far better than Swing at handling graphics because it uses a hardware-accelerated graphics pipeline called *Prism* to do the rendering job. In other words JavaFX is designed to make good use of fast, powerful modern hardware. Rendering, the process of placing images onto screens, is hardware processor intensive and best handled by the underlying operating system and not the Java Virtual Machine. Software rendering by JavaFX is also possible if the hardware graphics is not available. Prism is designed to use either a hardware or software rendering mechanism and, behind the scenes, uses DirectX or OpenGL to fully accelerate graphic usage. DirectX or OpenGL are software libraries for making 3D images. However, on encountering an incompatible underlying piece of hardware, Prism will fall back to Java2D (software) for rendering.

## Important Differences between JavaFX and Swing

Just for the record here are the main reasons programmers need to be able to use JavaFX. Oracle has decided that it will dominate Java's future in graphics and user interfaces.

**1. The Way Elements are Grouped Together.**

JavaFX uses the theater model to represent the top level containers of an application.

A stage represents the highest level container — typically, a window. The individual controls and other components that make up the user interface are contained in a scene . An application can have more than one scene, but only one of the scenes can be displayed on the stage at any given time.

A scene contains a scene graph, which is an important concept in JavaFX. The scene graph is a collection of all the elements that make up a user interface — groups, layouts, controls, and shapes. These objects are called nodes and are all derived from the Node class. The Node class has many useful features and capabilities that are automatically made available to any object that we can add to our user interface. For example, the Node class defines a setRotate method that allows you to rotate any node in the scene graph.

In Swing, the class that holds your user interface components is called a frame. A frame is essentially an empty window to which you can add a panel, which serves as a container for your user-interface elements. A panel is defined by the JPanel class.

A Swing application is actually a class that extends the JFrame class. To display user-interface components, you add components to a JPanel and then add the panel to the frame.

**2. Layout Management**

In Swing, a layout is associated with a JPanel. The top-level JPanel gives the basic layout for the frame. If you want to nest additional layouts within the top-level layout, you must create additional JPanels, set their associated layouts, and then add them to the higher-level layout.

In JavaFX, layouts are subclasses of the Node class just like controls and shapes. Layouts contain a collection of nodes, and any node contained in a layout can be any kind of node: a control, a shape, or another layout. This scheme is much less cumbersome than Swing's association of layouts with panels.

**3. Event Handling**

Both JavaFX and Swing use event handling to respond to user input events such as mouse movement or the pushing of buttons. Event handling in JavaFX is better designed. It is more consistent than their equivalents in Swing. But the biggest reason that event handling is improved in JavaFX, is because of its reliance on properties.

**4. Properties**

JavaFX uses properties extensively throughout its classes. Simply put, a property is a variable whose value can be observed. You can register a listener with any property, allowing you to write code that's triggered automatically whenever the property changes. In addition, you can bind properties to each other, meaning that if one property value changes, the other property value automatically changes with it.

Because nearly all characteristics of user-interface elements are managed through properties, JavaFX provides event handling that is not possible in Swing. For example, in JavaFX, you can attach an event listener to the color of a shape. If the shape changes color, your event listener code is called and executed.

**5. Skinnibility with Cascading Style Sheets (CSS).**

In graphic programming the word skin refers to the visual look, color, texture etc. of objects.

With JavaFX you can control formatting with Cascading Style Sheets (CSS). Just about every aspect of the appearance of your user interface can be set by a style rule, and you can easily allow the user to select which of several available style sheets to apply to the scene. Thus, you can change the entire appearance of your application with a single method call.

**6. Consistent Controls**

The JavaFX control hierarchy is more complete than Swing's. Both have all the basic controls — buttons, check boxes, combo boxes, and the like. But JavaFX has several controls that Swing doesn't have, such as the collapsible TitledPane control and the Accordion control that arranges multiple TitledPane controls in a stack. And the fact that all these controls are skinnable by CSS gives them a huge advantage over Swing.

**7. Special Effects**

The javafx.scene.effect package contains a number of classes that can easily apply special effects to any node in the scene graph. These classes let you apply shadows, reflections, blurs, and other interesting visual effects that can alter the appearance of your user interface.

**8. Animation**

Animation is possible in Swing, but Swing does not provide any inherent support for it. That is, Swing does not have robust and convenient functions (methods) to make animation simple. To animate a Swing component, you must set up your own timers and build your own logic to perform the animation. The animation will not be smooth.

In contrast, JavaFX has built-in support for sophisticated animations that can be applied to any node in the scene graph. You can use one of several built-in transition classes to perform common animations such as fades, rotations, or motion paths. To construct our own special purpose animtions we can use the KeyFrame and Timeline classes.

### 9. Touch Devices

Swing lacks any support for modern touch devices like smart-phones with their touch-screen and swipe gestures. In contrast, JavaFX has built-in support for common touch gestures such as scrolling, swiping, rotating, and zooming. Handling these events in JavaFX is the same as handling any other type of event: we simply install an event listener on the touch event and then write code that responds appropriately.

### Where to next?

We must have the knowledge and expertise to draw lines, circles, ellipses, rectangles, polygons and complex curves. In addition we also must have complete control of color.

# Chapter 2

## PRIMITIVES

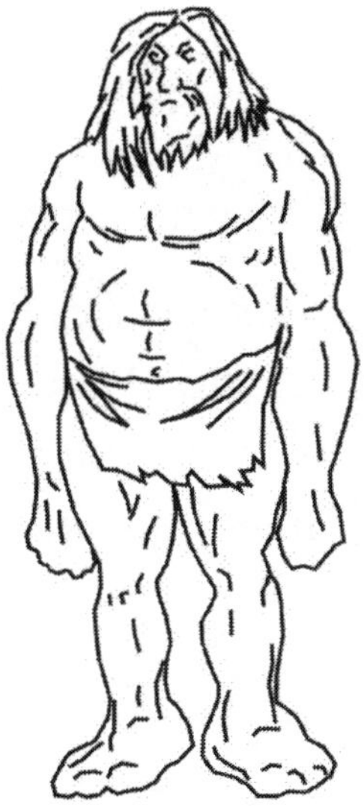

In this chapter we will cover:

The basic (primitive) drawing components of JavaFX. There is a single, simplified example of each of the following primitive JavaFX shapes:

- The line
- The rectangle
- The circle
- The ellipse
- The polyline
- The polygon
- The Quadratic curve

- The Cubic curve
- The path

This chapter is a basic reference set of examples presented in the simplest form. Only default values of line parameters like line width, color and pattern are used. In the chapters that follow the richer complexities of the primitives are expanded on.

The Quick Tour of JavaFX primitives

It is of great assistance to understanding a new field if we can get a some kind of high altitude view, the so-called helicopter view, of the landscape. We do that now. We take in a helicopter view of the graphics primitives (the fundamental shapes) that JavaFX uses. We have reduced them down to very simplified versions.

In subsequent chapter we explore them more deeply.

The examples that follow here are intended to be easy to verify. Not a lot of typing of code is necessary. In each of the 10 examples that follow about 80% of the code is the same in each example. So we do not need to re-type each example – just change the code between the lines //*********************************************.

If you are learning this stuff for the first time it will useful to have a copy of each of the ten examples saved in a folder called something like"javafx_primitives".

Then when we get confused with other complexities we can go back to simple basics to remember how to get the grammar (syntax) correct.

This is handy when we cannot remember exact syntax or when we want to experiment with alternative ways of doing things.

## ***Draw a line!***

**Line(startX, startY, endX, endY) ;**

```
// LineSimplest.java
/*
The class: javafx.scene.shape.Line
Constructor:
Line(startX, startY, endX, endY) ;

Tested on: java version "java-8-oracle"
Author: Mike Ohlson de Fine
*/
import javafx.application.Application;
import javafx.stage.Stage;
import javafx.scene.*;
import javafx.scene.shape.*; // Graphic primitives library.

public class LineSimplest extends Application
{
  public void start(Stage stage)
   {
        Group root = new Group();
     //**********************************************
     Line line1 = new Line(10, 10, 120, 30);
     //**********************************************
     root.getChildren().add(line1);

        Scene scene = new Scene(root, 200, 50);
        stage.setTitle("Line on Stage (canvas), JavaFX");
        stage.setScene(scene);
        stage.show();
   }
}
```

**Points to note**

It is important to note that the 'computer-graphics' way of locating positions on a drawing area using pairs of x, y coordinates has the world turned upside down. When the y (vertical) values get larger the locations of points move downwards as shown in the accompanying pictures.

An artist would find the coordinates used in Java confusing – the picture would be upside down.

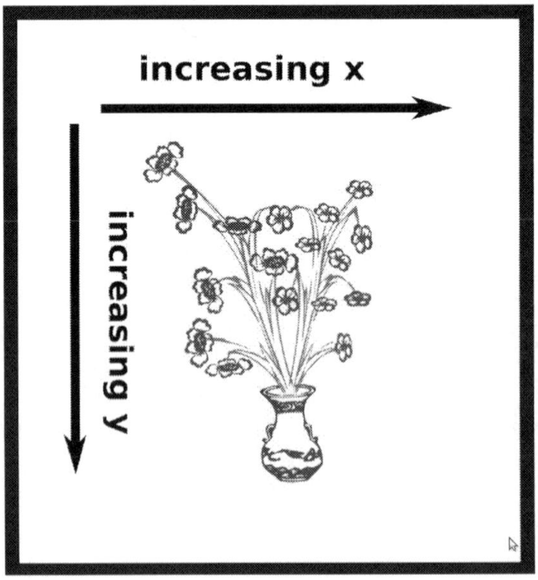


Inside a JavaFX pane the drawn shape starts at x=0, y=0 which is the top-left corner.

# A Circle

## Circle(centerX, centerY, radius);

```
// CircleSimplest.java
/*
Circle : class: javafx.scene.shape.Circle
An instance of Circle with given position and size.
Constructor:
Circle(centerX, centerY,  radius);

Tested on: java version "java-8-oracle"
Author: Mike Ohlson de Fine
*/
import javafx.application.Application;
import javafx.stage.Stage;
import javafx.scene.*;
import javafx.scene.shape.*; // Graphic primitives library.

public class CircleSimplest extends Application
{
   public void start(Stage stage)
   {
         Group root = new Group();
      //****************************************
      Circle circle1 = new Circle(100, 50, 40);
      //****************************************
      root.getChildren().add(circle1);

         Scene scene = new Scene(root, 200, 100);
         stage.setTitle("Circle on Stage (canvas), JavaFX");
         stage.setScene(scene);
         stage.show();
   }
}
```

# *An Ellipse*

**Ellipse(centerX, centerY, radiusX, radiusY);**

```
// EllipseSimplest.java
/*
Ellipse : class: javafx.scene.shape.Ellipse
-------------------------------------
An instance of an Ellipse with given position and size.
Constructor:
Ellipse(centerX, centerY, radiusX, radiusY);

Tested on: java version "java-8-oracle"
Author: Mike Ohlson de Fine
*/
import javafx.application.Application;
import javafx.stage.Stage;
import javafx.scene.*;
import javafx.scene.shape.*; // Graphic primitives library.

public class EllipseSimplest extends Application
{
   public void start(Stage stage)
   {
        Group root = new Group();
      //****************************************
      Ellipse ellipse1 = new Ellipse(100, 50, 80, 20);
      //****************************************
      root.getChildren().add(ellipse1);

         Scene scene = new Scene(root, 200, 100);
         stage.setTitle("Ellipse on Stage (canvas), JavaFX");
         stage.setScene(scene);
         stage.show();
   }
}
```

# *A Rectangle*

## Rectangle(x, y, width, height);

```
// RectangleSimplest.java
/*
Rectangle : class: javafx.scene.shape.Rectangle
-------------------------------------
An instance of a Rectangle with given position and size.
Constructor:
Rectangle(x, y, width, height);

Tested on: java version "java-8-oracle"
Author: Mike Ohlson de Fine
*/
import javafx.application.Application;
import javafx.stage.Stage;
import javafx.scene.*;
import javafx.scene.shape.*; // Graphic primitives library.

public class RectangleSimplest extends Application
{
   public void start(Stage stage)
   {
        Group root = new Group();
     //****************************************
     Rectangle rectangle1 = new Rectangle(30, 20, 80, 20);
     //****************************************
     root.getChildren().add(rectangle1);

         Scene scene = new Scene(root, 160, 50);
         stage.setTitle("Rectangle on Stage (canvas), JavaFX");
         stage.setScene(scene);
         stage.show();
   }
}
```

# *A Polygon*

## Polygon(x1, y1, x2, y2, x3, y3, etc);

```
// PolygonSimplest.java
/*
Polygon : class: javafx.scene.shape.Polygon
-------------------------------------
An instance of a Rectangle with given position and size.
Constructor:
Polygon(x1, y1, x2, y2, x3, y3, etc);

Tested on: java version "java-8-oracle"
Author: Mike Ohlson de Fine
*/
import javafx.application.Application;
import javafx.stage.Stage;
import javafx.scene.*;
import javafx.scene.shape.*; // Graphic primitives library.

public class PolygonSimplest extends Application
{
   public void start(Stage stage)
   {
         Group root = new Group();
     //**************************************************
     Polygon polygon1 = new Polygon(10, 10, 50, 50, 100, 10);
     //**************************************************
     root.getChildren().add(polygon1);

          Scene scene = new Scene(root, 160, 60);
          stage.setTitle("Polygon on Stage (canvas), JavaFX");
          stage.setScene(scene);
          stage.show();
   }
}
```

# A Polyline

## Polyline(x1, y1, x2, y2, x3, y3, etc);

```
// PolylineSimplest.java
/*
class: javafx.scene.shape.Polyline
```

```
-------------------------------------
An instance of a Polyline with given positions.
Constructor:
Polyline(x1, y1, x2, y2, x3, y3, etc);

Tested on: java version "java-8-oracle"
Author: Mike Ohlson de Fine
*/
import javafx.application.Application;
import javafx.stage.Stage;
import javafx.scene.*;
import javafx.scene.shape.*; // Graphic primitives library.

public class PolylineSimplest extends Application
{
   public void start(Stage stage)
   {
        Group root = new Group();
      //*********************************************************
      Polyline polyline1 = new Polyline(10, 10, 50, 50, 100, 10);
      //*********************************************************
      root.getChildren().add(polyline1);

        Scene scene = new Scene(root, 160, 60);
        stage.setTitle("Polyline on Stage (canvas), JavaFX");
        stage.setScene(scene);
        stage.show();
   }
}
```

# A QuadCurve

## QuadCurve(startX, startY, controlX, controlY, endX, endY)

**// QuadCurveSimplest.java**

```
/*
class: javafx.scene.shape.QuadCurve
-------------------------------------
Constructor:
QuadCurve(startX, startY, controlX, controlY, endX, endY)
```

```
Tested on: java version "java-8-oracle"
Author: Mike Ohlson de Fine
*/
import javafx.application.Application;
import javafx.stage.Stage;
import javafx.scene.*;
import javafx.scene.shape.*; // Graphic primitives library.

public class QuadCurveSimplest extends Application
{
  public void start(Stage stage)
  {
      Group root = new Group();
    //*************************************************************
    QuadCurve quadCurve1 = new QuadCurve(10, 10, 50, 100, 100, 10);
    //*************************************************************
    root.getChildren().add(quadCurve1);

      Scene scene = new Scene(root, 160, 60);
       stage.setTitle("QuadCurve on Stage (canvas), JavaFX");
       stage.setScene(scene);
       stage.show();
  }
}
```

# A CubicCurve

**CubicCurve(startX, startY, controlX1, controlY1, controlX2, controlY2, endX, endY);**

```
// CubicCurveSimplest.java
/*
class: javafx.scene.shape.CubicCurve
-------------------------------------
Constructor:
CubicCurve(startX, startY, controlX1, controlY1, controlX2, controlY2, endX,
endY);

Tested on: java version "java-8-oracle"
Author: Mike Ohlson de Fine
*/
import javafx.application.Application;
import javafx.stage.Stage;
```

```
import javafx.scene.*;
import javafx.scene.shape.*; // Graphic primitives library.

public class CubicCurveSimplest extends Application
{
   public void start(Stage stage)
   {
        Group root = new Group();
     //*********************************************************************
     CubicCurve cubicCurve1 = new CubicCurve(10, 10, 50, 100, 100, -60, 200, 80);
     //*********************************************************************
     root.getChildren().add(cubicCurve1);

        Scene scene = new Scene(root, 220, 100);
        stage.setTitle("CubicCurve on Stage (canvas), JavaFX");
        stage.setScene(scene);
        stage.show();
   }
}
```

# An ArcTo Path

## ArcTo(radiusX,radiusY, AxisRotation, x,y, largeArcFlag, sweepFlag) ;

```
// ArcToPathSimplest.java
/*
class: javafx.scene.shape.ArcTo
-------------------------------------
Constructor:
ArcTo(radiusX,radiusY, AxisRotation, x,y, largeArcFlag, sweepFlag) ;

Tested on: java version "java-8-oracle"
Author: Mike Ohlson de Fine
*/
import javafx.application.Application;
import javafx.stage.Stage;
import javafx.scene.*;
import javafx.scene.shape.*; // Graphic primitives library.

public class ArcToPathSimplest extends Application
{
   public void start(Stage stage)
```

```
 {
    Group root = new Group();Inkscape is professional quality vector graphics
software which runs on Linux, Mac OS X and Windows desktop computers.
    Path path = new Path();
    MoveTo moveTo1 = new MoveTo(40, 20); // Start position x,y

//*********************************************************************
        ArcTo arcTo1 = new ArcTo(80,30,   30,    100,100,   true, true);
    // ArcTo(radiusX,radiusY, AxisRotation, Endx,Endy, largeArcFlag,
sweepFlag) ;

//*********************************************************************
    path.getElements().add(moveTo1);
    path.getElements().add(arcTo1);
    root.getChildren().add(path);

    Scene scene = new Scene(root, 240, 130);
    stage.setTitle("ArcTo Path on Stage (canvas), JavaFX");
    stage.setScene(scene);
    stage.show();
  }
}
```

## A QuadcurveTo Path

**QuadCurve(controlX1, controlY1, endX, endY) ; //StartX,Y from MoveTo.**

```
// PathSimplest.java
/*
class: javafx.scene.shape.Path
-------------------------------------
Note: QuadCurve(startX, startY, controlX1, controlY1, endX, endY) ;
Constructor for path omits first point for each additional segment because
the first point is taken from the current position,
That is, the last point of the previous segment is treated as the first point of the
current segment:
MoveTo(startX, startY);
QuadCurve(controlX1, controlY1, endX, endY) ; //StartX,Y from MoveTo.

Tested on: java version "java-8-oracle"
Author: Mike Ohlson de Fine
*/
```

```
import javafx.application.Application;
import javafx.stage.Stage;
import javafx.scene.*;
import javafx.scene.shape.*; // Graphic primitives library.

public class PathSimplest extends Application
{
  public void start(Stage stage)
  {
    Group root = new Group();
    Path path = new Path();
   //**********************************************************************
    MoveTo moveTo1 = new MoveTo(40, 20); // Start position x,y
    QuadCurveTo quad1 = new QuadCurveTo(80,80,  120,20); // 1st point is
current position.
    QuadCurveTo quad2 = new QuadCurveTo(80,80,  160,130);
    QuadCurveTo quad3 = new QuadCurveTo(80,80,  80,170);
    QuadCurveTo quad4 = new QuadCurveTo(80,80,  20,130);
    QuadCurveTo quad5 = new QuadCurveTo(80,80,   40,20);
     /
/**********************************************************************
    path.getElements().add(moveTo1);
    path.getElements().add(quad1);
    path.getElements().add(quad2);
    path.getElements().add(quad3);
    path.getElements().add(quad4);
    path.getElements().add(quad5);

    root.getChildren().add(path);

    Scene scene = new Scene(root, 200, 200);
    stage.setTitle("Quad Path on Stage (canvas), JavaFX");
   stage.setScene(scene);
    stage.show();
  }
}
```

# The parent class of the Primitives: the shape class

All the primitive shapes above belong the *shape class* of JavaFX. They are the children (subclasses) of shape. We incorporate them into our programs with the line import javafx.scene.shape.*; // Graphic primitives library.

It is a good idea to start getting used to the Java documents from Oracle, who purchased Java from Sun. The documents are not easy to interpret because they sometimes use unfamiliar terms without explanation. They do not illustrate usage with examples, which is why this book was written. However they are part of the helicopter view we need to be aware of. For example the summary of the shape class will be found at

https://docs.oracle.com/javase/8/javafx/api/javafx/scene/shape/package-summary.html
If we click on words in grey-blue colored type then this will pull up a detailed page on the particular topic of that word. We can get further detail by clicking on the blue-grey words on that new page.

## *Java FX shape class Summary*

The definitions below are provided by the package *javafx.scene.shape* so we will always need an *import javafx.scene.shape.** statement at the top of our application code if we use any of the primitive shape subclasses below.

### Subclasses of shape

**Arc** - The Arc class represents a 2D arc, which is a portion of a circle or ellipse object, defined by a center point, a start angle (in degrees), an angular extent (length of the arc in degrees), and an arc type (ArcType.OPEN, ArcType.CHORD, or ArcType.ROUND). The arc type controls whether the arc is open between the ends, is closed off by a straight line (known as the chord in geometry) or is closed off by lines going to the center like a slice of pizza pie.

**ArcTo** - A path that forms an arc from the previous coordinates to the specified x and y coordinates using the specified radius.

**Circle** - a new circle with the specified radius and center location measured in pixels

**ClosePath** - A path element which closes the current path. It makes a straight line form the first point of the path to the final point.

**CubicCurve** – This draws a smooth cubic Bézier curve segment. A cubic curve is a curge that can have two humps and a point of inflection. It is very useful for making smooth drawings.

**CubicCurveTo** - Creates a curved path element from the current coordinate to a new point (x, y). The amount of bend or curvature is given by two so-called control points, (controlX1, controlY1) and (controlX2,controlY2).

**Ellipse** - an ellipse with the specified size (width and height) and location in pixels

HlineTo - a horizontal line the current point to x.

**VLineTo** - a vertical line segment from the current point to y.

**Line** - a straight line segment in (x,y) coordinate space.

**LineTo** – a straight line from the current coordinate to the new coordinates.

**MoveTo** – go to a new coordinate (x,y) without drawing a visible line.

**Path** - represents a shape made up of straight lines and curves.

**PathElement** - an element of the Path that can represent geometric objects like straight lines, arcs, quadratic curves and cubic curves.

**Polygon** - a shape made up of straight lines joining a list of (x,y) points. The shape is closed off by joining the first point to the last point.

**PolyLine** - a shape made up of straight lines joining a list of (x,y) points. The shape is not closed off.

**QuadCurve** - a quadratic smooth curve.

**QuadCurveTo** - a quadratic smooth curve, defined by two new points, by drawing a quadratic curve that intersects both the current coordinates and the specified coordinates (x, y), using the specified point (controlX, controlY) as a Bézier control point.

**Rectangle** - a rectangle with the specified size (width and height) and location (position of the top left corner).

**Shape** - definitions of common properties for objects that represent a geometric shape.

**SVGPath** - a simple shape that is constructed from SVG (Scaled Vector Graphics) path data. SVG is the standard for graphic drawings in HTML code, the standard web programming language.

## Controlling Properties of Shapes

Color, line width, outline character, transparency, size, position can all be modified after a graphic shape has been created or instantiated using the *new* keyword. The process of creating an object from a class, that can be seen on a computer screen, is called **instantiation.** An instance of a class is an **object**. We can create thousands of instances from one class by repeated us of the ***new*** magic keyword.

### Geometric shape object properties that can be altered.

**fill** - to fill the interior of an Shape using a Color specification. The default value is Color.BLACK for all shapes except Line, Polyline, and Path. The default value is null for those shapes. Use getFill(), setFill(Color) to discover or modify the color.

**smooth** - Defines whether antialiasing hints are used or not for this Shape. In JavaFX version 8 smoothing is automatically applied.

**StrokeDashOffset** - A distance specified in user coordinates that represents an offset into the dashing pattern.

StrokeLineCap - The style of cap at the end of lines. They can be swuare or rounded.

**strokeLineJoin** - the style of bend or corner where path segments meet. It should be: *StrokeLineJoin.MITER, StrokeLineJoin.BEVEL, and StrokeLineJoin.ROUND.*

**strokeMiterLimit** - Defines the limit for the StrokeLineJoin.MITER line join style.

**stroke** - a color of the line around the outline of a Shape. The default value is null for all shapes except Line, Polyline, and Path. The default value is Color.BLACK for those shapes. Use getStroke() and setStroke() to discover or modify the color.

**strokeType** - the location (inside, centered, or outside) that the strokeWidth is used around the shape.

**strokeWidth** - The line width in pixels. A value of 0.0 specifies a hairline stroke. A value of less than 0.0 will be treated as 0.0.

## Line

startX - The X coordinate of the start point of the line segment.
startY - The Y coordinate of the start point of the line segment.
endX - The X coordinate of the end point of the line segment.
endY - The Y coordinate of the end point of the line segment.

## Rectangle

Height - the vertical height of the rectangle.
Width - the horizontal width of the rectangle.
x - the X coordinate of the upper-left corner of the rectangle.
y - the Y coordinate of the upper-left corner of the rectangle.

### Circle

centerX - the horizontal position of the center of the circle in pixels.
centerY - the vertical position of the center of the circle in pixels.
radius - the radius of the circle in pixels.

### Ellipse

centerX - the horizontal position of the center of the circle in pixels.
centerY - the vertical position of the center of the circle in pixels.
radiusX - the width of the ellipse in pixels.
radiusY - the height of the ellipse in pixels.

### Poloygon & PolyLine

A polyline is a line made by joining many straight segments together. Each join is specified as a X,Y coordinate pair:

**x1, y1, x2, y2, x3, y3, etc.**

## The Role of Constructors

Constructors are critical in the use of java - a constructor is the mechanism that creates the software objects that we are trying to control. We, as programmers, cannot create constructors because they are pre-defined, intrinsic components of classes. All we can do is use the pre-defined constructors that come with a class to instantiate objects and then create our own methods that manipulate the variables that alter the values of the object properties. Java classes often have several constructors available to choose from. Which should we use? In the end it does not matter too much because the classes specializes methods that allow use to modify the properties of the object we are working on. So no matter what properties the object started with, they can all be changed later.
How does Java know which constructor to use? Java figures out which particular constructor we are using from the nature of the arguments being used in it. The number of arguments and their data type.

# Chapter 3

## LINES AND POLYLINES

"*A drawing is simply a line going for a walk*" Paul Klee.

In this chapter we will cover:

- All the different properties of a line.
- Basic use of color
- The control and design of shapes using polylines.

**The basis of all drawing is the line**
By controlling position, width and color we can draw any shape.

There are additional properties like the shapes of free ends, the types of corners and the way junctions at joins between lines can be made. Finally there is the property that controls aliasing which has a strong effect on how smooth the edges of a line appear.

# The Simplest Line

In the previous chapter we wrote the following code to draw a basic thin black line:

```
import javafx.application.Application;
import javafx.stage.Stage;
import javafx.scene.*;
import javafx.scene.shape.*;

public class LineSimplest extends Application
{
   public void start(Stage stage)
   {
         Group root = new Group();
         Line line1 = new Line(10, 10, 120, 30);
         // Line constructor: Line(startX, startY, endX, endY)

         root.getChildren().add(line1);
          Scene scene = new Scene(root, 200, 50);
          stage.setScene(scene);
          stage.show();
   }
}
```

We were able to keep the code relatively brief by allowing the *default* values of properties to operate. Default values are the ones that will be used if we do not actually specify different ones. The default properties for a line are color=BLACK, width= 1 pixel, no breaks or dot-dash patterns.

### The Constructors of the Line Class

1. **Line();** Instantiates a line with no length. Default start position is x=0, y=0.

2. **Line(startX, startY, endX, endY);** Instantiates a line starting at the position x=startX, y=startY and ending at the position x=endX,

y=endY.

What is the purpose of a constructor?

Why not just draw the line with a minimum of fuss?

The answer is that Java is an Object Oriented Programming language (OOP) and this means that every piece of code that executes has to be part of a method inside a class that has been instantiated. The word "instantiate" here means "turned into a real code object (ie. an instance) that exists in the RAM memory of our computer". Prior to being instantiated the class is just a plan for construction of an object. The magic spell that turns a class into an executable object is the CONSTRUCTOR. The word "new" is

the word that triggers the construction process. So in the program above the line

Line line1 = **new** Line(10, 10, 120, 30);,

take the plans for assembling the RAM and microcode for painting little colored pixels on a screen, and turns the plan into computer reality. So construction (or instantiation) is the action of transforming abstract plans into instructions in RAM waiting for execution. We can draw a million or more lines based on on this single constructor. All we need to do is to add each additional line to a JavaFX group: *root.getChildren().add(line1);* This makes a kind of permanent copy of the line ready for showing on the stage. Now we can change everything about the instance *line1*, like color, width and position and add THAT to the rendering list by executing another *root.getChildren().add(line1);* which does not wipe out the previous line provided this is all done inside a *for* loop. We do a lot of this later in the book.

# Aliasing or antialiasing?

JavaFX misleads us on antialiasing.

We think that we can enable or disable it with *setSmooth(**true**);* or *setSmooth(**false**);*

This is incorrect – the edges of vector graphic objects in JavaFX (version 8) are always smooth. If we use JavaFX graphics then all lines and shapes are already smoothed by default – anti-aliasing is always ON and we cannot turn it off.

If, on the other hand, we use Java Swing graphics instead of JavaFX then we have the option to select smoothing either ON or OFF. Swing is yesterday's technology and JavaFX is going to replace it completely sometime.

For completeness's sake here is the output of a Swing program with no anti-aliasing on the left followed on the right by the same set of lines **with anti-aliasing**.

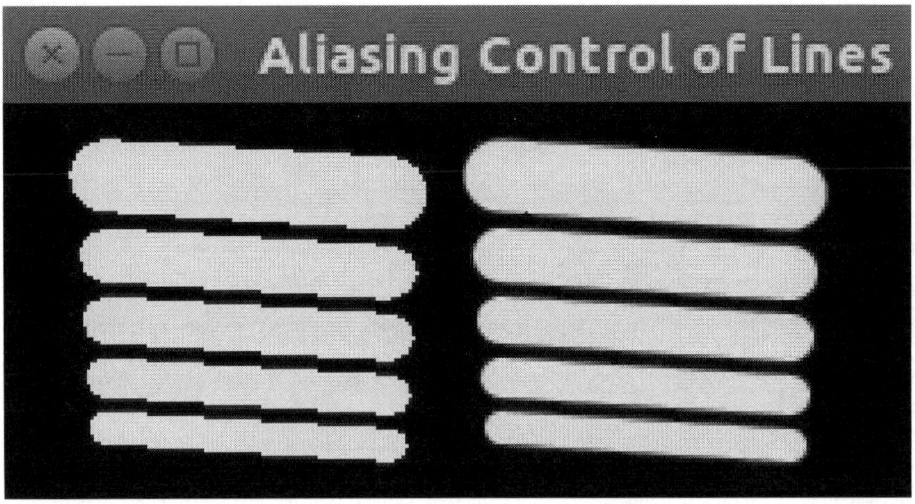


## The Basic Line

The simplest way to specify and construct a line is:

*Line line1 = new Line(10, 11, 120, 30);*
This is a line starting at (x=10, y=11) and ending at (x=120, y=30)

The line is by default solid (not dotted), one pixel wide and colored black.

Line width, color, dash-dot patterned and have various kinds of end shapes. We control these using specifiers like:

```
setStrokeWidth(8);                           // Width of the line, pixels.

setStrokeLineCap(StrokeLineCap.ROUND);  // Rounded ends of lines.
setStroke(Color.BLUE);                       // Color of line.
getStrokeDashArray().addAll(14d);            // Dash pattern: fill, blank, etc
setStrokeDashOffset(10);                     //Dash pattern: to shift the
beginning of the dash.
```

# A Completely Specified Line in JavaFX.

```
// LineProperties.java
/*
Line : javafx.scene.shape.Line

This is a fully specified dashed Line.

Line properties (inherited from javafx.scene.shape.Shape):
stroke, fill, strokeType, strokeWidth, strokeDashOffset, strokeLineCap,
strokeLineJoin, strokeMitreLimit

Constructor
a) Line( startX, startY, endX,  endY) // An instance of Line from start to
finish.

Tested on: java version "java-8-oracle"
Author: Mike Ohlson de Fine
*/
import javafx.application.Application;
import javafx.stage.Stage;
import javafx.scene.*;
import javafx.scene.paint.*;
import javafx.scene.shape.*;
```

```
public class LineProperties extends Application {
  public void start(Stage stage)

  {
         Group root = new Group();

         Line line1 = new Line(); // Create an instance of a line object.

         // Set the line properties below:
         line1.setStartX(40.0f);
         line1.setStartY(40.0f);
         line1.setEndX(580.0f);
         line1.setEndY(60.0f);
         line1.setStrokeWidth(8.0f);                          // Width of the line,
pixels.
         line1.setStrokeLineCap(StrokeLineCap.ROUND); // Rounded ends of
lines.
         line1.setStroke(Color.BLUE);                         // Color of line.
         line1.getStrokeDashArray().addAll(14d);              // Dash pattern: fill,
blank, etc
         line1.setStrokeDashOffset(10); //Dash pattern: to shift the beginning
of the dash.

         root.getChildren().add(line1);

       Scene scene = new Scene(root, 600, 80);
       stage.setTitle("Fully specified Line, JavaFX");
       stage.setScene(scene);
       stage.show();

   }
}
```

## Using Dashed Lines

In the above example the instruction

*line1.getStrokeDashArray().addAll(14d);*

is responsible for producing the dashed line. What it specifies is that the solid portions of the line should be 14 user units long and the blank or invisible portions of the line should also be 14 units long. Why then are the solid portions of the line obviously longer? The reason for this is that the round end caps of the line require extra space. The radius of the end cap is half the width of the line. In the example the width is 8 units the blank portions are shorter by one line width (two end cap radii). Thus the blank portions are 14 – 8 = 6 units.

Lines that have chopped off ends ( that is, square ends ) have the identical problem

because the lines are lengthened by one half-width so that the gaps between the lines are actually less than expected by one line width.

The program below maintains the solid-blank ratio at 40 units but progressively increases the line width.

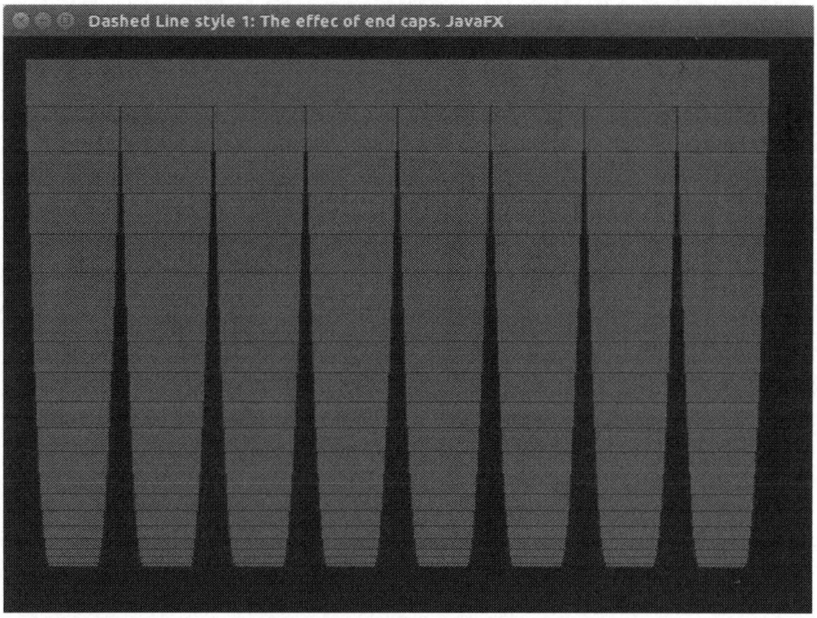


The inter-line gaps are reduced by one line width for both round and square-ended dashed lines for bot square-ended or round-ended lines.

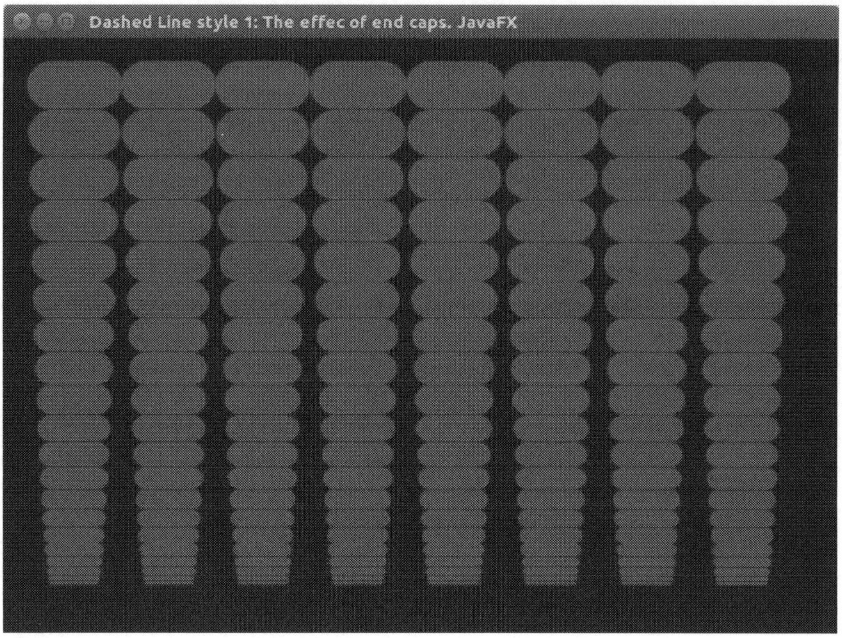


## The Styles of Dashed Lines.

Dashed lines in Java can be thought of as conforming to different styles based on the way their dashArrays are specified:

Style 1: line1.getStrokeDashArray().addAll(dash_length);

Style 2: line2.getStrokeDashArray().addAll(dash_length, gap_length);

Style 3: line3.getStrokeDashArray().addAll(dash_length1, gap_length2, dash_length3, gap_length4, .... dash_lengthN, gap_lengthN+1 );

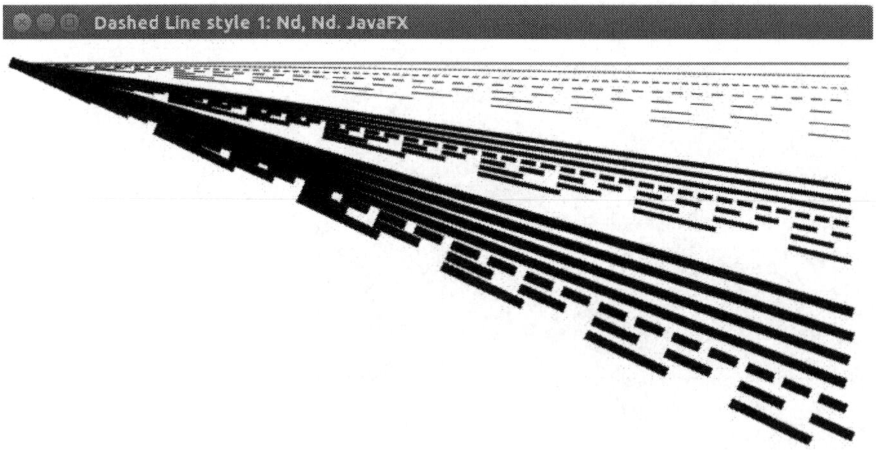
Dashed Line style 1: Nd, Nd. JavaFX

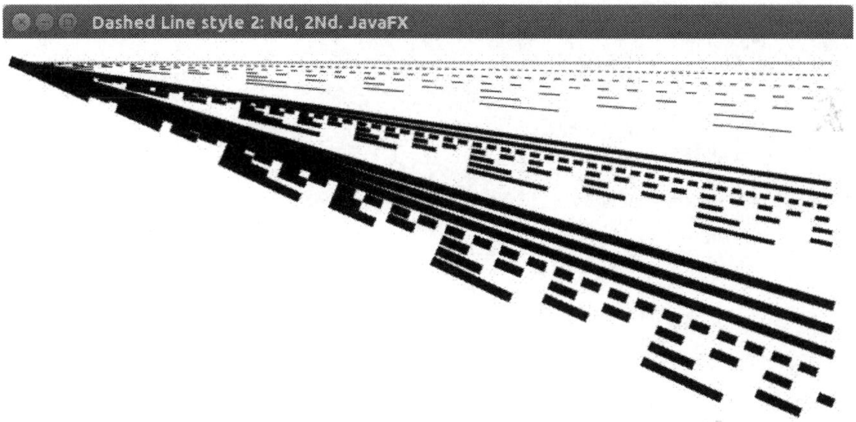
Dashed Line style 2: Nd, 2Nd. JavaFX

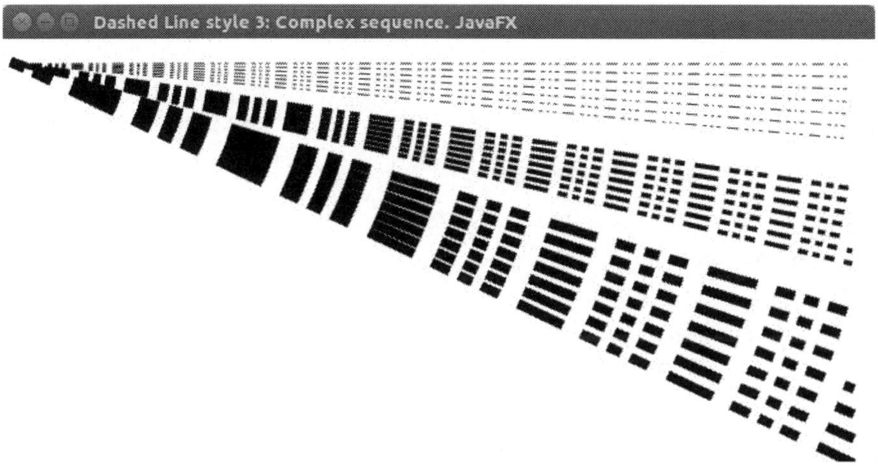
Dashed Line style 3: Complex sequence. JavaFX

## A Sunburst of Dashed Lines

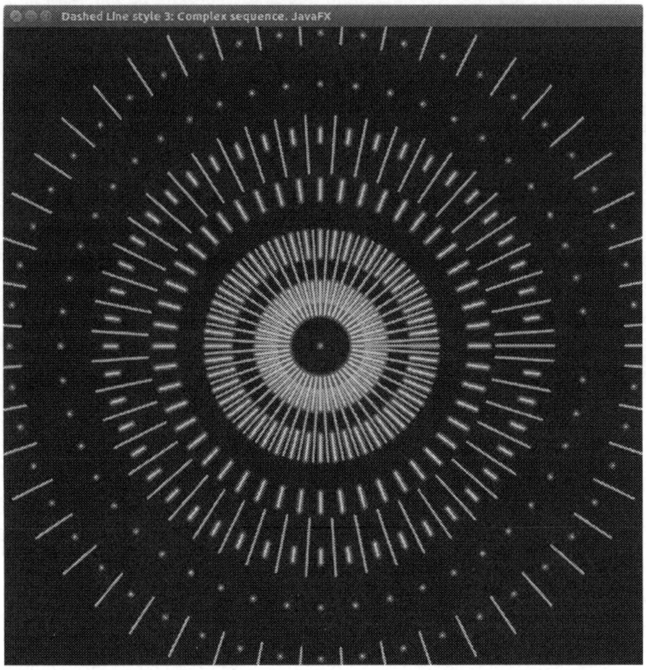


# Polyline

A polyline is a line made by joining many straight segments together. In principle a polyline can be used to draw any 2D shape, even perfectly smooth looking curves.

The polyline constructor:

**Polyline(x1, y1, x2, y2, x3, y3, etc);**

```
// PolylineSimplest.java
/*
class: javafx.scene.shape.Polyline
-------------------------------------
Constructor:
Polyline(x1, y1, x2, y2, x3, y3, etc);

Tested on: java version "java-8-oracle"
Author: Mike Ohlson de Fine
```

```
*/
import javafx.application.Application;
import javafx.stage.Stage;
import javafx.scene.*;
import javafx.scene.shape.*; // Graphic primitives library.

public class PolylineSimplest extends Application
{
   public void start(Stage stage)
   {
       Group root = new Group();
    //*****************************************************
    Polyline polyline1 = new Polyline(10, 10, 50, 50, 100, 10);
    //*****************************************************
    root.getChildren().add(polyline1);

        Scene scene = new Scene(root, 160, 60);
        stage.setTitle("Polyline on Stage (canvas), JavaFX");
        stage.setScene(scene);
        stage.show();
    }
  }
}
```

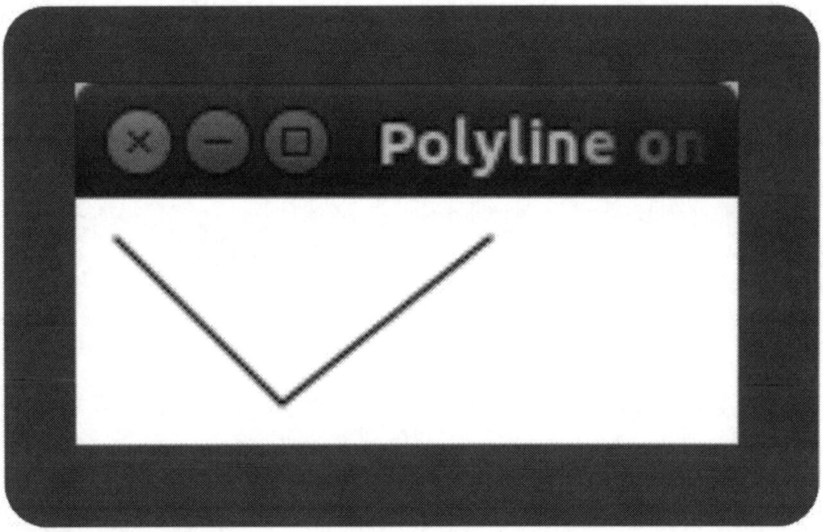

# A Polygon

A polygon is practically identical to a polyline with the difference that the first and last points are joined together to create an enclosed area that can be filled with color. If the segments of the polygon cross over each other then the class behavior  determines which enclosed areas get filled with color.
Constructor:
**Polygon(x1, y1, x2, y2, x3, y3, etc);**

```
// PolygonSimplest.java
/*
class: javafx.scene.shape.Polygon
-------------------------------------
Constructor:
Polygon(x1, y1, x2, y2, x3, y3, etc);

Tested on: java version "java-8-oracle"
Author: Mike Ohlson de Fine
*/
import javafx.application.Application;
import javafx.stage.Stage;
import javafx.scene.*;
import javafx.scene.shape.*; // Graphic primitives library.

public class PolygonSimplest extends Application
{
   public void start(Stage stage)
   {
        Group root = new Group();
     //**************************************************
     Polygon polygon1 = new Polygon(10, 10, 50, 50, 100, 10);
     //**************************************************
     root.getChildren().add(polygon1);

        Scene scene = new Scene(root, 160, 60);
        stage.setTitle("Polygon on Stage (canvas), JavaFX");
        stage.setScene(scene);
        stage.show();
   }
}
```

## Complex Polygon Shapes and Transforms.

## How to Manage Large Collections of Lines

Each individual segment of line we display has to be a unique object with its entire collection of properties that describe it kept in a portion of our computer RAM reserved exclusively for this one line segment. To display a second segment we need an additional and separate portion of RAM set aside to keep track of it's properties.
If there are one hundred segements of line making up a complete drawing then we need to construct 100 separate instances of a straight line in memory.
There is a neat and tidy way of handling such collections that uses a special type of Java data called an Array. Without delving into theory we have an example of using Arrays to produce a complex drawing made up of 81 straight line segments.

Straight Lines,

```
// LineLady2.java
/*
Line : javafx.scene.shape.Line
------------------------------------
This is a drawing composed of 81 straight lines.
The objective is to have suitable, compact code to
encapsulate complex drawings.

The line segments were produced from a drawing in Inkscape.
The SVG paths were converted to line segments using inkscape2python.

Constructor:
a) Line(startX, startY, endX, endY) ;

Tested on: java version "java-8-oracle"
Author: Mike Ohlson de Fine
*/
import javafx.application.Application;
import javafx.stage.Stage;
import javafx.scene.*;
import javafx.scene.paint.*;
import javafx.scene.shape.*;

public class LineLady2 extends Application {

   public void start(Stage stage)
   {
        Group root = new Group();

         /* The 1-dimensional arrays of the positions of independent line
segments
           making up each straight line segment of the drawing.*/
        // Segments 1 - 10
        double[] xy1 = {84.7, 127.3, 67.3, 134.6};
        double[] xy2 = {69.0, 135.7, 53.3, 168.7};
        double[] xy3 = {53.6, 170.9, 124.9, 314.6};
        double[] xy4 = {93.1, 255.1, 91.9, 277.8};
        double[] xy5 = {93.3, 279.7, 137.8, 352.9};
        double[] xy6 = {130.0, 343.7, 132.7, 380.3};
        double[] xy7 = {130.5, 375.8, 138.6, 387.0};
        double[] xy8 = {143.9, 386.5, 157.4, 387.1};
```

```
double[] xy9 = {160.7, 385.7, 147.9, 376.1};
double[] xy10 = {148.4, 384.0, 132.5, 320.2};

// Segments  11- 20
double[] xy11  = {112.1, 254.8, 109.3, 278.6};
double[] xy12  = {110.7, 276.6, 137.5, 350.7};
double[] xy13  = {90.8, 160.6, 117.1, 281.1};
double[] xy14  = {110.9, 266.8, 119.9, 285.5};
double[] xy15  = {119.6, 286.7, 138.6, 347.};
double[] xy16  = {64.3, 199.7, 57.3, 218.2};
double[] xy17  = {57.3, 218.2, 31.0, 242.0};
double[] xy18  = {29.9, 242.5, 19.8, 316.3};
double[] xy19  = {19.0, 293.4, 8.6, 309.6};
double[] xy20  = {10.3, 309.0, 22.9, 336.5};

// Segments 21- 30
double[] xy21  = {24.8, 337.0, 34.3, 338.7};
double[] xy22  = {31.8, 339.0, 47.8, 333.9};
double[] xy23  = {44.7, 332.8, 29.9, 326.9};
double[] xy24  = {27.6, 326.7, 27.3, 293.7};
double[] xy25  = {24.3, 304.9, 64.5, 221.8};
double[] xy26  = {118.5, 148.6, 49.7, 257.6};
double[] xy27  = {95.3, 167.3, 115.1, 149.1};
double[] xy28  = {119.3, 148.3, 115.1, 135.7};
double[] xy29  = {111.8, 154.4, 123.5, 108.9};
double[] xy30  = {123.5, 108.6, 112.6, 80.1};
// Segments 31- 40
double[] xy31  = {114.3, 82.9, 100.3, 60.8};
double[] xy32  = {122.5, 99.1, 126.3, 87.6};
double[] xy33  = {126.6, 85.4, 107.3, 68.0};
double[] xy34  = {112.6, 75.6, 148.1, 20.8};
double[] xy35  = {145.9, 17.7, 98.6, 7.9};
double[] xy36  = {98.4, 57.4, 136.7, 20.5};
double[] xy37  = {137.5, 33.6, 100.3, 9.6};
double[] xy38  = {102.3, 151.6, 109.8, 111.4};
double[] xy39  = {87.7, 130.4, 113.7, 98.2};
double[] xy40  = {84.7, 142.7, 87.5, 117.3};

// Segments 41- 50
double[] xy41  = {91.1, 118.1, 57.8, 85.4};
double[] xy42  = {56.1, 86.2, 78.5, 58.2};
```

```
double[] xy43  = {56.1, 82.9, 60.1, 57.4};
double[] xy44  = {59.2, 52.7, 51.1, 51.0};
double[] xy45  = {51.4, 52.7, 56.7, 12.4};
double[] xy46  = {62.6, 21.6, 77.7, 4.8};
double[] xy47  = {65.1, 83.4, 63.1, 22.7};
double[] xy48  = {68.4, 73.6, 84.9, 27.5};
double[] xy49  = {85.8, 25.8, 80.2, 7.6};
double[] xy50  = {81.0, 7.1, 79.1, 5.1};

 // Segments 51- 60
double[] xy51  = {81.9, 46.2, 92.8, 61.3 };
double[] xy52  = { 80.2, 44.3, 97.8, 49.9 };
double[] xy53  = { 98.4, 49.9, 104.5, 27.8 };
double[] xy54  = { 104.8, 26.6, 101.7, 20.5 };
double[] xy55  = { 102.8, 20.5, 107.3, 16.0 };
double[] xy56  = { 105.1, 15.2, 95.8, 5.4 };
double[] xy57  = { 85.5, 19.4, 94.5, 6.5 };
double[] xy58  = { 93.9, 6.8, 81.6, 9.9 };
double[] xy59  = { 70.7, 10.2, 57.8, 14.1 };
double[] xy60  = { 105.4, 21.9, 95.3, 12.4 };

 // Segments 61- 70
double[] xy61  = { 83.5, 26.9, 95.3, 14.1 };
double[] xy62  = { 86.4, 37.3, 98.1, 38.1 };
double[] xy63  = { 93.3, 60.8, 89.1, 49.3 };
double[] xy64  = { 74.6, 54.1, 87.2, 57.7 };
double[] xy65  = {75.4, 58.2, 105.6, 86.5 };
double[] xy66  = { 107.9, 87.9, 102.8, 101.3 };
double[] xy67  = { 81.9, 110.8, 100.9, 100.5 };
double[] xy68  = { 77.1, 103.3, 82.4, 85.4 };
double[] xy69  = {86.9, 87.0, 72.9, 62.4 };
double[] xy70  = {98.4, 97.1, 83.3, 88.2 };78
 // Segments 71- 81
double[] xy71  = { 88.6, 168.1, 92.8, 145.2 };
double[] xy72  = { 94.2, 153.9, 87.7, 131.2 };
double[] xy73  = { 83.8, 151.4, 102.0, 222.9 };
double[] xy74  = { 75.2, 133.5, 85.5, 151.6 };
double[] xy75  = { 67.1, 136.8, 87.5, 159.7 };
double[] xy76  = { 62.9, 148.3, 85.8, 164.8 };
double[] xy77  = { 106.5, 100.5, 89.7, 114.4 };
double[] xy78  = { 82.1, 128.4, 89.7, 156.9 };
```

```
        double[] xy79  = { 93.9, 118.1, 58.9, 84.0 };
        double[] xy80  = { 96.1, 111.1, 61.5, 82.3 };
        double[] xy81  = {96.4, 104.9, 64.5, 77.5 };

        /* The 2-dimensional array of the line segments
           making up the complete drawing.*/
        double[][] xy_all = { xy1,  xy2,  xy3,  xy4 , xy5,  xy6,  xy7,  xy8 , xy9, xy10,
                    xy11, xy12, xy13, xy14, xy15, xy16, xy17, xy18, xy19, xy20,
                    xy21, xy22, xy23, xy24, xy25, xy26, xy27, xy28, xy29, xy30,
                    xy31, xy32, xy33, xy34, xy35, xy36, xy37, xy38, xy39, xy40,
                    xy41, xy42, xy43, xy44, xy45, xy46, xy47, xy48, xy49, xy50,
                    xy51, xy52, xy53, xy54, xy55, xy56, xy57, xy58, xy59, xy60,
                    xy61, xy62, xy63, xy64, xy65, xy66, xy67, xy68, xy69, xy70,
                    xy71, xy72, xy73, xy74, xy75, xy76, xy77, xy78, xy79, xy80,
                    xy81 };

        for (int i =1;  i< xy_all.length; i++ )
        {
          Line line1 = new Line(xy_all[i][0], xy_all[i][1], xy_all[i][2], xy_all[i]
[3] );
          line1.setStrokeWidth(5.0f);                  // Width of the line, pixels.
          line1.setStrokeLineCap(StrokeLineCap.ROUND);  // Rounded ends
of lines.
          line1.setStroke(Color.SILVER);                // Color of line.
          root.getChildren().add(line1);

          Line line2 = new Line(xy_all[i][0], xy_all[i][1], xy_all[i][2], xy_all[i]
[3] );
          line2.setStrokeWidth(1.0f);                  // Width of the line, pixels.
          line2.setStrokeLineCap(StrokeLineCap.ROUND); // Rounded ends of
lines.
          line2.setStroke(Color.GREY);                 // Color of line.
          root.getChildren().add(line2);
        }

      Scene scene = new Scene(root, 200, 400);
      stage.setTitle("Straight Lines, JavaFX");
      stage.setScene(scene);
      stage.show();
   }
}
```

## What is the simplest way to Draw complex Shapes?

The polygons we want to use in Java are vector shapes. That is, each point on the shape is specified as a (x, y) coordinate on the X-Y plane. There are many software drawings tools available for producing vector graphics. One of the best is Inkscape. Inkscape is professional quality vector graphics software which runs on Linux, Mac OS X and Windows desktop computers. It has the great advantage that it widely available for free on the internet and has an extremely well written user manual always available on the web.
Inkscape can found at https://inkscape.org/en/download/

Typically with Applications like Inkscape there are three ways to produce vector line shapes in Java:
First produce the drawing in Inkscape and save it as a .svg file.
1. Write a java application that will parse through the vector .svg file (which is a subset of html code). The parsing program will re-assemble relevant parts of the .svg code as Java compatible arrays that can be used in Java Polygon and Polyline methods.
2. Use a pre-existing application (that can be in any other language) that does the necessary parsing and re-packing as Java arrays.
3. Use a particular Java class that uses .svg files directly.

These topics are covered in chapters 10 and 11.

# Chapter 4

## RECTANGLES

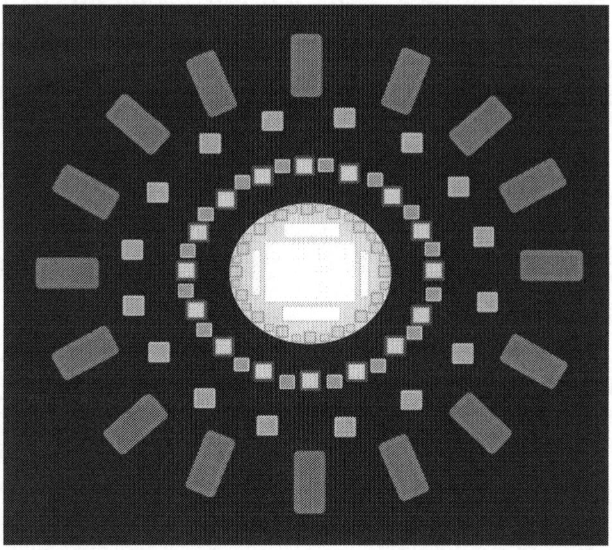

*"Art is the space between the viewer and the rectangle that hangs on the wall."* T. Allen Lawson.

In this chapter we will cover:

- All the different properties of rectangles.
- An extra freedom in handling color.
- Outline choices: inner, outer and center.
- Gradient fill - linear.
- Gradient fill with transparency.
- Gradient fill radial.
- Compiling classes separately, and combining them for execution.

Rectangles have corners and corner styles are different

Rectangles consist of an outline and a interior area. The outline is the line that defines the edge and this line can have the same variation in properties that a simple line has as well as some additional ones. The interior can be colored, transparent or partially transparent - this allows greater scope for creativity.

## The Simplest Rectangle

In the previous chapter we wrote the following code to draw a basic thin black line:

```
// RectangleSimplest.java
/*
Constructor:
Rectangle(double x, double y, double width, double height);

Tested on: java version "java-8-oracle"
Author: Mike Ohlson de Fine
*/
import javafx.application.Application;
import javafx.stage.Stage;
import javafx.scene.*;
import javafx.scene.shape.*; // Graphic primitives library.

public class RectangleSimplest extends Application
{
   public void start(Stage stage)
   {
        Group root = new Group();
       //***************************************************
       Rectangle rectangle1 = new Rectangle(30, 20, 80, 20);
       //***************************************************
       root.getChildren().add(rectangle1);

         Scene scene = new Scene(root, 160, 50);
         stage.setTitle("Rectangle on Stage (canvas), JavaFX");
         stage.setScene(scene);
```

```
        stage.show();
    }
}
```

The code is brief because we use the *default* values of properties like line color and width to be used. The default color is black and the default width is one pixel.

**Rectangle Constructors**

1. ***Rectangle();*** Create an empty instance of a rectangle. Meaningful properties can be specified later.

2. **Rectangle(Width, Height);** Create a rectangle Width pixels wide and Pixels high located with the top-left corner at (x=0, y=0) . Default parameter will be used for color etc.

3. **Rectangle(positionX, positionY, Width, Height);** Create a rectangle Width pixels wide and Pixels high located with the top-left corner at (x=positionX, y=positionX) . Default parameter will be used for color etc.

4. **Rectangle( Width, Height, fill color);** Create a rectangle Width pixels wide and Height pixels high, located with the top-left corner at (x=0, y=0) .

**Making Choices for Outline and Fill**

The outline of a rectangle is just a line with the difference that it has corners and corner style makes a big difference to the visual impact that a rectangle has.

Rectangle outline line-width, color, dash-dot patterns, end-caps and corner shapes are the parameters we can control. The interior fill of the rectangle allows us to vary color and transparency as well.

So for outlines we exercise control using specifiers like:

```
setStrokeWidth(8);                    // Width of the line, pixels.
```

*setStrokeLineCap(StrokeLineCap.ROUND); // Rounded ends of lines.*
*setStroke(Color.BLUE); // Color of line.*
*getStrokeDashArray().addAll(14d); // Dash pattern: fill, blank, etc*
*setStrokeDashOffset(10); //Dash pattern: to shift the beginning of the dash.*

For interior we can control color and transparency as follows:

# Specifying a Rectangle Completely in JavaFX.

// ***RectangleProperties1.java***
*/**
*A Rectangle with properties explicitly defined (no default values used).*

*Rectangle properties(inherited from javafx.scene.shape.Shape):*
*stroke, fill, strokeType, strokeWidth, strokeDashOffset, strokeLineCap, strokeLineJoin, strokeMitreLimit, smooth.*

*Setting the Rectangle properties.*
*setFill(Paint value) : Sets the fill color.*
*setStrokeType(StrokeType value) : Stroke position - CENTERED, INSIDE, OUTSIDE.*
*setStrokeWidth(double value) : Sets the stroke width.*
*setStroke(Paint value) : Sets the color and transparency of the interior fill.*
*setStrokeDashOffset(double value) : Sets the dashed outline if needed.*
*setStrokeLineCap(StrokeLineCap value) : Sets the stroke end-cap shape (only affects dashed lines).*

*setStrokeLineJoin(...): Corner style - ROUND,BEVEL or MITER where:*
*MITER: Joins path segments by extending their outside edges until they meet.*
*setStrokeMiterLimit(double value) : Sets the value of the property strokeMiterLimit.*
*ROUND:Joins path segments by rounding off the corner at a radius of half the line width.*
*BEVEL: Joins path segments by connecting the outer corners of their wide outlines with a straight segment.*

*Constructors*
*1. Rectangle(width, height)*
*2. Rectangle( x, y, width, height)*
*3. Rectangle( width, height, Paint fill)*

```
Tested on: java version "java-8-oracle"
Author: Mike Ohlson de Fine
*/
import javafx.application.Application;
import javafx.stage.Stage;
import javafx.scene.*;
import javafx.scene.paint.*;
import javafx.scene.shape.*;

public class RectangleProperties1 extends Application {
   public void start(Stage stage)
   {
         Group root = new Group();

         Rectangle rect1 = new Rectangle();

         // Size and location on the JavaFX scene.
         rect1.setX(40.0f);
         rect1.setY(20.0f);
         rect1.setWidth(220.0f);
         rect1.setHeight(100.0f);

         // Appearance of the outline.
         rect1.setStrokeWidth(10.0f);
        rect1.setStrokeLineCap(StrokeLineCap.ROUND);
         rect1.setStroke(Color.BLUE);

         rect1.setSmooth(true);
         rect1.getStrokeDashArray().addAll(40d);    // fill-blank pattern of
dashes.
         //rect1.setStrokeType(StrokeType.CENTERED); // Stroke halfway
across inner rectangle.
         //rect1.setStrokeType(StrokeType.INSIDE); //Stroke insides inner
rectangle.
         rect1.setStrokeType(StrokeType.OUTSIDE); //Strokeoutside inner
rectangle.

         // Corner Style: Default - square corners.

         // Fill Properties
         rect1.setFill(Color.VIOLET);
```

```
        root.getChildren().add(rect1);    // Add the rectangle to the group.

      Scene scene = new Scene(root, 290, 150);
      stage.setTitle("Outside stroke, JavaFX");
      stage.setScene(scene);
      stage.show();
   }
}
```

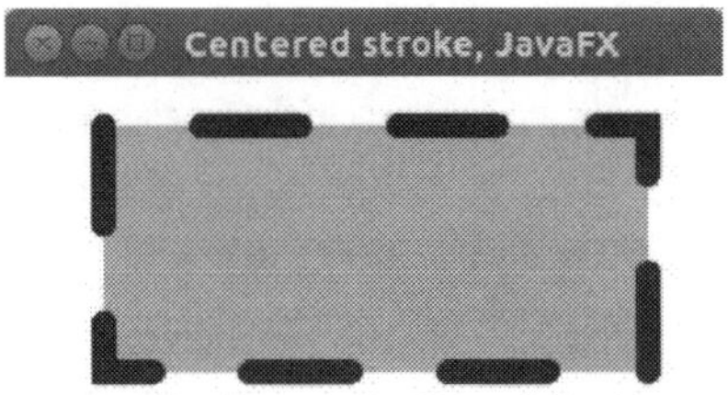


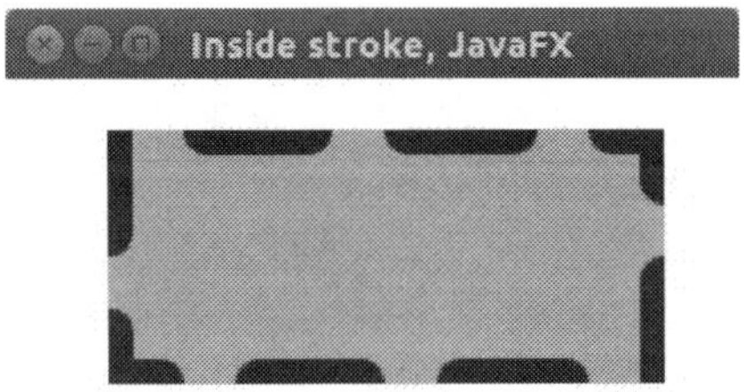


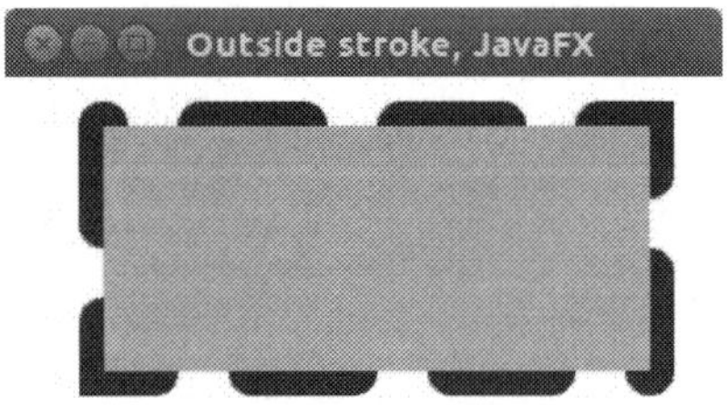


## Gradient Fill Specifications for Rectangles

To create a linear gradient paint, we specify startX, startY, endX, and endY for the start and end points. The start and end point coordinates specify where the gradient pattern begins and stops.

The linear gradient properties are:

startX: Set X coordinate of the gradient axis start point

startY: Set Y coordinate of the gradient axis start point

endX:  Set X coordinate of the gradient axis end point.

endY: Set Y coordinate of the gradient axis end point.

**proportional: true or false.** Set whether the coordinates are proportional to the shape. true will use unit square coordinates, otherwise use screen coordinate system.

cycleMethod: Set cycle method applied to the gradient.

stops: Set stop list for gradient's color specification.

```
// GradientFillRectangle1.java
/*
A Rectangle with properties explicitly defined (no default values used).

Constructors
1. LinearGradient(startX,  startY,  endX, endY, proportional, cycleMethod,
List of stops)
2. LinearGradient(startX, startY, endX, endY, proportional, cycleMethod,
stops)

Linear Gradient:
The LinearGradient class fills a shape with a linear color gradient pattern.
The user may specify two or more gradient colors.

Linear gradient creates a gradient going through all the stop colors along the
line between the "from" and the "to" .
If the points are percentages, then they are relative to the size of the area being
filled.
Percentage and length sizes cannot be mixed in a single gradient function

The an array of Stops specifys how to distribute the colors along the gradient.
The Stop#offset variable must be the range 0.0 to 1.0 and act like keyframes
along the gradient.
The offsets mark where the gradient should be exactly a particular color.

Tested on: java version "java-8-oracle"
Author: Mike Ohlson de Fine
*/
import javafx.application.Application;
import javafx.stage.Stage;
import javafx.scene.*;
import javafx.scene.paint.*;
import javafx.scene.shape.*;
```

```
public class GradientFillRectangle1 extends Application {
  public void start(Stage stage)
  {
        Group root = new Group();
        Rectangle rect1 = new Rectangle();

        // Size and location of rectangle on the JavaFX scene.
        rect1.setX(40.0f);
        rect1.setY(20.0f);
        rect1.setWidth(220.0f);
        rect1.setHeight(100.0f);

        // Appearance of the outline.
        rect1.setStrokeWidth(6.0f);
        rect1.setStroke(Color.BLUE);

        // Gradient Fill (Linear) Properties
        Stop[] stops = new Stop[] { new Stop(0, Color.BLACK), new Stop(0.5,
Color.RED)};
        LinearGradient lingrad1 = new LinearGradient(0, 0, 1, 0, true,

CycleMethod.NO_CYCLE, stops);

        rect1.setFill(lingrad1);
        root.getChildren().add(rect1);   // Add the rectangle to the group.

      Scene scene = new Scene(root, 300, 160);
      stage.setTitle("Linear Gradient Fill, JavaFX");
      stage.setScene(scene);
      stage.show();

  }
}
```

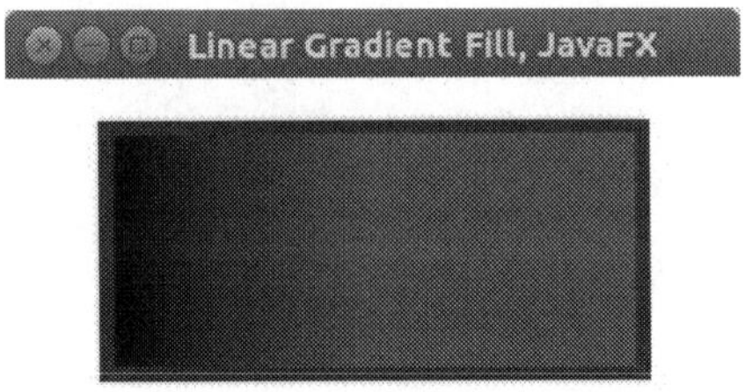

# Using Transparency/Opacity as a 'color'.

```
// GradientFillOpacityRectangle1.java
/*
Three Rectangles with various opacities.

Constructor
LinearGradient(double startX, double startY, double endX, double endY,
boolean proportional, CycleMethod cycleMethod, Stop... stops).

Opacity.
Opacity is a measure of how non-transparent a 'paint' is.
It is specified as a number between 0.0 (fully transparent) and 1.0 (fully
opaque).
For example, Color.rgb( 0,   255,  255,  0.8) is yellow an 80% opaque.

Linear Gradient:
The LinearGradient class fills a shape with a linear color gradient pattern.
The user may specify two or more gradient colors, and this Paint will provide
an interpolation between each color.

Tested on: java version "java-8-oracle"
Author: Mike Ohlson de Fine
*/
import javafx.application.Application;
import javafx.stage.Stage;
import javafx.scene.*;
import javafx.scene.paint.*;
import javafx.scene.shape.*;

public class GradientFillOpacityRectangle1 extends Application {
  public void start(Stage stage)
  {
        Group root = new Group();

        Rectangle rect1 = new Rectangle();
        rect1.setX(40.0f);           // Size and location on the JavaFX scene.
        rect1.setY(20.0f);
        rect1.setWidth(260.0f);
```

```
        rect1.setHeight(160.0f);
        rect1.setStrokeWidth(6.0f); // Appearance of the outline.
        rect1.setStroke(Color.BLUE);
        rect1.setStrokeType(StrokeType.INSIDE); //Stroke insides inner
rectangle.

        Rectangle rect2 = new Rectangle();
        rect2.setX(80.0f);          // Size and location on the JavaFX scene.
        rect2.setY(60.0f);
        rect2.setWidth(260.0f);
        rect2.setHeight(160.0f);
        rect2.setStrokeWidth(6.0f); // Appearance of the outline.
        rect2.setStroke(Color.RED);
        rect2.setStrokeType(StrokeType.INSIDE); //Stroke insides inner
rectangle.
        Rectangle rect3 = new Rectangle();
        rect3.setX(120.0f);          // Size and location on the JavaFX scene.
        rect3.setY(100.0f);
        rect3.setWidth(260.0f);
        rect3.setHeight(160.0f);
        rect3.setStrokeWidth(6.0f); // Appearance of the outline.
        rect3.setStroke(Color.GREEN);
        rect3.setStrokeType(StrokeType.INSIDE); //Stroke insides inner
rectangle.

        // Fill Properties 1
        LinearGradient lingrad1 = new LinearGradient(
            0,   // start X
            0,   // start Y
            0,   // end X
            1,   // end Y
            true, // proportional
            CycleMethod.NO_CYCLE, // cycle colors
            // stops: given by the two lines below  red, green, blue, opacity.
            new Stop(0.1f, Color.rgb(0,   250,    0,  .8)),
            new Stop(1.0f, Color.rgb(0,     0,  250,  .7)));

        // Fill Properties 2
        LinearGradient lingrad2 = new LinearGradient(
            0,   // start X
            0,   // start Y
```

```
            1,    // end X
            0,    // end Y
            true, // proportional
            CycleMethod.NO_CYCLE, // cycle colors
            // stops: given by the two lines below  red, green, blue, opacity
            new Stop(0.1f, Color.rgb( 0,   250,  250,  0.8)),
            new Stop(1.0f, Color.rgb(250,     0,    0,  .4)));

        // Fill Properties 3
        LinearGradient lingrad3 = new LinearGradient(
            0,    // start X
            0,    // start Y
            1,    // end X
            1,    // end Y
            true, // proportional
            CycleMethod.NO_CYCLE, // cycle colors
            // stops: given by the two lines below  red, green, blue, opacity
            new Stop(1.0f, Color.rgb( 0,     0,  250,  .6)),
            new Stop(0.1f, Color.rgb(250,  250,     0,  .8)));

        rect1.setFill(lingrad1);
        rect2.setFill(lingrad2);
        rect3.setFill(lingrad3);

        root.getChildren().add(rect1);   // Add the rectangles to the group.
        root.getChildren().add(rect2);
        root.getChildren().add(rect3);

      Scene scene = new Scene(root, 420, 300);
      stage.setTitle("Linear Gradients with opacity variation, JavaFX");
      stage.setScene(scene);
      stage.show();

   }
}
```

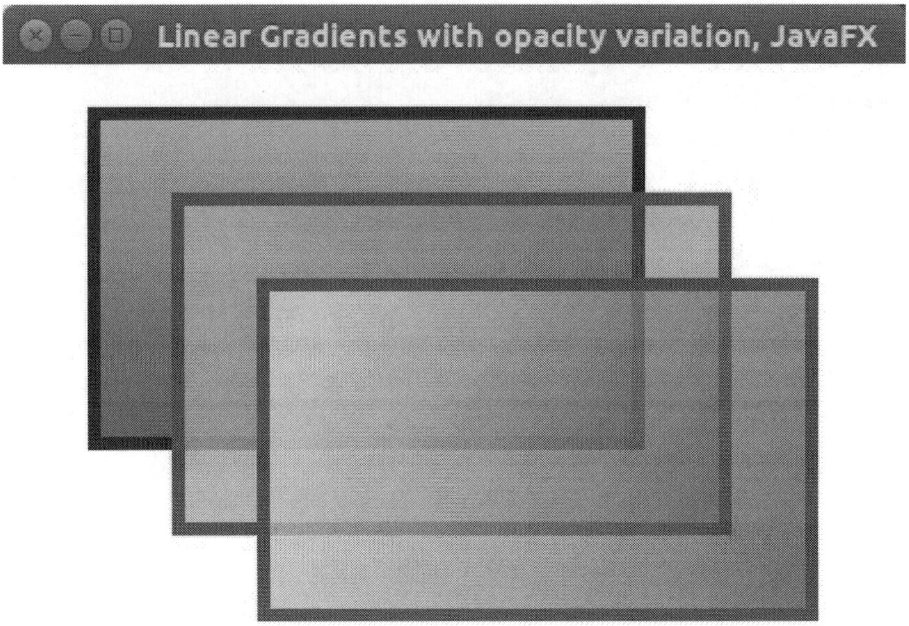


## Radial Gradient Specifications.

**startX, startY** – These double properties represent the x and y coordinates of the starting point of the gradient.

**endX, endY** – These double properties represent the x and y coordinates of the ending point of the gradient.

**CycleMethod** – This argument defines how the regions outside the color gradient bounds are defined by the starting and ending points and how they should be filled

**proportional** – This is a Boolean Variable; on setting this property to **true** the start and end locations are set to a proportion.

**Stop** – This argument defines the color-stop points along the gradient line.

**focus-distance**: (percentage) t is the distance from the center of the gradient to the focus point to which the first color is mapped. The value of the focus-distance is specified in "%". By default the focus is placed at the "center" of the gradient. The positive values will move the focus towards right and the negative values towards the left.

**Focus-angle**: (degrees from 0 to 360) Is the angle in degrees from the center of the gradient to the focus point to which the first color is mapped. Initially both the dots will be at same point (center). After applying some 'focus-distance' the green point will be moved towards right and by applying the 'focus-angle' the focus can be moved to the desired point.

**center:** (x%, y%) The 'center' is the co-ordinates of the center point of the gradient's circle. The value for the parameter is specified in "%" that is relative to the start point of the node on which the gradient is applied.

x - The X coordinate of the center point of the gradient's circle.
y - The Y coordinate of the center point of the gradient's circle.

**radius:** (length of percentage) It is the radius of the circle defining the extents of the color gradient. This is a mandatory parameter and if it is not included an exception will be thrown.
This radius unit can be in "%" or "px".

**repeat/reflect** Applying this parameter will make the gradient to repeat in cycles. If neither repeat nor reflect are given, then the CycleMethod defaults "NO_CYCLE".

*// **RadialGradientFillRectangle1.java***
*/**
*A Rectangle with a radial fill pattern.*
*We may specify 2 or more gradient colors.*
*We specify the circle controlling the gradient pattern, which is defined by a center point and a radius.*
*We can also specify a separate focus point within that circle, which controls the location of the first color of the gradient. By default the focus is set to be the center of the circle.*

*The center and radius are specified relative to a unit square, unless the*

*proportional variable is false.*
*By default proportional is true, and the gradient will be scaled to fill whatever shape it is applied to.*
*The focus point is always specified relative to the center point by an angle and a distance*
*relative to the radius.*

*The first color of the gradient will be the focus point, and the last color at the perimeter of the circle.*
*Any line drawn from the focus point to the circumference will thus span all of the gradient colors.*

*The focus distance will be clamped to the range (-1, 1) so that the focus point is always strictly inside the circle.*

*The stops: The array of Stops specifies how to distribute the colors along the gradient.*
*They mark where the gradient should be exactly a particular color.*

*Constructor*
*RadialGradient(focusAngle,*
*focusDistance,*
*centerX,*
*centerY,*
*radius,*
*proportional,*
*cycleMethod,*
*stops)*
*where:*
*focusAngle - the angle in degrees from the center of the gradient to the focus point to which the first color is mapped*
*focusDistance - the distance from the center of the gradient to the focus point to which the first color is mapped*
*centerX - the X coordinate of the center point of the gradient's circle*
*centerY - the Y coordinate of the center point of the gradient's circle*
*radius - the radius of the circle defining the extent of the color gradient*
*proportional - whether the coordinates and sizes are proportional to the shape which this gradient fills*
*cycleMethod - cycle method applied to the gradient*
*stops - the gradient's color specification using a list of stops.*

```
Tested on: java version "java-8-oracle"
Author: Mike Ohlson de Fine
*/
import javafx.application.Application;
import javafx.stage.Stage;
import javafx.scene.*;
import javafx.scene.paint.*;
import javafx.scene.shape.*;

public class RadialGradientFillRectangle1 extends Application {
   public void start(Stage stage)
   {
        Group root = new Group();
        Rectangle rect1 = new Rectangle();

        // Size and location of rectangle on the JavaFX scene.
        rect1.setX(40.0f);
        rect1.setY(20.0f);
        rect1.setWidth(300.0f);
        rect1.setHeight(200.0f);

        // Appearance of the outline.
        rect1.setStrokeWidth(6.0f);
        rect1.setStroke(Color.BLUE);

        //Stops: Set the radial gradient stop list.
        Stop[] stops = new Stop[]
        {
        new Stop(0.0, Color.WHITE),
        new Stop(0.3, Color.RED),
        new Stop(1.0, Color.DARKRED)
        };

        // Radial gradient set up.
        RadialGradient radialGradient = new RadialGradient(
             0,  // start X
             0,  // start Y
           180,  // end X
           100,  // end Y
            60,  // radius of the circle defining the extent of the color gradient
         false,  // proportional
```

```
            CycleMethod.NO_CYCLE, // Don't cycle colors
            stops);    // stops: given by the the 'stops' list above.

        //For rect1 set the radial fill pattern as specified above.
        rect1.setFill(radialGradient);
        root.getChildren().add(rect1);   // Add the rectangle to the group.

    Scene scene = new Scene(root, 400, 260);
    stage.setTitle("Radial Gradient Fill, JavaFX");
    stage.setScene(scene);
    stage.show();

  }
}
```

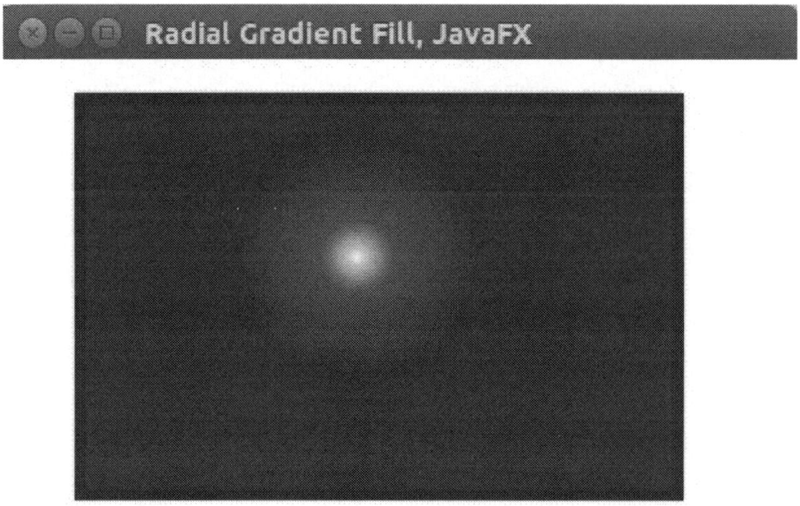


## Splitting Source Files.

If we need to develop a large application program the total code can be many thousands of lines long. Such long programs become progressively unwieldy and difficult to edit. The probability of introducing programmers errors also grows.

Therefore we need program architectures that can be split up into separate, smaller and easy to handle parts. The natural part in Java is the class.

We now introduce the type of program structure that separates code into different source files. Each source file can be written, compiled and debugged separately.

## Combine all Class source code into one document

This is the code structure we use mainly in this book. Although it is not best practice, it gives us code that is easier to understand. We can see it all at once and do not need to remember what instructions are written in files we cannot see simultaneously.

Diagrammatically this style of code looks like:

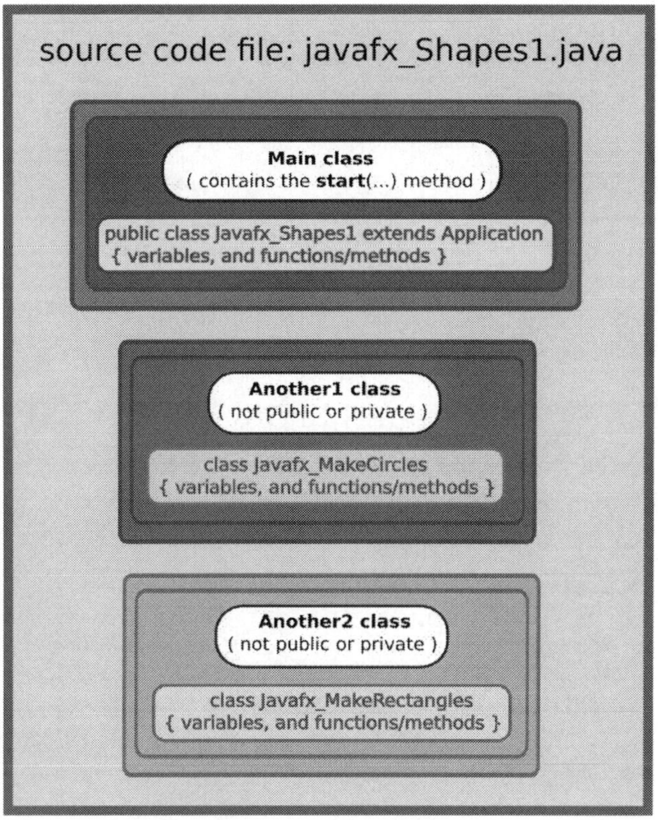


## Constructing Separate Source files that work together.

We can separate the classes by typing each one into a separate text document and saving it under the correct file name. For instance if we were writing a class named “Elephant_Ears” then the first line would be:

*public class Elephant_Ears*

and the file name must be **Elephant_Ears.java**

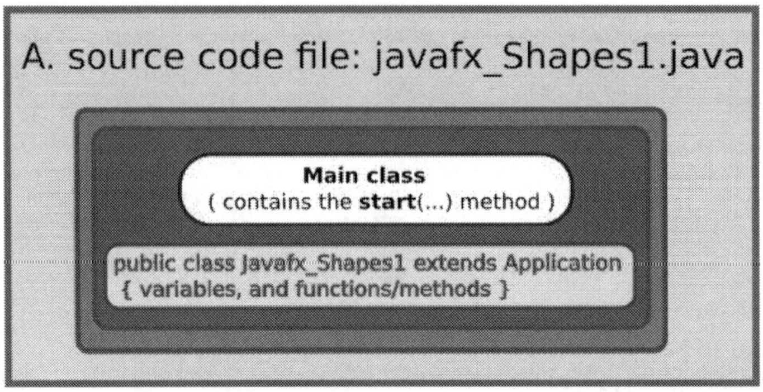


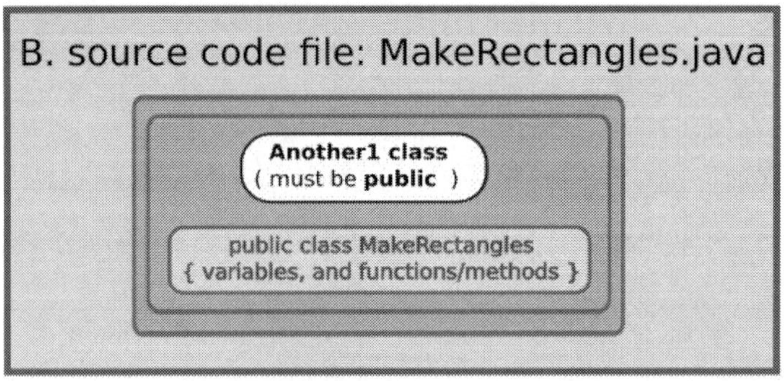


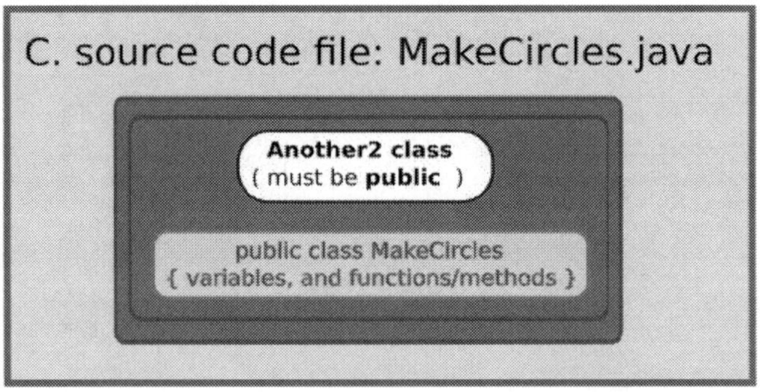


So far we have not dealt with circles. Drawing circles will be handled in detail in chapter 6. Therefore we give the code for class to draw circles below without explanation. The main point we want to make is how the three separately written files get compiled and how they can "see" each other because they have saved inside the same folder (package).

## 1. The MakeRectangles class

The source code is:

```
// MakeRctangles.java
/*
An experiment in class architecture.
Create a function that draws any rectangles with no default parameters.
All parameters are specified explicitly.
This class is instantiated and used in "Javafx_Shapes1".

Tested on: java version "java-8-oracle"
Author: Mike Ohlson de Fine
*/

import javafx.scene.paint.*;
import javafx.scene.shape.*;

public class MakeRectangles
{

    /* Method: Set up Rectangles, each with unique appearance.
       Parameters: position x, y, 3 fill colors, 3 stroke colors, stroke width.
       Note that the parameters can still be modified within the method as
       we have done with the setStrokeWidth(...) parameter. */

    public Rectangle make_rec1(double xx, double yy, double xwidth, double
yheight,
                    Color kula1fill,
                    Color kula1stroke,
                    double strokew)

    {
    // Rectangle instantiation:
    Rectangle rect1 = new Rectangle();

      // Size and location on the JavaFX scene.
```

```
        rect1.setX(xx);
        rect1.setY(yy);
        rect1.setWidth(xwidth);
        rect1.setHeight(yheight);

        // Appearance of the outline.
        rect1.setStrokeWidth(strokew);
        rect1.setStrokeLineCap(StrokeLineCap.ROUND);
        rect1.setStroke(kula1stroke);

        rect1.setSmooth(true);
        rect1.getStrokeDashArray().addAll(20d); // fill and blank pattern.
        rect1.setStrokeType(StrokeType.CENTERED); // CENTERED,
INSIDE or OUTSIDE.

        // Corner Style.
        rect1.setStrokeLineJoin(StrokeLineJoin.ROUND) ; // BEVEL,
MITER, ROUND

        // Fill Properties
        rect1.setFill(kula1fill);

        // Return a Rectangle object with detailed parameter specifications.
        return rect1 ;
    }
}
```

**Points to note.**

1.This must be a public class explicitly as specified in the first line:

*public class MakeRectangles*

2. This source code must be saved under the file name **MakeRectangles.java.**

3. The command, in the terminal, for compiling the file will be:

**javac MakeRectangles.java**

4. Proof of successful compilation will be the sudden appearance of a file named

**MakeRectangles.class** inside the same folder that contained the MakeRectangles.java source code.

## 2. Make the MakeCircles class.

The source code is:

```
// MakeCircles.java
/*
An experiment in class architecture.
Create a function that draws any circles with no default parameters.
All parameters are specified explicitly.
This class is instantiated and used in "Javafx_Shapes1".

Tested on: java version "java-8-oracle"
Author: Mike Ohlson de Fine
*/

import javafx.scene.paint.*;
import javafx.scene.shape.*;

public class MakeCircles
{

    /* Method: Set up circles. The parameters give a unique appearance.
       Parameters: position x, y, fill colors, stroke colors, stroke width.
       Note that the parameters can still be modified within the method as
       we have done with the setStrokeWidth(...) parameter.  */

    public Circle make_cir1(double xx, double yy, double radius,
                Color kula1fill,
                Color kula1stroke,
                double outlineWidth)
    {
    // Outer Circle: Position, radius and fill color.
    Circle circ1 = new Circle();
    circ1.setCenterX(xx);
    circ1.setCenterY(yy);
    circ1.setRadius(radius);
    circ1.setFill(kula1fill);
    // Outer Circle: outline width, color and dash pattern.
```

```
    circ1.setStroke(kula1stroke);
    circ1.setStrokeWidth(outlineWidth+8);
    circ1.setStrokeLineCap(StrokeLineCap.ROUND);
    circ1.getStrokeDashArray().addAll(40d);// fill, blank.
    return circ1 ;
    }
}
```

Similarly to the MakeRectangles class:

1. This must be a public class explicitly as specified in the first line:

*public class MakeCircles*

2. This source code must be saved under the file name **MakeCircles.java.**

3. The command, in the terminal, for compiling the file will be:

**javac MakeCircles.java**

4. Proof of successful compilation will be the sudden appearance of a file named

**MakeCircles.class** inside the same folder that contained the MakeRectangles.java source code.

## 3. Make the main class, instantiating both previously complied classes MakeRectangles and MakeCircles.

The very important point now is that inside this main Application class we need to create instances (class objects) of each of the previously compiled classes we want to make use of. This class object creation occurs when the instructions:

**MakeRectangles make_rect = new MakeRectangles();**

and

**MakeCircles make_circ = new MakeCircles();**

are executed.

```
// Javafx_Shapes1.java
/*
An experiment in class architecture - Separately compiled classes.
1. This class Javafx_CircleSet1 is only able to draw circles using the methods
defined
 in completely separate classs: "MakeCircles" and "MakeRectangles".
2a. MakeCircles is a completely separeate source file, compiled separately as a
public class.
2b. MakeRectangles is a completely separeate source file, compiled separately
as a public class.
3. The compiled classes are all inside a common directory folder, making them
components of the same package.
4. Note that if the classes were included in the "Javafx_CircleSet1" cource code
then they
   may not be classified as a public class. They have to be private.

Draws three concentric circles and then three rectangles with no default
parameters.
All parameters are specified explicitly in the "make_cir1" method.

Tested on: java version "java-8-oracle"
Author: Mike Ohlson de Fine
*/
import javafx.application.Application;
import javafx.stage.Stage;
import javafx.scene.*;
import javafx.scene.paint.*;
import javafx.scene.shape.*;

public class Javafx_Shapes1 extends Application
{
      Group root_node_grp = new Group();

      // Purples.
      final Color purp1 = Color.web("rgb(81%, 55%, 70%)");   // rgb percent
web color.
      final Color purp2 = Color.web("rgb(55%, 19%,  39%)");
      final Color purp3 = Color.web("rgb(28%, 0.4%, 16%)");
```

```
        // Red-violets.
        final Color yell1 = Color.web("rgb(80%, 60%, 100%)");
        final Color yell2 = Color.web("rgb(80%, 20%, 60%)");
        final Color yell3 = Color.web("rgb(80%,  0%, 20%)");

    public void start(Stage stage)
    {
        // Position.
        double xx = 300;
        double yy = 220;
        double radiu1 = 100;
        double radiu2 = 120;
        double radiu3 = 160;

        // Instantiate our external classes.
        MakeCircles mkcir = new MakeCircles(); // Instantiate an external class
        MakeRectangles mkrec = new MakeRectangles(); // Instantiate an
external class

        // Parameters: position x, y, radius, fill colors,stroke colors, stroke
width.
        Circle circ1 = mkcir.make_cir1( xx,  yy, radiu1, yell1, purp1, 3);
        Circle circ2 = mkcir.make_cir1( xx,  yy, radiu2, yell2, purp2, 5);
        Circle circ3 = mkcir.make_cir1( xx,  yy, radiu3, yell3, purp3, 7);

        // Insert the drawings of circles.
        root_node_grp.getChildren().add(circ3);
        root_node_grp.getChildren().add(circ2);
        root_node_grp.getChildren().add(circ1);


        xx = 40 ;
        yy = 30 ;
        double width1 = 160 ;
        double height1 = 220 ;
        // Parameters: position x, y, width, , height, fill colors, stroke colors,
stroke width.
        Rectangle rect1 = mkrec.make_rec1( xx,  yy, width1, height1, yell1, purp1,
3);
        Rectangle rect2 = mkrec.make_rec1( xx+20,  yy+20, width1-40, height1-
40, yell2, purp2, 5);
```

```
Rectangle rect3 = mkrec.make_rec1( xx+40,  yy+40, width1-80, height1-
80, yell3, purp3, 7);

/* Note that once the graphic objects have been assigned as children of
the root node,
   their parameter values are cast in concrete and cannot be changed.
   assigning new a different values to position, size and color will have no
effect
  on graphic objects already assigned. However any new graphic children
created will have
   the new parameter values.
*/

// Insert the drawings of circles.
root_node_grp.getChildren().add(rect1);
root_node_grp.getChildren().add(rect2);
root_node_grp.getChildren().add(rect3);

Scene scene = new Scene(root_node_grp, 500, 400, Color.web("#2c8437"));
stage.setTitle("Multiple Source files. Specify Rectangle and Circle
Parameters");
stage.setScene(scene);
stage.show();
  }
}
```

# Chapter 5

## COLOR

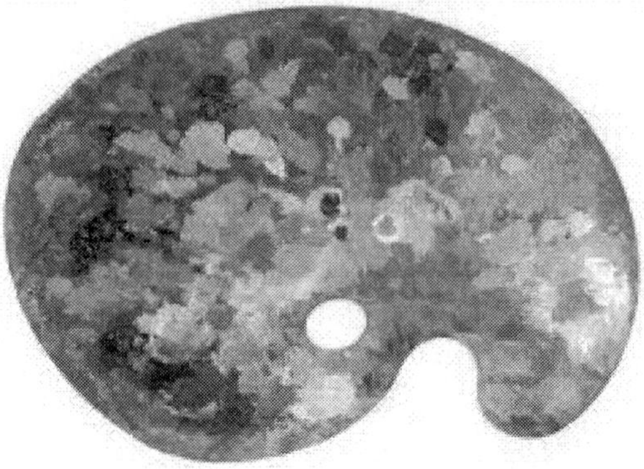

*"Sunset is still my favorite color, and rainbow is second."* Mattie Stepanek

*"A poplar tree is not green. It is a mix of blue green, lime green, silver green, light brown, cool grey and white."* four anonymous design professionals, *Thou Shall Not Use Comic Sans.*

In this chapter we will cover:

- how to control color
- using named web colors
- a minimal palette of named colors
- hue, saturation and brightness
- color scheme design using web tools
- construction of smoothly mixed color swatches
- Construction of a general paint box to mix colors.

# Controlling Color

Color is complicated. There are too many choices. Three primary colors, each divided into 256 levels of intensity give us 1.65 million choices. Plus there is a fourth "color" for specifying opacity (or transparency). This raises the number of choices to 420 million. In addition we humans have thought up semi-arbitrary rules about which colors may be placed near each other to produce a pleasant mood or an unpleasant one if the scenario demands it. Artists and paint manufacturers have narrowed the choices down to a few hundred by giving them names and packing them in tubes and cans. It is all a bit daunting. Our task of controlling color digitally has apparently been simplified by confining our options to 256 levels of three primary colors of red, green and blue. Controlling color is difficult when they are expressed purely as numbers. Color is a vocabulary of visual communication. Colors evoke an emotional response in us and this introduces an extra dimension in how colors are used. For drawings to be effective and valued, color should be handled with the same thought and sensitivity as choice of words in spoken communication.

Artists refer to colors by names like vermillion, burnt umber, burnt sienna, cobalt blue. Vendors of commercial house paints give them romantic names like hot pink, lavender blush or misty rose.

Using colors by name in Java gives rise to the following difficulties:

- we have difficulty remembering which names are valid and recognized in the FavaFX.Paint library. Is the name in upper case or lower? Should we qualify a color as 'light' or 'pale'.
- Which 5 colors form a good shaded sequence from dark to light?
- There are often several valid names for the same color. There is a huge array of 'whites'.

- There is nothing in the name that indicates that color's relationship to other colors.

If colors are expressed purely as numbers then it becomes possible to control, combine and manipulate colors in systematic, programmable ways. We end this chapter with methods for achieving this.

In this chapter we deal with both named colors and numerically defined colors.

We also briefly discuss how to combine colors in ways that should be appealing. A desirable tool that we want is the equivalent of an artist's mixing palette where we can place two end-colors and then mix various intermediate colors to create transitional colors. We create such a tool for ourselves.

## The Named Colors

The javafx.scene.,Paint.* library will recognize the following color names.

The list is flawed. Some of the names are wrong because the color they paint is incorrect for it name. There are also redundant names for the same color. So the recommendation is not to use these colors unless you have tested them individually.

"ALICEBLUE", "ANTIQUEWHITE", "AQUA", "AQUAMARINE", "AZURE", "BEIGE"
"BISQUE", "BLACK", "BLANCHEDALMOND", "BLUE", "BLUEVIOLET", "BROWN",
"BURLYWOOD", "CADETBLUE", "CHARTREUSE", "CHOCOLATE", "CORAL",
"CORNFLOWERBLUE", "CORNSILK", "CRIMSON", "CYAN", "DARKBLUE", "DARKCYAN",
"DARKGOLDENROD", "DARKGRAY", "DARKGREEN", "DARKGREY", "DARKKHAKI",
"DARKMAGENTA","DARKOLIVEGREEN", "DARKORANGE", "DARKORCHID", "DARKRED",

"DARKSALMON", "DARKSEAGREEN", "DARKSLATEBLUE",
"DARKSLATEGRAY",
"DARKSLATEGREY", "DARKTURQUOISE", "DARKVIOLET", "DEEPPINK",
"DEEPSKYBLUE",
"DIMGRAY", "DIMGREY", "DODGERBLUE", "FIREBRICK", "FLORALWHITE",
"FORESTGREEN", "FUCHSIA", "GAINSBORO", "GHOSTWHITE", "GOLD",
"GOLDENROD",
"GRAY", "GREEN", "GREENYELLOW", "GREY", "HONEYDEW", "HOTPINK",
"INDIANRED",
"INDIGO", "IVORY", "KHAKI", "LAVENDER", "LAVENDERBLUSH",
"LAWNGREEN",
"LEMONCHIFFON", "LIGHTBLUE", "LIGHTCORAL", "LIGHTCYAN",
"LIGHTGOLDENRODYELLOW", "LIGHTGRAY", "LIGHTGREEN",
"LIGHTGREY",
"LIGHTPINK", "LIGHTSALMON", "LIGHTSEAGREEN", "LIGHTSKYBLUE",
"LIGHTSLATEGRAY", "LIGHTSLATEGREY", "LIGHTSTEELBLUE",
"LIGHTYELLOW", "LIME",
"LIMEGREEN", "LINEN", "MAGENTA", "MAROON",
"MEDIUMAQUAMARINE",
"MEDIUMBLUE", "MEDIUMORCHID", "MEDIUMPURPLE",
"MEDIUMSEAGREEN",
"MEDIUMSLATEBLUE", "MEDIUMSPRINGGREEN", "MEDIUMTURQUOISE",
"MEDIUMVIOLETRED", "MIDNIGHTBLUE", "MINTCREAM", "MISTYROSE",
"MOCCASIN",
"NAVAJOWHITE", "NAVY", "OLDLACE", "OLIVE", "OLIVEDRAB", "ORANGE",
"ORANGERED",
"ORCHID", "PALEGOLDENROD", "PALEGREEN", "PALETURQUOISE",
"PALEVIOLETRED",
"PAPAYAWHIP", "PEACHPUFF", "PERU", "PINK", "PLUM", "POWDERBLUE",
"PURPLE", "RED",
"ROSYBROWN", "ROYALBLUE", "SADDLEBROWN", "SALMON",
"SANDYBROWN",
"SEAGREEN", "SEASHELL", "SIENNA", "SILVER", "SKYBLUE",
"SLATEBLUE", "SLATEGRAY",
"SLATEGREY", "SNOW", "SPRINGGREEN", "STEELBLUE", "TAN", "TEAL",
"THISTLE",
"TOMATO", "TURQUOISE", "VIOLET", "WHEAT", "WHITE",
"WHITESMOKE", "YELLOW",
"YELLOWGREEN"

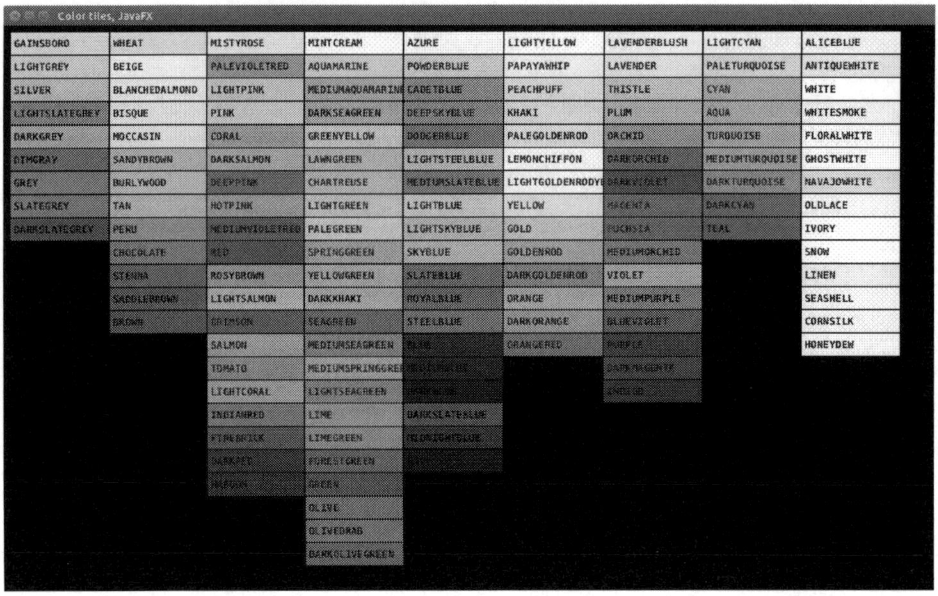


If we eliminate redundancies and errors we end up with the following digital pallette of colors that are practically useful.

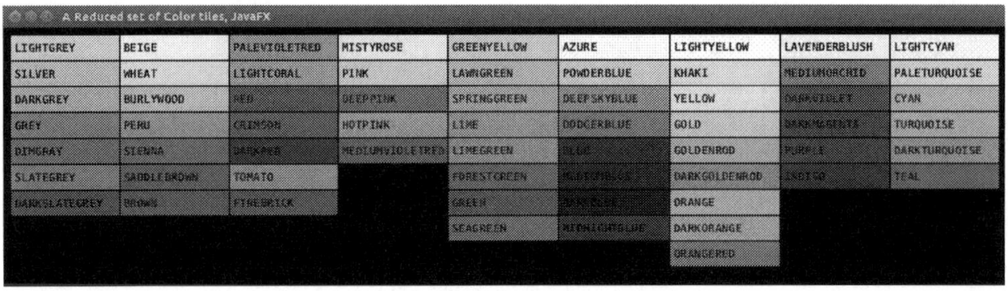


The Java code to achieve this is:

```
// ColorPalletteMinimized2.java
/*
An array of rectangular Color samples arranged by hue.

Tested on: java version "java-8-oracle"
Author:Mike Ohlson de Fine
*/
import javafx.application.Application;
import javafx.stage.Stage;
```

```
import javafx.scene.*;
import javafx.scene.paint.*;
import javafx.scene.shape.*;

import javafx.scene.text.Font;
import javafx.scene.text.FontWeight;
import javafx.scene.text.Text;

public class ColorPalletteMinimized2 extends Application
{
   public void start(Stage stage)
   {
      Group root = new Group();

// Reds
 Color[] colorRed =
   {

      Color.PALEVIOLETRED,
      Color.LIGHTCORAL,
      Color.RED,
      Color.CRIMSON,
      Color.DARKRED,
      Color.TOMATO,
      Color.FIREBRICK,
   };

String[] NameReds =
   {
      "PALEVIOLETRED",
      "LIGHTCORAL",
      "RED",
      "CRIMSON",
      "DARKRED",
      "TOMATO",
      "FIREBRICK",
   };

 // Pinks
 Color[] colorPink =
   {
```

```
        Color.MISTYROSE,
        Color.PINK,
        Color.DEEPPINK,
        Color.HOTPINK,
        Color.MEDIUMVIOLETRED,
    };

String[] NamePinks =
    {
        "MISTYROSE",
        "PINK",
        "DEEPPINK",
        "HOTPINK",
        "MEDIUMVIOLETRED"
    };

// Greens
Color[] colorGreen =
    {
        Color.GREENYELLOW,
        Color.LAWNGREEN,
        Color.SPRINGGREEN,
        Color.LIME,
        Color.LIMEGREEN,
        Color.FORESTGREEN,
        Color.GREEN,
        Color.SEAGREEN,
    };

String[] NameGreens =
    {
        "GREENYELLOW",
        "LAWNGREEN",
        "SPRINGGREEN",
        "LIME",
        "LIMEGREEN",
        "FORESTGREEN",
        "GREEN",
        "SEAGREEN",
    };
```

```
// Yellows
Color[] colorYellow =
  {
   Color.LIGHTYELLOW,
   Color.KHAKI,
   Color.YELLOW,
   Color.GOLD,
   Color.GOLDENROD,
   Color.DARKGOLDENROD,
   Color.ORANGE,
   Color.DARKORANGE,
   Color.ORANGERED,
  };
String[] NameYellows =
  {
    "LIGHTYELLOW",
    "KHAKI",
    "YELLOW",
    "GOLD",
    "GOLDENROD",
    "DARKGOLDENROD",
    "ORANGE",
    "DARKORANGE",
    "ORANGERED",
  };


// Blues
Color[] colorBlue =
  {
   Color.AZURE,
   Color.POWDERBLUE,
   Color.DEEPSKYBLUE,
   Color.DODGERBLUE,
   Color.BLUE,
   Color.MEDIUMBLUE,
   Color.DARKBLUE,
   Color.MIDNIGHTBLUE,
   } ;

String[] NameBlues =
```

```
 {
  "AZURE",
  "POWDERBLUE",
  "DEEPSKYBLUE",
  "DODGERBLUE",
  "BLUE",
  "MEDIUMBLUE",
  "DARKBLUE",
  "MIDNIGHTBLUE",
 };

// Cyans
Color[] colorCyan =
 {
  Color.LIGHTCYAN,
  Color.PALETURQUOISE,
  Color.CYAN,
  Color.TURQUOISE,
  Color.DARKTURQUOISE,
  Color.TEAL,
 };

String[] NameCyans =
 {
  "LIGHTCYAN",
  "PALETURQUOISE",
  "CYAN",
  "TURQUOISE",
  "DARKTURQUOISE",
  "TEAL",
 };

// Violets
Color[] colorViolet =
 {
  Color.LAVENDERBLUSH,
  Color.MEDIUMORCHID,
  Color.DARKVIOLET,
  Color.DARKMAGENTA,
  Color.PURPLE,
  Color.INDIGO,
```

```
    };

String[] NameViolets =
    {
      "LAVENDERBLUSH",
      "MEDIUMORCHID",
      "DARKVIOLET",
      "DARKMAGENTA",
      "PURPLE",
      "INDIGO",
    };

// Browns
Color[] colorBrown =
    {
    Color.BEIGE,
    Color.WHEAT,
    Color.BURLYWOOD,
    Color.PERU,
    Color.SIENNA,
    Color.SADDLEBROWN,
    Color.BROWN,
    };

String[] NameBrowns =
    {
     "BEIGE",
     "WHEAT",
     "BURLYWOOD",
     "PERU",
     "SIENNA",
     "SADDLEBROWN",
     "BROWN",
    };

// Greys
Color[] colorGrey =
    {
     Color.LIGHTGREY,
     Color.SILVER,
     Color.DARKGREY,
```

```
    Color.GREY,
    Color.DIMGRAY,
    Color.SLATEGREY,
    Color.DARKSLATEGREY,
   Color.BLACK,
  };

String[] NameGreys =
  {
    "LIGHTGREY",
    "SILVER",
    "DARKGREY",
    "GREY",
    "DIMGRAY",
    "SLATEGREY",
    "DARKSLATEGREY",
    "BLACK"
  };

   int colorGreyLen = colorGrey.length ;
   int colorBrownLen = colorBrown.length ;
   int colorVioletLen = colorViolet.length ;
   int colorCyanLen = colorCyan.length ;
   int colorBlueLen = colorBlue.length ;
   int colorYellowLen = colorYellow.length ;
   int colorGreenLen = colorGreen.length ;
   int colorRedLen = colorRed.length ;
   int colorPinkLen = colorPink.length ;

   System.out.println("Length of colorGrey " + colorGreyLen);
        double xx, yy, ww, hh, gap, txtOffset ;
        xx = 10;
        yy = 10;
        ww = 134;
        hh = 30;
        gap = 2;
        txtOffset = 4 ;
          for(int i=0; i<colorGrey.length; i++)
          {
             Text txt1 = new Text(xx+txtOffset, yy+20, NameGreys[i]);
             txt1.setFill(Color.BLACK);
```

```
            txt1.setFont(Font.font(java.awt.Font.MONOSPACED,
FontWeight.BOLD, 14));

            Rectangle rect = new Rectangle(xx,yy,ww,hh);
            yy += hh + gap ;
            rect.setFill(colorGrey[i]);
            root.getChildren().add(rect);
            root.getChildren().add(txt1);

        }

    xx += ww + gap ;
    yy = 10;
    System.out.println("Length of colorBrown " + colorBrownLen);
        for(int i=0; i<colorBrown.length; i++)
        {
            Text txt1 = new Text(xx+txtOffset, yy+20, NameBrowns[i]);
            txt1.setFill(Color.BLACK);
            txt1.setFont(Font.font(java.awt.Font.MONOSPACED,
FontWeight.BOLD, 14));

            Rectangle rect = new Rectangle(xx,yy,ww,hh);
            yy += hh + gap ;
            rect.setFill(colorBrown[i]);
            root.getChildren().add(rect);
            root.getChildren().add(txt1);
        }

    xx += ww + gap ;
    yy = 10;
    System.out.println("Length of colorRed " + colorRedLen);
        for(int i=0; i<colorRed.length; i++)
        {
            Text txt1 = new Text(xx+txtOffset, yy+20, NameReds[i]);
            txt1.setFill(Color.BLACK);
            txt1.setFont(Font.font(java.awt.Font.MONOSPACED,
FontWeight.BOLD, 14));

            Rectangle rect = new Rectangle(xx,yy,ww,hh);
            yy += hh + gap ;
            rect.setFill(colorRed[i]);
```

```
            root.getChildren().add(rect);
            root.getChildren().add(txt1);
        }

    xx += ww + gap ;
    yy = 10;
    System.out.println("Length of colorPink " + colorPinkLen);
        for(int i=0; i<colorPink.length; i++)
        {
            Text txt1 = new Text(xx+txtOffset, yy+20, NamePinks[i]);
            txt1.setFill(Color.BLACK);
            txt1.setFont(Font.font(java.awt.Font.MONOSPACED,
FontWeight.BOLD, 14));

            Rectangle rect = new Rectangle(xx,yy,ww,hh);
            yy += hh + gap ;
            rect.setFill(colorPink[i]);
            root.getChildren().add(rect);
            root.getChildren().add(txt1);
        }

    xx += ww + gap ;
    yy = 10;
    System.out.println("Length of colorGreen " + colorGreenLen);
        for(int i=0; i<colorGreen.length; i++)
        {
            Text txt1 = new Text(xx+txtOffset, yy+20, NameGreens[i]);
            txt1.setFill(Color.BLACK);
            txt1.setFont(Font.font(java.awt.Font.MONOSPACED,
FontWeight.BOLD, 14));

            Rectangle rect = new Rectangle(xx,yy,ww,hh);
            yy += hh + gap ;
            rect.setFill(colorGreen[i]);
            root.getChildren().add(rect);
            root.getChildren().add(txt1);
        }

    xx += ww + gap ;
    yy = 10;
    System.out.println("Length of colorBlue " + colorBlueLen);
```

```
        for(int i=0; i<colorBlue.length; i++)
        {
           Text txt1 = new Text(xx+txtOffset, yy+20, NameBlues[i]);
           txt1.setFill(Color.BLACK);
           txt1.setFont(Font.font(java.awt.Font.MONOSPACED,
FontWeight.BOLD, 14));

           Rectangle rect = new Rectangle(xx,yy,ww,hh);
           yy += hh + gap ;
           rect.setFill(colorBlue[i]);
           root.getChildren().add(rect);
           root.getChildren().add(txt1);
        }

        xx += ww + gap ;
        yy = 10;
        System.out.println("Length of colorYellow " + colorYellowLen);
        for(int i=0; i<colorYellow.length; i++)
        {
           Text txt1 = new Text(xx+txtOffset, yy+20, NameYellows[i]);
           txt1.setFill(Color.BLACK);
           txt1.setFont(Font.font(java.awt.Font.MONOSPACED,
FontWeight.BOLD, 14));

           Rectangle rect = new Rectangle(xx,yy,ww,hh);
           yy += hh + gap ;
           rect.setFill(colorYellow[i]);
           root.getChildren().add(rect);
          root.getChildren().add(txt1);
        }


    xx += ww + gap ;
    yy = 10;
    System.out.println("Length of colorViolet " + colorVioletLen);
        for(int i=0; i<colorViolet.length; i++)
        {
           Text txt1 = new Text(xx+txtOffset, yy+20, NameViolets[i]);
           txt1.setFill(Color.BLACK);
           txt1.setFont(Font.font(java.awt.Font.MONOSPACED,
FontWeight.BOLD, 14));
```

```
            Rectangle rect = new Rectangle(xx,yy,ww,hh);
            yy += hh + gap ;
            rect.setFill(colorViolet[i]);
            root.getChildren().add(rect);
            root.getChildren().add(txt1);
        }

    xx += ww + gap ;
    yy = 10;
    System.out.println("Length of colorCyan " + colorCyanLen);
        for(int i=0; i<colorCyan.length; i++)
        {
            Text txt1 = new Text(xx+txtOffset, yy+20, NameCyans[i]);
            txt1.setFill(Color.BLACK);
            txt1.setFont(Font.font(java.awt.Font.MONOSPACED,
FontWeight.BOLD, 14));

            Rectangle rect = new Rectangle(xx,yy,ww,hh);
            yy += hh + gap ;
            rect.setFill(colorCyan[i]);
            root.getChildren().add(rect);
            root.getChildren().add(txt1);
        }

    Scene scene = new Scene(root, 1240, 320, Color.BLACK);
     stage.setTitle("A Reduced set of Color tiles, JavaFX");
     stage.setScene(scene);
     stage.show();
  } }
```

Because it is difficult and time consuming to produce and test the above color palette the code has been given here in full. This means that anyone can copy it and run it on any device that runs a modern java and verify which named colors appear correctly on that device.

## *Numerically Constructed Colors*

To have complete control over colors we mix the three primary colors of red, green and blue to provide any color we desire.

There are more than one way of assembling the red, green and blue, abbreviated RGB, components as demonstrated below. Borrowing from the old Television transmission technology red, green and blue portions are often referred to as channels.

In specifying color for computer graphics there is a fourth channel that goes by the name alpha. Alpha is opacity, the measure of how transparent or opaque the final mix of color should appear. The alpha value varies from 0.0 which is totally see through, to 1.0 which is totally opaque. If alpha is 0.5 then the object is 50% opaque and an object with this color will allow other objects to show through as shown in the diagram below.

## Alpha channel opacity values

### Color specification syntax

JavaFX allows us to specify colors in at least 22 different ways. Most of them give the values of the red, green and blue components separately. The alpha (opacity) value can be specified optionally or allowed to take on the default value of 1 (fully opaque).

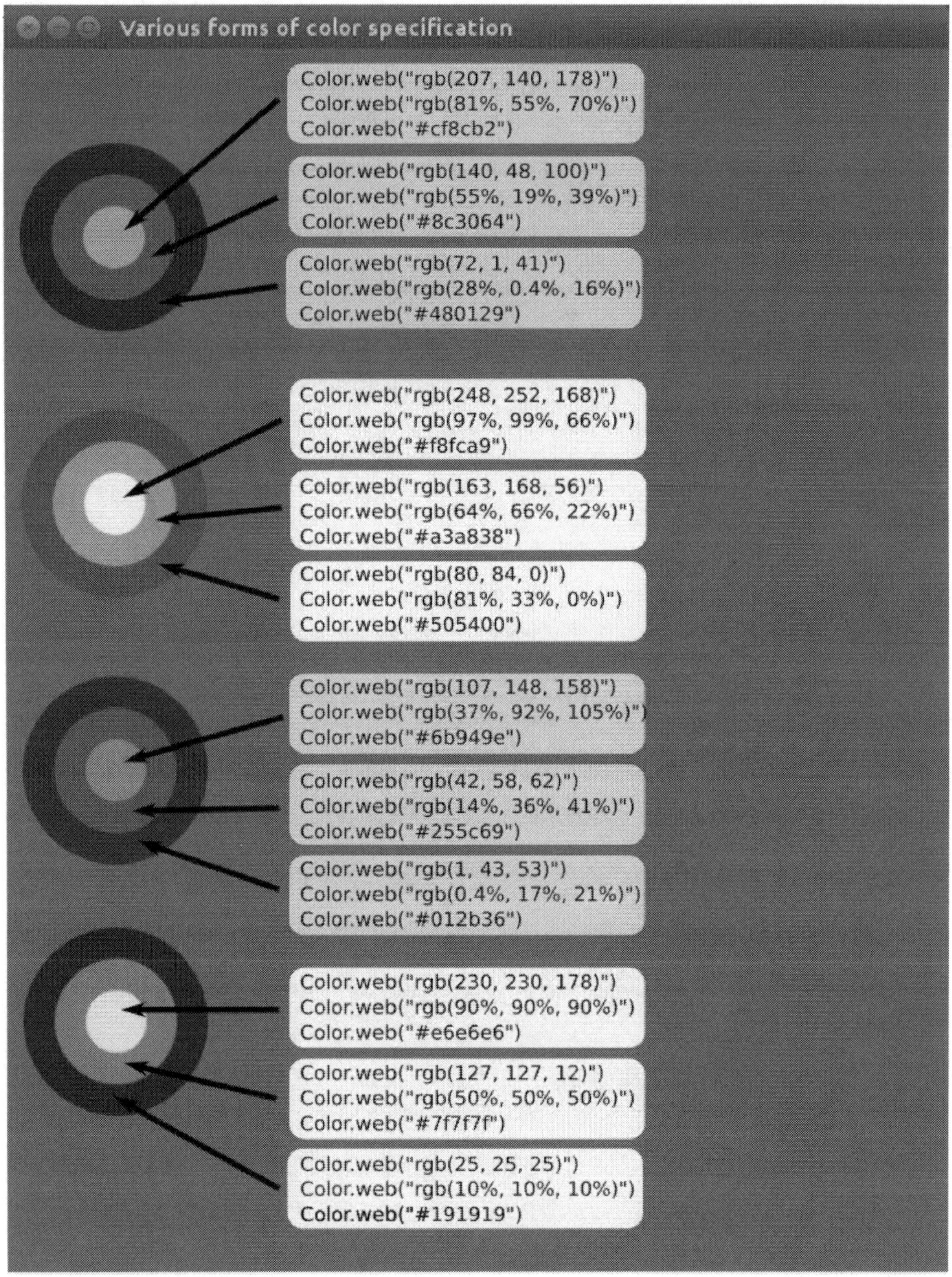
Various forms of color specification
Color.web("rgb(207, 140, 178)")
Color.web("rgb(81%, 55%, 70%)")
Color.web("#cf8cb2")
Color.web("rgb(140, 48, 100)")
Color.web("rgb(55%, 19%, 39%)")
Color.web("#8c3064")
Color.web("rgb(72, 1, 41)")
Color.web("rgb(28%, 0.4%, 16%)")
Color.web("#480129")
Color.web("rgb(248, 252, 168)")
Color.web("rgb(97%, 99%, 66%)")
Color.web("#f8fca9")
Color.web("rgb(163, 168, 56)")
Color.web("rgb(64%, 66%, 22%)")
Color.web("#a3a838")
Color.web("rgb(80, 84, 0)")
Color.web("rgb(81%, 33%, 0%)")
Color.web("#505400")
Color.web("rgb(107, 148, 158)")
Color.web("rgb(37%, 92%, 105%)")
Color.web("#6b949e")
Color.web("rgb(42, 58, 62)")
Color.web("rgb(14%, 36%, 41%)")
Color.web("#255c69")
Color.web("rgb(1, 43, 53)")
Color.web("rgb(0.4%, 17%, 21%)")
Color.web("#012b36")
Color.web("rgb(230, 230, 178)")
Color.web("rgb(90%, 90%, 90%)")
Color.web("#e6e6e6")
Color.web("rgb(127, 127, 12)")
Color.web("rgb(50%, 50%, 50%)")
Color.web("#7f7f7f")
Color.web("rgb(25, 25, 25)")
Color.web("rgb(10%, 10%, 10%)")
Color.web("#191919")

Here is a list of examples of the different ways color can be specified.

## Color Construction with explicit alpha (opacity/transparency) channel.

Color kula = new Color( 0,   0, 1,   1.0); // The standard color constructor, using 0->1.0 values.

Color kula = Color.color(0,   0, 1.0, 1.0); // Use 0->1.0 values. 0 is dark, 1.0 the brightest.

Color kula = Color.rgb( 0,   0, 255, 1.0); // Use integers in the range 0->255, going from dark to bright.

Color kula = Color.hsb(270, 0.9, 0.7, 1.0); //hue = 270, saturation & brightness = 1.0.

Color kula = Color.web("rgba(0,   0, 255, 1.0)");   // Red-Green-Blue-alpha web values.

Color kula = Color.web("rgba(0.0%, 100%, 0.0%, 1.0)"); // Green as an rgb percent web value.

Color kula = Color.web("hsla(270, 100%, 100%, 1.0)"); // Blue as an Hue-Saturation-Luminosity web value.

Color kula = Color.web("0x0000FF", 1.0); // Blue - Hex (hexadecimal) website value.

Color kula = Color.web("#000FF00", 1.0); // Green - Hex (hexadecimal) website value.

Color kula = Color.web("FF0000",  1.0); // Red - Hex (hexadecimal) website value.

## Fully opaque colors (implicit alpha = 1.0).

Color kula = Color.BLUE;         //The blue constant

```
Color kula = Color.color(0.8,      0.8,    0.8);  // Light grey in 0->1.0 values.

Color kula = Color.rgb( 0,      0,    255);        //Use the integer range 0->255.

Color kula = Color.hsb(270,   1.0,    1.0);          //hue-saturation-brightness.


Color kula = Color.web("rgb(0,       0,   255)");  // blue as an rgb web value in the range 0 to 255.

Color kula = Color.web("rgb(0,       0,  100%)");        // blue as an rgb percent web value.

Color kula = Color.web("hsl(270,  100%,  100%)");  // blue as an hue-saturation-luminance (hsl) web value.

Color kula = Color.web("0x0000FF");            // blue as a hex web value.

Color kula = Color.web("0x00F");               // blue as a short hex web value.

Color kula = Color.web("#0000FF");             // blue as a hex web value.

Color kula = Color.web("#00F");                // blue as a short hex web value.

Color kula = Color.web("0000FF");              // blue as a hex web value.

Color kula = Color.web("00F");                 // blue as a short hex web value.
```

These 23 different ways of defining color can be divided up into five categories defined by the format of of numbers used to represent color.

**Category 1: The named colors.**

Here the color is specified by a unique name, represented as a string value. These are the names listed on the second page of this chapter.

**Category 2: The range 0 to 1. (double floating point values).**

This method is the easiest and simplest to use and we use it in this book mostly.

RGB values going from low value 0.0 to highest value 1.0

Pure red is Color.color(1.0, 0, 0),

pure green is Color.color(0, 1.0, 0),

yellow, an equal parts mixture of green and blue is Color(0, 1.0, 1.0)

**Category 3: The range 0 to 255 (integer values).**

RGB values going from low value 0 to highest value 255

Pure red is Color(255, 0, 0),

pure green is Color(0, 255, 0),

yellow, an equal parts mixture of green and blue is Color(0, 255, 255)

**Category 4: The hexadecimal range 0 to FF.**

RGB values going from low value 0 to highest value FF

Pure red is Color(FF0000),

pure green is Color(00FF00),

yellow, an equal parts mixture of green and blue is Color(FFFF00)

**Category 5: Hue, saturation and brightness also called HSB**

The range of hues is 0 to 360, saturation in the range 0.0 to 1.0, and brightness also in the range 0.0 to 1.0.

This method is very technical and can only be accurately explained using mathematical terminology. However the underlying ideas are not difficult to understand and are illustrated in the diagrams below.

**Hue** – the amount or red-green-blue represented as an angle in degrees.

**Saturation** - the amount of pure color

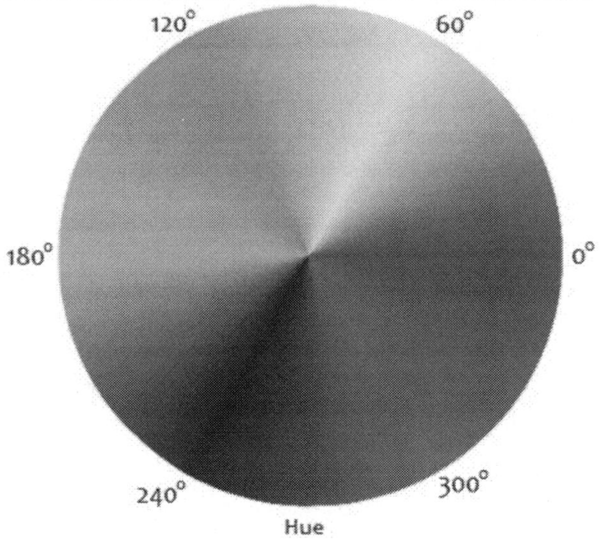


**Brightness** – the brightness is like the paleness of a color which is achieved by adding increasing amounts of all the colors. Full brightness is 100% of red, 100% green, and 100% blue.

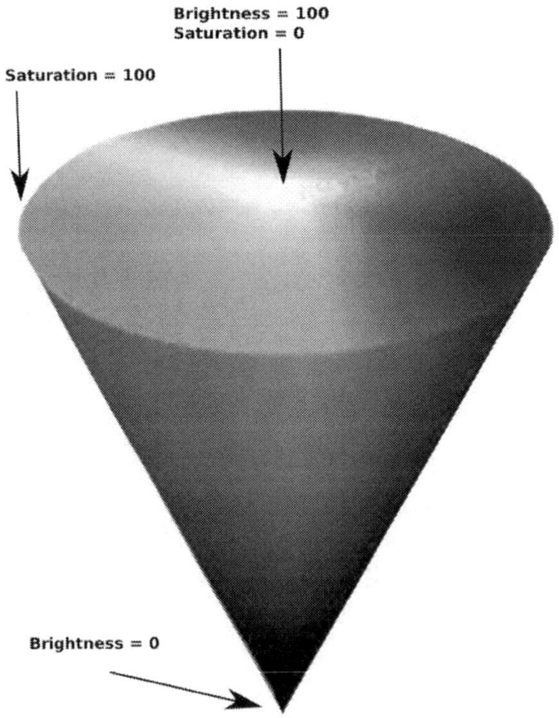

# The simplest way to control color

The form of color specification that is easiest to control and vary with Java instructions are:
***Color kula = Color.color(rr, gg, bb, alpha);***

This format gives an explicit value to the alpha (opacity) channel which can be made any value between zero an one. Each value ***rr, gg, bb, alpha*** is a double and therefore easily modified using simple arithmetic.

Later we have examples of Java code that begin with one color (rr1, gg1, bb1, alfa1) and transforms it in small adjustments until it ends up as a final color (rr2, gg2, bb2, alfa2).

# JavaFX Color Manipulation Methods

In addition to specifying the numerical value of color in each color channel, JavaFX provides some methods that allow us to achieve some more sophisticated operations on a color as listed below.

**brighter()** Creates a new Color that is a brighter version of this Color.
**Darker()** Creates a new Color that is a darker version of this Color.
**Invert()** Creates a new Color that is inversion of this Color. Similar to a color negative used in old fashioned wet chemical photography.
**Saturate()** Creates a new Color that is a more saturated (more intense) version of this Color.
**Desaturate()** Creates a new Color that is a less saturated version of this Color.
**deriveColor( hueShift, saturationFactor, brightnessFactor, opacityFactor)**
Creates a new Color based on this Color with hue, saturation, brightness and opacity values altered.
**interpolate(Color endValue, double t)**
The function calculates an interpolated value along the fraction t between 0.0 and 1.0.

## To discover properties

**getBrightness()** Gets the brightness component of this Color.
**GetHue()** Gets the hue component of this Color.
**GetSaturation()** Gets the saturation component of this Color.
**GetOpacity()** The opacity of the Color, in the range 0.0-1.0.
**getRed()** The red component of the Color, in the range 0.0-1.0.
**getGreen()** The green component of the Color, in the range 0.0-1.0.
**getBlue()** The blue component of the Color, in the range 0.0-1.0.

## General Color Specification

**gray( gray)** Creates an opaque grey color.
**gray( gray, opacity)** Creates a grey color.
**grayRgb( gray)** A shortcut for rgb(gray, gray, gray).
**grayRgb( gray, opacity)** A shortcut for rgb(gray, gray, gray, opacity).
**Grayscale()** A new Color that is grayscale equivalent of this Color.
**HashCode()** Returns a hash code for this Color object.
**hsb(hue, saturation, brightness)** An opaque Color based on the specified values in the HSB color model.
**hsb( hue, saturation, brightness, opacity)** A Color based on the specified values in the HSB color model, and a given opacity.
**rgb(red, green,blue)**
An opaque sRGB color with the specified RGB values in the range 0-255.
**rgb(red, green, blue, opacity)**
An RGB color with the specified RGB values in the range 0-255, and a given opacity.
**ToString()** Returns a string representation of this Color.
**valueOf(java.lang.String value)** A color value from a string representation.
**web(java.lang.String colorString)** An RGB color specified with an HTML or CSS attribute string.
**web(java.lang.String colorString, opacity)** An RGB color specified with an HTML or CSS attribute string.

# Numerical Color Synthesis and Interpolation

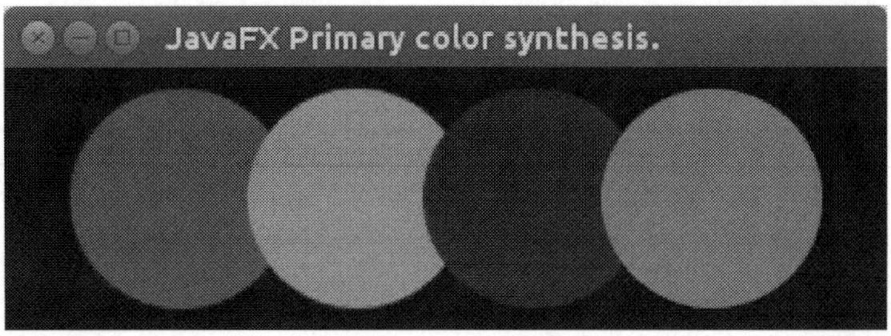


## 1. Simple color construction using arrays of RGB values.

Here we confirm the way we will be constructing color objects from a string with double precision values embedded in them. The format is:

***Color red1 = Color.web("rgb("+kul1[0]+"%,"+kul1[1]+"%,"+kul1[2]+"%)");***

where

kul1 is a Java array of values like ***double[] kul1 = { 100, 0, 0 };*** where each value in the array represents the amount of primary color in the red, green and blue channels.

```
// ColorArraySeries1.java
/*
Colors are synthesized from numerical % values kept in
simple arrays in the format: double[] kul1 = { 50,   80,   100 };
Thes numerical arrays are used to assemble color specifications in the
form:
Color kula_1 = Color.web("rgb(47%, 27%,  75%)");

Tested on: java version "java-8-oracle"
Author: Mike Ohlson de Fine
*/
import javafx.application.Application;
import javafx.stage.Stage;
import javafx.scene.*;
import javafx.scene.paint.*;
import javafx.scene.shape.*;

public class ColorArraySeries1 extends Application
 {
```

```
    Group root = new Group();
    double xx = 80;
    double yy = 60;

  public void start(Stage stage)
  {
    // Define Primary color arrays.
    double[] kul1 = {  100,   0,   0 };  // Red
    double[] kul2 = {   0,  100,   0 };  // Green
    double[] kul3 = {   0,    0, 100 };  // Blue
    double[] kul4 = {  50,  50,  50 };  // Grey

    Color red1    =
Color.web("rgb("+kul1[0]+"%,"+kul1[1]+"%,"+kul1[2]+"%)");
    Color green1 =
Color.web("rgb("+kul2[0]+"%,"+kul2[1]+"%,"+kul2[2]+"%)");
    Color blue1  =
Color.web("rgb("+kul3[0]+"%,"+kul3[1]+"%,"+kul3[2]+"%)");
    Color grey1  =
Color.web("rgb("+kul4[0]+"%,"+kul4[1]+"%,"+kul4[2]+"%)");

    // This is a way of  displaying the synthesized colors.
    double radiu1 = 50;

    Circle circ1 = new Circle(xx, yy, radiu1, red1); // Red
    root.getChildren().add(circ1);

    xx = 160;
    Circle circ2 = new Circle(xx, yy, radiu1, green1); // Green
    root.getChildren().add(circ2);

    xx = 240;
    Circle circ3 = new Circle(xx, yy, radiu1, blue1); // Blue
    root.getChildren().add(circ3);

    xx = 320;
    Circle circ4 = new Circle(xx, yy, radiu1, grey1); // Grey
    root.getChildren().add(circ4);

    Scene scene = new Scene(root, 400, 120, Color.web("rgb(6%, 3%,  8%)"));
    stage.setTitle("JavaFX Primary color synthesis.");
```

```
        stage.setScene(scene);
        stage.show();

    }
}
```

In the next example we make a method (aka function) for gradually changing from one color to another in separate steps. This is interpolation.

## 2. Interpolation between two colors.

Here we define a method called *kulaInterpolate()* to interpolate between two colors. We have a start color and an end color and we split up the color change in each of the primary color channels of red, green and blue. We decide how many slices to split the color transition from start color to end color. This is the integer numkulas.

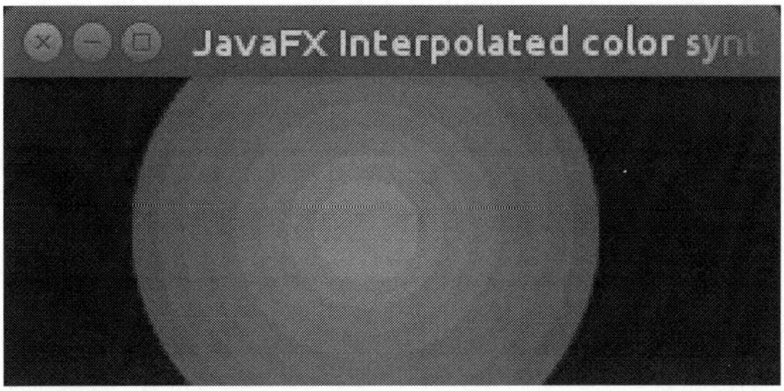


```
// ColorArraySeries2.java
/*
Colors are synthesized from numerical % values kept in
simple arrays in the format: double[] kul1 = { 50,   80,   100 };
Thes numerical arrays are used to assemble color specifications in the
form:
Color kula_1 = Color.web("rgb(47%, 27%,  75%)");

Tested on: java version "java-8-oracle"
Author: Mike Ohlson de Fine
*/
```

```
import javafx.application.Application;
import javafx.stage.Stage;
import javafx.scene.*;
import javafx.scene.paint.*;
import javafx.scene.shape.*;

public class ColorArraySeries2 extends Application {

    Group root = new Group();
    double xx = 140;
    double yy = 60;
    Color kula_1, kula_2, kula_3, kula_4, kula_5, kula_6, kula_7, kula_8,
kula_9 ;
    Color[] kulaArray = { kula_1, kula_2, kula_3, kula_4, kula_5, kula_6,
kula_7, kula_8, kula_9 } ;

  public void start(Stage stage)
  {
    // Define Primary color arrays.
    double[] kul1 = { 100,   0,   0 };  //Red
    double[] kul2 = {   0, 100,   0 };  //Green

    // This is a method for displaying the synthesized colors.
    double radiu1 = 100;
    double radiu2 = 90;
    double radiu3 = 80;
    double radiu4 = 70;
    double radiu5 = 60;
    double radiu6 = 50;
    double radiu7 = 40;
    double radiu8 = 30;
    double radiu9 = 20;

    Color[] kulaSet1 = kulaInterpolate(kul1[0], kul1[1], kul1[2],    kul2[0],
kul2[1], kul2[2],  8 )  ;

    Circle circ1 = new Circle(xx, yy, radiu1, kulaSet1[0]); // Red
    root.getChildren().add(circ1);
    Circle circ2 = new Circle(xx, yy, radiu2, kulaSet1[1]);
    root.getChildren().add(circ2);
    Circle circ3 = new Circle(xx, yy, radiu3, kulaSet1[2]);
```

```
root.getChildren().add(circ3);
Circle circ4 = new Circle(xx, yy, radiu4, kulaSet1[3]);
root.getChildren().add(circ4);
Circle circ5 = new Circle(xx, yy, radiu5, kulaSet1[4]);
root.getChildren().add(circ5);
Circle circ6 = new Circle(xx, yy, radiu6, kulaSet1[5]);
root.getChildren().add(circ6);
Circle circ7 = new Circle(xx, yy, radiu7, kulaSet1[6]);
root.getChildren().add(circ7);
Circle circ8 = new Circle(xx, yy, radiu8, kulaSet1[7]);
root.getChildren().add(circ8);
Circle circ9 = new Circle(xx, yy, radiu9, kulaSet1[8]); // Green
root.getChildren().add(circ9);


 Scene scene = new Scene(root, 300, 120, Color.web("rgb(6%, 3%,  8%)"));
 stage.setTitle("JavaFX Interpolated color synthesis.");
 stage.setScene(scene);
 stage.show();
}

public Color[] kulaInterpolate(double rr1, double gg1, double bb1,
                  double rr2, double gg2, double bb2, int numkulas )
{
    /* The colors must be specified as the Color.web("rgb(rr%, gg%,  bb%)")
format.
     The start and end colors are respectively Color.web("rgb(1rr%, 1gg%,
1bb%)")
     and Color.web("rgb(2rr%, 2gg%,  2bb%)").
    */
    double rrdel = (rr1-rr2)/numkulas ;   // The increment vlaue in red
channel.
    double ggdel = (gg1-gg2)/numkulas ; // The increment vlaue in green
channel.
    double bbdel = (bb1-bb2)/numkulas ; // The increment vlaue in blue
channel.
    double rr, gg, bb ;
    double rr0, gg0, bb0 ;
    rr0 = rr1 + rrdel ;
    gg0 = gg1 + ggdel ;
    bb0 = bb1 + bbdel ;
```

```
        for (int i=0; i<numkulas; i++ )
        {
            rr = rr1 - i*rrdel ;
            gg = gg1 - i*ggdel ;
            bb = bb1 - i*bbdel ;
            kulaArray[i+1] = Color.web("rgb("+rr+"%,"+gg+"%,"+bb+"%)");
        }
    return kulaArray;
    }
}
```

## 3. Multiple Interpolation between colors.

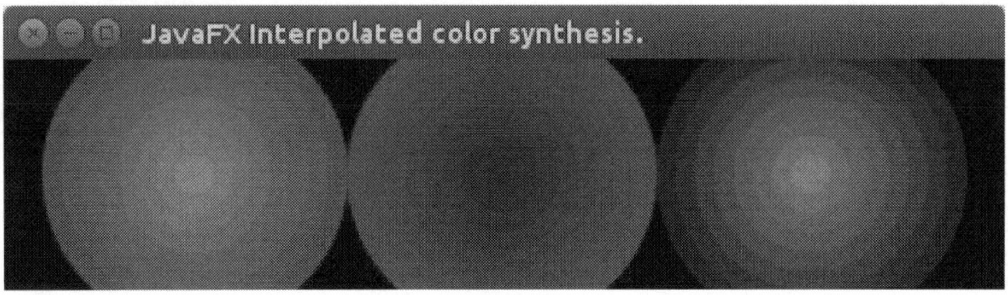


Now we explore a way of interpolating between several start and end colors.

To achieve code economy we use arrays to contain the following series of quantities:

- colors series,
- radii of concentric circles,
- start and end color sets.

## *A note of caution when copying Objects.*

We cannot replicate or make independent copies of arrays by assignment.

For example

*array_A = array_B ;* will be disastrous if we wanted array_A to have

different and independent values from array_B. All the assignment
*array_A = array_B ;*

achieves is to to give two names to the same object inside computer memory.

For array_A and array_B to be independent of each other they each have to be defined from scratch independently. For for color arrays we achieve this with the three separate definitions:

```
// We want three independent color arrays. This is why these are defined
separately.
    Color[] kulaArray1 = { kula_1, kula_2, kula_3, ... kula_8, kula_9 } ;
    Color[] kulaArray2 = { kula_1, kula_2, kula_3, ... kula_8, kula_9 } ;
    Color[] kulaArray3 = { kula_1, kula_2, kula_3, ... kula_8, kula_9 } ;
```

The color variables *kula_1, kula_2, kula_3, ... kula_8, kula_9* are dummy variables that allow the correct amount of computer memory to be reserved for our color arrays. Later in the *kulaInterpolate()* method our color arrays will be given concrete color values in each red, green and blue channel.

```
// ColorArraySeries3.java
/*
When creating more than one arry of any particular type of object,
for example an array of colors, care must be taken to ensure each
object is independent and merely a new label added to a prviously
defined object.

Tested on: java version "java-8-oracle"
Author: Mike Ohlson de Fine
*/
import javafx.application.Application;
import javafx.stage.Stage;
import javafx.scene.*;
import javafx.scene.paint.*;
import javafx.scene.shape.*;

public class ColorArraySeries3 extends Application {
```

```
        Group root = new Group();
        double xx = 100;
        double yy = 60;

        Color kula_1, kula_2, kula_3, kula_4, kula_5, kula_6, kula_7, kula_8,
kula_9 ;

        // We want three independent color arrays. This is why these are defined
separately.
        Color[] kulaArray1 = { kula_1, kula_2, kula_3, kula_4, kula_5, kula_6,
kula_7, kula_8, kula_9 } ;
        Color[] kulaArray2 = { kula_1, kula_2, kula_3, kula_4, kula_5, kula_6,
kula_7, kula_8, kula_9 } ;
        Color[] kulaArray3 = { kula_1, kula_2, kula_3, kula_4, kula_5, kula_6,
kula_7, kula_8, kula_9 } ;

    public void start(Stage stage)
    {
        // Define Primary color arrays.
        double[] kul1 = { 100,   0,   0 };     //Red
        double[] kul2 = {   0, 100,   0 };     //Green
        double[] kul3 = {   0,   0,  100 };    //Blue

        // This is a method for displaying the synthesized colors.
        double[] radi = { 90, 80, 70, 60, 50, 40, 30, 20, 10 };

       Color[] kulaSet1 = kulaInterpolate(kul1[0], kul1[1], kul1[2],    kul2[0],
kul2[1], kul2[2], 8, kulaArray1);
       Color[] kulaSet2 = kulaInterpolate(kul1[0], kul1[1], kul1[2],    kul3[0],
kul3[1], kul3[2], 8, kulaArray2);
       Color[] kulaSet3 = kulaInterpolate(kul3[0], kul3[1], kul3[2],    kul2[0],
kul2[1], kul2[2], 8, kulaArray3);

       int arrlen = kulaSet1.length;

       for (int k=0; k< arrlen; k++ )  // The array of red-green circles.
       {
          Circle circ1 = new Circle(xx, yy, radi[k], kulaSet1[k]);
          root.getChildren().add(circ1);
       }
```

```
xx = 260 ;
for (int k=0; k< arrlen; k++ )  // The array of red-blue circles.
{
   Circle circ2 = new Circle(xx, yy, radi[k], kulaSet2[k]);
   root.getChildren().add(circ2);
}

xx = 420 ;
for (int k=0; k< arrlen; k++ )  // The array of blue-green circles.
{
   Circle circ3 = new Circle(xx, yy, radi[k], kulaSet3[k]);
   root.getChildren().add(circ3);
}


 Scene scene = new Scene(root, 520, 120, Color.web("rgb(6%, 3%,  8%)"));
 stage.setTitle("JavaFX Interpolated color synthesis.");
 stage.setScene(scene);
 stage.show();
}

public Color[] kulaInterpolate(double rr1, double gg1, double bb1,
                        double rr2, double gg2, double bb2, int numkulas,
                        Color[]  kulaArray )
{
    /* The colors must be specified as the Color.web("rgb(rr%, gg%,  bb%)")
format.
     The start and end colors are respectively Color.web("rgb(1rr%, 1gg%,
1bb%)")
     and Color.web("rgb(2rr%, 2gg%,  2bb%)").
    */
    double rrdel = (rr1-rr2)/numkulas ;
    double ggdel = (gg1-gg2)/numkulas ;
    double bbdel = (bb1-bb2)/numkulas ;
    double rr, gg, bb ;
    double rr0, gg0, bb0 ;
    rr0 = rr1 + rrdel ;
    gg0 = gg1 + ggdel ;
    bb0 = bb1 + bbdel ;
    for (int i=0; i<numkulas; i++ )
```

```
        {
            rr = rr1 - i*rrdel ;
            gg = gg1 - i*ggdel ;
            bb = bb1 - i*bbdel ;
           kulaArray[i+1] = Color.web("rgb("+rr+"%,"+gg+"%,"+bb+"%)");
        }
    return kulaArray;
    }
}
```

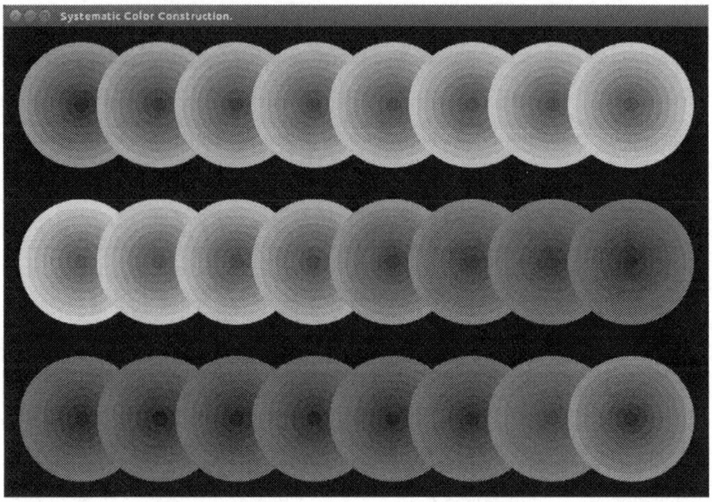


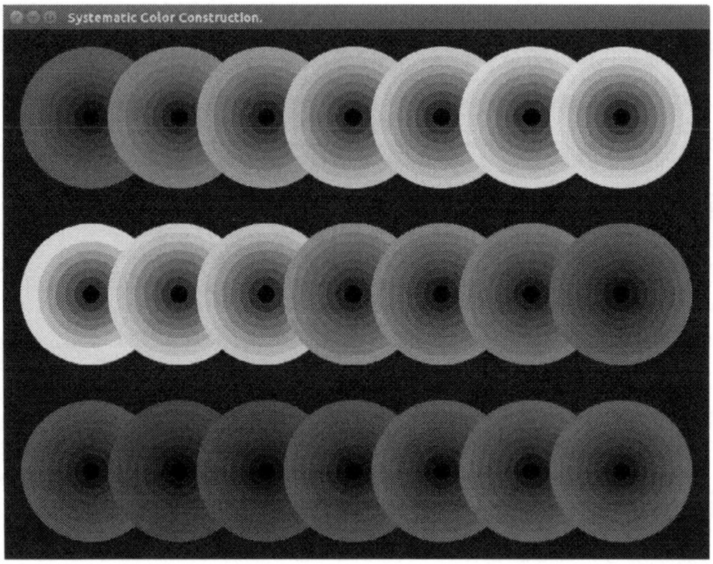

## Programming Efficiency in Color Handling

The code examples given above in the chapter are longer than they need to be.

We have written them in this form in the interest of clarity. Now we use example that are more streamlined in terms of code usage.

# A Numerical Paint Box

We set up a numerical paint box that gives us samples of the primary colors of red, green and blue as well as selected mixtures of the two. We use the color specification format ***Color kula = Color.color(rr, gg, bb, alpha);***

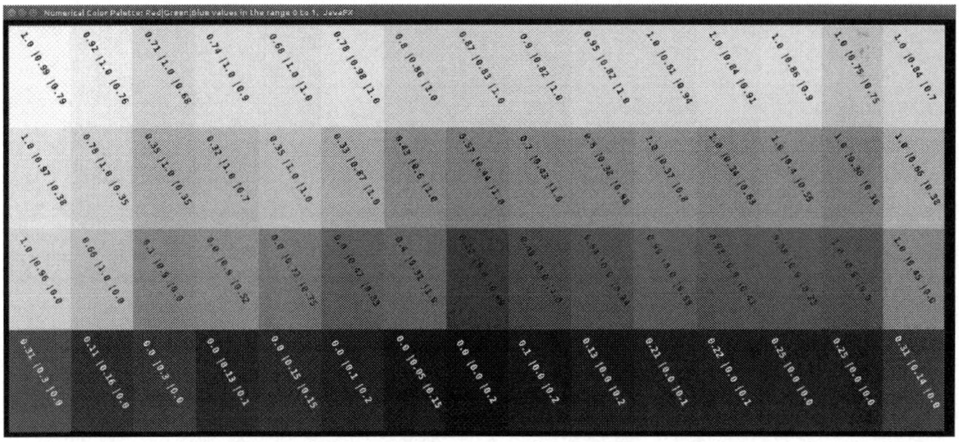

The code that produces this follows here.

```
// ColorPalletteNumerical3.java
/*
A reasonably compact color pallette of Primary and
intermediate colors in four levels of brightness.
The numerical values of each color channel are shown.

Tested on: java version "java-8-oracle"
Author:Mike Ohlson de Fine
*/
import javafx.application.Application;
```

```
import javafx.stage.Stage;
import javafx.scene.*;
import javafx.scene.paint.*;
import javafx.scene.shape.*;
import java.lang.reflect.Array;

import javafx.scene.text.Font;
import javafx.scene.text.FontWeight;
import javafx.scene.text.Text;

public class ColorPalletteNumerical3 extends Application
{
   public void start(Stage stage)
   {

      Group root = new Group();

/*
Transparency can be added to a color by including an additional parameter
defining the transparency in the range [0.0-1.0]

Key Variables
^^^^^^^^^^^^^^^^
red The RGB red value in the range [0.0-1.0]
green The RGB green value in the range [0.0-1.0]
blue The RGB blue value in the range [0.0-1.0]
opacity The transparency of the color in the range [0.0-1.0]
*/

// Handy Colors - numerical specification.
double[] Red1 = {  1, .75, .75 }; // Pale
double[] Red2 = {  1, .36, .36 }; // Light
double[] Red3 = {  1,   0,   0 }; // Saturated
double[] Red4 = {.25,   0,   0 }; // Dark

double[] Orange1 = {  1, .84, .7 }; //2
double[] Orange2 = {  1, .66, .38 };
double[] Orange3 = {  1, .45, .0 };
double[] Orange4 = {.31, .14, .0 };

double[] Yellow1 = {   1, .99, .79 }; //3
```

```
double[] Yellow2 = {   1, .97, .38 };
double[] Yellow3 = {   1, .96, 0 };
double[] Yellow4 = { .31, .30, 0 };

double[] Olive1 = { .95, 1, .75 }; //4
double[] Olive2 = { .82, 1, .33 };
double[] Olive3 = { .73, .98, 0 };
double[] Olive4 = { .17, .2, 0};

double[] LimeGreen1 = { .92,   1, .76 }; //5
double[] LimeGreen2 = { .78,   1, .35 };
double[] LimeGreen3 = { .66,   1, 0 };
double[] LimeGreen4 = { .11, .16, .0 };

double[] Green1 = {.71,  1, .68 }; //6
double[] Green2 = {.35,  1, .35 };
double[] Green3 = { .1, .9,  0 };
double[] Green4 = { 0,  .3,  0 };

double[] Forest1 = {.74,  1, .9 }; //7
double[] Forest2 = {.32,  1, .7 };
double[] Forest3 = { 0,  .9,  .52 };
double[] Forest4 = { 0, .13,  0.1 };


double[] PastelBlue1 = {.68,  1, 1 }; //8
double[] PastelBlue2 = {.35,  1, 1 };
double[] PastelBlue3 = { 0, .72, .75 };
double[] PastelBlue4 = { 0, .15, .15 };

double[] SkyBlue1 = { .78, .98,  1 }; //9
double[] SkyBlue2 = { .33, .87,  1 };
double[] SkyBlue3 = {   0, .47, .83 };
double[] SkyBlue4 = {   0,  .1, .2 };

double[] Blue1 = {  .8, .86,   1 }; //10
double[] Blue2 = { .43,  .6,   1 };
double[] Blue3 = {  .4, .31,   1 };
double[] Blue4 = {   0, .05, .15 };

double[] DeepPurple1 = { .87, .83,   1 }; // 11
```

```
double[] DeepPurple2 = { .57, .44,   1 };
double[] DeepPurple3 = { .22,   0, .89 };
double[] DeepPurple4 = {   0,   0, .2 };

double[] Purple1 = { .9, .82,  1 };  //12
double[] Purple2 = { .7, .43,  1 };
double[] Purple3 = {.49,   0,  1 };
double[] Purple4 = { .1,   0, .2 };

double[] Violet1 = { .95, .82,   1 }; //13
double[] Violet2 = {  .8, .38, .98 };
double[] Violet3 = { .64,   0, .94 };
double[] Violet4 = { .13,  .0,  .2 };

double[] PalePink1 = {  1, .81, .94 }; //14
double[] PalePink2 = {  1, .37, .80 };
double[] PalePink3 = {.98,   0, .68 };
double[] PalePink4 = { .21,  .0, .1 };

double[] DeepPink1 = {  1, .84, .91 }; //15
double[] DeepPink2 = {  1, .34, .63 };
double[] DeepPink3 = {.93,   0, .41 };
double[] DeepPink4 = {.22,   0, .1 };

double[] FireRed1 = {   1, .86,  .9 }; //16
double[] FireRed2 = {   1,  .4, .55 };
double[] FireRed3 = { .98,   0, .25 };
double[] FireRed4 = { .25,   0, .0};

/* Arbitrary names. The important thing is to be able to assemble the array
called "pallette1" through which each color can be accessed using the integer
indices of the pallette1 array.
*/
double[][] yellow_pure   = { Yellow1, Yellow2, Yellow3, Yellow4 };
double[][] lime_green    = { LimeGreen1, LimeGreen2, LimeGreen3,
LimeGreen4 };
double[][] green_green   = { Green1, Green2, Green3, Green4 };
double[][] forest_green  = { Forest1, Forest2, Forest3,Forest4 };
double[][] pastel_blue   = { PastelBlue1, PastelBlue2, PastelBlue3, PastelBlue4
};
double[][] sky_blue      = { SkyBlue1, SkyBlue2, SkyBlue3, SkyBlue4 };
```

```
double[][] blue_blue     = { Blue1, Blue2, Blue3, Blue4 };
double[][] deep_purple   = { DeepPurple1, DeepPurple2, DeepPurple3,
DeepPurple4 };
double[][] purple_purple = { Purple1, Purple2, Purple3, Purple4 };
double[][] violet_violet = { Violet1, Violet2, Violet3, Violet4 };
double[][] pale_pink     = { PalePink1, PalePink2, PalePink3, PalePink4 };
double[][] deep_pink     = { DeepPink1, DeepPink2, DeepPink3, DeepPink4 };
double[][] fire_red      = { FireRed1, FireRed2, FireRed3, FireRed4 };
double[][] red_red       = { Red1, Red2, Red3, Red4 };
double[][] orange_red    = { Orange1, Orange2, Orange3, Orange4 };

// Assemble the 3-dimensional color pallette.
double[][][] pallette1 = { yellow_pure, lime_green, green_green, forest_green,
pastel_blue,
sky_blue, blue_blue, deep_purple,  purple_purple, violet_violet, pale_pink,
deep_pink,
fire_red, red_red, orange_red };

        double xx, yy, ww, hh, gap, txtOffset ;
        xx = 10;
        yy = 10;
        ww = 110;
        hh = 180;
        gap = 0;
        txtOffset = 10 ;
        int num_colors = Array.getLength(pallette1) ;

        for (int j=0; j< num_colors; j++)
        {

          yy = 10;
          for(int i=0; i<4; i++)
          {
            String str1 = String.valueOf(pallette1[j][i][0]) ;
            String str2 = String.valueOf(pallette1[j][i][1]) ;
            String str3 = String.valueOf(pallette1[j][i][2]) ;

            Text txt1 = new Text(xx-txtOffset, yy+80, str1 + " | " + str2 + " | " +
str3);
            txt1.setRotate(60); // angle the text to fit inside the color swatch.
            if (i==0 || i==1 || i==2) txt1.setFill(Color.BLACK); // For light
```

```
colored swatches.
            if (i==3) txt1.setFill(Color.WHITE);          // For dark colored
swatches.
            txt1.setFont(Font.font(java.awt.Font.MONOSPACED,
FontWeight.BOLD, 16));

            Rectangle rect = new Rectangle(xx,yy,ww,hh);
            yy += hh + gap ;
            Color kula = Color.color(pallette1[j][i][0],
                            pallette1[j][i][1],
                            pallette1[j][i][2]);
            rect.setFill(kula);
            root.getChildren().add(rect);
            root.getChildren().add(txt1);
         }
         xx += ww;
      }

      Scene scene = new Scene(root, 1680, 740, Color.BLACK);
      stage.setTitle("Numerical Color Palette: Red | Green | Blue values in the
range 0 to 1,  JavaFX");
      stage.setScene(scene);
     stage.show();
  }
}
```

## Fine Color Interpolation

```
//Color_Fine_Interpolation2.java
/*
A color interpolator. We start with a source and a target color and construct
an
```

```
interpolation method that will bridge a transitional series of colors between
the two.
The basic assumption is that the numerical increment from one intermediate
color
to the next is a steady value (the color intervals in each color channel are
identical.

The format of color specification is:
Color kula_1 = Color.color(red, green, blue, alpha);
where red, green, and blue values are in the range 0 to 1.
The alpha channels are not modified.

For Color design see http://paletton.com/ or
http://colorschemedesigner.com/

Tested on: java version "java-8-oracle"
Author: Mike Ohlson de Fine
*/
import javafx.application.Application;
import javafx.stage.Stage;
import javafx.scene.*;
import javafx.scene.paint.*;
import javafx.scene.shape.*;
import java.lang.Math;
import java.util.Random;

public class Color_Fine_Interpolation2 extends Application {

      Group root = new Group();

   public Color[] kulaInterpolate(double rr1, double gg1, double bb1,double
alfa1,
                          double rr2,  double gg2, double bb2, double alfa2,
                          int numkulas )
   {
      /* Create an interpolated sequence of colors.
       Color format:  Color.color(red, green, blue, alpha) format.
       The start and end colors are respectively Color.color(rr1, gg1, bb1,
alfa1)
       and Color.color(rr2, gg2, bb2, alfa2).
       numkulas is the total number of separate colors required.
```

```
    */

    double rrdelta = (rr1-rr2)/numkulas ;
    double ggdelta = (gg1-gg2)/numkulas ;
    double bbdelta = (bb1-bb2)/numkulas ;
    double rr, gg, bb , alfa;
    double rr0, gg0, bb0, alfa0;
    Color[] kulaArray = new Color[numkulas];

    for (int i=0; i<numkulas; i++ )
    {
        rr = rr1 - i*rrdelta ;
        gg = gg1 - i*ggdelta ;
        bb = bb1 - i*bbdelta ;
       kulaArray[i] = Color.color(rr, gg, bb, alfa1);
    }
return kulaArray;
}


Rectangle general_rectangle(double x_start, double y_start, double width,
                    double height, Color kula)
{     // A general rectangle constructed for coding convenience.
      Rectangle rect = new Rectangle();
     rect.setX(x_start);             // Size and location on the JavaFX scene.
     rect.setY(y_start);
     rect.setWidth(width);
     rect.setHeight(height);
     rect.setFill(kula);
    return rect;
 }


public void start(Stage stage)
{
   double x_center = 500;   // The center of all circles.
   double y_center = 500;

   double xx = 10 ;
   double yy = 10 ;
   double width = 16 ;
```

```
        double height = 80 ;

        // Color channels.
        double rr1 = 0;
        double gg1 = 1;
        double bb1 = 0;
        double alfa1 = 0;

        double rr2 = 0;
        double gg2 = 0;
        double bb2 = 1;
        double alfa2 = 0;

          int numkulas = 30 ;  // The number of colors generated.
        Color[] kula_sequence = kulaInterpolate(rr1, gg1, bb1, 1,   rr2, gg2, bb2,
1, numkulas ) ;
          for (int i=0; i<numkulas; i++)
          {
             Rectangle rect1 =  general_rectangle(xx, yy, width, height,
kula_sequence[i]);
             xx += width;
             root.getChildren().add(rect1);
          }

        Scene scene = new Scene(root, 500, 100, Color.color(0, 0 , 0));
        stage.setTitle("Interpolation between two Colors.");
        stage.setScene(scene);
        stage.show();
    }
}
```

# CHAPTER 6

## CIRCLE AND ELLIPSE

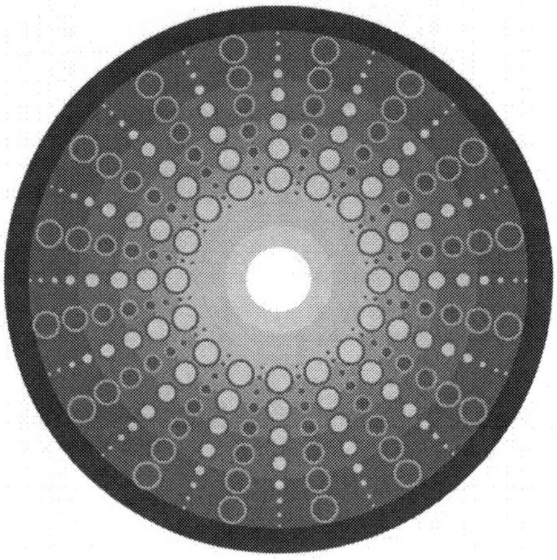

In this chapter we will cover:

- All the different properties of circles.
- The use of constructors in Java.
- The properties of ellipses.

Primitive graphic objects in Java like circles, rectangles and polygons have many properties such as line fill color, outline thickness, outline color, outline pattern ( solid or dashed) and transparency. When a primitive object is created and drawn all these properties are specified. Most of them have default values. A default value is a value that is pre-allocated by the Java class definition for the particular object. Typical default values for circles and ellipses are black outline, one pixel width, and a solid black fill interior which is fully opaque. Some of these properties can be set when the object is constructed using the appropriate constructor. The circle class provides several different constructors each with a different set of parameters that we may find useful. In this chapter we will pay some attention to constructors and how we can use them. We will also explore Java Arrays because they are extremely useful in making complicated drawings.

## The Simplest Circle

A basic circle using the default properties of line width and color:

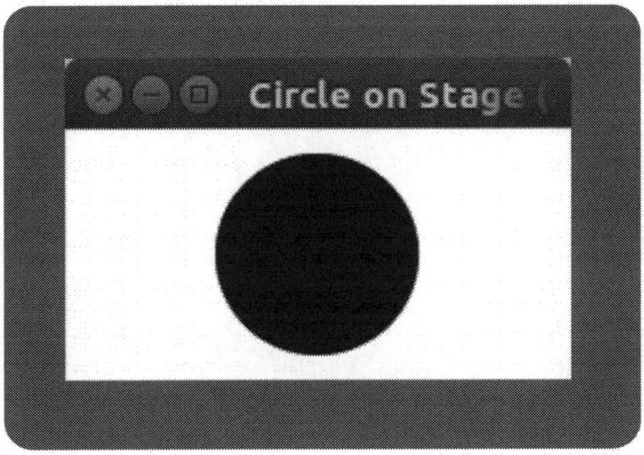


```
// CircleSimplest.java
/*
Circle : class: javafx.scene.shape.Circle
----------------------------------------
An instance of Circle with given position and size.
Constructor:
Circle(centerX, centerY,  radius);

Tested on: java version "java-8-oracle"
Author: Mike Ohlson de Fine
*/
import javafx.application.Application;
import javafx.stage.Stage;
```

```
import javafx.scene.*;
import javafx.scene.shape.*; // Graphic primitives library.

public class CircleSimplest extends Application
{
  public void start(Stage stage)
  {
      Group root = new Group();
    //****************************************
    Circle circle1 = new Circle(100, 50, 40);
    //****************************************
    root.getChildren().add(circle1);

       Scene scene = new Scene(root, 200, 100);
       stage.setTitle("Circle on Stage (canvas), JavaFX");
       stage.setScene(scene);
       stage.show();
  }
}
```

## What are the native constructors belonging to the JavaF Circle Class?

1. Circle() ; This creates an instance of a circle with no specifications like position and radius. So although the circle exists inside computer memory, thee will be nothing on the stage. The stage is the screen area where JavaFX will place any images.

2. Circle(radius); This creates an instance of a circle with a radius specified and default center position at x = 0, y = 0.

3. Circle(centerX, centerY, radius); This creates an instance of a circle with a radius specified and position x = centerX, y = centerY. The example CircleSimples1.java above uses this constructor.

4. Circle(centerX, centerY, radius, fill); This creates an instance of a circle with a color specified in addition to position x = centerX, y = centerY.

5. Circle(radius, fill); This creates an instance of a circle with a color

and radius specified as well as default center (0,0). We can re-position a circle constructed this way using the special methods setCenterX and setCenterY that belong to the Circle class.

The Circle constructors do not allow us to do anything about specifying outline width, color or dash patterns. We must either alter those properties individually after the object, a circle in this case, has been constructed.

The way to modify all these properties of a circle is to code a special method to achieve particular modifications. We show how this can be done using the function

*CircleSet(... )*

## Constructing an Ellipse

An ellipse is a distorted circle with the radius changing around the circumference. The simplest way of specifying an ellipse is give the radius in the X-directions and the radius in the Y-direction. The direction with the longest radius is called the major axis of the ellipse. The shorter radius defines the minor axis. This means that the ellipse is always aligned with its major axis along either the X or the Y direction but not at any angle in between. However it is simple to rotate the major axis to any angle using a Rotate transform.

## Ellipse Constructors

**Ellipse();** An ellipse with no size or location given at the time of construction. The defining parameters can be specified later. See the examples below.
**Ellipse(radiusX, radiusY);** An ellipse with the major and minor radii given but not its position. The position can be specified later.
**Ellipse(centerX, centerY, radiusX, radiusY);** An ellipse with the major and minor radii given as well as its position.

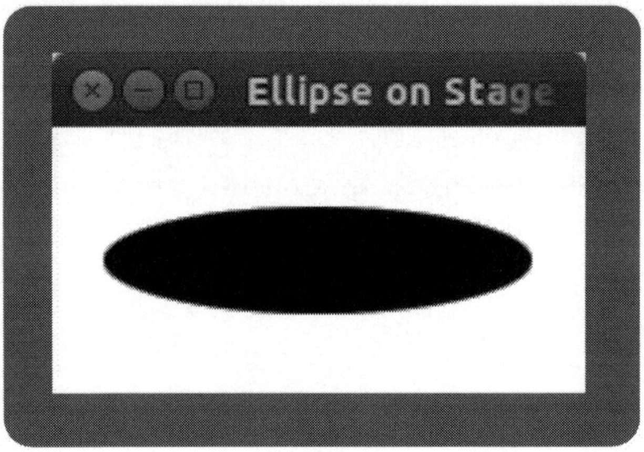


```
// EllipseSimplest.java
/*
Ellipse : class: javafx.scene.shape.Ellipse
-------------------------------------
Constructors:
1. Ellipse(); An ellipse with no size or location given.
2. Ellipse(radiusX, radiusY); An ellipse with the major and minor radii given.
3. Ellipse(centerX, centerY, radiusX, radiusY); An ellipse with radii and
position specified.

Tested on: java version "java-8-oracle"
Author: Mike Ohlson de Fine
*/
import javafx.application.Application;
import javafx.stage.Stage;
import javafx.scene.*;
import javafx.scene.shape.*; // Graphic primitives library.

public class EllipseSimplest extends Application
{
   public void start(Stage stage)
   {
         Group root = new Group();
      //**************************************
      Ellipse ellipse1 = new Ellipse(180, 50, 80, 30); // center, radii.
      //**************************************
      root.getChildren().add(ellipse1);
```

```
        Scene scene = new Scene(root, 360, 100);
        stage.setTitle("Ellipsee on Stage (ie. canvas), JavaFX");
        stage.setScene(scene);
        stage.show();
    }
}
```

## Making Choices for Outline and Fill

The outline of a circle or an ellipse is just a line and we may specify line-width, color, dash-dot patterns as we see fit. The interior fill of the circle allows us to vary color and transparency as well.

So for outline we exercise control using specifiers like:

```
setStrokeWidth(8);                          // Width of the line, pixels.
setStrokeLineCap(StrokeLineCap.ROUND);      // Rounded ends of lines.
setStroke(Color.BLUE);                      // Color of line.
getStrokeDashArray().addAll(14d);           // Dash pattern: fill, blank,
etcsetStrokeDashOffset(10);   //Dash pattern: to shift the beginning of the dash.
```

## Can we make our own constructors?

Constructors aren't polymorphic - we cannot *override* them at all.

A constructor is very different from an ordinary method/function because a constructor literally constructs an entire class in computer memory. This is a big deal. Remember this. That little keyword "new" is a powerful spell.

We cannot override (change properties) of a constructor – it is not alterable. The constructor is invoked by the name of the class it constructs.

We could make a new subclass that has it's own constructors. Such a subclass constructor must chain inherit the properties of their superclass constructor that they are descended from as well as having any additional ones we code into it. When you create a child class it's parent, the super-class, will be instantiated first then subclass will be instantiated. This is called chaining. *The Child can not exist without its parent.*

The Java compiler will automatically call the super-class constructor from subclass constructor.

This kind of programming is risky because we need remember that we have created objects with unexpected behavior - it is fundamentally a bad idea. Errors can be difficult to trace. It is better to create a special method that gives the facilities we desire without tinkering with the rules of class constructors.

## How can we make entire tribes of ellipses?

When we instantiate graphic objects we are setting aside exclusive memory areas for them in the RAM of our computing platform whether it be a desktop, laptop, tablet or smart-phone.

If we actually want to display the graphic objects on a screen we need to place them on a stage using an instruction like *root.getChildren().add(ellipse1);* Adding a node to a root node completes it and dispatches it 'out the door' – it has gone onto the stage and cannot be recalled. BUT we can use the same object ellipse1 and give it amakeover -. different color, size, outline an then add this same but different looking ellipse1 using the same *root.getChildren().add(ellipse1);* -the altered ellipse1 will be added to the old one as a child of the same group. However this only allowed to happen inside a *for* loop.

There is another way to make many similar copies of the same object: give every displayed object its own exclusive constructor. One neat way to create tribes of similar is to makes each separate object an element of a Java Array. We do this at the end of this chapter. It is an important strategy in Java graphic applications.

## Specifying and controlling Circle properties.

How can we give values for stroke color, width and pattern? Well the Shape class, which is the parent of the circle class, has special methods for the following parameters:

- **setStroke** – this sets the color of the outline of the circle.
- **SetStrokeWidth** - this sets the width of the outline of the circle.
- **SetStrokeType** – this determines whether the stroke is inside, outside or centered to the boundary of the shape. Examples are given in chapter 4.
- **SetStrokeLineCap** – if the circle outline is dashed then this controls whether the ends of line segments are round (StrokeLineCap.BUTT) or flat (StrokeLineCap.ROUND).

In addition to controlling the properties of the outline we can alter the color of the fill of the circle interior with **setFill**.

All these characterestic attributes like stroke width and colors can be altered after the circle has been constructed but once it has been drawn (by *stage.show();* ) nothing about can be changed. If we wanted to redraw the same circle but in a different color then we would have to create a completely new instance of the circle using the *new* keyword to do so.

The following example illustrates control of the parameters as well as construction of multiple instances. We do this without any attempt as reducing code in order to try and keep the code obvious and therefore easier to decipher. Later on we develop techniques to making the code more compact more universally usable.

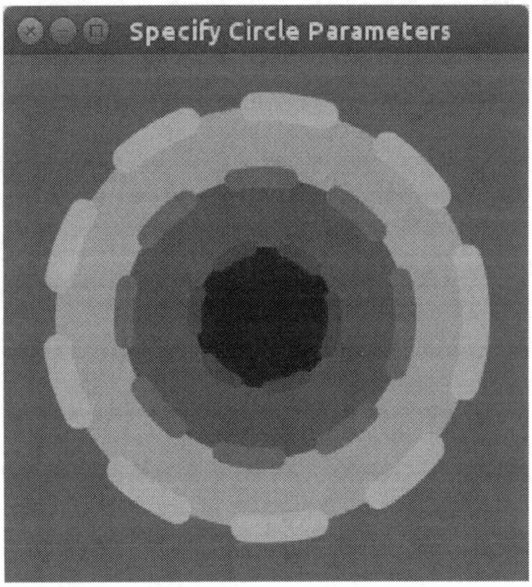


```
// CircleSet1.java
/*
Create a function that draws three concentric circles with no default
parameters.
All parameters are specified explicitly.

Tested on: java version "java-8-oracle"
Author: Mike Ohlson de Fine
*/
import javafx.application.Application;
import javafx.stage.Stage;
import javafx.scene.*;
import javafx.scene.paint.*;
import javafx.scene.shape.*;

public class CircleSet1 extends Application
{
	Group root = new Group();

	// Purples.
	final Color purp1 = Color.web("rgb(81%, 55%, 70%)");	// rgb percent
web color.
	final Color purp2 = Color.web("rgb(55%, 19%, 39%)");
	final Color purp3 = Color.web("rgb(28%, 0.4%, 16%)");
```

```
    // Red-violets.
    final Color yell1 = Color.web("rgb(80%, 60%, 100%)");
    final Color yell2 = Color.web("rgb(80%, 20%, 60%)");
    final Color yell3 = Color.web("rgb(80%,  0%, 20%)");

public void start(Stage stage)
{
    // Position.
    double xx = 150;
    double yy = 150;
    CircleSet(xx, yy, purp1, purp2, purp3, yell1, yell2, yell3, 8 ) ;
    // Parameters: position x, y, 3 fill colors, 3 stroke colors, stroke width.

    Scene scene = new Scene(root, 300, 300, Color.web("#2c8437"));
    stage.setTitle("Specify Circle Parameters");
    stage.setScene(scene);
    stage.show();
}


public void CircleSet(double xx, double yy,
                Color kula1fill, Color kula2fill, Color kula3fill,
                Color kula1stroke, Color kula2stroke, Color kula3stroke,
                double outlineWidth )

{  /* Method: Draw three concentric circles, each with unique appearance.
      Parameters: position x, y, 3 fill colors, 3 stroke colors, stroke width.
      Note that the parameters can still be modified within the method as
      we have done with the setStrokeWidth(...) parameter.  */

    double radiu1 = 40;
    double radiu2 = 80;
    double radiu3 = 120;

   // Outer Circle: Position, radius and fill color.
   Circle circ1 = new Circle();
   circ1.setCenterX(xx);
   circ1.setCenterY(yy);
   circ1.setRadius(radiu3);
   circ1.setFill(kula1fill);
```

```
    // Outer Circle: outline width, color and dash pattern.
    circ1.setStroke(kula1stroke);
    circ1.setStrokeWidth(outlineWidth+8);
    circ1.setStrokeLineCap(StrokeLineCap.ROUND);
    circ1.getStrokeDashArray().addAll(40d);// fill, blank.
    root.getChildren().add(circ1);

    // Middle circle: Position, radius and fill color.
    Circle circ2 = new Circle();
    circ2.setCenterX(xx);
    circ2.setCenterY(yy);
    circ2.setRadius(radiu2);
    circ2.setFill(kula2fill);

    circ2.setStrokeLineCap(StrokeLineCap.ROUND); // Middle Circle:
outline
    circ2.getStrokeDashArray().addAll(30d);
    circ2.setStroke(kula2stroke);
    circ2.setStrokeWidth(outlineWidth+4);
    root.getChildren().add(circ2);

    // Inner circle: Position, radius and fill color..
    Circle circ3 = new Circle();
    circ3.setCenterX(xx);
    circ3.setCenterY(yy);
    circ3.setRadius(radiu1);
    circ3.setFill(kula3fill);

    circ3.setStroke(kula3stroke); // Inner Circle: outline
    circ3.setStrokeLineCap(StrokeLineCap.ROUND);
    circ3.getStrokeDashArray().addAll(20d);
    circ3.setStrokeWidth(outlineWidth);
    root.getChildren().add(circ3);
    }
}
```

## Arrays of objects

We first encountered Java arrays in the example *ColorArraySeries1.java* in chapter 5 where we used arrays to hold color % values:

```
// Define Primary color arrays.

double[] kul1 = {  100,   0,   0 };    // Red
double[] kul2 = {    0, 100,   0 };    // Green
double[] kul3 = {    0,   0, 100 };    // Blue
double[] kul4 = {   50,  50,  50 };    // Grey
```

These are arrays of double precision floating point numbers. The definition of Java arrays allows the objects inside the array to be any valid Java object regardless of complexity. Each object in an array could be a three dimensional simulation of a dinosaur with wings and knitted socks called a Gruffalump. All that is necessary for the array to be valid is that it must be declared as an array of Gruffalumps:

*Gruffalump[] pink_blue_green_GRUFFS = { pinkGruff, BlueGruff, greenGruff };*

In the examples below we make use of arrays of Colors, circles, x-coordinates, y-coordinates and radii. All these are very different types of objects and have no real connection to each other. However we create connections by coordinating their indices in *for loops* so that they match up to produce well behaved circular color patterns.

## *Duplicating Arrays is not simple - A note of caution.*

We cannot replicate or make independent copies of arrays by assignment.

For example:

*array_A = array_B ;* will be disastrous if we wanted array_A to have different and independent values from array_B.

All the assignment *array_A = array_B ;*

achieves is to to give two names to the **same object** inside computer memory.

For array_A and array_B to be separate and independent of each other they each have to be defined from scratch independently. For for color arrays we achieve this with the three separate definitions:

```
// We want three independent color arrays. This is why these are defined
separately.
    Color[] kulaArray1 = { kula_1, kula_2, kula_3, ... kula_8, kula_9 } ;
    Color[] kulaArray2 = { kula_1, kula_2, kula_3, ... kula_8, kula_9 } ;
    Color[] kulaArray3 = { kula_1, kula_2, kula_3, ... kula_8, kula_9 } ;
```

The color variables *kula_1, kula_2, kula_3, ... kula_8, kula_9* are dummy variables, previously declared as Colors, that allow the correct amount of computer memory to be reserved for our color arrays. Later in the *kulaInterpolate()* method our color arrays will be given definite color values in each red, green and blue channel.

We take care to point this out with comments in the code below.

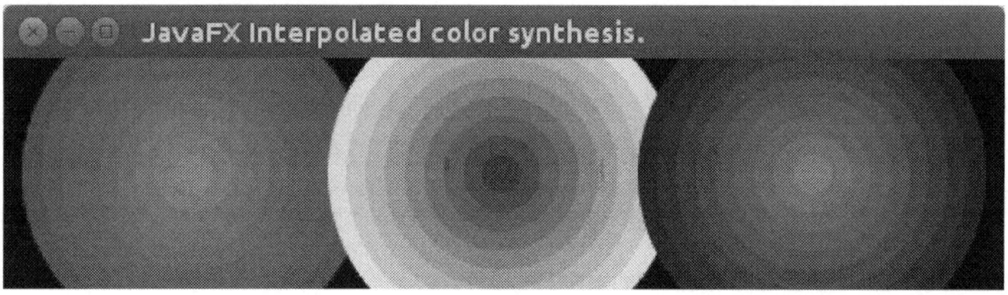


In the program below we make use of two different types of arrays:

- Arrays of colors – Color[]
- Arrays of double precision decimal numbers - double[]

```
// ColorArraySeries3.java
/*
When creating more than one array of any particular type of object,
for example an array of colors, care must be taken to ensure each
object is independent and not merely an extra label added to a prviously
defined object.
Tested on: java version "java-8-oracle"
```

```
Author: Mike Ohlson de Fine
*/
import javafx.application.Application;
import javafx.stage.Stage;
import javafx.scene.*;
import javafx.scene.paint.*;
import javafx.scene.shape.*;

public class ColorArraySeries3 extends Application {

        Group root = new Group();
        double xx = 100;
        double yy = 60;

        /* The Color variables here are dummy variables. This type declaration
ensure that 9 separate areas of memory are reserved for Color objects.
         They are then used in the array declarations Color[] to force the Java
compiler to reserve memory for three totally independent arrays of such Color
objects. */
        Color kula_1, kula_2, kula_3, kula_4, kula_5, kula_6, kula_7, kula_8,
kula_9 ;

         /* We want three independent color arrays. This is why these are
defined separately.
           The dummy Color variables are used like empty boxes to ensure that
sufficient space
           is reserved for actual color values that will be created later. */
        Color[]  kulaArray1 =  { kula_1, kula_2, kula_3, kula_4, kula_5, kula_6,
kula_7, kula_8, kula_9 } ;
        Color[]  kulaArray2 =  { kula_1, kula_2, kula_3, kula_4, kula_5, kula_6,
kula_7, kula_8, kula_9 } ;
        Color[]  kulaArray3 =  { kula_1, kula_2, kula_3, kula_4, kula_5, kula_6,
kula_7, kula_8, kula_9 } ;

    public void start(Stage stage)
    {
        //  Define Primary color arrays.
        double[] kulRed = { 100,   0,   0 };        //Red
        double[] kulGreen = {   0, 100,   0 };      //Green
        double[] kulBlue = {   0,   0, 100 };       //Blue
        double[] kulYell = { 100, 100,   0 };       //Yellow
```

```
    // These are the radii of circles for displaying the synthesized colors.
    double[] radi = { 90, 80, 70, 60, 50, 40, 30, 20, 10 };

   // Here the interpolated colors arrays are created.
    Color[] kulaSet1 = kulaInterpolate(kulRed[0], kulRed[1], kulRed[2],
kulGreen[0], kulGreen[1], kulGreen[2], 9, kulaArray1);
    Color[] kulaSet2 = kulaInterpolate(kulYell[0], kulYell[1], kulYell[2],
kulBlue[0], kulBlue[1], kulBlue[2], 9, kulaArray2);
    Color[] kulaSet3 = kulaInterpolate(kulBlue[0], kulBlue[1], kulBlue[2],
kulGreen[0], kulGreen[1], kulGreen[2], 9, kulaArray3);

    int arrlen = kulaSet1.length;

    for (int k=0; k< arrlen; k++ )  // The array of red-green circles.
    {
      Circle circ1 = new Circle(xx, yy, radi[k], kulaSet1[k]);
      root.getChildren().add(circ1);
    }

    xx = 260 ;
    for (int k=0; k< arrlen; k++ )  // The array of yellow-blue circles.
    {
      Circle circ2 = new Circle(xx, yy, radi[k], kulaSet2[k]);
      root.getChildren().add(circ2);
    }

    xx = 420 ;
    for (int k=0; k< arrlen; k++ )  // The array of blue-green circles.
    {
      Circle circ3 = new Circle(xx, yy, radi[k], kulaSet3[k]);
      root.getChildren().add(circ3);
    }

    Scene scene = new Scene(root, 520, 120, Color.web("rgb(6%, 3%,  8%)"));
    stage.setTitle("JavaFX Interpolated color synthesis.");
    stage.setScene(scene);
    stage.show();
    }

  // The color interpolation method.
```

```
  public Color[] kulaInterpolate(double rr1, double gg1, double bb1,
                           double rr2, double gg2, double bb2, int numkulas,
                           Color[]  kulaArray )
  {
      /* The colors must be specified as the Color.web("rgb(rr%, gg%,  bb%)")
format.
      The start and end colors are respectively Color.web("rgb(1rr%, 1gg%,
1bb%)")
      and Color.web("rgb(2rr%, 2gg%,  2bb%)").
      */
      double rrdel = (rr1-rr2)/numkulas ;
      double ggdel = (gg1-gg2)/numkulas ;
      double bbdel = (bb1-bb2)/numkulas ;
      double rr, gg, bb ;
      double rr0, gg0, bb0 ;
      rr0 = rr1 + rrdel ;
      gg0 = gg1 + ggdel ;
     bb0 = bb1 + bbdel ;
      for (int i=0; i<numkulas; i++ )
      {
         rr = rr1 - i*rrdel ;
         gg = gg1 - i*ggdel ;
         bb = bb1 - i*bbdel ;
        kulaArray[i] = Color.web("rgb("+rr+"%,"+gg+"%,"+bb+"%)");
      }
  return kulaArray;
  }
}
```

## Using Arrays for Decorative Frames.

Now we construct the code for a frame of shaded circles. Each shaded group is in a different location and starts with a different radius. These different positions and radii are specified by numerical arrays xxc, yyc and radius. This arrangement was designed using Inkscape as the drafting tool as shown here.

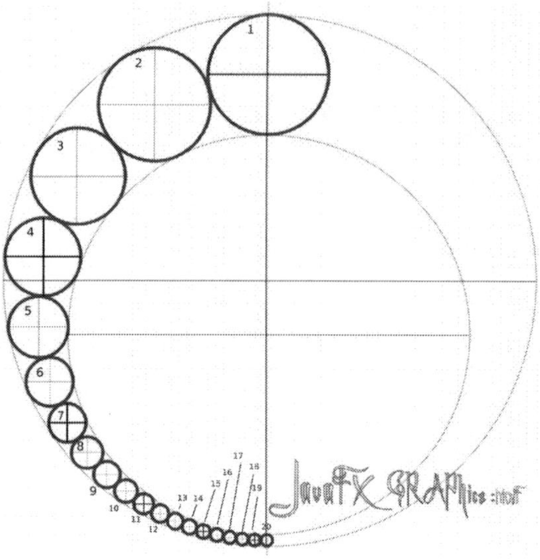

```
// ColorHaloFrame1.java
/*
When creating more than one array of any particular type of object,
for example an array of colors, care must be taken to ensure each
object is independent and merely a new label added to a prviously
defined object.

Tested on: java version "java-8-oracle"
Author: Mike Ohlson de Fine
*/
import javafx.application.Application;
import javafx.stage.Stage;
import javafx.scene.*;
import javafx.scene.paint.*;
import javafx.scene.shape.*;

public class ColorHaloFrame1 extends Application {

        Group root = new Group();
        double xx = 100;
        double yy = 60;
        Color kula_1, kula_2, kula_3, kula_4, kula_5, kula_6, kula_7, kula_8,
kula_9 ;

        // We want nine independent color arrays.
```

```
        Color[] kulaArray1 = { kula_1, kula_2, kula_3, kula_4, kula_5, kula_6,
kula_7, kula_8, kula_9 } ;
        Color[] kulaArray2 = { kula_1, kula_2, kula_3, kula_4, kula_5, kula_6,
kula_7, kula_8, kula_9 } ;
        Color[] kulaArray3 = { kula_1, kula_2, kula_3, kula_4, kula_5, kula_6,
kula_7, kula_8, kula_9 } ;
        Color[] kulaArray4 = { kula_1, kula_2, kula_3, kula_4, kula_5, kula_6,
kula_7, kula_8, kula_9 } ;
        Color[] kulaArray5 = { kula_1, kula_2, kula_3, kula_4, kula_5, kula_6,
kula_7, kula_8, kula_9 } ;
        Color[] kulaArray6 = { kula_1, kula_2, kula_3, kula_4, kula_5, kula_6,
kula_7, kula_8, kula_9 } ;
        Color[] kulaArray7 = { kula_1, kula_2, kula_3, kula_4, kula_5, kula_6,
kula_7, kula_8, kula_9 } ;
        Color[] kulaArray8 = { kula_1, kula_2, kula_3, kula_4, kula_5, kula_6,
kula_7, kula_8, kula_9 } ;
        Color[] kulaArray9 = { kula_1, kula_2, kula_3, kula_4, kula_5, kula_6,
kula_7, kula_8, kula_9 } ;

    public void start(Stage stage)
    {
        // Define Primary color arrays.
        double[] kul1 = { 100,   0,   0 };     //Red
        double[] kul2 = {   0, 100,   0 };     //Green
        double[] kul3 = {   0,   0, 100 };     //Blue
        double[] kul4 = { 100, 100,   0 };     //Yellow
        double[] kul5 = {  44,   4,  67 };     //Purple
        double[] kul6 = {   0,   0,   0 };     //Black

        // The radii for displaying the synthesized colors..
        double[] radi1 = { 1.00, .99, .98, .96, .94, .91, .88, .84, .80 };
        double[] radi2 = { 1.00, .92, .86, .80, .76, .73, .70, .68, .66 };


        Color[] kulaSet1 = kulaInterpolate(kul1[0], kul1[1], kul1[2],    kul2[0],
kul2[1], kul2[2], 8, kulaArray1); // Red to Green.
        Color[] kulaSet2 = kulaInterpolate(kul1[0], kul1[1], kul1[2],    kul3[0],
kul3[1], kul3[2], 8, kulaArray2); // Red to Blue.
        Color[] kulaSet3 = kulaInterpolate(kul3[0], kul3[1], kul3[2],    kul2[0],
kul2[1], kul2[2], 8, kulaArray3); // Blue to Green.
        Color[] kulaSet4 = kulaInterpolate(kul3[0], kul3[1], kul3[2],    kul4[0],
```

```
kul4[1], kul4[2], 8, kulaArray4); // Blue to Yellow.
    Color[] kulaSet5 = kulaInterpolate(kul5[0], kul5[1], kul5[2],    kul1[0],
kul1[1], kul1[2], 8, kulaArray5); // Purple to Red.
    Color[] kulaSet6 = kulaInterpolate(kul6[0], kul6[1], kul6[2],    kul5[0],
kul5[1], kul5[2], 8, kulaArray6); // Black to Purple.
    Color[] kulaSet7 = kulaInterpolate(kul6[0], kul6[1], kul6[2],    kul3[0],
kul3[1], kul3[2], 8, kulaArray7); // Black to Blue.
    Color[] kulaSet8 = kulaInterpolate(kul6[0], kul6[1], kul6[2],    kul1[0],
kul1[1], kul1[2], 8, kulaArray8); // Black to Red.
    Color[] kulaSet9 = kulaInterpolate(kul3[0], kul3[1], kul3[2],    kul5[0],
kul5[1], kul5[2], 8, kulaArray8); // Blue to Purple.

    double[] mainCenter = { 344.8, 559.1, 163.6 }; // x, y, radius.

    // The arrangement of circles to form an elliptical frame.
    double[] xxc    = { 344.5,   203.1, 106.2,  62.4,  56.8,  71.4,  93.9, 119.5,
144.1, 168.2, 190.3, 211.1, 230.6, 249.2, 266.6, 283.4, 299.4, 315.3, 330.7,
346.0 };
    double[] yyc    = { 840.7,   802.7, 713.2, 612.2, 523.9, 455.5, 404.4,   367,
339.1, 318.2, 302.2, 290.4, 280.8, 273.6, 267.8, 263.6, 260.6, 258.5, 257.4,
257.1 };
    double[] radius = {  75.1,    70.9,  60.1,  48.8,  38.5,  30.6,  24.2,  20.2,
16.7,  14.2,  12.6,  11.1,  10.2,   9.3,   8.6,   8.1,   7.8,   7.5,   7.3,   7.3 };

    int halolen = xxc.length; // The number of circles in half the frame.

    double xxr, xxl, yoffset;
    double xoffset = 100;
    double yyv;
    int arrlen = kulaSet1.length;

   // Left-hand side of the frame of circles.
  for (int k=0; k< halolen; k++ )  // The array of blue circles in the frame.
    {
       xxl = xxc[k] + xoffset ;
       yyv = 3*mainCenter[0] - yyc[k];
       Circle circ1 = new Circle(xxl, yyv, radius[k], Color.web("rgb(0%, 0%,
30%)"));
       circ1.setFill(null);
       circ1.setStroke(Color.web("rgb(0%, 0%,  50%)"));
       root.getChildren().add(circ1);
```

```
    for (int j=0;j< arrlen;j++ )  // Blue-to-purple transition.
    {  Circle circ2 = new Circle(xxl, yyv, radi1[j]*radius[k], kulaSet9[j]);
    root.getChildren().add(circ2);
    }

    for (int j=0;j< arrlen;j++ ) // Purple-to-red transition.
    {  Circle circ3 = new Circle(xxl, yyv, radi2[j]*radius[k], kulaSet5[j]);
       root.getChildren().add(circ3);
    }

    // Right-hand side of the frame of circles.
    xxr = 153 + xoffset + 2*mainCenter[0] - xxc[k];
    Circle circ4 = new Circle(xxr, yyv, radius[k], Color.BLUE);
    circ4.setFill(null);
    circ4.setStroke(Color.web("rgb(0%, 0%,  50%)"));
    root.getChildren().add(circ4);

    for (int j=0;j< arrlen;j++ )  // Blue-to-purple transition.
    {  Circle circ5 = new Circle(xxr, yyv, radi1[j]*radius[k], kulaSet9[j]);
    root.getChildren().add(circ5);
    }

    for (int j=0;j< arrlen;j++ ) // Purple-to-red transition.
    {  Circle circ6 = new Circle(xxr, yyv, radi2[j]*radius[k], kulaSet5[j]);
       root.getChildren().add(circ6);
    }
  }

  Scene scene = new Scene(root, 1000, 900, Color.web("rgb(6%, 3%,  8%)"));
  stage.setTitle("JavaFX Interpolated color synthesis.");
  stage.setScene(scene);
  stage.show();
 }

public Color[] kulaInterpolate(double rr1, double gg1, double bb1,
                    double rr2, double gg2, double bb2, int numkulas,
                    Color[]  kulaArray )
{
    /* The colors must be specified as the Color.web("rgb(rr%, gg%,  bb%)")
format.
```

```
        The start and end colors are respectively Color.web("rgb(1rr%, 1gg%,
1bb%)")
        and Color.web("rgb(2rr%, 2gg%,  2bb%)").
        */
        double rrdel = (rr1-rr2)/numkulas ; // The increment vlaue in red
channel.
        double ggdel = (gg1-gg2)/numkulas ; // The increment vlaue in red
channel.
        double bbdel = (bb1-bb2)/numkulas ; // The increment vlaue in red
channel.
        double rr, gg, bb ;
        double rr0, gg0, bb0 ;
        rr0 = rr1 + rrdel ;
        gg0 = gg1 + ggdel ;
        bb0 = bb1 + bbdel ;
        for (int i=0; i<numkulas; i++ )
        {
            rr = rr1 - i*rrdel ;
            gg = gg1 - i*ggdel ;
            bb = bb1 - i*bbdel ;
            kulaArray[i+1] = Color.web("rgb("+rr+"%,"+gg+"%,"+bb+"%)");
        }
      return kulaArray;
    }
}
```

# Gradient Fill Specifications for Circles and Rectangles.

To create a linear gradient paint, we specify startX, startY, endX, and endY for the start and end points. The start and end point coordinates specify where the gradient pattern begins and stops.

The linear gradient properties are:

startX: Set X coordinate of the gradient axis start point

startY: Set Y coordinate of the gradient axis start point

endX: Set X coordinate of the gradient axis end point.

endY: Set Y coordinate of the gradient axis end point.

proportional: true or false. Set whether the coordinates are proportional to the shape. true will use unit square coordinates, otherwise use screen coordinate system.

cycleMethod: Set cycle method applied to the gradient.

stops: Set stop list for gradient's color specification.

# CHAPTER 7

## POLYGON

In this chapter we will cover:

- All the different properties of polygons.
- Arrays for polygons
- Multi Array Polygons
- Intersections of shapes
- Unions of shapes
- Subtractions of shapes

# *The Simplest Polygon*

Here is a program for a basic triangle polygon using the default properties of line width and color:

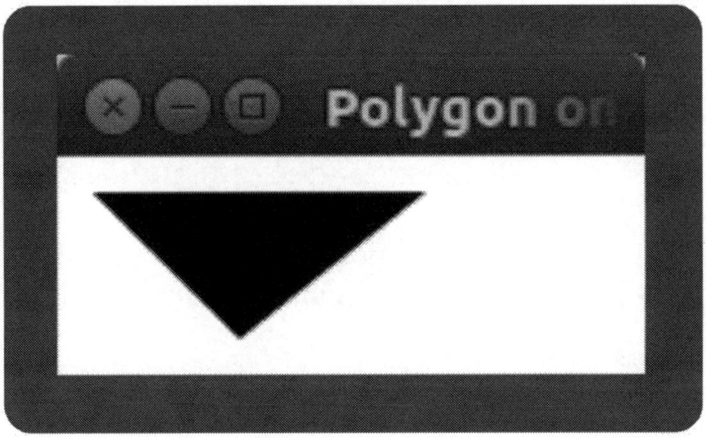


```
// PolygonSimplest.java
/*
Polygon : class: javafx.scene.shape.Polygon
--------------------------------------
An instance of a Triangle with given position.
The Parameters are simply a list of (x,y) postitions called vertexes.
Constructor:
Polygon(x1, y1, x2, y2, x3, y3, etc);

Tested on: java version "java-8-oracle"
Author: Mike Ohlson de Fine
*/
import javafx.application.Application;
import javafx.stage.Stage;
import javafx.scene.*;
import javafx.scene.shape.*; // Graphic primitives library.

public class PolygonSimplest extends Application
{
   public void start(Stage stage)
   {
        Group root = new Group();
     ///////////////////////////////////////////
     Polygon polygon1 = new Polygon(10, 10, 50, 50, 100, 10);
```

```
    ////////////////////////////////////////////
    root.getChildren().add(polygon1);

        Scene scene = new Scene(root, 160, 60);
        stage.setTitle("Polygon on Stage (canvas), JavaFX");
        stage.setScene(scene);
        stage.show();
  }
}
```

## Polygon Constructors

1. **Polygon();** Create an instance of a polygon that is empty. This means that space in memory has been reserved for the polygon but no explicit values have been specified
yet.
2. **Polygon(x0, y0, x1, y1 .... xn, yn);** Create an instance of a polygon with all the vertices specified. The values of these (x, y) vertexes can be changed later but the number of vertices cannot be changed.

We are going to use the polygon shown below to create a graphic sun with sunbeams radiating outward. We use rotation and translation transforms from the
*import javafx.scene.transform.*;* module.
The vertices for each point in this polygon are contained in the array:

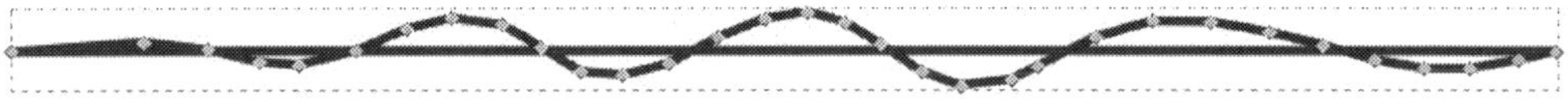

```
Double[] sunbeam1 = {0.2, 0.3, 29.0, -1.6, 43.6, 0.0, 54.9, 2.7, 63.7, 3.3, 76.3,
0.3, 87.7, -4.5, 97.3, -6.8, 108.2, -5.4, 116.9, -0.5, 125.3, 4.8, 134.4, 5.6, 144.1,
3.2, 154.9, -2.5, 165.2, -6.6, 174.7, -8.2, 182.8, -5.9, 190.7, -1.2, 199.5, 4.8,
208.0, 7.9, 219.4, 6.5, 225.1, 3.6, 237.3, -2.6, 249.6, -6.1, 262.2, -6.0, 274.5,
-3.7, 285.9, -1.0, 297.2, 2.3, 307.9, 4.2, 317.9, 4.2, 328.6, 2.3, 336.8, 0.4 } ;
```

# *Transformations (Translation and rotation) on Polygons*

```
// PolygonSunburst1.java
/*
Polygon : javafx.scene.shape.Polygon
This is a long segmented Line. Because it is a polygon
the last point is joined to the first by straight line.

Transforms that can be applied to the Polygon.
1. Rotate(angle, pivotX,  pivotY) / / Rotation.
2. Translate( x, y) / / Translation
3. Scale( x,  y)      / / Scaling (size changing in x and y separately).
4. Scale( x,  y,  pivotX,  pivotY)  / / Scale about a pivot point.

Tested on: java version "java-8-oracle"
Author: Mike Ohlson de Fine
*/
import javafx.application.Application;
import javafx.stage.Stage;
import javafx.scene.*;
```

```
import javafx.scene.paint.*;
import javafx.scene.shape.*;
import javafx.scene.transform.*;

public class PolygonSunburst1 extends Application {

   public void start(Stage stage)
   {
         double width =  1;
         double alphadeg = 7.5 ;
         double alphaIncrement = alphadeg ;
         Group root = new Group();

         for (int i = 0; i < 48; i++)  // 48 segments at 7.5 degree intervals
         {
          Polygon polyline1 = new Polygon();
          polyline1.getPoints().addAll(new Double[]{0.2, 0.3, 29.0, -1.6, 43.6, 0.0,
54.9, 2.7, 63.7, 3.3, 76.3, 0.3, 87.7, -4.5, 97.3, -6.8, 108.2, -5.4, 116.9, -0.5,
125.3, 4.8, 134.4, 5.6, 144.1, 3.2, 154.9, -2.5, 165.2, -6.6, 174.7, -8.2, 182.8,
-5.9, 190.7, -1.2, 199.5, 4.8, 208.0, 7.9, 219.4, 6.5, 225.1, 3.6, 237.3, -2.6, 249.6,
-6.1, 262.2, -6.0, 274.5, -3.7, 285.9, -1.0, 297.2, 2.3, 307.9, 4.2, 317.9, 4.2,
328.6, 2.3, 336.8, 0.4 });

            polyline1.setStroke(Color.RED) ;
            polyline1.setStrokeWidth(width) ;
            polyline1.getTransforms().add(new Translate(300, 300)); //  shift to
x,y
            polyline1.getTransforms().add(new Rotate(alphadeg,0,0)); //  angle,
pivotX, pivotY
            root.getChildren().add(polyline1) ;

            alphadeg += alphaIncrement ;
         }
       Scene scene = new Scene(root, 600, 600, Color.DARKBLUE);
       stage.setTitle("A Polygon Rotated and Translated. JavaFX");
       stage.setScene(scene);
       stage.show();

   }
}
```

## *Multiple Polygons from the same array.*

Now we make a more complex pattern by making a second version of the radiating sunbeam pattern using different colors.

```
// PolygonSunburst2.java
/*
Polygon : javafx.scene.shape.Polygon
This is a long segmented Line. Because it is a polygon
the last point is joined to the first by straight line.

Transforms that can be applied to the Polygon.
1. Rotate(angle, pivotX,  pivotY) // Rotation.
2. Translate( x, y) // Translation
3. Scale( x,  y)    // Scaling (size changing in x and y separately).
4. Scale( x,  y,  pivotX,  pivotY)  // Scale about a pivot point.

Tested on: java version "java-8-oracle"
Author: Mike Ohlson de Fine
*/
import javafx.application.Application;
import javafx.stage.Stage;
import javafx.scene.*;
import javafx.scene.paint.*;
```

```
import javafx.scene.shape.*;
import javafx.scene.transform.*;

public class PolygonSunburst2 extends Application {

   public void start(Stage stage)
   {
         double width =  2;
         double alphadeg = 7.5 ;
         double alphaIncrement = alphadeg ;
         Group root = new Group();
         double[] sunbeam1 = {0.2, 0.3, 29.0, -1.6, 43.6, 0.0, 54.9, 2.7, 63.7, 3.3,
76.3, 0.3, 87.7, -4.5, 97.3, -6.8, 108.2, -5.4, 116.9, -0.5, 125.3, 4.8, 134.4, 5.6,
144.1, 3.2, 154.9, -2.5, 165.2, -6.6, 174.7, -8.2, 182.8, -5.9, 190.7, -1.2, 199.5,
4.8, 208.0, 7.9, 219.4, 6.5, 225.1, 3.6, 237.3, -2.6, 249.6, -6.1, 262.2, -6.0, 274.5,
-3.7, 285.9, -1.0, 297.2, 2.3, 307.9, 4.2, 317.9, 4.2, 328.6, 2.3, 336.8, 0.4 } ;

         //int len = sunbeam1.length ;
         for (int i = 0; i < 48; i++) // 48 segments at 7.5 degree intervals
         {
          Polygon polygon1 = new Polygon();
          polygon1.getPoints().addAll(sunbeam1); // Use"sunbeam1" to
populate polygon1

            polygon1.setStroke(Color.RED) ;
            polygon1.setStrokeWidth(width) ;
            polygon1.getTransforms().add(new Translate(300, 300)); //  shift to
x,y
            polygon1.getTransforms().add(new Rotate(alphadeg,0,0)); //  angle,
pivotX, pivotY
            root.getChildren().add(polygon1) ;

            alphadeg += alphaIncrement ;
         }

         alphadeg = 3.75;
         alphaIncrement = 7.5;

         for (int i = 0; i < 48; i++) // 48 segments at 7.5 degree intervals
         {
          Polygon polygon2 = new Polygon();
```

```
        polygon2.getPoints().addAll(sunbeam1);// Use"sunbeam1" to populate
polygon2

            polygon2.setStroke(Color.YELLOW) ;
            polygon2.setStrokeWidth(width) ;

            polygon2.getTransforms().add(new Translate(300, 300));    // shift
to x,y
            polygon2.getTransforms().add(new Scale(0.94, 0.94));      // Shrink
by 0.94
            polygon2.getTransforms().add(new Rotate(alphadeg,0,0)); // angle,
pivotX, pivotY
            root.getChildren().add(polygon2) ;

            alphadeg += alphaIncrement ;
        }

        Scene scene = new Scene(root, 600, 600, Color.DARKBLUE);
        stage.setTitle("A Polygon Rotated and Translated. JavaFX");
        stage.setScene(scene);
        stage.show();

    }
}
```

## Size Transformation on One Axis only

The figure below is a polygon intended to form the basis of a kind of radiating sun image. We intend to add new versions of the same polygon to each other but with a change of height and color each time, while leaving the width unaltered. So we need some java code to achieve this with reasonably economic, efficient code.

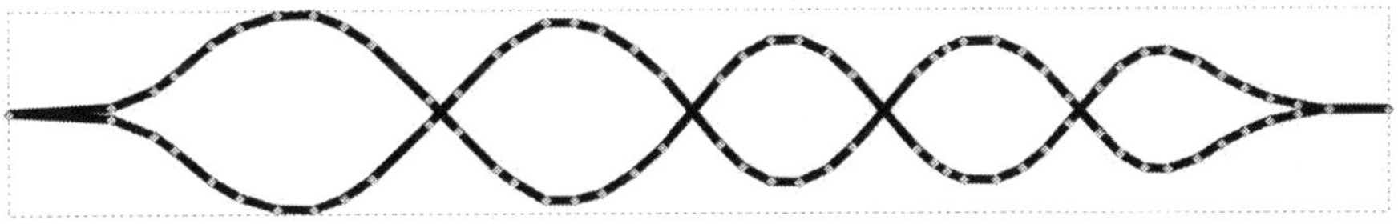

The program shown below produces the desired image. There is a sequence of code that constructs each of four polygons and each is a different size and color. In the example following this one we do better by replacing the similar sequences of polygon construction instructions with a general purpose Method that achieves a similar and much more flexible results.

```
// PolygonSunburst3.java
/*
Polygon : javafx.scene.shape.Polygon
This is a long segmented Line. Because it is a polygon
the last point is joined to the first by straight line.

Transforms that can be applied to the Polygon.
1. Rotate(angle, pivotX,  pivotY) // Rotation.
2. Translate( x, y) // Translation
3. Scale( x,  y)    // Scaling (size changing in x and y separately).
4. Scale( x,  y,  pivotX,  pivotY)  // Scale about a pivot point.
Tested on: java version "java-8-oracle"
Author: Mike Ohlson de Fine
*/
import javafx.application.Application;
import javafx.stage.Stage;
import javafx.scene.*;
import javafx.scene.paint.*;
import javafx.scene.shape.*;
import javafx.scene.transform.*;
import java.lang.reflect.Array;

public class PolygonSunburst3 extends Application {

   public void start(Stage stage)
   {
         double width =  2;
         double alphadeg = 7.5 ;
         double alphaIncrement = alphadeg ;
         Group root = new Group();
         Double[] spindle = { 589.2,0.294, 575.3,2.794, 562.8,5.594, 551.4,10.29,
540.7,15.6,530.,22.4, 516.7,27.1, 506.4,26.4, 495.7,19.9, 487.1,10.59,
473.2,-5.106, 462.5,-17.2, 452.5,-25.4, 441.,-30.4, 426.7,-30.1,
419.2,-26.9, 413.5,-22.9, 406.,-16.5, 377.5,16.7, 366.7,26.4, 353.5,32.4,
340.7,32.1, 328.2,25.3, 318.2,15.3, 292.5,-15.4, 279.6,-26.9, 265.3,-35.8,
252.8,-39., 240.3,-39., 226.4,-30.8, 218.9,-25.4, 201.7,-7.91, 188.9,5.994,
163.5,30.6, 151.4,38.85, 137.8,44.21, 121.7,43.85, 105.,38.49, 92.14,31.,
75.74,17.4, 66.44,10.59, 47.54,3.094, 1.397,0.4256, 47.54,-1.886, 66.44,
-9.386, 75.74,-16.19, 92.14,-29.79, 105.,-37.28, 121.7,-42.64, 137.8,-43.,
151.4,-37.64, 163.5,-29.39, 188.9,-4.786, 201.7,9.114, 218.9,26.61,
226.4,32.01, 240.3,40.21, 252.8,40.21, 265.3,37.01, 279.6,28.11,
```

```
292.5,16.61, 318.2,-14.09, 328.2,-24.09, 340.7,-30.89, 353.5,-31.19,
366.7,-25.19, 377.5,-15.49, 406.,17.71, 413.5,24.11, 419.2,28.11,
 426.7,31.31, 441.,31.61, 452.5,26.61, 462.5,18.41, 473.2,6.314,
487.1,-9.386, 495.7,-18.69, 506.4,-25.19, 516.7,-25.89, 530.,-21.19,
540.7,-14.39, 551.4,-9.086, 562.8,-4.386, 575.3,-1.586, 589.2,0.9143, 616.2,0.4254
  };

        int len_spindle =  Array.getLength(spindle);
        Double[] spindle2 = new Double[len_spindle]; // make an independent array.
        Double[] spindle3 = new Double[len_spindle]; // make an independent array.
        Double[] spindle4 = new Double[len_spindle]; // make an independent array.

        for ( int k=0; k<len_spindle/2; k++)
        {
            spindle2[2*k]   =  spindle[2*k] * 1.0;
            spindle2[1+2*k] =  spindle[1+2*k] * 0.8;

            spindle3[2*k]   =  spindle[2*k] * 1.0;
            spindle3[1+2*k] =  spindle[1+2*k] * 0.6;

            spindle4[2*k]   =  spindle[2*k] * 1.0;
            spindle4[1+2*k] =  spindle[1+2*k] * 0.4;
        };

        for (int i = 0; i < 48; i++) // 48 segments at 7.5 degree intervals
        {
           Polygon polyline1 = new Polygon();
           polyline1.getPoints().addAll(spindle);
           polyline1.setStroke(Color.RED) ;
           polyline1.setStrokeWidth(width) ;
           polyline1.setFill(null) ;
           polyline1.getTransforms().add(new Translate(300, 300)); //  shift to x,y
           polyline1.getTransforms().add(new Rotate(alphadeg,0,0)); //  angle, pivotX,
pivotY

           Polygon polyline2 = new Polygon();
           polyline2.getPoints().addAll(spindle2);
           polyline2.setStroke(Color.ORANGE) ;
           polyline2.setStrokeWidth(width) ;
           polyline2.setFill(null) ;
           polyline2.getTransforms().add(new Translate(300, 300)); //  shift to x,y
           polyline2.getTransforms().add(new Rotate(alphadeg,0,0)); //  angle, pivotX,
pivotY

           Polygon polyline3 = new Polygon();
           polyline3.getPoints().addAll(spindle3);
           polyline3.setStroke(Color.YELLOW) ;
           polyline3.setStrokeWidth(width) ;
```

```
        polyline3.setFill(null) ;
        polyline3.getTransforms().add(new Translate(300, 300)); // shift to x,y
        polyline3.getTransforms().add(new Rotate(alphadeg,0,0)); // angle, pivotX,
pivotY

        Polygon polyline4 = new Polygon();
        polyline4.getPoints().addAll(spindle4);
        polyline4.setStroke(Color.WHITE) ;
        polyline4.setStrokeWidth(width) ;
        polyline4.setFill(null) ;
        polyline4.getTransforms().add(new Translate(300, 300)); // shift to x,y
        polyline4.getTransforms().add(new Rotate(alphadeg,0,0)); // angle, pivotX,
pivotY

        root.getChildren().add(polyline4) ;
        root.getChildren().add(polyline3) ;
        root.getChildren().add(polyline2) ;
        root.getChildren().add(polyline1) ;

        alphadeg += alphaIncrement ;
      };

    Scene scene = new Scene(root, 1000, 1000, Color.DARKBLUE);
    stage.setTitle("A Multi-Polygon Rotated and Translated. JavaFX");
    stage.setScene(scene);
    stage.show();
  }
}
```

## A Better Way to do Repetition

We make should be smarter and more professional in the way we handle repeated actions. In the example above we make four versions of the spindle shapes. Each has different parameters like line width, color etc.

In the example below we make a general purpose method *make_Polygon,* that allows us to generate polygons with unique attributes.

```
// PolygonSunburst5.java
/*
Construntion of a custom method or function to make polygons with
particular properties.

Tested on: java version "java-8-oracle"
Author: Mike Ohlson de Fine
*/
import javafx.application.Application;
import javafx.stage.Stage;
import javafx.scene.*;
import javafx.scene.paint.*;
import javafx.scene.shape.*;
import javafx.scene.transform.*;
import java.lang.reflect.Array;

public class PolygonSunburst5 extends Application {

//=============================================================
//  Method/Function
//=============================================================
Polygon make_Polygon(Double[] poly_shape, Color kulaStroke, Color kulaFill, int
width,
            double shiftX, double shiftY, double rotateAlpha)
```

```
    {
            Polygon poly = new Polygon();
            poly.getPoints().addAll(poly_shape);
            poly.setStroke(kulaStroke) ;
            poly.setFill(kulaFill) ;
            poly.setStrokeWidth(width) ;
            poly.getTransforms().add(new Translate(shiftX, shiftY)); //  shift to x,y
            poly.getTransforms().add(new Rotate(rotateAlpha,0,0)); //  angle, pivotX,
pivotY
            return poly;
    }

//============================================================
//  Main Execution
//============================================================

   public void start(Stage stage)
   {
        int width =  2;
        double alphadeg = 7.5 ;
        double alphaIncrement = alphadeg ;
        Group root = new Group();
        Double[] spindle = { 589.2,0.294, 575.3,2.794, 562.8,5.594, 551.4,10.29,
540.7,15.6,530.,22.4, 516.7,27.1, 506.4,26.4, 495.7,19.9, 487.1,10.59,
473.2,-5.106, 462.5,-17.2, 452.5,-25.4, 441.,-30.4, 426.7,-30.1,
419.2,-26.9, 413.5,-22.9, 406.,-16.5, 377.5,16.7, 366.7,26.4, 353.5,32.4,
340.7,32.1, 328.2,25.3, 318.2,15.3, 292.5,-15.4, 279.6,-26.9, 265.3,-35.8,
252.8,-39., 240.3,-39., 226.4,-30.8, 218.9,-25.4, 201.7,-7.91, 188.9,5.994,
163.5,30.6, 151.4,38.85, 137.8,44.21, 121.7,43.85, 105.,38.49, 92.14,31.,
75.74,17.4, 66.44,10.59, 47.54,3.094, 1.397,0.4256, 47.54,-1.886, 66.44,
-9.386, 75.74,-16.19, 92.14,-29.79, 105.,-37.28, 121.7,-42.64, 137.8,-43.,
151.4,-37.64, 163.5,-29.39, 188.9,-4.786, 201.7,9.114, 218.9,26.61,
226.4,32.01, 240.3,40.21, 252.8,40.21, 265.3,37.01, 279.6,28.11,
292.5,16.61, 318.2,-14.09, 328.2,-24.09, 340.7,-30.89, 353.5,-31.19,
366.7,-25.19, 377.5,-15.49, 406.,17.71, 413.5,24.11, 419.2,28.11,
 426.7,31.31, 441.,31.61, 452.5,26.61, 462.5,18.41, 473.2,6.314,
487.1,-9.386, 495.7,-18.69, 506.4,-25.19, 516.7,-25.89, 530.,-21.19,
540.7,-14.39, 551.4,-9.086, 562.8,-4.386, 575.3,-1.586, 589.2,0.9143, 616.2,0.4254
  };

        int len_spindle =  Array.getLength(spindle);
        Double[] spindle2 = new Double[len_spindle]; // make an independent array.
        Double[] spindle3 = new Double[len_spindle]; // make an independent array.
        Double[] spindle4 = new Double[len_spindle]; // make an independent array.
        Double[] spindle5 = new Double[len_spindle]; // make an independent array.

        for ( int k=0; k<len_spindle/2; k++)
        {
```

```
        spindle2[2*k]   = spindle[2*k] * 1.0;
        spindle2[1+2*k] = spindle[1+2*k] * 0.8;

        spindle3[2*k]   = spindle[2*k] * 1.0;
        spindle3[1+2*k] = spindle[1+2*k] * 0.6;

        spindle4[2*k]   = spindle[2*k] * 1.0;
        spindle4[1+2*k] = spindle[1+2*k] * 0.4;

        spindle5[2*k]   = spindle[2*k] * 1.0;
        spindle5[1+2*k] = spindle[1+2*k] * 0.2;
      };

      for (int i = 0; i < 48; i++) // 48 segments at 7.5 degree intervals
      {

        Polygon poly5 = make_Polygon(spindle5, Color.CYAN, Color.CYAN, width,
          300, 300, alphadeg) ;
        root.getChildren().add(poly5) ;

        Polygon poly4 = make_Polygon(spindle4, Color.WHITE, null, width,
          300, 300, alphadeg) ;
        root.getChildren().add(poly4) ;

        Polygon poly3 = make_Polygon(spindle3, Color.YELLOW, null, width,
          300, 300, alphadeg) ;
        root.getChildren().add(poly3) ;

        Polygon poly2 = make_Polygon(spindle2, Color.ORANGE, null, 3,
          300, 300, alphadeg) ;
        root.getChildren().add(poly2) ;

        Polygon poly1 = make_Polygon(spindle, Color.RED, null, 4,
          300, 300, alphadeg) ;
        root.getChildren().add(poly1) ;

        alphadeg += alphaIncrement ;
      };

//==================================================
//  Graphic Drawing
//==================================================
      Scene scene = new Scene(root, 1000, 1000, Color.DARKBLUE);
      stage.setTitle("A Multi-Polygon Rotated and Translated. JavaFX");
      stage.setScene(scene);
      stage.show();
  }
}
```

### Can a Polygon be made smooth?

A polygon is a many sided figure made up of straight line segments. Where one segment joins the next there will always be a sharp corner. Can we make the sharp corners rounder and smoother? In computer programming languages with vector graphic objectives it is possible to create smooth curves from sequences of points. For

example if we had three points which were the corners, called apexes, of a triangle it is possible to create many smooth curves that go through each of the three points. A circle is the curve that will neatly go through any three random points. For more than three points the curves get morc complicated. These problems are solved using elliptic arcs or Bezier quadratic curves and Bezier cubic curves. Each of these topics is dealt with in a separate chapter later in this book. Bezier cubic curves are very useful because we can make absolutely shape of line with them.

## Combining Shapes: Intersection, Subtraction and Union

We can make new shapes by means of three operations on any shapes:

- Adding two shapes to each other, called their union,
- Subtracting one shape from the other,
- Taking the shapes of the overlap of the shapes, called their intersection

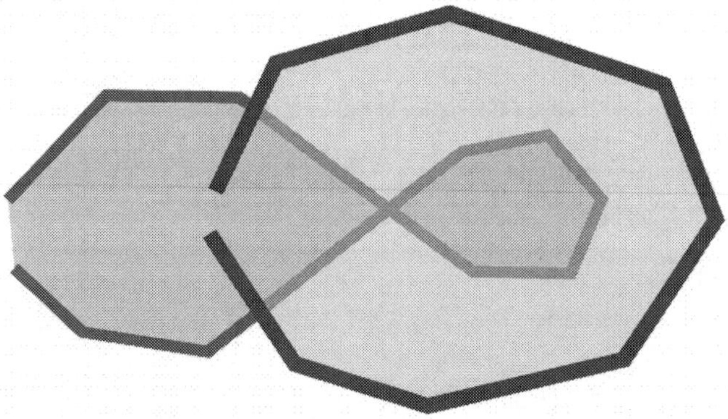

The operations will work on and 2D shapes including, circles, ellipses, rectangles, paths and polygons. In the program below we demonstrate all three  shpae combinations.

To test each combination in turn compile the program three times, each time with a different line below executing (ie. uncommented).

```
// Try out each in turn: intersection, subtraction and then union.

        //root.getChildren().add(intersection) ;  //Test 1. intersection.

        //root.getChildren().add(subtraction) ;  //Test 2. subtraction.

        root.getChildren().add(uniona) ;         //Test 3. union.
```

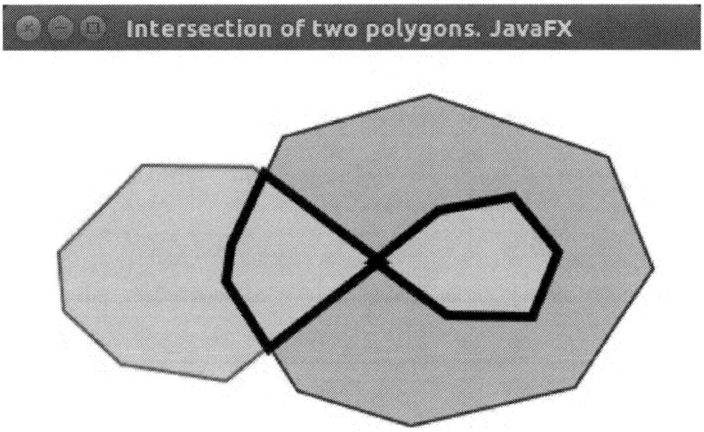

Note that with subtraction there are two separate results that depend of which shape is being subtracted:

Shape subtraction = Shape.subtract(polygon1, polygon2);

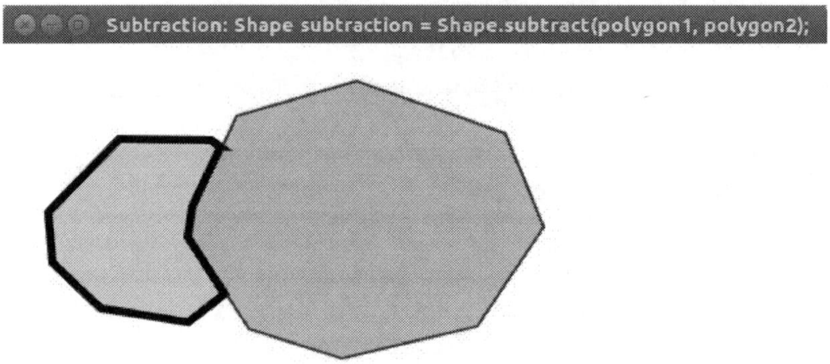


Shape subtraction = Shape.subtract(polygon2, polygon1);

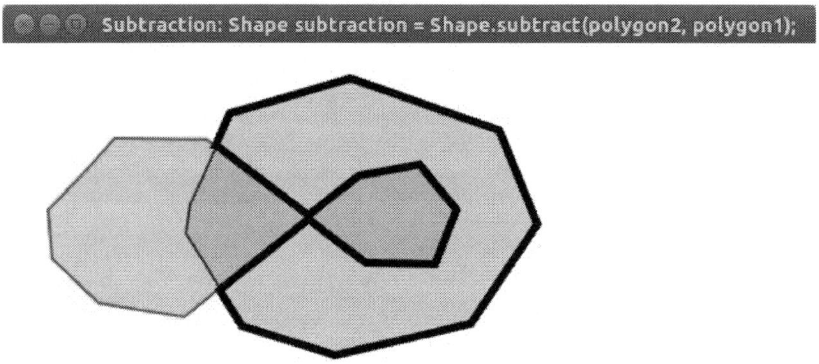


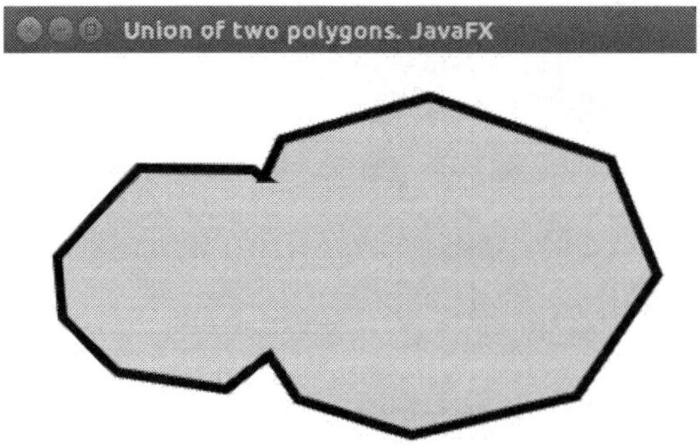

```
// PolygonsUnion.java
/*
Display the intersection, subtraction and union of two shapes.
Polyine : javafx.scene.shape.Polyine

Tested on: java version "java-8-oracle"
Author: Mike Ohlson de Fine
*/
import javafx.application.Application;
import javafx.stage.Stage;
import javafx.scene.*;
import javafx.scene.paint.*;
import javafx.scene.shape.*;
import javafx.scene.transform.*;

public class PolygonsUnion extends Application
 {
   public void start(Stage stage)
   {
        Group root = new Group();

        // The arrays that will be make up the Polygons.
       Double[] polypoints1 = {33.,121. , 83.,69. , 149.,70. , 265.,158. , 314.,159.
, 329.,121. , 303.,89. , 260.,97. , 133.,198. , 70.,188. , 36.,156. };
       Double[] polypoints2 = {137.,117. , 167.,52. , 254.,27. , 360.,64. ,
387.,131. , 340.,202. , 243.,225. , 176.,204. , 134.,138.};

         // Construct or instantiate two polygons
         Polygon polygon1 = new Polygon();
         Polygon polygon2 = new Polygon();

         // Make arrays into a polygons.
         polygon1.getPoints().addAll(polypoints1); // Add first array to a
Polygon.
         polygon2.getPoints().addAll(polypoints2); // Add second array to a
Polygon.
           polygon1.setStroke(Color.RED) ;
           polygon1.setStrokeWidth(2) ;
           polygon1.setFill(Color.PINK) ;

           polygon2.setStroke(Color.BLUE) ;
```

```
        polygon2.setStrokeWidth(2) ;
        polygon2.setFill(Color.SKYBLUE) ;

       // Construct or instantiate the intersection of two polygons.
       Shape intersection = Shape.intersect(polygon1, polygon2);
       intersection.setStroke(Color.BLACK);
       intersection.setStrokeWidth(6) ;
       intersection.setFill(Color.LIGHTGRAY);

       // Construct or instantiate the subtraction of two polygons.
       // Note the two possibilities, subtract(polygon1, polygon2) or
subtract(polygon2, polygon3),
       //  that give different results.
       //Shape subtraction = Shape.subtract(polygon1, polygon2);
       Shape subtraction = Shape.subtract(polygon2, polygon1);
       subtraction.setStroke(Color.BLACK);
       subtraction.setStrokeWidth(6) ;
       subtraction.setFill(Color.LIGHTGRAY);

       // Construct or instantiate the union of two polygons.
       Shape uniona = Shape.union(polygon1, polygon2);
       uniona.setStroke(Color.BLACK);
       uniona.setStrokeWidth(6) ;
       uniona.setFill(Color.LIGHTGRAY);

        // Show the two original polygons.
        root.getChildren().add(polygon1) ;
        root.getChildren().add(polygon2) ;

        // Try out each in turn: intersection, subtraction and then union.
        //root.getChildren().add(intersection) ;  //Test 1. intersection.
        //root.getChildren().add(subtraction) ;  //Test 2. subtraction.
        root.getChildren().add(uniona) ;         //Test 3. union.

    Scene scene = new Scene(root, 800, 800, Color.WHITE);
    stage.setTitle("Union of two polygons. JavaFX");
    stage.setScene(scene);
    stage.show();

  }
}
```

# CHAPTER 8

## ARC

*"The earth together with its surrounding waters must in fact have such a shape as its shadow reveals, for it eclipses the moon with the arc of a perfect circle."* Nicolaus Copernicus.

In this chapter we will cover:

- All the different properties of arcs.
- The use of constructors in Java.

- Arcs and using them.
- ArcTo and Path creation.

Arcs like other primitive graphic objects in JavaFX have many properties such as  line fill color, outline thickness, outline color, outline pattern ( solid or dashed) and transparency. When a primitive object is created and drawn all these properties are specified. Most of them have default values. A default value is a value that is pre-allocated by the Java class definition for the particular object. Typical default values for circles and ellipses are black outline, one pixel width, and a solid black fill interior which is fully opaque. Some of these properties can be set when the object is constructed using the appropriate constructor. The circle class provides several different constructors, each with a different set of parameters that we may find useful. In this chapter we will pay some attention to constructors and how we can use them. We will also explore Java Arrays because they are extremely useful in making complicated drawings.

## Arc Specification Parameters

The Arc class represents a 2D portion of a circle or ellipse, defined by a center point, a start angle (in degrees), an angular extent (length of the arc in degrees), and an arc type (ArcType.OPEN, ArcType.CHORD, or ArcType.ROUND).

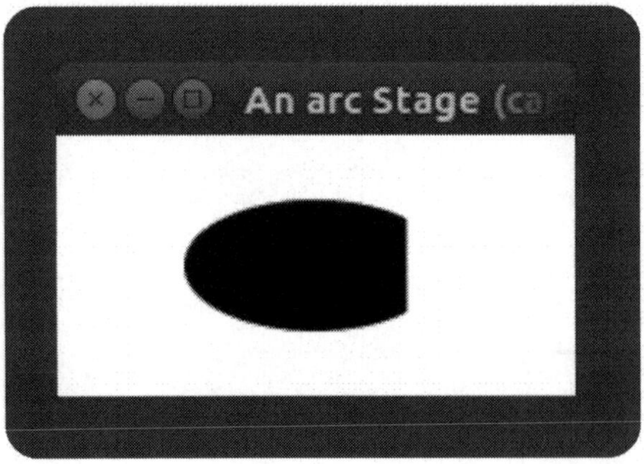

# *The Simplest Arc*

A basic circle using the default properties of line width and color:

```
// ArcSimplest.java
/*
Arc : class: javafx.scene.shape.Arc
-------------------------------------
An instance of Arc with given position and size.
Constructor:
Arc(CenterX, CenterY,  RadiusX, RadiusY, StartAngle, ArcLength);

Tested on: java version "java-8-oracle"
Author: Mike Ohlson de Fine
*/
import javafx.application.Application;
import javafx.stage.Stage;
import javafx.scene.*;
import javafx.scene.shape.*;

public class ArcSimplest extends Application
{
   public void start(Stage stage)
   {
        Group root = new Group();
     //****************************************
    //    X, Y,  RadX, RadY, StartAnd, ExtentAng)
     Arc arc = new Arc(100, 50, 50, 25, 45, 270);
     //****************************************
     root.getChildren().add(arc);

         Scene scene = new Scene(root, 200, 100);
         stage.setTitle("An arc Stage (canvas), JavaFX");
         stage.setScene(scene);
         stage.show();
   }
}
```

## *Ways to Close an Arc*

The arc can be completed in one of three ways as illustrated below.

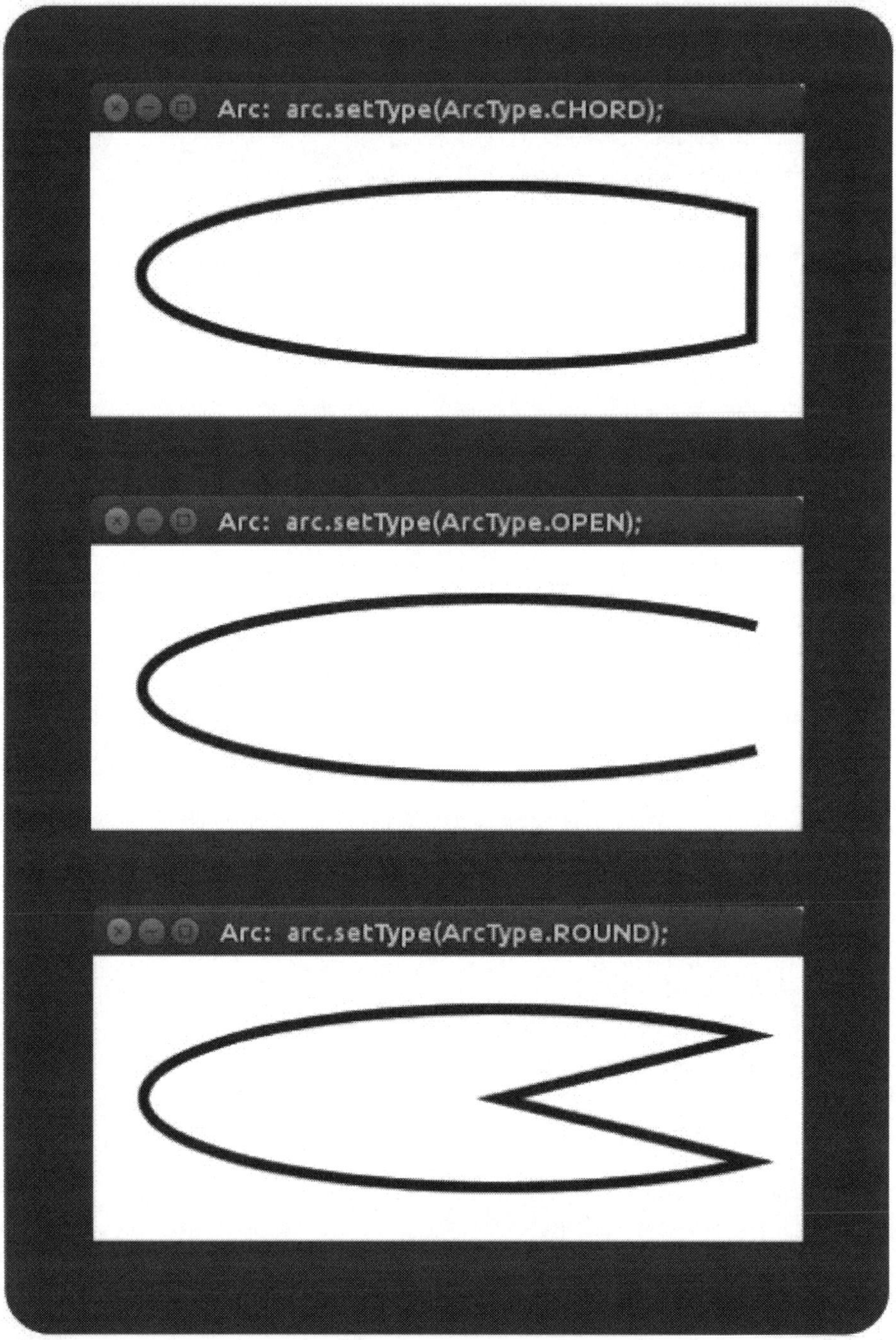

```
// ArcRoundChordOpen.java
/*
Arc : class: javafx.scene.shape.Arc
------------------------------------
An instance of Arc with given position and size.
Constructor:
Arc(CenterX, CenterY,  RadiusX, RadiusY, AtartAngle, ArcLength);
Closure default is OPEN.
Other optionsa are CHORD and ROUND.

Tested on: java version "java-8-oracle"
Author: Mike Ohlson de Fine
*/
import javafx.application.Application;
import javafx.stage.Stage;
import javafx.scene.*;
import javafx.scene.shape.*;
import javafx.scene.paint.Color;

public class ArcRoundChordOpen extends Application
{
   public void start(Stage stage)
   {
        Group root = new Group();
      //****************************************
      Arc arc = new Arc(230, 80, 200, 50, 45, 270);
      arc.setFill(null);
      arc.setStrokeWidth(6);
      arc.setStroke(Color.DARKBLUE);
      arc.setType(ArcType.ROUND); // Round - "Pie slice shape"
      //arc.setType(ArcType.CHORD); // Chord - A straight line across the
end.
      //arc.setType(ArcType.OPEN);  // Open - Simply not closed.
      //****************************************
      root.getChildren().add(arc);

          Scene scene = new Scene(root, 400, 160);
          stage.setTitle("Arc:  arc.setType(ArcType.ROUND);");
          //stage.setTitle("Arc:  arc.setType(ArcType.CHORD);");
          //stage.setTitle("Arc:  arc.setType(ArcType.OPEN);");
```

```
        stage.setScene(scene);
        stage.show();
    }
}
```

## Connecting Points – ArcTo(...)

Using the Arc(…) method we draw arcs specifying two radii, a start angle, an extent angle ("length") and a center.
As we shall see in chapter 11 Paths are a useful, versatile and efficient way of making intricate drawings. We jump a little bit ahead in this chapter to explore the particular Path method named ArcTo(…) because it is an extension of arc drawing but with some important differences. The chief difference is that we the programmer do not decide on

the start angle or extent angle of the arc. We only decide on the radii RadiusX and RadiusY as well as start and end position. The software machine, JavaFX makes decisions about size without consulting us.

## *The Simplest ArcTo*

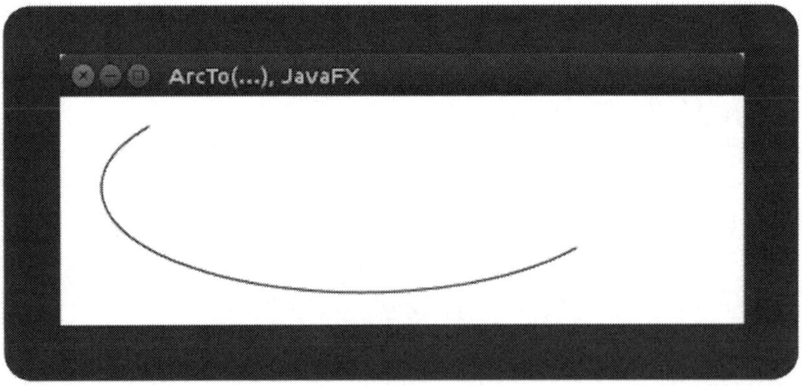


```
// ArcToSimplest.java
/*
Arc : class: javafx.scene.shape.ArcTo
------------------------------------
```

```
An instance of ArcTo with given position and size.
Constructors:
1. ArcTo(); or
2. ArcTo(RadiusX, RadiusY, StartAngle, xAxisRotation, x, y, largeArcFlag,
sweepFlag);
where:
RadiusX and RadiusY are the radii of the ellipse being used to form the arc,

Tested on: java version "java-8-oracle"
Author: Mike Ohlson de Fine
*/
import javafx.application.Application;
import javafx.stage.Stage;
import javafx.scene.*;
import javafx.scene.shape.*;

public class ArcToSimplest extends Application
{
   public void start(Stage stage)
   {
     Group root = new Group();
        //****************************************
        ArcTo arcTo = new ArcTo();
        arcTo.setX(340);       // End position
        arcTo.setY(100);       // End position
        arcTo.setRadiusX(100);
        arcTo.setRadiusY(40);

        Path path1 = new Path(new MoveTo(60,  20), arcTo);  // Start position,
an arc
        root.getChildren().add(path1);
        //****************************************

     Scene scene = new Scene(root, 450, 150);
     stage.setTitle("ArcTo(...), JavaFX");
     stage.setScene(scene);
     stage.show();
   }
}
```

## ArcTo: LargeArcFlag and SweepFlag

When we draw an arc of given radii between two points there are four possibilities.

There are two lengths of path – a short path or the long path. For each of these two options  the arc can be drawn clockwise from start to end or the car can be drawn anti-clockwise.

```
// ArcToSweepFlag1.java
/*
The state of the SweepFlag determines whether the path is
clockwise [ SweepFlag(true) ],
or
anticlockwise [ SweepFlag(false) ].
Arc : class: javafx.scene.shape.ArcTo
-------------------------------------
An instance of ArcTo with given position and size.
Constructors:
1. ArcTo();  or
2. ArcTo(RadiusX, RadiusY, StartAngle, xAxisRotation, x, y, largeArcFlag,
sweepFlag);

Tested on: java version "java-8-oracle"
Author: Mike Ohlson de Fine
*/
import javafx.application.Application;
import javafx.stage.Stage;
import javafx.scene.*;
import javafx.scene.paint.*;
import javafx.scene.shape.*;

public class ArcToSweepFlag1 extends Application
{
  public void start(Stage stage)
  {
   Group root = new Group();

     // ArcTo1 with LargeArcFlag(true)
     ArcTo arcTo1 = new ArcTo();
     arcTo1.setX(360);      // End position
```

```
        arcTo1.setY(60);       // End position
        arcTo1.setRadiusX(160);
        arcTo1.setRadiusY(40);
        //**********************************************************
        arcTo1.setSweepFlag(true); // "true" go clockwise from the start.
        arcTo1.setLargeArcFlag(true); // "true" go the long way around
        //**********************************************************
        Path path1 = new Path(new MoveTo(80,  60), arcTo1);  // Start
position, an arc
        path1.setStroke(Color.GREEN);
        path1.setStrokeWidth(6.);
        root.getChildren().add(path1);


        // ArcTo2 with LargeArcFlag(false)
        ArcTo arcTo2 = new ArcTo();
        arcTo2.setX(360);      // End position
        arcTo2.setY(60);       // End position
        arcTo2.setRadiusX(160);
        arcTo2.setRadiusY(40);
        //**********************************************************
        arcTo2.setLargeArcFlag(false); // "true" go the long way around
        //arcTo2.setSweepFlag(false); // "false" is the default, anti-clockwise.
        //**********************************************************
        Path path2 = new Path(new MoveTo(80,  60), arcTo2);  // Start
position, an arc
        path2.setStroke(Color.GREY);
        path2.setStrokeWidth(10.);
        root.getChildren().add(path2);

      Scene scene = new Scene(root, 450, 150);
      stage.setTitle("ArcTo(...), SweepFlag=true ->clockwise sweep");
      stage.setScene(scene);
      stage.show();
    }
}
```

# *Arc Paths – Collections of ArcTo*

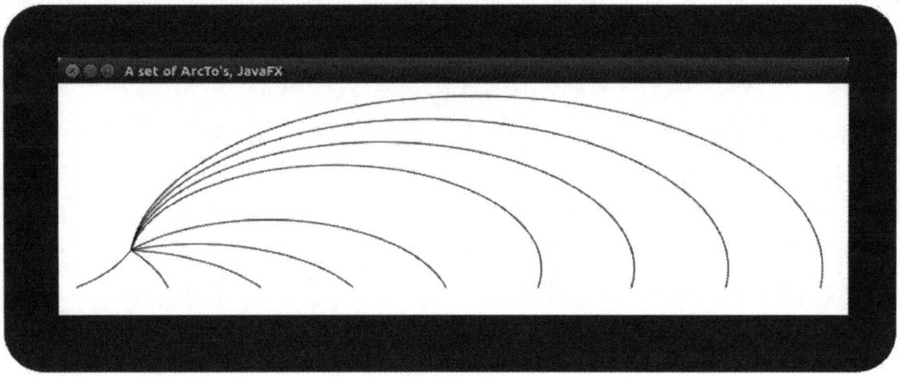


```
//ArcToSet1.java
/*
Arc : class: javafx.scene.shape.Arc
-------------------------------------
An instance of Arc with given position and size.
Constructors:
ArcTo();
ArcTo(RadiusX, RadiusY, StartAngle, xAxisRotation, x, y, largeArcFlag,
sweepFlag);
where:
RadiusX and RadiusY are the radii of the ellipse being used to form the arc,
xAxisRotation rotates the entire arc clockwise or anticlockwise.
x,y is the arc end point.

largArcFlag, if true will go the long way around to make the arc, the short arc
if false.
sweepFlag will determine the direction of the arc.

Tested on: java version "java-8-oracle"
Author: Mike Ohlson de Fine
*/
import javafx.application.Application;
import javafx.stage.Stage;
import javafx.scene.*;
import javafx.scene.shape.*;
```

```
public class ArcToSet1 extends Application
{
   public void start(Stage stage)
   {
        Group root = new Group();
     //****************************************

    // The common end position of 9 separate arcs.
    ArcTo arcTo = new ArcTo();
    arcTo.setX(80);
    arcTo.setY(180);
    arcTo.setRadiusX(200);
    arcTo.setRadiusY(100);

    // 9 separate arcs, each starting in a different position.
    Path path1 = new Path(new MoveTo(20,  220), arcTo);
    Path path2 = new Path(new MoveTo(120, 220), arcTo);
    Path path3 = new Path(new MoveTo(220, 220), arcTo);
    Path path4 = new Path(new MoveTo(320, 220), arcTo);
    Path path5 = new Path(new MoveTo(420, 220), arcTo);
    Path path6 = new Path(new MoveTo(520, 220), arcTo);
    Path path7 = new Path(new MoveTo(620, 220), arcTo);
    Path path8 = new Path(new MoveTo(720, 220), arcTo);
    Path path9 = new Path(new MoveTo(820, 220), arcTo);

      root.getChildren().add(path1);
      root.getChildren().add(path2);
      root.getChildren().add(path3);
      root.getChildren().add(path4);
      root.getChildren().add(path5);
      root.getChildren().add(path6);
      root.getChildren().add(path7);
      root.getChildren().add(path8);
      root.getChildren().add(path9);
     //****************************************
          Scene scene = new Scene(root, 850, 250);
         stage.setTitle("A set of ArcTo's, JavaFX");
         stage.setScene(scene);
         stage.show();
   }
}
```

# ArcTo largeArcFlag and sweepFlag

ArcTo will draw an arc (portion of a circle or ellipse) from the previous coordinates to the specified x and y coordinates using the specified existing radius.

There are four options of how to draw an arc from starting point to given end coordinates.

They are:

- **largeArcFlag == true** This means that the arc greater than 180 degrees will

be drawn.

- **sweepFlag == true** means that the arc will be drawn in the positive angle direction - i.e. the angle in the ellipse formula will increase from [fromX, fromY] to [x,y].

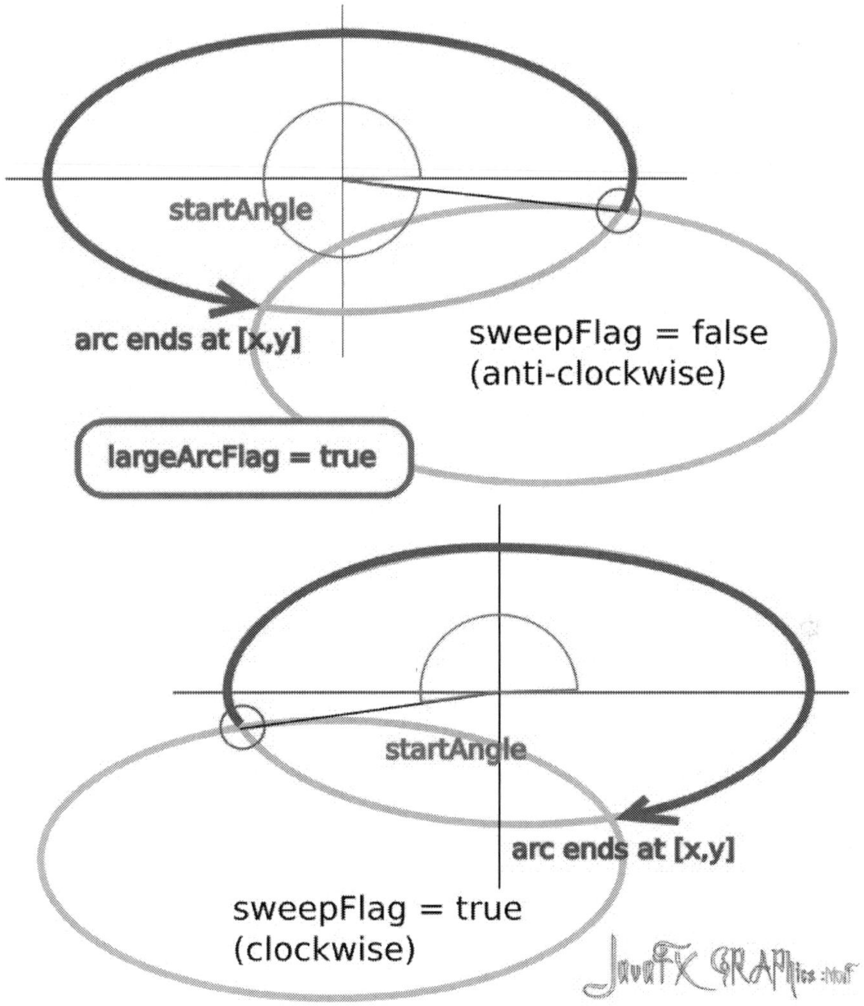


## Making Choices for Outline and Fill

The outline of a circle is just a line and we may specify line-width, color, dash-dot patterns. The interior fill of the circle allows us to vary color and transparency as well.

Similarly the outline and fill color of ellipses may be specified in the same way. So for outlines we exercise control using specifiers like:

*setStrokeWidth(8);* *// Width of the line, pixels.*

*setStrokeLineCap(StrokeLineCap.ROUND);* *// Rounded ends of lines.*

```
setStroke(Color.BLUE);                    // Color of line.
getStrokeDashArray().addAll(14d);         // Dash pattern: fill, blank, etc
setStrokeDashOffset(10);                  //Dash pattern: to shift the
beginning of the dash.
```

For interior areas we can control color and transparency as follows:

## The constructors belonging to the JavaFX Arc Class

1. **Arc() ;** This creates an instance of an arc with no specifications like position, radii ans srart and extent angle. So although the circle exists inside computer memory, there will be nothing to see on the stage.

2. **Arc(centerX, centerY, radiusX, , radiusY, startAngle, length);** This creates an instance of a arc with the following specifications:

centerX - the X coordinate of the center point of the arc.

CenterY - the Y coordinate of the center point of the arc.

RadiusX - the overall width (horizontal radius) of the full ellipse of which this arc is a partial section

RadiusY - the overall height (vertical radius) of the full ellipse of which this arc is a partial section

startAngle – The starting angle of the arc in degrees.

Length – the angular extent of the arc in degrees.

The Arc constructors do not allow us to do anything about specifying outline width, color or dash patterns. We must either alter those properties individually after the object, a arc in this case, has been constructed.

The way to modify all these properties of an arc is to code a special method to achieve particular modifications. We show this can be done using the function ***ArcSet(... )*** **.**

## *Specifying and controlling Arc properties.*

The drawing of arcs requires us to make many choices.

The key choices that could be made are:

1. Where is the center

2. What are the radii (for ellipses there are two different "radiuses").

3. What is the start angle.

4. How far should the drawn angle go? That is, what is the angular extent (degrees).

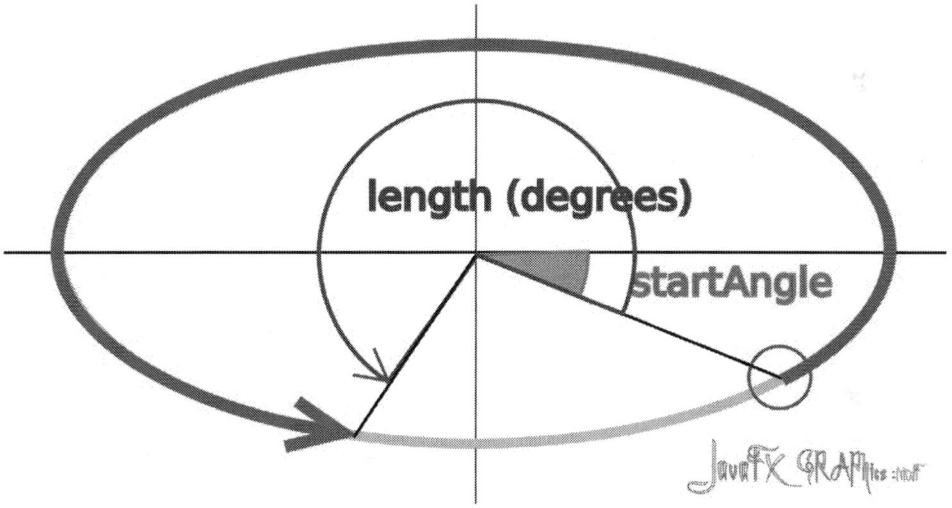


In addition the parent class of the arcs allows us to specify the character of the arc curve such as stroke width and color as well as a dash pattern if we choose.

So we can explicitly give numerical values to the parameters below or we can let them take on default values.

- setCenterX - Specifies the X coordinate of the center of the arc.
- setCenterY - Specifies the Y coordinate of the center of the arc.

- setRadiusX – Specifies the overall width (horizontal radius) of the full ellipse of which this arc is a partial section
- setRadiusY - Specifies the overall height (vertical radius) of the full ellipse of which this arc is a partial section
- setStartAngle – The start angle anticlockwise measured from the horizontal.
- setLength - The arc exten angle anticlockwise measured from the Start.
- setType – Specifies the closure type for the arc: ArcType.OPEN, ArcType.CHORD, ArcType.ROUND (ROUND=>Arc closed with line radii. ).
- **setStroke** – this sets the color of the outline of the circle.
- **setStrokeWidth** - this sets the width of the outline of the circle.
- **setStrokeType** – this determines whether the stroke is inside, outside or centered to the boundary of the shape. Examples are given in chapter 4.
- **setStrokeLineCap** – if the circle outline is dashed then this controls whether the ends of line segments are round (StrokeLineCap.BUTT) or flat (StrokeLineCap.ROUND).

In addition to controlling the properties of the outline we can alter the color of the fill of the circle interior with **setFill**.

Also we can rotate the principal axes of the ellipses of which the arcs are pieces of. The way to do this is to use the rotation(…) method belonging to the Transform class. See chapter 20.

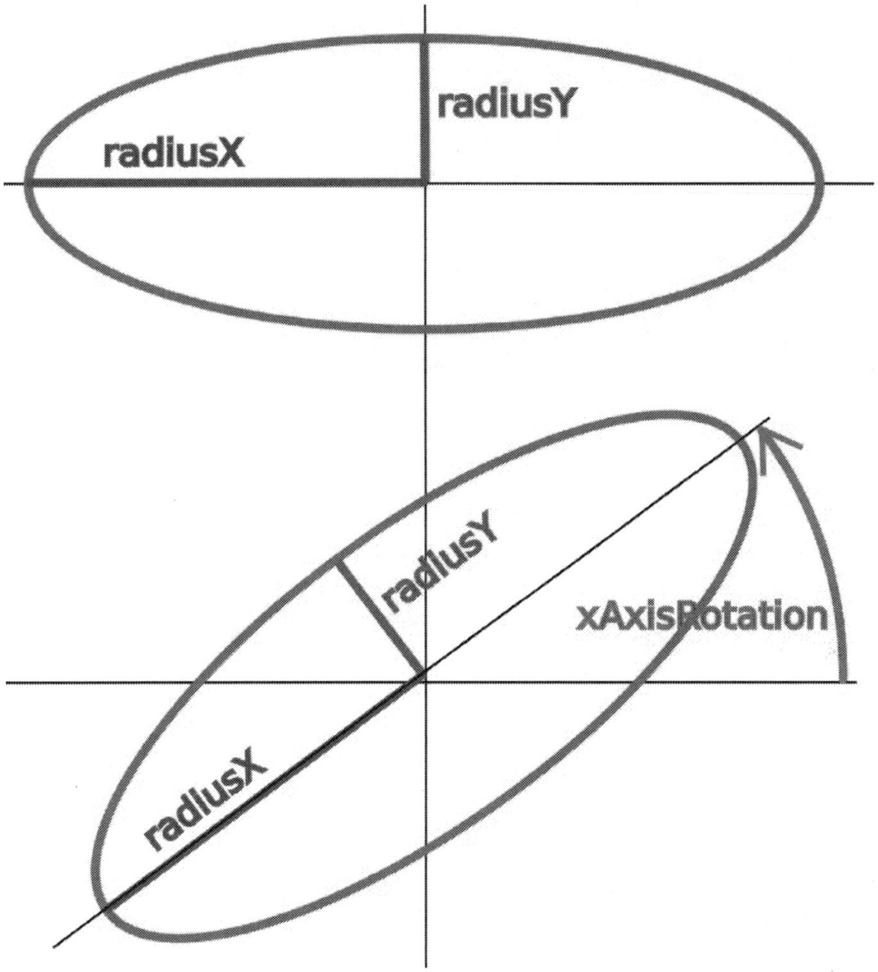


All these characteristic attributes like stroke width and colors can be altered after the circle has been constructed but once it has been drawn (by *stage.show()*; ) nothing about it can be changed. If we wanted to redraw the same circle but in a different color then we would have to create a completely new instance of the circle using the *new* keyword to do so.

The following example illustrates control of the parameters as well as construction of multiple instances. We do this without any attempt at reducing code in order to try and keep the code obvious and therefore easier to decipher. Later on we develop techniques to making the code more compact and more universally usable.

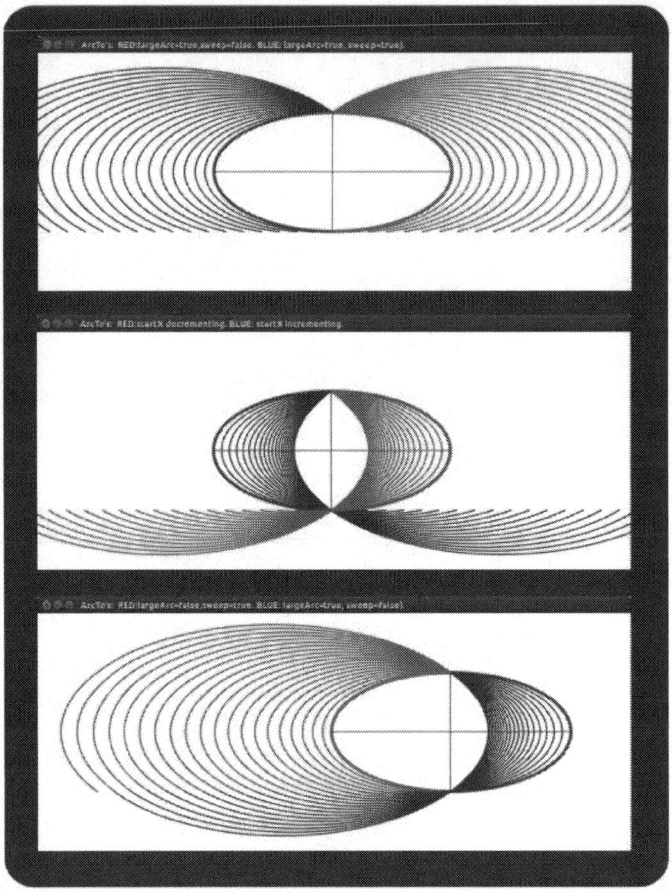


## ArcTo Patterns for Creative Experimentation

The three applications below were used to produce the images above. The possibilities are without limit. You dear reader are encouraged to hack (alter and modify) these applications. Imagine producing images of lurid sunrises or starry nights, peacocks, dragons and neon lizards. The only limit is your imagination.

### ArcTo Creative 1

```
// ArcTo_Creative1.java
/*
```

```
Tested on: java version "java-8-oracle"
Author: Mike Ohlson de Fine
*/
import javafx.application.Application;
import javafx.stage.Stage;
import javafx.scene.*;
import javafx.scene.shape.*;

public class ArcTo_Creative1 extends Application
{
   public void start(Stage stage)
   {
        Group root = new Group();
   //****************************************
   ArcTo arcTo1 = new ArcTo();
   arcTo1.setX(400);
   arcTo1.setY(200);
   arcTo1.setRadiusX(200);
   arcTo1.setRadiusY(100);

   //arcTo1.setSweepFlag(false); // true=anti-clockwise,
false=clockwise.
   arcTo1.setLargeArcFlag(true); // ==default. True and false seem to
be the same.

   double endX1 = 300 ;
   double endY = 400 ;
   for (int i = 0; i<20; i++)
   {  Path path1 = new Path(new MoveTo(endX1, endY), arcTo1);
      path1.setStrokeWidth(2);
      root.getChildren().add(path1);
       endX1 += 20 ;
  }
   //****************************************

         Scene scene = new Scene(root, 1100, 450);
         stage.setTitle(" ArcTo's, default setSweepFlag=default,
setLargeArcFlag=true");
```

```
        stage.setScene(scene);
        stage.show();
    }
}
```

## ArcTo Creative 2

```
// ArcTo_Creative2.java
/*
Tested on: java version "java-8-oracle"
Author: Mike Ohlson de Fine
*/
import javafx.application.Application;
import javafx.stage.Stage;
import javafx.scene.*;
import javafx.scene.shape.*;
import javafx.scene.paint.*;

public class ArcTo_Creative2 extends Application
{
  public void start(Stage stage)
  {
      Group root = new Group();
    //***********************************

  double cenX = 700 ;
  double cenY = 200 ;
  double radX = 200 ;
  double radY = 100 ;
  double startX = cenX ;
  double startY = cenY+radY ;
  double endX = cenX ;
  double endY = cenY-radY ;


  Ellipse ellip1 =  new Ellipse(cenX, cenY, radX, radY);
  ellip1.setFill(null) ;
  ellip1.setStroke(Color.GREY) ;
  ellip1.setStrokeWidth(6) ;
  ellip1.setFill(null) ;
```

```
root.getChildren().add(ellip1);

Line lineV = new Line(cenX, cenY-radY, cenX, cenY+radY);
root.getChildren().add(lineV);
 Line lineH = new Line(cenX-radX, cenY, cenX+radX, cenY);
root.getChildren().add(lineH);


ArcTo arcTo1 = new ArcTo();
arcTo1.setX(endX);
arcTo1.setY(endY);
arcTo1.setRadiusX(radX);
arcTo1.setRadiusY(radY);
arcTo1.setSweepFlag(false);
arcTo1.setLargeArcFlag(true);
System.out.println("largeArcFlag = " + arcTo1.isLargeArcFlag()); // false
is the default.
System.out.println("sweepFlag = " + arcTo1.isSweepFlag());      // false is
the default.

ArcTo arcTo2 = new ArcTo();
arcTo2.setX(endX);
arcTo2.setY(endY);
arcTo2.setRadiusX(radX);
arcTo2.setRadiusY(radY);
arcTo2.setSweepFlag(true);
arcTo2.setLargeArcFlag(false);
System.out.println("largeArcFlag = " + arcTo2.isLargeArcFlag()); // false
is the default.
System.out.println("sweepFlag = " + arcTo2.isSweepFlag());      // false is
the default.


for (int i = 0; i<20; i++)
{  Path path1 = new Path(new MoveTo(startX, startY), arcTo1);
   path1.setStrokeWidth(2);
   path1.setStroke(Color.BLUE);
   root.getChildren().add(path1);
    startX -= 30 ;

   Path path2 = new Path(new MoveTo(startX, startY), arcTo2);
```

```
        path2.setStrokeWidth(2);
        path2.setStroke(Color.RED);
        root.getChildren().add(path2);

    }
      //****************************************

          Scene scene = new Scene(root, 1000, 400);
          stage.setTitle("ArcTo's:  RED:largeArc=false,sweep=true. BLUE:
largeArc=true, sweep=false). ");
          stage.setScene(scene);
          stage.show();
    }
}
```

## ArcTo Creative 3

```
// ArcTo_Creative3.java
/*
Tested on: java version "java-8-oracle"
Author: Mike Ohlson de Fine
*/
import javafx.application.Application;
import javafx.stage.Stage;
import javafx.scene.*;
import javafx.scene.shape.*;
import javafx.scene.paint.*;

public class ArcTo_Creative3 extends Application
{
   public void start(Stage stage)
   {
        Group root = new Group();
      //****************************************
   double cenX = 500 ;
   double cenY = 200 ;
   double radX = 200 ;
   double radY = 100 ;
   double startX = cenX ;
   double startY = cenY+radY ;
```

```
double endX = cenX ;
double endY = cenY-radY ;

Ellipse ellip1 =  new Ellipse(cenX, cenY, radX, radY);
ellip1.setFill(null) ;
ellip1.setStroke(Color.GREY) ;
ellip1.setStrokeWidth(6) ;
ellip1.setFill(null) ;
root.getChildren().add(ellip1);

Line lineV = new Line(cenX, cenY-radY, cenX, cenY+radY);
root.getChildren().add(lineV);
 Line lineH = new Line(cenX-radX, cenY, cenX+radX, cenY);
root.getChildren().add(lineH);


ArcTo arcTo1 = new ArcTo(); // BLUE
arcTo1.setX(endX);
arcTo1.setY(endY);
arcTo1.setRadiusX(radX);
arcTo1.setRadiusY(radY);
arcTo1.setSweepFlag(true);
arcTo1.setLargeArcFlag(true);
System.out.println("Blue: largeArcFlag = " + arcTo1.isLargeArcFlag()); //
false is the default.
System.out.println("Blue: sweepFlag = " + arcTo1.isSweepFlag());       //
false is the default.

ArcTo arcTo2 = new ArcTo();  // RED
arcTo2.setX(endX);
arcTo2.setY(endY);
arcTo2.setRadiusX(radX);
arcTo2.setRadiusY(radY);
arcTo2.setSweepFlag(false);
arcTo2.setLargeArcFlag(true);
System.out.println("Red: largeArcFlag = " + arcTo2.isLargeArcFlag()); //
false is the default.
System.out.println("Red: sweepFlag = " + arcTo2.isSweepFlag());       //
false is the default.
```

```
    for (int i = 0; i<20; i++)
    {  Path path1 = new Path(new MoveTo(startX, startY), arcTo1);
       path1.setStrokeWidth(2);
       path1.setStroke(Color.BLUE);
       root.getChildren().add(path1);
        startX += 30 ;
    }

    startX = cenX ;
    for (int i = 0; i<20; i++)
    {
       Path path2 = new Path(new MoveTo(startX, startY), arcTo2);
       path2.setStrokeWidth(2);
       path2.setStroke(Color.RED);
       root.getChildren().add(path2);
        startX -= 30 ;
    }
      //*************************************
          Scene scene = new Scene(root, 1000, 400);
          stage.setTitle("ArcTo's:  RED:startX decrementing. BLUE: startX
incrementing. ");
          stage.setScene(scene);
          stage.show();
    }
}
```

# CHAPTER 9

## QUADRATIC CURVE

*"A quadratic equation (from the Latin quadratus for "square") is any equation having the form* $ax^2 + bx + c = 0$*.*

*The Egyptian Berlin Papyrus, dating back to the Middle Kingdom (2050 BC to 1650 BC), contains the solution to a two-term quadratic equation. In the Indian Sulba Sutras, about 800 BC, quadratic equations of the form ax2 = c and ax2 + bx = c were explored using geometric methods. Babylonian mathematicians from circa 400 BC and Chinese mathematicians from circa 200 BC used geometric methods of dissection to solve quadratic equations with positive roots."* WikipediA.

In this chapter we will cover:

- What a Bezier curve is.
- All the different properties of quatratics.
- The properties of ellipses.
- Arcs and using them.

## About Bezier Curves

This chapter and the next three are about how to use Bezier splines to draw smooth curves.

Here is a bit of history that explains the word *Bezier* and *spline* in connection to drawn curves. In 1959 Paul de Casteljau working for the world famous French motor car producer Citroen, developed reliable mathematical expressions that will always produce beautifully smooth curves. De Castlejau created these for the purpose of designing lovely car bodies for his company. Before this the best way to draw smooth curves was to to use thin, flexible strips of wood called splines. The splines would be fixed to a drawing table with thin nails and bent in curves to draw the curved sections of car bodies. Another car body designer, Pierre Bézier, at a rival French car manufacturer Renault, published these formulae in 1962.

What makes the Bézier curves special is that there are straight lines which we can control the shape of the curve. The ends of the smooth curves line up exactly with the straight lines controlling the curves. We say the curves are tangential to the straight lines at the end points.

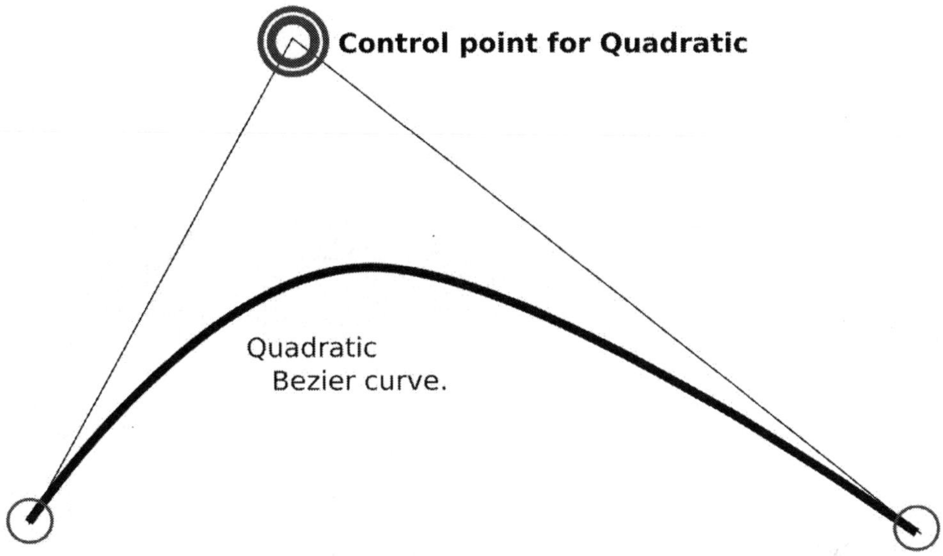


# Quadratics, an important shape.

**Class javafx.scene.shape.QuadCurve**
The Quadcurve class of JavaFX defines a quadratic Bézier parametric curve segment in (x,y) coordinate space. Drawing a curve that intersects both the specified coordinates (startX, startY) and(endX, enfY), using the specified point (controlX, controlY) as the Bézier control point.

**The constructors**
QuadCurve();
QuadCurve(startX, startY, controlX, controlY, endX, endY)

**Specifying the control points individually:**
```
QuadCurve quad = QuadCurve();

quad.setStartX(0.0f);    // x start point.

quad.setStartY(50.0f); // y start point.

quad.setEndX(50.0f); // x end point.
```

quad.setEndY(50.0f); // y end point.

quad.setControlX(25.0f); // x control point.

quad.setControlY(0.0f); // x control point.

# The Simplest Quadratic Bezier Spline Curve.

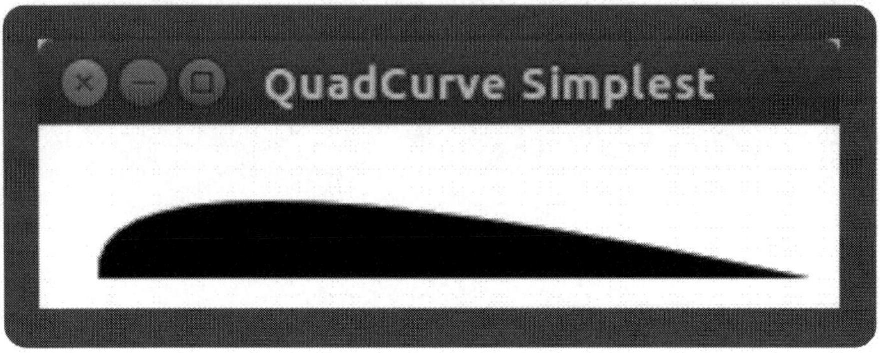


```
// QuadCurveSimplest.java
/*
Quadcurve : class: javafx.scene.shape.QuadCurve
---------------------------------------------
Constructor:
1. QuadCurve( );   - to create an empty instance.
2. QuadCurve( StartX, StartY, EndX, EndY, ControlX, ControlY);

Tested on: java version "java-8-oracle"
Author: Mike Ohlson de Fine
*/
import javafx.application.Application;
import javafx.stage.Stage;
import javafx.scene.*;
import javafx.scene.shape.*; // Graphic primitives library.

public class QuadCurveSimplest extends Application
{
   public void start(Stage stage)
   {
        Group root = new Group();
     ////////////////////////////////////////
     QuadCurve quad = new QuadCurve();
     quad.setStartX(20);      // x start point.
```

```
    quad.setStartY(50);       // y start point.
    quad.setEndX(250);        // x end point.
    quad.setEndY(50);         // y end point.
    quad.setControlX(15);     // x control point.
    quad.setControlY(0);      // x control point.
    ////////////////////////////////////////
    root.getChildren().add(quad);

        Scene scene = new Scene(root, 260, 60);
        stage.setTitle("QuadCurve Simplest");
        stage.setScene(scene);
        stage.show();
  }
}
```

**Why create an EMPTY Instance?**

The instruction *QuadCurve quad = new QuadCurve();* creates an empty instance of QuadCurve. The six parameter specifications follow:

```
    quad.setStartX(20);       // x start point.

    quad.setStartY(50);       // y start point.
    quad.setEndX(250);        // x end point.
    quad.setEndY(50);         // y end point.
    quad.setControlX(15);     // x control point.
    quad.setControlY(0);      // x control point.
```

The specifications determine the precise shape of the curve. By default the fill color is black.

The instruction *QuadCurve quad = new QuadCurve(20, 50, 250, 50, 15, 0);* which is the alternative form of the constructor will create the exact same curve and saves six lines of code. However it is more difficult to recognise which numbers affect each part of the curve. It is better programming to make things simple and obvious. When we come to use our code in six months time it is much easier to read and understand.

# Mouse Controlled QuadCurve

Here we demonstrate in the most obvious way the influence how the positions of the tips (vertices) of the triangle that contains the QuadCurve, control it's shape.

We use some unfamiliar instructions and methods that allow active mouse interaction. Do not try to figure out how these work yet. We explore this mouse event handling in chapter 15. For now it is sufficient to just use the code without being concerned how it works.

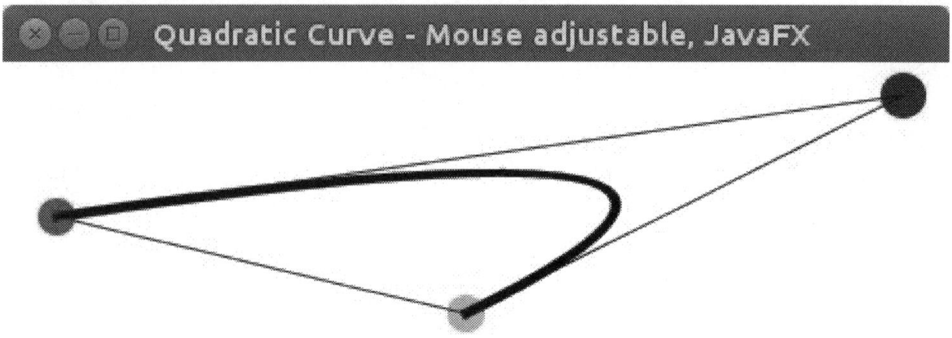


```
//MouseDragQuadCurve1.java
/*
Use setOnMouseDragged : class: javafx.scene.input.MouseEvent;
----------------------------------------------------------
Line line = new Line(StartX, startY, endX, endY); // Line constructor
line.setStartX(x0);
line.setStartY(y0);
line.setEndX(x1);
line.setEndY(y1);

QuadCurve quad = new QuadCurve();      // QuadCurve constructor.
quad.setStartX(x0);    // First point.
quad.setStartY(y0);
quad.setControlX1(X);  //Control lever.
quad.setControlY1(Y);
quad.setEndX(x1);      // Last point.
quad.setEndY(y1);

Tested on: java version "java-8-oracle"
Author: Mike Ohlson de Fine
*/

import javafx.application.Application;
import javafx.scene.Scene;
import javafx.scene.layout.Pane;
```

```
import javafx.scene.paint.Color;
import javafx.scene.shape.*;
import javafx.stage.Stage;
import java.awt.geom.GeneralPath ;

import javafx.event.EventHandler;       // For Mouse detection.
import javafx.scene.input.MouseEvent; // For mouse position capture.

public class MouseDragQuadCurve1 extends Application
{

   public void start(Stage primaryStage)
   {
      Pane root = new Pane();

      Circle circ_A = new Circle(100,100, 11, Color.BLUE) ;
      Circle circ_B = new Circle(80, 200, 9, Color.RED) ;
      Circle circ_C = new Circle(170,220, 9, Color.VIOLET) ;

      Line line_AB = new Line(100,100,  80, 200) ;
      Line line_BC = new Line(80 ,200, 170, 220) ;
      Line line_CA = new Line(170,220, 100,  100) ;

                              // Vertices          B           A           C
      QuadCurve quad1 = new QuadCurve(80,200,  100,100, 170,220);
      quad1.setFill(null);
      quad1.setStrokeWidth(5);
      quad1.setStroke(Color.BLACK);

      root.getChildren().add(circ_A);
      root.getChildren().add(circ_B);
      root.getChildren().add(circ_C);

      root.getChildren().add(line_AB);
      root.getChildren().add(line_BC);
      root.getChildren().add(line_CA);

      root.getChildren().add(quad1);

      ////////////////////////////////////////////////////////////
      /* Below are three mouse handling methods - one for each vertex
```

```
  of the triangle that controls the shape of the Quadratic curve */

/* Event handler for dragging inside circ_A - Blue */
circ_A.setOnMouseDragged(new EventHandler<MouseEvent>()
{
   public void handle(MouseEvent event)
   {
      circ_A.setCenterX(event.getX());
      circ_A.setCenterY(event.getY());
      line_AB.setStartX(event.getX());
      line_AB.setStartY(event.getY());
      line_CA.setEndX(event.getX());
      line_CA.setEndY(event.getY());
      quad1.setControlX(event.getX());
      quad1.setControlY(event.getY());
   }
});

/* Event handler for dragging inside circ_B - Red*/
circ_B.setOnMouseDragged(new EventHandler<MouseEvent>()
{
   public void handle(MouseEvent event)
   {
      circ_B.setCenterX(event.getX());
      circ_B.setCenterY(event.getY());
      line_BC.setStartX(event.getX());
      line_BC.setStartY(event.getY());
      line_AB.setEndX(event.getX());
      line_AB.setEndY(event.getY());

      quad1.setStartX(event.getX());
      quad1.setStartY(event.getY());
   }
});

/* Event handler for dragging inside circ_C - Violet */
circ_C.setOnMouseDragged(new EventHandler<MouseEvent>()
{
   public void handle(MouseEvent event)
   {
      circ_C.setCenterX(event.getX());
```

```
            circ_C.setCenterY(event.getY());
            line_CA.setStartX(event.getX());
            line_CA.setStartY(event.getY());
            line_BC.setEndX(event.getX());
            line_BC.setEndY(event.getY());

            quad1.setEndX(event.getX());
            quad1.setEndY(event.getY());
        }
    });

    ////////////////////////////////////////////////////////////
    Scene scene = new Scene(root, 500, 300);
    primaryStage.setTitle("Quadratic Curve - Mouse adjustable, JavaFX");
    primaryStage.setScene(scene);
    primaryStage.show();
```

## Parametric control of curves

We use the word parameter here to mean some kind of *variable* control that specifies the shape of the curve. The curves are specified by some general purpose equations and the parameters are the 'control knobs' that adjust the final shape.

```
// QuadCurveSet.java
/*
Repeated constructors creating a set of progressively different
quadrativ curves.

Tested on: java version "java-8-oracle"
Author: Mike Ohlson de Fine
*/
import javafx.application.Application;
import javafx.stage.Stage;
import javafx.scene.*;
import javafx.scene.paint.*;
import javafx.scene.shape.*; // Graphic primitives library.

public class QuadCurveSet extends Application
{
    double m1, c1, deltx;
```

```
    double x1 = 50 ;
    double y1 = 300 ;
    double x2 = 210 ;
    double y2 = 280 ;
    double x3 = 500 ;
    double y3 = 250 ;

  public void start(Stage stage)
  {
        Group root = new Group();

    for (int i = 0; i<60; i++ )
    {
      QuadCurve QCSet = new QuadCurve() ;
      QCSet.setStartX(x1);     //  x start point.
      QCSet.setStartY(y1);     //  y start point.
      QCSet.setEndX(x2);       //  x end point.
      QCSet.setEndY(y2);       //  y end point.
      QCSet.setControlX(x3);   //  x control point.
      QCSet.setControlY(y3);   //  y control point.
      QCSet.setFill(null);
      QCSet.setStrokeWidth(1);
      QCSet.setStroke(Color.BLACK);
      root.getChildren().add(QCSet);
      y2 -= 4 ;
      y3 += 8 ;
      x3 += 5 ;
    };
        Scene scene = new Scene(root, 500, 500);
        stage.setTitle("Quadratic Bezier curve on Stage, JavaFX");
        stage.setScene(scene);
        stage.show();
  }
}
```

# Generating Sets of Similar Curves

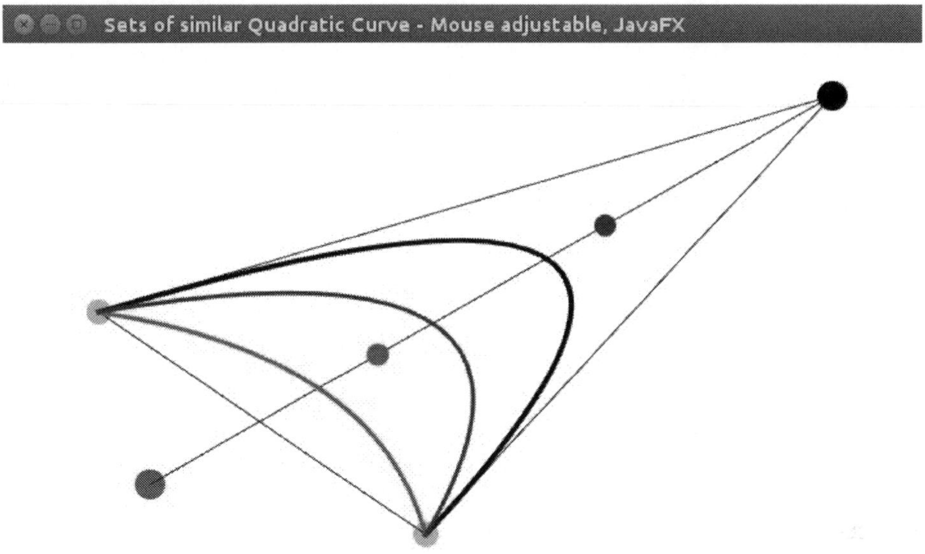


```
// MouseDragQuadSet5.java
/*
Generate and control families of cubic curves.
---------------------------------------------

Tested on: java version "java-8-oracle"
Author: Mike Ohlson de Fine
*/
import javafx.application.Application;
import javafx.scene.Scene;
import javafx.scene.layout.Pane;
import javafx.scene.paint.Color;
import javafx.scene.shape.*;
import javafx.stage.Stage;
import java.awt.geom.GeneralPath ;

import javafx.event.EventHandler;
import javafx.scene.input.MouseEvent;
import java.lang.Math ;
```

```
public class MouseDragQuadSet5 extends Application
{  /* Generate arrays of control points for the families of quadratic curves */
   double xx ;
   double yy ;
   double xa = 300 ; // Control point A.
   double ya = 100 ;
   double xb = 80  ; // Start point B.
   double yb = 200 ;
   double xc = 400 ; // End point B.
   double yc = 320 ;
   double xd = 100 ; // Auxiliary control point D.
   double yd = 400 ;
   int num_divisions = 3; // Number of quadratics to be drawn.

    private double[][] line_parameters(double xm, double ym, double xn, double
yn, int num_divisions)
    {
       double len =  Math.sqrt( (yn-ym)*(yn-ym) + (xn-xm)*(xn-xm) );
       double m = (yn - ym)/(xn - xm);
       double c = ym - m * xm;
       double theta = Math.atan(m);
       double delta_x = len/num_divisions;

       double[][] xy_intermediates  ;
       xy_intermediates = new double[2][num_divisions] ;
       double next_x ;

        for (int i=0; i<num_divisions; i++)
        {  next_x = i* delta_x ;
           xy_intermediates[0][i] = xm +  next_x *Math.cos(theta); // X-
compoment.
           xy_intermediates[1][i] = ym +  next_x *Math.sin(theta); // Y-
compoment.
        }
       return xy_intermediates ;
     }

    public void start(Stage primaryStage)
    {
      Pane root = new Pane();
```

```
Circle circ_A = new Circle(xa, ya, 11, Color.BLACK) ;
Circle circ_B = new Circle(xb, yb, 9, Color.ORANGE) ;
Circle circ_C = new Circle(xc, yc, 9, Color.VIOLET) ;

Line line_AB = new Line(xb, yb,  xa, ya) ;
Line line_BC = new Line(xb, yb,  xc, yc) ;
Line line_CA = new Line(xc, yc,  xa, ya) ;

Circle circ_D = new Circle(xd, yd, 11, Color.BROWN) ;
Line line_AD  = new Line(xa, ya,  xd, yd) ;

                                   // Vertices  B     A     C
QuadCurve quad1 = new QuadCurve(xb,yb,  xa,ya, xc,yc);
quad1.setFill(null);
quad1.setStrokeWidth(4);
quad1.setStroke(Color.BLACK);

QuadCurve quad2 = new QuadCurve(xb,yb,  80,80, xc,yc);
quad2.setFill(null);
quad2.setStrokeWidth(3);
quad2.setStroke(Color.RED);

QuadCurve quad3 = new QuadCurve(xb,yb,  60,60, xc,yc);
quad3.setFill(null);
quad3.setStrokeWidth(3);
quad3.setStroke(Color.BLUE);

root.getChildren().add(circ_A);
root.getChildren().add(circ_B);
root.getChildren().add(circ_C);
root.getChildren().add(circ_D);

root.getChildren().add(line_AB);
root.getChildren().add(line_BC);
root.getChildren().add(line_CA);
root.getChildren().add(line_AD);

root.getChildren().add(quad1);
root.getChildren().add(quad2);
root.getChildren().add(quad3);
```

```
        double[][] xy_intermediates =  line_parameters(xd, yd, xa, ya,
num_divisions);

        Circle cirqu2 = new Circle(xy_intermediates[0][1], xy_intermediates[1][1],
8, Color.RED) ;
        root.getChildren().add(cirqu2);

        Circle cirqu3 = new Circle(xy_intermediates[0][2], xy_intermediates[1][2],
8, Color.BLUE) ;
        root.getChildren().add(cirqu3);


      ///////////////////////////////////////////////////////////////
      ///          EVENT HANDLING                                 ///
      ///////////////////////////////////////////////////////////////
      // Event handler for dragging inside circ_A - Black
      circ_A.setOnMouseDragged(new EventHandler<MouseEvent>()
       {
        public void handle(MouseEvent event)
        {
          xx = event.getX();
          yy = event.getY();

          circ_A.setCenterX(xx);
          circ_A.setCenterY(yy);
          line_AB.setEndX(xx);
          line_AB.setEndY(yy);
          line_CA.setEndX(xx);
          line_CA.setEndY(yy);
          line_AD.setStartX(xx);
          line_AD.setStartY(yy);

           xa = xx ;
           ya = yy ;
           double[][] xy_intermeds1 =  line_parameters(xd, yd, xa, ya,
num_divisions);
           quad1.setControlX(xx);
           quad1.setControlY(yy);
           quad2.setControlX(xy_intermeds1[0][1]) ;
           quad2.setControlY(xy_intermeds1[1][1]) ;
           quad3.setControlX(xy_intermeds1[0][2]) ;
```

```
        quad3.setControlY(xy_intermeds1[1][2]) ;

        cirqu2.setCenterX(xy_intermeds1[0][1]) ;
        cirqu2.setCenterY(xy_intermeds1[1][1]) ;
        cirqu3.setCenterX(xy_intermeds1[0][2]) ;
        cirqu3.setCenterY(xy_intermeds1[1][2]) ;
      }
    });
    ////////////////////////////////////////////////////////////
    // Event handler for dragging inside circ_B - Brown
    circ_D.setOnMouseDragged(new EventHandler<MouseEvent>()
    {
      public void handle(MouseEvent event)
      {
        xx = event.getX();
        yy = event.getY();
        xd = xx ;
        yd = yy ;

        circ_D.setCenterX(xx);
        circ_D.setCenterY(yy);
        line_AD.setEndX(xx);
        line_AD.setEndY(yy);

        double[][] xy_intermeds1 =  line_parameters(xd, yd, xa, ya,
num_divisions);
        quad1.setControlX(xa);  // This remains unchanged when circle D is
adjusted.
        quad1.setControlY(ya);
        quad2.setControlX(xy_intermeds1[0][1]);
        quad2.setControlY(xy_intermeds1[1][1]);
        quad3.setControlX(xy_intermeds1[0][2]);
        quad3.setControlY(xy_intermeds1[1][2]);
        cirqu2.setCenterX(xy_intermeds1[0][1]) ;
        cirqu2.setCenterY(xy_intermeds1[1][1]) ;
        cirqu3.setCenterX(xy_intermeds1[0][2]) ;
        cirqu3.setCenterY(xy_intermeds1[1][2]) ;
      }
    });

    ////////////////////////////////////////////////////////////
```

```
// Event handler for dragging inside circ_B - Orange
circ_B.setOnMouseDragged(new EventHandler<MouseEvent>()
 {
   public void handle(MouseEvent event)
   {
     xx = event.getX();
     yy = event.getY();

     circ_B.setCenterX(xx);
     circ_B.setCenterY(yy);
     line_BC.setStartX(xx);
     line_BC.setStartY(yy);
     line_AB.setStartX(xx);
     line_AB.setStartY(yy);
     quad1.setStartX(xx);
     quad1.setStartY(yy);
     quad2.setStartX(xx);
     quad2.setStartY(yy);
     quad3.setStartX(xx);
     quad3.setStartY(yy);
   }
 });

// Event handler for dragging inside circ_C - Violet
circ_C.setOnMouseDragged(new EventHandler<MouseEvent>()
 {
   public void handle(MouseEvent event)
   {
     xx = event.getX();
     yy = event.getY();

     circ_C.setCenterX(xx);
     circ_C.setCenterY(yy);
     line_CA.setStartX(xx);
     line_CA.setStartY(yy);
     line_BC.setEndX(xx);
     line_BC.setEndY(yy);
     quad1.setEndX(xx);
     quad1.setEndY(yy);
     quad2.setEndX(xx);
     quad2.setEndY(yy);
```

```
            quad3.setEndX(xx);
            quad3.setEndY(yy);
          }
      });

   ////////////////////////////////////////////////////////////////
      Scene scene = new Scene(root, 800, 800);
      primaryStage.setTitle("Sets of similar Quadratic Curve - Mouse
adjustable, JavaFX");
      primaryStage.setScene(scene);
      primaryStage.show();
   }
}
```

## *Generating Large sets of QuadCurves*

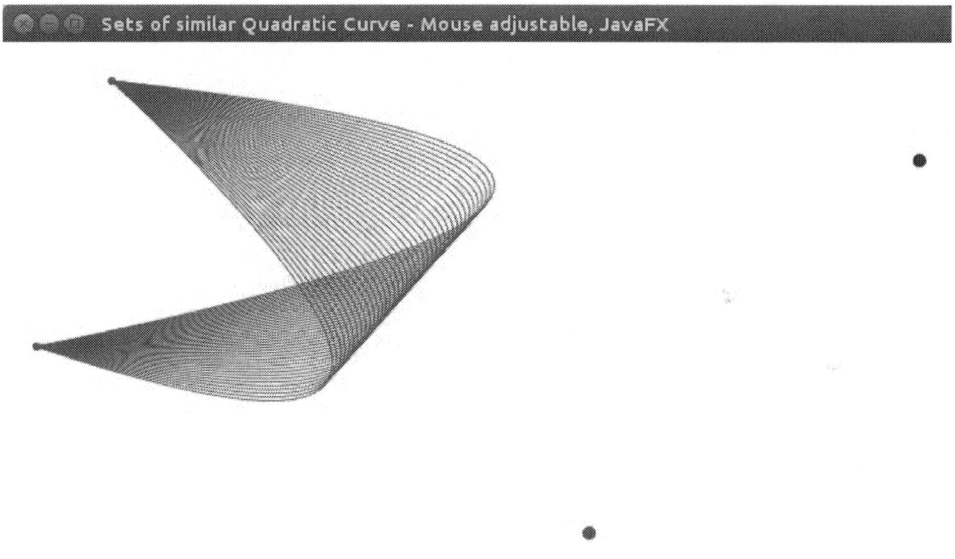


```
//MouseDragQuadSet10.java
/*
Generate and control families of cubic curves.
-----------------------------------------------
Various ways of declaring QuadCurve arrays:
QuadCurve[] quadCArray = new QuadCurve[30]; // Number of quad-curves
= 30.
```

```
QuadCurve[] quadCArray = {...member quad-curves...};
QuadCurve[] quadCArray = new QuadCurve[]{...member quad-curves...};

Tested on: java version "java-8-oracle"
Author: Mike Ohlson de Fine
*/
import javafx.application.Application;
import javafx.scene.Scene;
import javafx.scene.layout.Pane;
import javafx.scene.paint.Color;
import javafx.scene.shape.*;
import javafx.stage.Stage;
import java.awt.geom.GeneralPath ;

import javafx.event.EventHandler;
import javafx.scene.input.MouseEvent;
import java.lang.Math ;

public class MouseDragQuadSet10 extends Application
{
  double xx ;
  double yy ;
  double xa = 300 ; // Control point A.
  double ya = 100 ;
  double xb = 80  ; // Start point B.
  double yb = 200 ;
  double xc = 400 ; // End point B.
  double yc = 320 ;
  double xd = 100 ; // Auxiliary control point D.
  double yd = 400 ;
  int num_curves = 40; // Number of quadratics to be drawn.

   private double[][] line_parameters(double xm, double ym, double xn, double
yn, int num_curves)
   {  /* Generate arrays of control points for the families of quadratic curves.
        Equi-spaced control points are distributed along the line
        which joins the points (xm,ym) to (xn,yn).  */
      double len =  Math.sqrt( (yn-ym)*(yn-ym) + (xn-xm)*(xn-xm) );
      double m = (yn - ym)/(xn - xm);
      double c = ym - m * xm;
      double theta = Math.atan(m);
```

```
    double delta_x = len / num_curves;

     double[][] xy_intermediates  ;
     xy_intermediates = new double[2][num_curves] ;
     double next_x ;

       for (int i=0; i<num_curves; i++)
       {  next_x = i* delta_x ;
          xy_intermediates[0][i] = xm +  next_x *Math.cos(theta);  // X-
compoment.
          xy_intermediates[1][i] = ym +  next_x *Math.sin(theta);  // Y-
compoment.
        }
      return xy_intermediates ;  // The array of (x,y) control points.
   }

  public void start(Stage primaryStage)
  {
     Pane root = new Pane();
     Circle circ_A = new Circle(xa, ya, 5, Color.BLUE) ;
     Circle circ_B = new Circle(xb, yb, 3, Color.GREEN) ;
     Circle circ_C = new Circle(xc, yc, 3, Color.GREEN) ;
     Circle circ_D = new Circle(xd, yd, 5, Color.BROWN) ;

//************************************************************
//************************************************************
// A Loop controlled method of generating Quadcurves
  QuadCurve[] quads = new QuadCurve[num_curves];

   /* Here we instantiate an array og Quadrurves "quads[ ]"
     Each must be given distinct properties even though they
     will be modulated as a group.
     They have been added as items that will show on the stage.      */
  for (int i = 0 ; i<num_curves ;  i++)
  {
    quads[i] = new QuadCurve(xb,yb,  xa,ya,  xc,yc);
    quads[i].setFill(null);
    quads[i].setStrokeWidth(1);
    quads[i].setStroke(Color.GREEN);
    root.getChildren().add(quads[i]);
   }
```

```
//***************************************************************
//***************************************************************
    root.getChildren().add(circ_A);
    root.getChildren().add(circ_B);
    root.getChildren().add(circ_C);
    root.getChildren().add(circ_D);

    double[][] xy_intermeds1 =  line_parameters(xd, yd, xa, ya, num_curves);

    for (int i = 0; i<num_curves; i++)
    {
      quads[i].setControlX(xy_intermeds1[0][i]) ;
      quads[i].setControlY(xy_intermeds1[1][i]) ;
    };

   ////////////////////////////////////////////////////////////
   ///       EVENT  HANDLING            //////////////////////
   ////////////////////////////////////////////////////////////
   // Event handler for dragging inside circ_A - Blue
   circ_A.setOnMouseDragged(new EventHandler<MouseEvent>()
   {
     public void handle(MouseEvent event)
     {
       xx = event.getX();
       yy = event.getY();

       circ_A.setCenterX(xx);
       circ_A.setCenterY(yy);

       xa = xx ;
       ya = yy ;

       double[][] xy_intermeds1 =  line_parameters(xd, yd, xa, ya,
num_curves);

       for (int i = 0; i<num_curves; i++)
       {
         quads[i].setControlX(xy_intermeds1[0][i]) ;
         quads[i].setControlY(xy_intermeds1[1][i]) ;
       };
     }
```

```
    });
    ////////////////////////////////////////////////////////////
    // Event handler for dragging inside circ_B - Brown
    circ_D.setOnMouseDragged(new EventHandler<MouseEvent>()
    {
      public void handle(MouseEvent event)
      {
        xx = event.getX();
        yy = event.getY();
        xd = xx ;
        yd = yy ;

        circ_D.setCenterX(xx);
        circ_D.setCenterY(yy);

        double[][] xy_intermeds1 =  line_parameters(xd, yd, xa, ya,
num_curves);

        for (int i = 0; i<num_curves; i++)
        {
          quads[i].setControlX(xy_intermeds1[0][i]) ;
          quads[i].setControlY(xy_intermeds1[1][i]) ;
        };
      }
    });

    ////////////////////////////////////////////////////////////
    // Event handler for dragging inside circ_B - Green
    circ_B.setOnMouseDragged(new EventHandler<MouseEvent>()
    {
       public void handle(MouseEvent event)
       {
         xx = event.getX();
         yy = event.getY();

         circ_B.setCenterX(xx);
         circ_B.setCenterY(yy);

         for (int i = 0; i<num_curves; i++)
         {
           quads[i].setStartX(xx) ;
```

```
            quads[i].setStartY(yy) ;
          };

        }
    });

    // Event handler for dragging inside circ_C - Green
    circ_C.setOnMouseDragged(new EventHandler<MouseEvent>()
    {
      public void handle(MouseEvent event)
      {
        xx = event.getX();
        yy = event.getY();

        circ_C.setCenterX(xx);
        circ_C.setCenterY(yy);

        for (int i = 0; i<num_curves; i++)
        {
          quads[i].setEndX(xx) ;
          quads[i].setEndY(yy) ;
        };
      }
    });

  ///////////////////////////////////////////////////////////////////////
      Scene scene = new Scene(root, 800, 800, Color.WHITE);
      primaryStage.setTitle("Sets of similar Quadratic Curve - Mouse
adjustable, JavaFX");
      primaryStage.setScene(scene);
      primaryStage.show();
  }
}
```

# CHAPTER 10

## CUBIC CURVE

*"A cubic equation is of the form* $ax^3 + bx^2 + cx + d = 0$.

*Babylonian (20th to 16th centuries BC) cuneiform tablets have been found with tables for calculating cubes and cube roots. The Babylonians could have used the tables to solve cubic equations, but no evidence exists to confirm that they did. Methods for solving cubic equations appear in The Nine Chapters on the Mathematical Art, a Chinese mathematical text compiled around the 2nd century BC."*
WikipediA.

In this chapter we will cover:

- The curvature controls of cubic curves.

- Comparison of cubics with quadratics.
- Construction of a mouse tool to create cubics.
- Making families of cubics.
- Making complex drawings with cubics.

## Cubics, a Most convenient shape.

### Class javafx.scene.shape.CubicCurve

The Cubic Bezier curve is the the crown jewel for graphic design. It is the curve that allows us to match up curves smoothly, without any kinks. We just need to ensure that the slope of the last control point of one curve is the same as the slope of the first control point of the next curve. This is easily understood from the diagrams below.

As we shall see in the next chapter on Paths, we can make extremely complicated artistic drawings with surprisingly little programming effort.

The CubicCurve class defines a cubic Bézier parametric curve segment in (x,y) coordinate space. Drawing a curve that intersects both the specified coordinates (startX, startY) and (endX, enfY), and using the two specified points (controlX1, controlY1) and (controlX2, controlY2) as Bézier control points.

**The constructor**

CubicCurve quad = new CubicCurve();

**CubicCurve**(startX, startY,controlX1, controlY1, controlX2, controlY2, endX, endY)

**Specifying parameters**

cubic.setStartX(0.0f); // x start point.

```
cubic.setStartY(50.0f);          //  y start point.
cubic.setEndX(50.0f);            //  x end point.
cubic.setEndY(50.0f);            //  y end point.
cubic.setControlX1(25.0f);  //  first x control point.
cubic.setControlY1(0.0f);     //  first y control point.
cubic.setControlX2(25.0f);  //  second x control point.
cubic.setControlY2(0.0f);     //  second y control point.
```

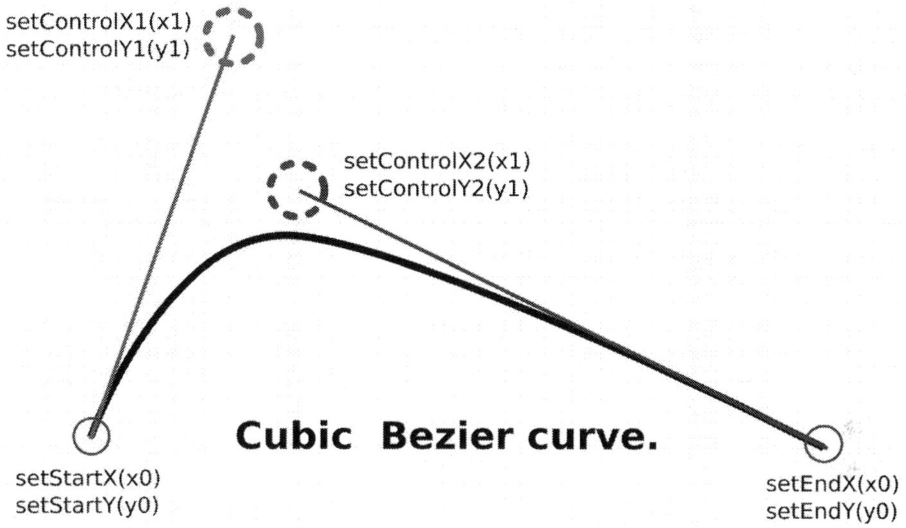


# The Simplest Cubic Bezier.

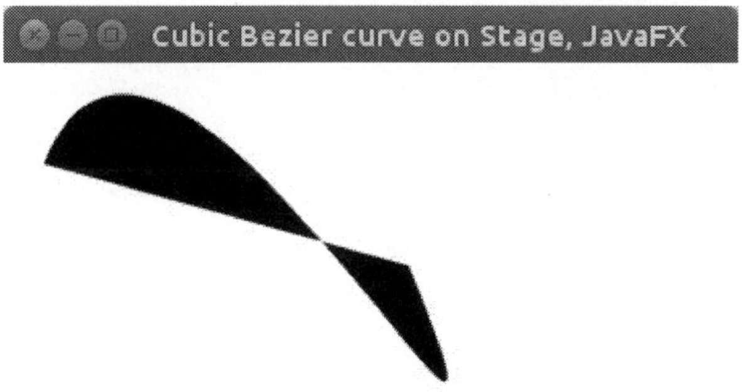

```
// CubicCurveSimplest.java
/*
CubicCurve : class: javafx.scene.shape.CubicCurve
------------------------------------
Constructor:
CubicCurve cubic = new CubicCurve(startX, startY, controlX1,  controlY1,
controlX2, controlY2, endX, endY);
or
CubicCurve cubic = new CubicCurve();
cubic.setStartX(0.0f);       // First point.
cubic.setStartY(50.0f);
cubic.setControlX1(25.0f);  // First control lever.
cubic.setControlY1(0.0f);
cubic.setControlX2(75.0f);  // Second control lever.
cubic.setControlY2(100.0f);
cubic.setEndX(100.0f);      // Last point.
cubic.setEndY(50.0f);
}

Tested on: java version "java-8-oracle"
Author: Mike Ohlson de Fine
*/
import javafx.application.Application;
import javafx.stage.Stage;
import javafx.scene.*;
import javafx.scene.shape.*; // Graphic primitives library.

public class CubicCurveSimplest extends Application
{
   public void start(Stage stage)
   {
        Group root = new Group();

     //**********************************************************
     CubicCurve cubic = new CubicCurve(20,50, 80,-100, 280,300, 200,100);
      //**********************************************************
     root.getChildren().add(cubic);

         Scene scene = new Scene(root, 260, 180);
         stage.setTitle("Cubic Bezier curve on Stage, JavaFX");
         stage.setScene(scene);
```

```
        stage.show();
    }
}
```

Instead of *CubicCurve cubic = new CubicCurve(20,50, 80,-100, 280,300, 200,100);*
*We could have written:*

```
CubicCurve cubic = new CubicCurve();

cubic.setStartX(20);      // x start point.
cubic.setStartY(50);      // y start point.

cubic.setControlX1(80);      // First control lever x coordinate.
cubic.setControlY1(-100);   // First control lever x coordinate.

cubic.setControlX2(280);   // Second control lever x coordinate.
cubic.setControlY2(300);   // Second control lever x coordinate.

cubic.setEndX(200);          // x endpoint.
cubic.setEndY(100);          // x endpoint.
}
```

This form is valuable if we want to control the parameters as variables as we will see later.

## Can we turn Quadratics into Cubics and visa versa?

The answer is yes we can and here is how:

A cubic Bézier curve can be made identical to a quadratic curve by

1. Copying the end points, and

2. Placing the 2 middle control points (dashed circles) 2/3 along line segments from the end points to the quadratic curve's middle control point (solid circles).

Will this always work? There is a problem when the Cubic has both a maximum and a minimum, that is if the cubic has two humps going in opposite directions. If this is the case then the cubic must be matched with two Quadratic curves. This idea is illustrated below.

# Comparison of Cubic with Quadratic.

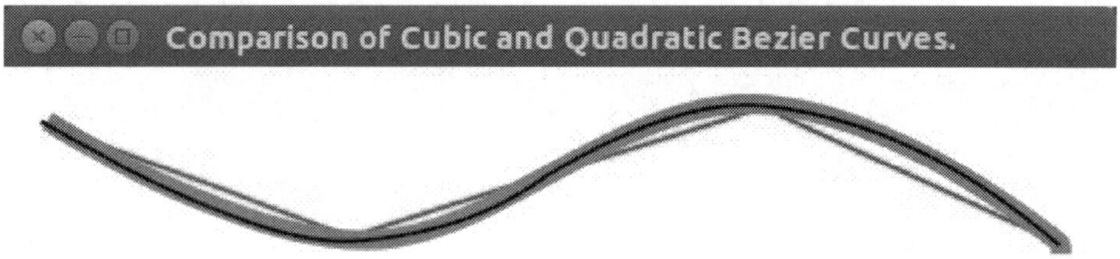


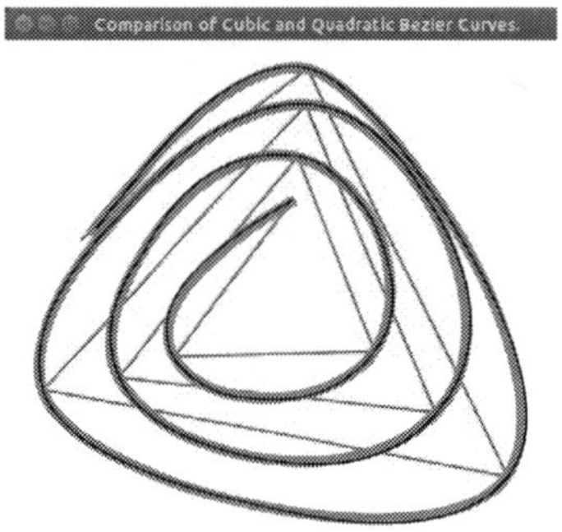


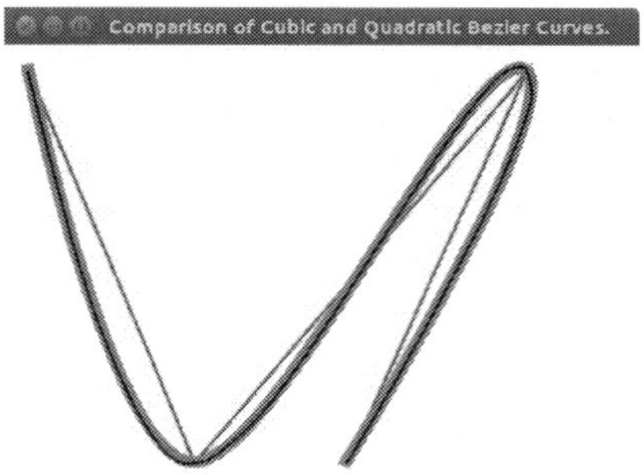


In the shapes shown above each curve consists of two lines, one on top of the other. The wide grey line was produced using quadratic Bezier curves while the thin black line was produces using cubic Bezier curves.

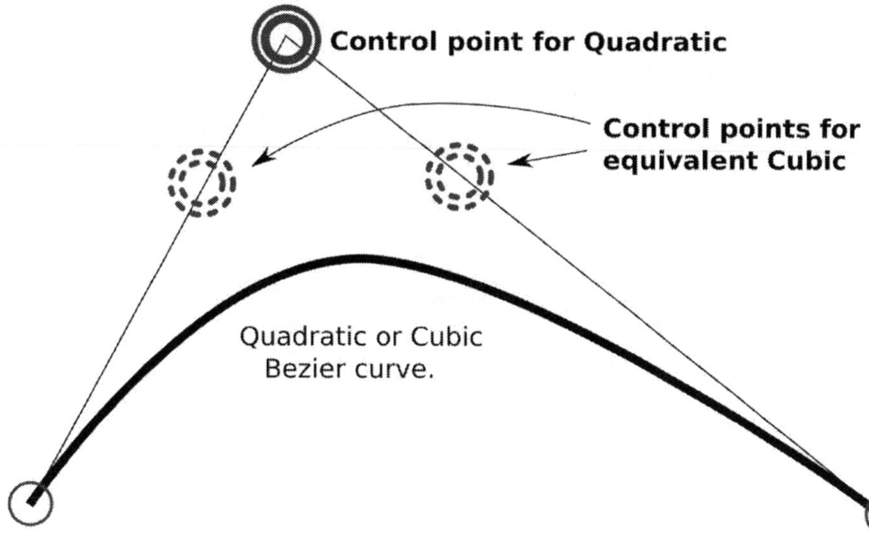


## Active Cubic Bezier Shape Design by Mouse Control

As we did in the previous chapter we now make use of a program that allows mouse

control of the cubic curve. This allows us to see exactly how the control points of a cubic Bezier curve influence the shape of the curve. As before we do not need to understand the instructions that handle the mouse. This is covered in chapter 17.

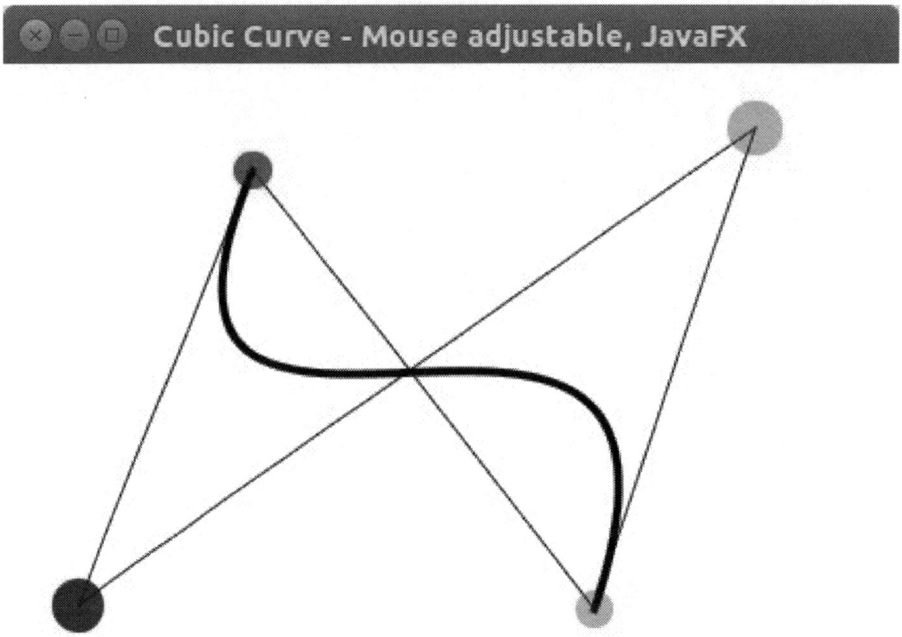


```
// MouseDragCubicCurve1.java
/*
Use setOnMouseDragged : class: javafx.scene.input.MouseEvent;
-------------------------------------

Tested on: java version "java-8-oracle"
Author: Mike Ohlson de Fine
*/import javafx.application.Application;
import javafx.scene.Scene;
import javafx.scene.layout.Pane;
import javafx.scene.paint.Color;
import javafx.scene.shape.*;
import javafx.stage.Stage;
import java.awt.geom.GeneralPath ;

import javafx.event.EventHandler;
import javafx.scene.input.MouseEvent;

public class MouseDragCubicCurve1 extends Application
{
   public void start(Stage primaryStage)
   {
      Pane root = new Pane();
```

```
    Circle circ_A = new Circle(100,100, 13, Color.BLUE) ;
    Circle circ_B = new Circle(80, 200, 9, Color.RED) ;
    Circle circ_C = new Circle(170,220, 9, Color.ORANGE) ;
    Circle circ_D = new Circle(150, 80, 13, Color.VIOLET) ;

    Line line_AB = new Line(100,100,  80, 200) ;
    Line line_BC = new Line(80 ,200, 170, 220) ;
    Line line_CD = new Line(170,220, 150,  80) ;
    Line line_DA = new Line(150, 80, 100, 100) ;

    CubicCurve cubic1 = new CubicCurve(80,200,  100, 100,  150,80,
170,220);
    cubic1.setFill(null);
    cubic1.setStrokeWidth(4);
    cubic1.setStroke(Color.BLACK);

    root.getChildren().add(circ_A);
    root.getChildren().add(circ_B);
    root.getChildren().add(circ_C);
    root.getChildren().add(circ_D);

    root.getChildren().add(line_AB);
    root.getChildren().add(line_BC);
    root.getChildren().add(line_CD);
    root.getChildren().add(line_DA);

    root.getChildren().add(cubic1);

    ////////////////////////////////////////////////////////
    /* Event handler for dragging inside circ_A */
    circ_A.setOnMouseDragged(new EventHandler<MouseEvent>()
    {
      public void handle(MouseEvent event)
      {
        circ_A.setCenterX(event.getX());
        circ_A.setCenterY(event.getY());
        line_AB.setStartX(event.getX());
        line_AB.setStartY(event.getY());
        line_DA.setEndX(event.getX());
        line_DA.setEndY(event.getY());
```

```
        cubic1.setControlX1(event.getX());
        cubic1.setControlY1(event.getY());
    }
});

/* Event handler for dragging inside circ_B */
circ_B.setOnMouseDragged(new EventHandler<MouseEvent>()
{
    public void handle(MouseEvent event)
    {
        circ_B.setCenterX(event.getX());
        circ_B.setCenterY(event.getY());
        line_BC.setStartX(event.getX());
        line_BC.setStartY(event.getY());
        line_AB.setEndX(event.getX());
        line_AB.setEndY(event.getY());

        cubic1.setStartX(event.getX());
        cubic1.setStartY(event.getY());
    }
});

/* Event handler for dragging inside circ_C */
circ_C.setOnMouseDragged(new EventHandler<MouseEvent>()
{
    public void handle(MouseEvent event)
    {
        circ_C.setCenterX(event.getX());
        circ_C.setCenterY(event.getY());
        line_CD.setStartX(event.getX());
        line_CD.setStartY(event.getY());
        line_BC.setEndX(event.getX());
        line_BC.setEndY(event.getY());

        cubic1.setEndX(event.getX());
        cubic1.setEndY(event.getY());
    }
});

/* Event handler for dragging inside circ_D */
circ_D.setOnMouseDragged(new EventHandler<MouseEvent>()
```

```
        {
            public void handle(MouseEvent event)
            {
                circ_D.setCenterX(event.getX());
                circ_D.setCenterY(event.getY());
                line_DA.setStartX(event.getX());
                line_DA.setStartY(event.getY());
                line_CD.setEndX(event.getX());
                line_CD.setEndY(event.getY());

                cubic1.setControlX2(event.getX());
                cubic1.setControlY2(event.getY());
            }
        });

        ///////////////////////////////////////////////////////////
        Scene scene = new Scene(root, 500, 300);
        primaryStage.setTitle("Cubic Curve - Mouse adjustable, JavaFX");
        primaryStage.setScene(scene);
        primaryStage.show();
    }
}
```

# Handling Arrays of Similar CubicCurves

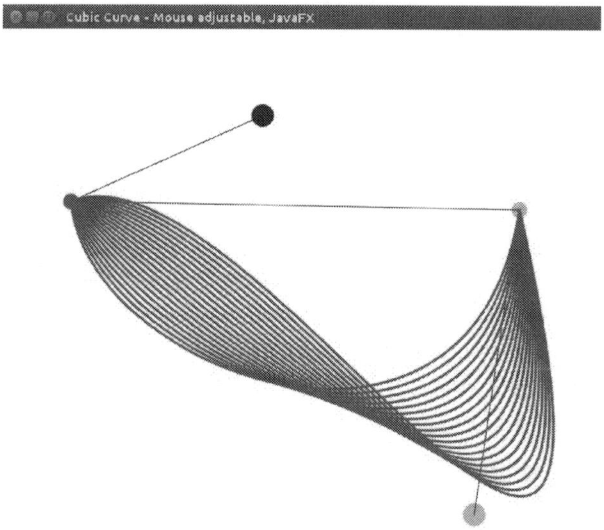

```
// MouseDragCubicSets1.java
/*
Use setOnMouseDragged : class: javafx.scene.input.MouseEvent;
-------------------------------------

Tested on: java version "java-8-oracle"
Author: Mike Ohlson de Fine
*/
import javafx.application.Application;
import javafx.scene.Scene;
import javafx.scene.layout.Pane;
import javafx.scene.paint.Color;
import javafx.scene.shape.*;
import javafx.stage.Stage;
import java.awt.geom.GeneralPath ;

import javafx.event.EventHandler;
import javafx.scene.input.MouseEvent;

public class MouseDragCubicSets1 extends Application
{
  double xx ;
  double yy ;
  double xa = 300 ; // Control point A.
  double ya = 100 ;
  double xb = 80  ; // Start point B.
  double yb = 200 ;
  double xc = 400 ; // End point C.
  double yc = 320 ;
  double xd = 100 ; // Second control point D.
  double yd = 400 ;
  int num_curves = 40; // Number of cubics to be drawn.

   private double[][] line_parameters(double xm, double ym, double xn, double
yn, int num_curves)
   {  /* Generate arrays of control points for the families of quadratic curves
*/
      double len =  Math.sqrt( (yn-ym)*(yn-ym) + (xn-xm)*(xn-xm) );
      double m = (yn - ym)/(xn - xm);
```

```
      double c = ym - m * xm;
      double theta = Math.atan(m);
      double delta_x = len / num_curves;

      double[][] xy_intermediates  ;
      xy_intermediates = new double[2][num_curves] ;
      double next_x ;

       for (int i=0; i<num_curves; i++)
       {  next_x = i* delta_x ;
          xy_intermediates[0][i] = xm +  next_x *Math.cos(theta);  // X-
compoment.
          xy_intermediates[1][i] = ym +  next_x *Math.sin(theta);  // Y-
compoment.
       }
      return xy_intermediates ;
   }
  public void start(Stage primaryStage)
  {
     Pane root = new Pane();

     Circle circ_A = new Circle(xa, ya, 13, Color.BLUE) ;
     Circle circ_B = new Circle(xb, yb, 9, Color.RED) ;
     Circle circ_C = new Circle(xc, yc, 9, Color.ORANGE) ;
     Circle circ_D = new Circle(xd, yd, 13, Color.VIOLET) ;

     Line line_AB = new Line(xa,ya,  xb,yb) ;
     Line line_BC = new Line(xb,yb,  xc,yc) ;
    Line line_CD = new Line(xc,yc,  xd,yd) ;

     root.getChildren().add(circ_A);
     root.getChildren().add(circ_B);
     root.getChildren().add(circ_C);
     root.getChildren().add(circ_D);

     root.getChildren().add(line_AB);
     root.getChildren().add(line_BC);
     root.getChildren().add(line_CD);

//*****************************************************************
//*****************************************************************
```

```
// A Loop controlled method of generating CubicCurves
  CubicCurve[] cubics = new CubicCurve[num_curves];

  /* Here we instantiate an array og CubicCurves "cubics[ ]"
    Each must be given distinct properties even though they
    will be modulated as a group.
    They have been added as items that will show on the stage.
  */
  for (int i = 0 ; i<num_curves ;  i++)
  {
    cubics[i] = new CubicCurve(xb,yb,  xa,ya,  xc,yc, xd,yd);
    cubics[i].setFill(null);
    cubics[i].setStrokeWidth(3);
    cubics[i].setStroke(Color.GREEN);
    root.getChildren().add(cubics[i]);
  }
//*********************************************************************
//*********************************************************************
     double[][] xy_intermeds1 =  line_parameters(xd, yd, xa, ya, num_curves);

     for (int i = 0; i<num_curves; i++)
     {
        cubics[i].setControlX1(xy_intermeds1[0][i]) ;
        cubics[i].setControlY1(xy_intermeds1[1][i]) ;
     };
    ////////////////////////////////////////////////////////////////
    ////////////////////////////////////////////////////////////////
    ///          EVENT HANDLING                              ///
    ////////////////////////////////////////////////////////////////
     /* Event handler for dragging inside circ_A */
     circ_A.setOnMouseDragged(new EventHandler<MouseEvent>()
     {
        public void handle(MouseEvent event)
        {
          xx = event.getX();
           yy = event.getY();
           xa = xx ;
           ya = yy ;
           circ_A.setCenterX(event.getX());
           circ_A.setCenterY(event.getY());
           line_AB.setStartX(event.getX());
```

```
        line_AB.setStartY(event.getY());

      double[][] xy_intermeds1 =  line_parameters(xd, yd, xa, ya,
num_curves);

      for (int i = 0; i<num_curves; i++)
      {
        cubics[i].setControlX1(xy_intermeds1[0][i]) ;
        cubics[i].setControlY1(xy_intermeds1[1][i]) ;
      };

      }
    });

    /* Event handler for dragging inside circ_B */
    circ_B.setOnMouseDragged(new EventHandler<MouseEvent>()
    {
      public void handle(MouseEvent event)
      {
        xx = event.getX();
        yy = event.getY();

        circ_B.setCenterX(xx);
        circ_B.setCenterY(yy);

       for (int i = 0; i<num_curves; i++)
       {
         cubics[i].setStartX(xx) ;
         cubics[i].setStartY(yy) ;
       };

         line_BC.setStartX(xx);
         line_BC.setStartY(yy);
         line_AB.setEndX(xx);
         line_AB.setEndY(yy);

      }
    });

    /* Event handler for dragging inside circ_C */
    circ_C.setOnMouseDragged(new EventHandler<MouseEvent>()
```

```
{
    public void handle(MouseEvent event)
    {
      xx = event.getX();
      yy = event.getY();

      circ_C.setCenterX(xx);
      circ_C.setCenterY(yy);

      for (int i = 0; i<num_curves; i++)
      {
        cubics[i].setEndX(xx) ;
        cubics[i].setEndY(yy) ;
      };

       line_CD.setStartX(xx);
       line_CD.setStartY(yy);
       line_BC.setEndX(xx);
       line_BC.setEndY(yy);

    }
  });

  /* Event handler for dragging inside circ_D */
  circ_D.setOnMouseDragged(new EventHandler<MouseEvent>()
  {
    public void handle(MouseEvent event)
    {
       xx = event.getX();
       yy = event.getY();
       xd = xx ;
       yd = yy ;

       line_CD.setEndX(xx);
       line_CD.setEndY(yy);

       cubics[0].setControlX2(xx);
       cubics[0].setControlY2(yy);

       circ_D.setCenterX(xx);
```

```
            circ_D.setCenterY(yy);

        double[][] xy_intermeds1 =  line_parameters(xd, yd, xa, ya,
num_curves);

        for (int i = 0; i<num_curves; i++)
        {
          cubics[i].setControlX2(xy_intermeds1[0][i]) ;
         cubics[i].setControlY2(xy_intermeds1[1][i]) ;
        };

        }
      });
      ////////////////////////////////////////////////////
      Scene scene = new Scene(root, 800, 800);
      primaryStage.setTitle("Cubic Curve Sets - Mouse adjustable, JavaFX");
      primaryStage.setScene(scene);
      primaryStage.show();
   }
}
```

# Making Complex Drawings.

Now we explore how we can begin to create complex shapes. We do not yet see how to discover and record the (x,y) coordinate positions that control the exact shape of the curves that make up our final drawing. We deal with this topic in chapter 12.

However some programmers notes or hints have been made in the comments at the top of the code. It is good programming practice, particularly in the beginning when we are tentatively starting to construct an application or program. These notes we make are ideas, plans or maps of where we want to go although we may not yet have discovered the best route to get there. Additionally, if our work on the program is interrupted for any length of time it helps us remember what we were trying to do. The act of making the notes in the first place also helps us to clarify our thinking during the exploratory phase of program construction.

The shape we work with now is an iconic version of an elephant. This particular drawing was used because it represents the shape of an elephant using a single unbroken curved line. The original shape was a Scaled Vector Graphics (.svg) file created using the Inkscape open source drawing package.

```
// arrayQuads_elephant1.java
/*
The SVG curves contain the parameters for two end-to-end Quad curves.
For example:
 d="M 273.4,66.24 C 273.4,66.24 233.7,105 197.3,88.14 C 180.3,80.24 190.7,60.04
190.7,60.04"
should be interpreted as containing the parapeters for two Bezier quadratics as follows:
d="M startX,startY C startX1,startY1  controlX1,controlY1  endX1, endY1 C
controlX2,controlY2  endX2, endY2 endX2, endY2"
Note that endX1, endY1 = startX2, startY2
so that the curve constructors would be:
1. QuadCurve(startX1,startY1,  controlX1,controlY1,  endX1, endY1);  and
2. QuadCurve(endX1, endY1, controlX2,controlY2,  endX2, endY2);

To generate curve segments using 'for' loops a hierarchy of arrays is constructed - 2
dimensional.
The idea is to be able to rever to any quadcurve by its loop index 'i'.

Declaring multidimensional arrays:
```

```
=======================================
int[][] num = new int[5][2];
Or
int num[][] = new int[5][2];
or
int[] num[] = new int[5][2];
or
int[][] num = {element1, element2, element3, ... , elementN};

Tested on: java version "java-8-oracle"
Author: Mike Ohlson de Fine
*/
import javafx.application.Application;
import javafx.scene.Group;
import javafx.scene.Scene;
import javafx.scene.shape.*;
import javafx.stage.Stage;
import javafx.scene.paint.*;

public class arrayQuads_elephant1 extends Application
{
   public void start(Stage stage)  throws Exception
   {
      final Group rootgroup = new Group();
      Color kula1 = Color.color(.05,  .05,  .9);

      //*************************************************************
      /* These are the parameters (start, end and control positions)
         for a family of Bezier QuadCurves that comprise the shape
         of an elephant.
         They are organized into a two dimensional array "dbl1" so each
         value can be accessed by using the array indices  */
     double[] Qary_1 = { 273.4,66.24,  233.7,105,   197.3,88.14 };
     double[] Qary_2 = { 197.3,88.14, 180.3,80.24, 190.7,60.04 };

     double[] Qary_3 = { 190.5,59.14,  194.9,46.06, 182.3,35.61};
     double[] Qary_4 = {182.3,35.61, 161.1,18.04, 120.6,24.68 };


     double[] Qary_5 = { 119.3,24.9,   71.93,30.04,   47.07,63.94 };
     double[] Qary_6 = { 47.07,63.94, 13,112.7,  37.86,155.8 };

     double[] Qary_7 = { 38.93,155.6, 46.65,123.6, 64.22,119.6 };
     double[] Qary_8 = { 64.22,119.6, 92.29,112.5, 87.36,153.9 };

     double[] Qary_9 = { 85.86,153.6, 62.72,137.6, 66.36,123.2 };
     double[] Qary_10 = { 66.36,123.2, 70.21,110, 97,104.1 };
```

```
double[] Qary_11 = { 97.86,103.5, 120.1,96.94, 131.8,106.7  };
double[] Qary_12 = { 131.8,106.7, 148.6,120.8, 147.2,155.8  };

double[] Qary_13 = { 148.7,153.2, 166,109.6, 179.1,106.3 };
double[] Qary_14 = { 179.1,106.3, 185.8,104.6, 194.8,110.3 };

double[] Qary_15 = {  194.8,110.3, 202.9,112.3, 201.2,119.4  };
double[] Qary_16 = {  201.2,119.4, 199.5,126.4, 171.4,132.6  };

double[] Qary_17 = { 171.2,131.6, 207.8,95.94, 197.1,87.94   };
double[] Qary_18 = {197.1,87.94, 188.7,81.64, 170.3,87.44   };

double[] Qary_19 = {  169.4,87.64, 150,93.74, 140.5,73.74 };
double[] Qary_20 = {  140.5,73.74, 130.1,51.94, 167.4,32.4  };

double[] Qary_21 = { 167.8,31.97, 195.2,17.35, 217,34.97  };
double[] Qary_22 = { 217,34.97, 250.5,62.04, 251.3,110.2  };

double[] Qary_23 = {  251.1,111.2, 254.9,130, 242.8,140.6    };
double[] Qary_24 = {  242.8,140.6, 227.5,154, 221.8,138    };

double[] Qary_25 = {  221.8,137.5, 221.1,130.1, 227.5,129.9  };
double[] Qary_26 = {  227.5,129.9, 232.6,129.8, 232,134  };

double[][] dbl1= { Qary_1,  Qary_2,  Qary_3,  Qary_4,  Qary_5,  Qary_6,
Qary_7,
              Qary_8,  Qary_9,  Qary_10,  Qary_11,  Qary_12,  Qary_13,
              Qary_14,  Qary_15,  Qary_16, Qary_17,  Qary_18,  Qary_19,
              Qary_20,  Qary_21,  Qary_22,  Qary_23,  Qary_24, Qary_25,  Qary_26
};

/* This will be a super array of QuadCurves. The plan is to be able to superimpose
  a number of identical shapes on top of each other and thus create interesting
  effects like glow.
  The curves will differ in width and color to create the effects.
 Declaration example: int[][] num = new int[5][2];
*/

 QuadCurve[][] QCrv = new QuadCurve[5][26];
/* Instantiate 26 QuadCurves. This DOES NOT construct the component
QuadCurves
    that comprise the final elephant shape. Each component curve gets constructed
    by the statement "QCrv[clyr][i] = new QuadCurve() ; ", which is inside the "for"
loop.

   (It is a happy quirk of the Java language that allows to repeatedly re-declare
objects
     inside for loops.)
```

```
    */

    int clyr = 0;  // Layer index (not used in this example).

     for (int i=0; i<26; i++)
     {
        QCrv[clyr][i] = new QuadCurve() ;  // CONSTRUCT the first QuadCurve
object.

        QCrv[clyr][i].setStartX(dbl1[i][0]);
        QCrv[clyr][i].setStartY(dbl1[i][1]);

        QCrv[clyr][i].setControlX(dbl1[i][2]);
        QCrv[clyr][i].setControlY(dbl1[i][3]);

        QCrv[clyr][i].setEndX(dbl1[i][4]);
        QCrv[clyr][i].setEndY(dbl1[i][5]);

        QCrv[clyr][i].setFill(null)  ;
        QCrv[clyr][i].setStroke(kula1) ;
        QCrv[clyr][i].setStrokeWidth(9.0) ;
        rootgroup.getChildren().add(QCrv[clyr][i]);
     }

     Scene scene = new Scene(rootgroup, 300, 200);
     stage.setScene(scene);
     stage.setTitle("SVG Vector Elephant from Inkscape");
     stage.show();
  }
}
```

# Neon Effect - Making the Elephant Glow.

We now modify the above program by having a method "draw_elephant(...)" that we use to draw five elephants of the same size but each of a different color and line width.

It is important to note that the order in which we draw the shapes is vital to producing the desired glow effect. The thickest lines have to be drawn first and the thinnest lines last. If this is not done then a thicker line drawn after a thinner one will simply hide the thinner one.

The sequence in which lines are drawn is just the sequence in which the shapes are added to the group using statements like *group.getChildren().add(some_shape1);*

In our program here the sequence is determined by the code:

```
// Here are 5 layers of quadcurves. Each layer has different parameters.

    draw_elephant(rootgroup, 0, dbl1, 15, kula1);
    draw_elephant(rootgroup, 1, dbl1, 10, kula2);
    draw_elephant(rootgroup, 2, dbl1, 6, kula3);
    draw_elephant(rootgroup, 3, dbl1, 3, kula4);
    draw_elephant(rootgroup, 4, dbl1, 1, kula5);
```

Because each of these methods " *draw_elephant(...)*" contains the rootgroup.getChildren().add(…) instruction, the sequence of shape drawing follows the sequence of instructions as they appear in the program. kula1 with a line width of 15 pixes will be drawn first and kula5 with a line width of one pixel will be drawn last.

```
// arrayQuads_neonElephant1.java
/*
Five layers of color are used to create the effect of a glowing neon tube.

Tested on: java version "java-8-oracle"
Author: Mike Ohlson de Fine
*/
import javafx.application.Application;
import javafx.scene.Group;
import javafx.scene.Scene;
import javafx.scene.shape.*;
import javafx.stage.Stage;
```

```
import javafx.scene.paint.*;

public class arrayQuads_neonElephant1 extends Application
{
   //==================================================
   //    Methods/Functions
   //==================================================
   public void draw_elephant(Group group, int layer, double[][] dbl1, double width,
Color kula)
      {
         /* This instantiates a two dimensional of memory reference to QuadCurve type
objects
            but does not instantiate any QuadCurves as such. That has to be done separately.
         */
         QuadCurve[][] QCrv = new QuadCurve[5][26];

          for (int i=0; i<26; i++)
          {
             QCrv[layer][i] = new QuadCurve() ;  // Constructor for each of 26
QuadCurves.

             QCrv[layer][i].setStartX(dbl1[i][0]);
             QCrv[layer][i].setStartY(dbl1[i][1]);

             QCrv[layer][i].setControlX(dbl1[i][2]);
             QCrv[layer][i].setControlY(dbl1[i][3]);

             QCrv[layer][i].setEndX(dbl1[i][4]);
             QCrv[layer][i].setEndY(dbl1[i][5]);


             QCrv[layer][i].setFill(null)  ;
             QCrv[layer][i].setStroke(kula) ;
             QCrv[layer][i].setStrokeWidth(width) ;
             group.getChildren().add(QCrv[layer][i]);
           }
      }

   //==================================================
   //    Main Execution
   //==================================================
   public void start(Stage stage)  throws Exception
   {
      final Group rootgroup = new Group();

      Color kula1 = Color.color(0,     0,  .5);
      Color kula2 = Color.color(.05, .05,  .7);
      Color kula3 = Color.color(.7,  .05, .05);
```

```
Color kula4 = Color.color(.1,   .2,  .2);
Color kula5 = Color.color(1,     1,  1);

/* These are the parameters (start, end and control positions)
   for a family of Bezier QuadCurves that comprise the shape
   of an elephant.
   They are organized into a two dimensional array "dbl1" so each
   value can be accessed by using the array indices  */
double[] Qary_1 = { 273.4,66.24,  233.7,105,   197.3,88.14 };
double[] Qary_2 = { 197.3,88.14, 180.3,80.24, 190.7,60.04 };

double[] Qary_3 = { 190.5,59.14,  194.9,46.06, 182.3,35.61};
double[] Qary_4 = {182.3,35.61, 161.1,18.04, 120.6,24.68 };

double[] Qary_5 = { 119.3,24.9,   71.93,30.04,   47.07,63.94 };
double[] Qary_6 = { 47.07,63.94, 13,112.7,  37.86,155.8 };


double[] Qary_7 = { 38.93,155.6, 46.65,123.6, 64.22,119.6 };
double[] Qary_8 = { 64.22,119.6, 92.29,112.5, 87.36,153.9 };

double[] Qary_9 = { 85.86,153.6, 62.72,137.6, 66.36,123.2 };
double[] Qary_10 = { 66.36,123.2, 70.21,110, 97,104.1 };

double[] Qary_11 = { 97.86,103.5, 120.1,96.94, 131.8,106.7  };
double[] Qary_12 = { 131.8,106.7, 148.6,120.8, 147.2,155.8  };

double[] Qary_13 = { 148.7,153.2, 166,109.6, 179.1,106.3 };
double[] Qary_14 = { 179.1,106.3, 185.8,104.6, 194.8,110.3 };

double[] Qary_15 = {  194.8,110.3, 202.9,112.3, 201.2,119.4  };
double[] Qary_16 = {  201.2,119.4, 199.5,126.4, 171.4,132.6  };

double[] Qary_17 = { 171.2,131.6, 207.8,95.94, 197.1,87.94   };
double[] Qary_18 = {197.1,87.94, 188.7,81.64, 170.3,87.44   };

double[] Qary_19 = {  169.4,87.64, 150,93.74, 140.5,73.74 };


double[] Qary_20 = {  140.5,73.74, 130.1,51.94, 167.4,32.4  };

double[] Qary_21 = { 167.8,31.97, 195.2,17.35, 217,34.97  };
double[] Qary_22 = { 217,34.97, 250.5,62.04, 251.3,110.2  };

double[] Qary_23 = {  251.1,111.2, 254.9,130, 242.8,140.6    };
double[] Qary_24 = {  242.8,140.6, 227.5,154, 221.8,138    };

double[] Qary_25 = {  221.8,137.5, 221.1,130.1, 227.5,129.9  };
```

```
    double[] Qary_26 = {  227.5,129.9, 232.6,129.8, 232,134  };

    double[][] dbl1= { Qary_1,  Qary_2,  Qary_3,  Qary_4,  Qary_5,  Qary_6,
Qary_7,
                Qary_8,  Qary_9,  Qary_10,  Qary_11,  Qary_12,  Qary_13,
                Qary_14,  Qary_15,  Qary_16, Qary_17,  Qary_18,  Qary_19,
                Qary_20,  Qary_21,  Qary_22,  Qary_23,  Qary_24, Qary_25,  Qary_26
};

    // Here are 5 layers of quadcurves. Each layer has different parameters.
    draw_elephant(rootgroup, 0, dbl1, 15, kula1);
    draw_elephant(rootgroup, 1, dbl1, 10, kula2);
    draw_elephant(rootgroup, 2, dbl1, 6, kula3);
    draw_elephant(rootgroup, 3, dbl1, 3, kula4);
    draw_elephant(rootgroup, 4, dbl1, 1, kula5);

  //===========================================================
  //    Draw Graphics
  //===========================================================
     Scene scene = new Scene(rootgroup, 350, 180, Color.BLACK);
     stage.setScene(scene);
     stage.setTitle("SVG Vector Elephant from Inkscape");
     stage.show();
  };
}
```

# CHAPTER 11

## PATHS

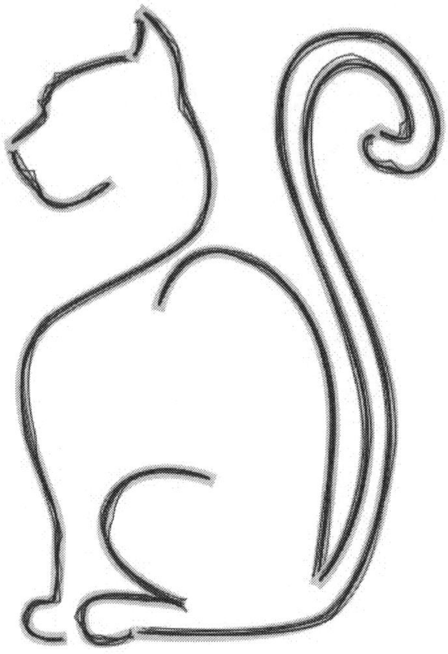

*"A path is a route, course, or track along which something moves".*

*" A path is a continuous curve that connects two or more points".*

In this chapter we will cover:

- The properties of paths.
- Arrays as containers of 2D positions
- Converting arrays of points into paths.
- Handling complex drawings as super-arrays of paths.
- Randomizing paths for realism.

## What is a Path?

The Path is a sequence of connected path elements that let us draw arbitrary shapes. These path elements can be straight lines, elliptical arcs, quadratic curves and cubic curves. The coordinate points can absolute or relative with absolute coordinates being the default.

The Path class, which belongs to the Shape class,  provides tools and methods for basic construction and management of a geometric path.

In the path specifiers listed below ArcTo, QuadCurveTo and CubicCurveTo are not fully explained because each of these topics is explained in detail in the three chapters that follow this one. However for the sake of completeness we will include short examples that make use of them.

The following Path specifiers are be used to make a path:

MoveTo: MoveTo Should always be the first element in a path – it is where the path will start.

If the first element of the path is not a MoveTo(x,y); then the start of the path is taken as the point (0,0).

LineTo: Creates a line segment by drawing a straight line from the current (x,y) coordinate to the new coordinate.

HLlneTo: draws a horizontal straight line from the current point to the specified x coordinate.

VLineTo: draws a vertical straight line from the current point to the specified y coordinate.

ArcTo: Creates a portion of an ellipse that intersects the current point and the specified end point.

QuadCurveTo: Creates a quadratic (a species of smooth mathematical curve) that starts at the current point and ends at the specified end point with one additional point, the control point, functioning as the typical Quadratic Bezier control point.

CubicCurveTo: Creates a cubic curve that starts at the current point and ends at the specified end point with additional points, the two control points, functioning as the typical Cubic Bezier control point. CubicCurveTos are most useful.

ClosePath: closes the current path by drawing a straight line segment from the current point to the original starting point of the path.

**Constructors for paths**

1, **Path();** Creates a path by reserving computer memory for a Path type of object without specifying all the parameters necessary. The necessary parameters can be supplied afterward.

2. **Path(Collection of path elements);**

3. **Path(A list of path elements);**

# 1. Simple Path – a single quadratic section

In Chapter 9 we explored how to draw Bezier Quadratic curves. We needed to specify start and end locations as well as one curvature control point – a total of three independent (x,y) positions on our stage. When we use the Path class of JavaFX we only specify two (x,y) positions – the curvature control position and the end position. This is because the Path class uses the (x.y) position of the previous path segment as the start position of the next path segment ("element" = "segment").

In the basic example below the first element of the path is specified as a MoveTo instruction. This MoveTo simply specifies where the path should begin. If this initial MoveTo is missing then JavaFX assumes it is at the default position (0,0) which is the top left corner of the scene.

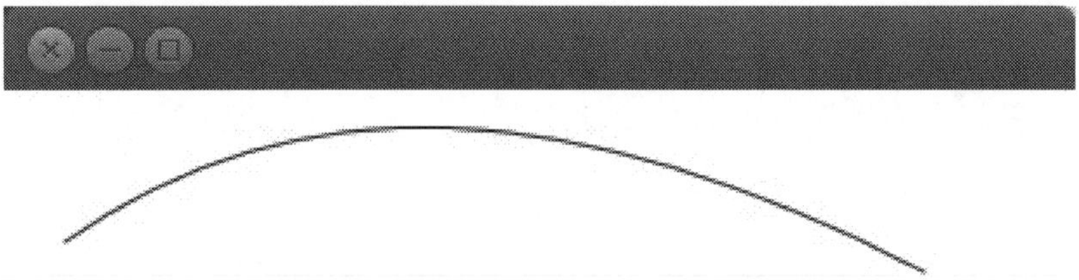

```
// pathSimple1.java
/*
A Simple Quadratic Bezier path.

Tested on: java version "java-8-oracle"
Author: Mike Ohlson de Fine
*/
import javafx.application.Application;
import javafx.scene.Group;
import javafx.scene.Scene;
import javafx.scene.shape.*;
import javafx.stage.Stage;

public class pathSimple1 extends Application
{
    public void start(Stage stage)  throws Exception
    {
       final Group group = new Group();
       Scene scene = new Scene(group, 350, 80);
       stage.setScene(scene);
//*************************************************************
      Path path1 = new Path();
      MoveTo moveTo1 = new MoveTo(20,50);  // Move to the start
      path1.getElements().add(moveTo1);

      QuadCurveTo qcrv1 = new QuadCurveTo(130,-30,   300,60); // Quad
section.
     path1.getElements().add(qcrv1);

      group.getChildren().addAll(path1);
//*************************************************************
        stage.show();
    }
```

```
}
```

## 2. Complex Path – four quadratic sections

Here we put together a complex path made up of five elements – a start given by a MoveTo(…) followed by four QuadCurveTo(...)s. The thing to take note of is that the four separate quadratic curves are joined together absolutely smoothly. There are no kinks or sudden changes of curvature where they are joined to each other. This is the great advantage of the Path method.

```
// pathQCurve1.java
/*
Make a path from four sections of Quadratic Bezier Curve.
Tested on: java version "java-8-oracle"
Author: Mike Ohlson de Fine
*/
import javafx.application.Application;
import javafx.scene.Group;
import javafx.scene.Scene;
import javafx.scene.shape.*;
import javafx.stage.Stage;

public class pathQCurve1 extends Application
{
    public void start(Stage stage)  throws Exception
    {
        final Group group = new Group();
        Scene scene = new Scene(group, 300, 100);
        stage.setScene(scene);
        stage.setTitle("A QuadCurve Path");
```

```
//***************************************************************************
      Path path1 = new Path(); // Instantiate a path.

      MoveTo moveTo1 = new MoveTo(273.4,66.24); // Define the start of the
path.
      QuadCurveTo qcrv1 = new QuadCurveTo(233.7,105,   197.3,88.14);//
QuadCurve from the start.
      QuadCurveTo qcrv2 = new QuadCurveTo(180.3,80.24, 190.7,60.04);
      QuadCurveTo qcrv3 = new QuadCurveTo(194.9,46.06, 182.3,35.61);
      QuadCurveTo qcrv4 = new QuadCurveTo(161.1,18.04, 120.6,24.68);

      path1.getElements().add(moveTo1); // Go to Start
      path1.getElements().add(qcrv1); // Add QuadCurve to last point (ie to
the start).
      path1.getElements().add(qcrv2); // Add QuadCurve to the previous
point.
      path1.getElements().add(qcrv3); // Add another QuadCurve to the
previous point.
      path1.getElements().add(qcrv4); // Add the final QuadCurve.

      group.getChildren().addAll(path1); // Add the complete path to the
group
//***************************************************************************
        stage.show();
    }
}
```

# 3. Four Cubic and Two Line elements.

Here we build our path of two Bezier Cubic curves followed by two straight lines and completed with another two cubic curves.

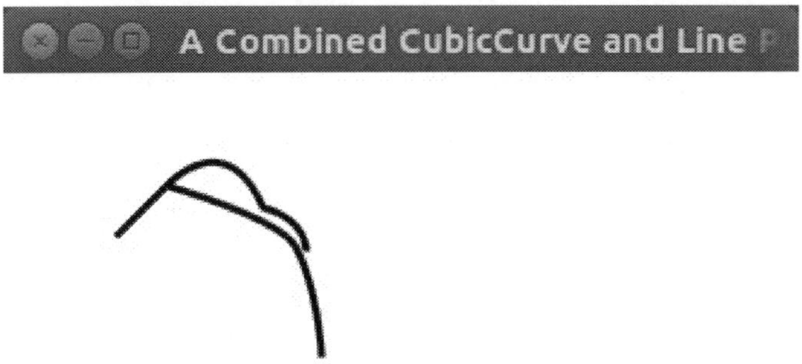

We need start and end locations as well as two curvature control points – a total of four independent (x,y) positions on our stage. The start position is taken as the current position in the path. This current position is always taken as the end point of the previous path element. So when we use the Path class of JavaFX we only need to specify three (x,y) positions – two curvature control position and the end position. Note that regardless of what type of elements are being used to build up a path, the last point of the of one element is used as the start position of the next.

```
// pathCubicCurve1.java
/*
Constructor:
CubicCurveTo(controlX1, controlY1, controlX2, controlY2, x, y)
Tested on: java version "java-8-oracle"
Author: Mike Ohlson de Fine
*/
import javafx.application.Application;
import javafx.scene.Group;
import javafx.scene.Scene;
import javafx.scene.shape.*;
import javafx.stage.Stage;
import javafx.stage.Stage;
import javafx.scene.paint.*;

public class pathCubicCurve1 extends Application
{
    public void start(Stage stage)  throws Exception
    {
        final Group group = new Group();
        Scene scene = new Scene(group, 330, 130);
        stage.setScene(scene);
        stage.setTitle("A Combined CubicCurve and Line Path");

       Path path1 = new Path();
       MoveTo moveTo1 = new MoveTo( 125.8,73.1   );
       CubicCurveTo crv1 = new CubicCurveTo( 125,73, 127,62, 108,56   );
       CubicCurveTo crv2 = new CubicCurveTo( 93,21, 69,46, 69,46  );
```

```
        LineTo crv3 = new LineTo(  47,68   );
        LineTo crv4 = new LineTo(  68,47   );
        CubicCurveTo crv5 = new CubicCurveTo(  68,47, 114,60, 121,72  );
        CubicCurveTo crv6 = new CubicCurveTo(  128,84, 131,104, 132,117   );

        path1.getElements().add(moveTo1);
        path1.getElements().add(crv1);
        path1.getElements().add(crv2);
        path1.getElements().add(crv3);
        path1.getElements().add(crv4);
        path1.getElements().add(crv5);
        path1.getElements().add(crv6);
        path1.setStrokeWidth(3);
        group.getChildren().addAll(path1);

        stage.show();
    }
}
```

## ***4. Very Complex Paths and Arrays.***

As this chapter progresses we make paths of increasing complexity. Any line drawing that an artist can draw can be emulated using JavaFX Path instructions. A typical artist's line drawing can consist of hundreds or even thousands of paths. So we need efficient ways of writing Java code to produce complex drawings. To write efficient code we need to make good use of Java arrays and so we shall explore arrays now.

Here is an array of bicycles. How would we handle arrays of Java objects, using bicycles as examples of objects that can be very complex.

# Java Arrays

An array is a collection of similar objects into a single container. Arrays are a **fixed size** sequential collection of objects of the same type. This restriction – the fact that array size ( the number of similar objects it may contain) – is fixed, has to be remembered carefully. So once an array has been declared we cannot make it longer or shorter. We can only modify the values of the parameters defining each element. For example if the array consisted of 50 circles, each circle could have a different color, size and outline width. At any time the size, color or outline width of any of the members of the array can be changed. The only thing we are not allowed to do is to make the array longer or shorter. Once declared the number of elements is fixed. However we can make the array longer that we need to begin with and then only use some but not all the elements.

The individual objects can be used and modified by accessing each object by using the name of the collection together with an integer index. This index is the key to being able to using and modifying individual objects sequentially inside ***for*** loops.

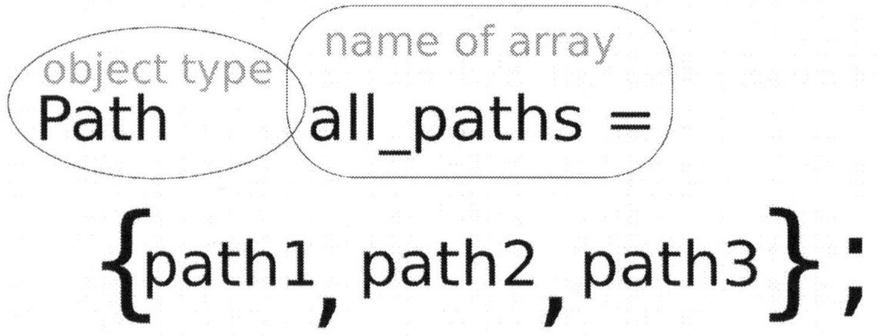


There are more than one way to declare arrays of objects in java. The one we shall be using is like:

***Object_type    name_of_array = {object1, object2, object3, ... };***

where object1, object2, object3 etc. have already been declared correctly somewhere.

In this chapter we use two dimensional arrays of double precision numbers like:

double[][] pp1 = {{108.,153, 102,157, 95,161}, {88,164, 79,169, 73,168},...};

Here below we illustrate the idea of array declarations graphically as arrays of bicycles and cats.

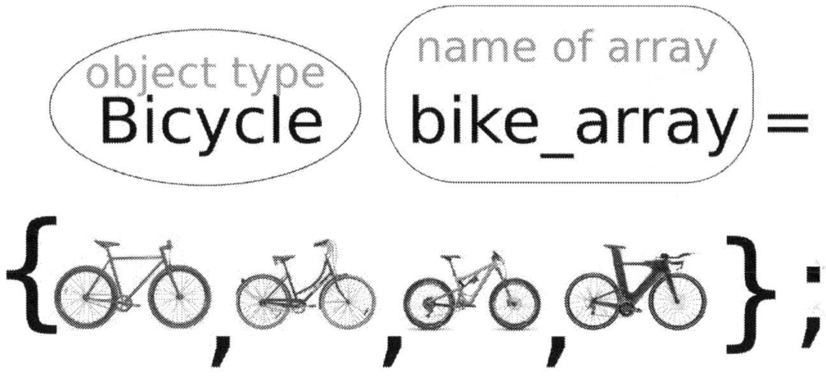


As with all Java objects we must declare what type of object they are before we can use them.

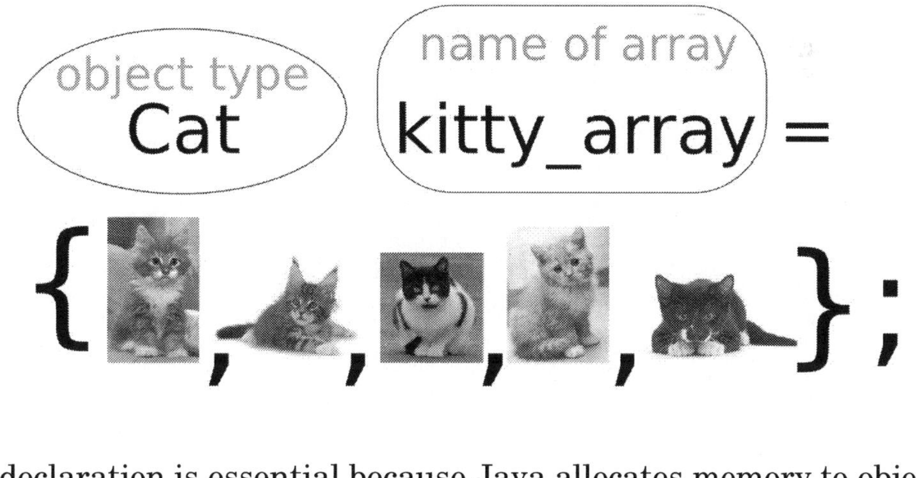


This declaration is essential because Java allocates memory to objects as a kind of planning phase. This is analogous to building a town on a vacant piece of land: first there is a requirement that the number and size of every building in the town must be specified so that the town can be laid out on a map before the town is constructed. In a Java application the size and structure of every object to be used must be reserved ahead of execution. When it comes to arrays of objects the same rules apply and the sequence of declaration is critical particularly when declaring arrays of paths.

How for loops allow complicated drawings to be made

Remember that arrays have a fixed length. Once we have declared an array we cannot add extra elements to it – we cannot make it longer. In the example of a cat shown below we collect all the eight curves that make up the cat into one array called path_n.

Then we assemble each of the eight separate CubicCurveTo elements the instruction:

```
crv_pth1 = new CubicCurveTo(path_points[j][0], path_points[j][1], path_points[j][2],
                                        path_points[j][3], path_points[j][4], path_points[j]
[5]);
```

and then add each of the cat drawing's elements to the path_n path using the for loop:

```
for (int j=0; j< num_cctos ; j++)
  {
      crv_pth1 = new CubicCurveTo(path_points[j][0], path_points[j][1], path_points[j]
[2],
                                        path_points[j][3], path_points[j][4], path_points[j]
[5]);
      path_n.getElements().add(crv_pth1);
  };
```

## Now here is a peculiarity worth remembering:

**We are allowed to *repeatedly* use the same declaration inside a**

***for* loop without restriction.**
In other words the Java compiler is happy to let us use the object constructor again and again **inside** a for loop. If we tried to do the same thing outside the loop we would not be allowed to. We make use of this fact many times when we draw objects.

## Paths to Draw a Cat

The drawing of a cat here is composed of eight separate paths. Each path is constructed from many Bezier Cubic curves.
The start and end points and the two control points are given in the arrays shown below.

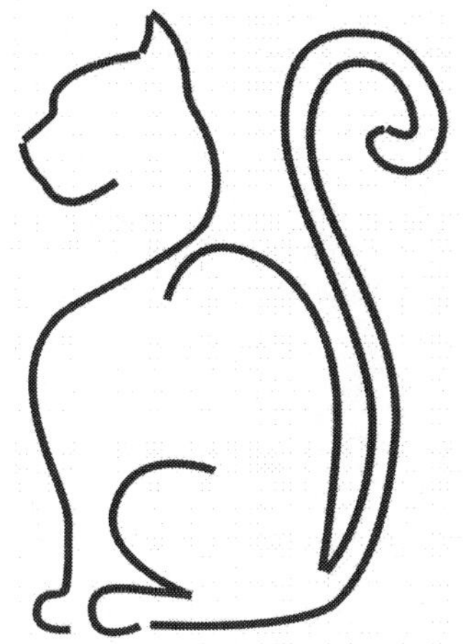

The important thing to note here is that the two dimensional arrays given below are not defined as path elements – they are merely arrays of numbers. We choose to handle our drawings this way because makes it easier to capture raw svg (scaled vector graphics) drawings. In chapter 12 we see how to make the raw drawings using vector graphic editors.

```
double[][] pp1 = {{108.,153, 102,157, 95,161},
            {88,164,  79,169, 73,168},
            {57,166,  57,156, 51,151},
            {39,141,  37,124, 37,124}};
```

```
double[][] pp2 = {{38,122, 58,106, 60,102},
        {61,100, 60,96,  61,91},
        {61,87,  64,82,  72,76},
        {89,64, 125,58, 125,58}};

double[][] pp3 = {{127,57, 131,48, 132,43},
        {133,38, 133,29, 133,29}};

double[][] pp4 = {{ 134,27, 146,34,  155,54},
        {163,74,  158,85,  165,98},
        {172,111, 194,145, 175,182},
        {162,209,  71,240,  60,257},
        {43,277,   40,302,  49,337},
        {58,371,   71,392,  71,411},
        {70,431,   71,440,  69,455},
        {67,465,   50,454,  47,471},
        {44,490,   72,487,  72,487}};

double[][] pp5 = {{181,369, 117,345, 105,398},
        {97,437,  163,462, 163,462},
       {154,460, 144,459, 135,458},
        {105,454,  89,454,  88,470},
        {88,478,   90,488, 102,489},
        {114,489, 124,484, 124,484}};

double[][] pp6 = {{145,241, 160,184, 210,208},
        {239,218, 278,263, 271,350},
        {266,409, 260,443, 260,443}};

double[][] pp7 = {{262,444, 294,411, 297,339},
        {300,270, 238,177, 234,120},
        {230,63,  252,35,  303,44},
        {324,48,  354,89,  349,117},
        {345,138, 333,150, 315,140},
        {297,140, 293,124, 297,119},
        {302,115, 306,115, 306,115}};

double[][] pp8 = {{308,114, 327,126, 328,114},
        {330,102, 319,65,  288,65},
        {262,63,  242,104, 258,156},
        {274,208, 321,272, 314,345},
```

*{306,417, 288,448, 272,465},*
*{249,491, 132,483, 132,483}};*

# Accessing array elements

Looking at the first array:

*double[][] pp1 = {{108.,153, 102,157, 95,161},*

*{88,164, 79,169, 73,168},*

*{57,166, 57,156, 51,151},*

*{39,141, 37,124, 37,124}};*

We see that is a two-dimensional array made up of four groups of elements with each element being an array of six double precision floating point numbers. Each of the four groups can be accessed by using its index.

That is:

pp1[ 0 ] = *{108.,153, 102,157, 95,161}*

pp1[ 1 ] = *{88,164, 79,169, 73,168}*

pp1[ 2 ] = *{57,166, 57,156, 51,151}*

pp1[ 3 ] = *{39,141, 37,124, 37,124}*

Individual values of the double precision values are obtained by a further level of indexing.

For instance:

pp1[ 0 ][ 1 ]= 153

pp1[ 2 ][ 3 ]= 156

pp1[ 3 ][ 5 ]= 124

## The Paths Making up the Cat.

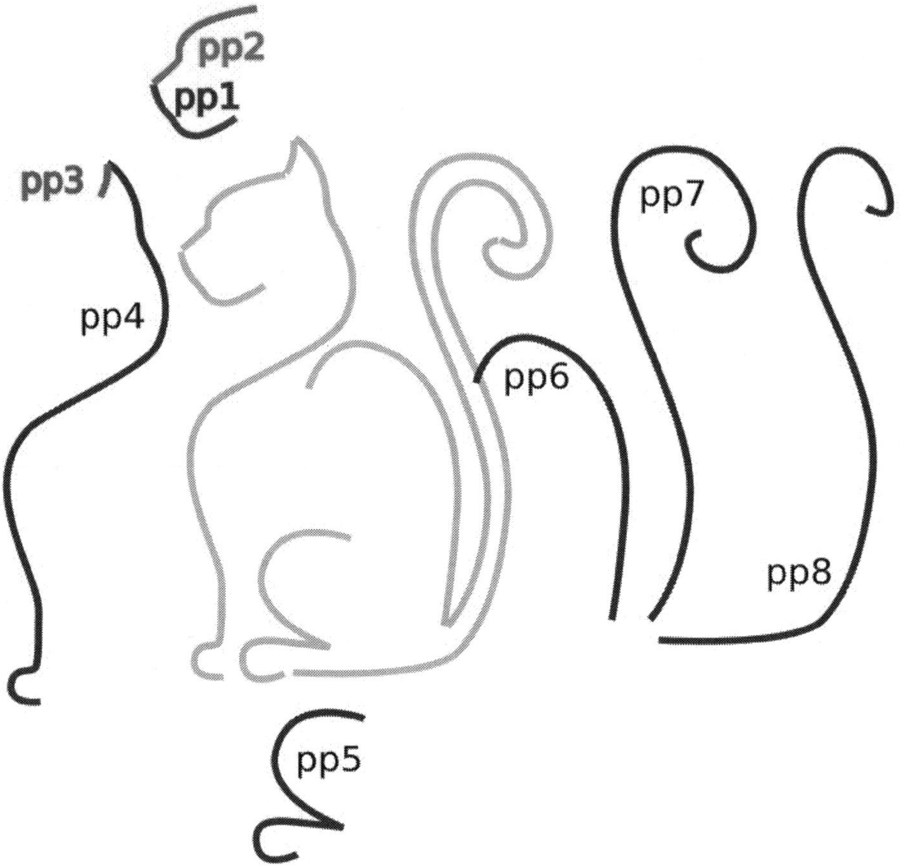

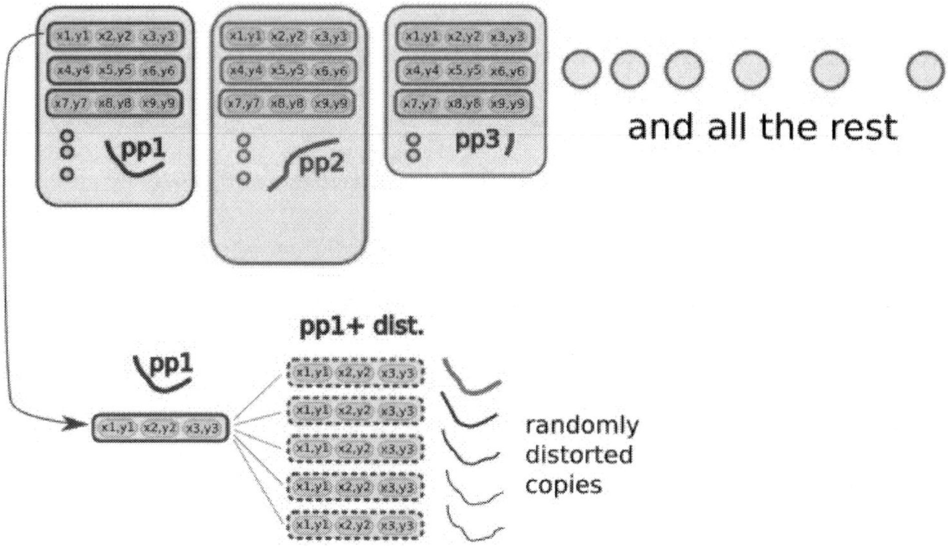


```
MoveTo moveTo1 = new MoveTo(108,153);
double[][] pp1 = {
{108,153, 102,157, 95,161},
{88,164, 79,169, 73,168},
{57,166, 57,156, 51,151},
{39,141, 37,124, 37,124}};
```

Each of the paths shown above corresponds to the similarly labeled array above namely pp1, pp2, pp3, pp4, pp5, pp6 and pp7.

The key problem now is to convert these raw arrays of numbers into CubicCurveTo(…)

instructions that Java can interpret as components of paths.

The specific Java instruction that populates the set of CubicCurveTo(…) instructions with the appropriate position coordinate is:

*crv_pth1 = new CubicCurveTo(path_points[j][0], path_points[j][1], path_points[j][2],*

*path_points[j][3], path_points[j][4], path_points[j][5]);*

There is a strange but useful piece of Java trickery that makes this possible.

This strange behavior is that although we need to create many CubicCurveTo(…) sets,

Java allows us to keep creating the **same** object over and over *inside* the for loop, but not outside it. If we tried to do this kind of repeated construction outside the loop the Java compiler would forbid it. Java would forbid the repeated declaration of the same name more than once. Inside a *for loop* we are allowed to do it without end and this is very, very convenient.

Each time a fresh version of our CubicCurveTo element of the path is created it is immediately added to the path via the *path_n.getElements().add(crv_pth1);* instruction. This means that new elements are added to the path each time the loop is executed. This makes it permanent and the *crv_pth1* element can be reused for a fresh CubicCurveTo element.

The method or function that achieves this is:

*Path Points2paths(double[][] path_points, MoveTo selected_moveTo, double Stroke_width, Color kula)*
*{*
*/* Applies to : One path - the raw points that will be used to construct all*

```
the
                CubicCurveTos that make up the sequence of drawn
CubicCurveTo parts.
      The first position in the path is the starting MoveTo (which could be the
first vertex/point
      of the first CubicCurveTo. The "path_index" selects the correct path
      to be worked on. path_points[A][B] - "A" is the index pointing to each
CubicCurveTo section,
      "B" refers to each of the three coordinates of the cubic curves.

      After the points have been randomized they must now be assembled into
      CubicCurveTo paths which are the output.

      The Output: An assembled path ready to be added to stage for display.
    */

    int num_cctos = Array.getLength(path_points) ; // Number of
CubicCurveTos making up the path.
    CubicCurveTo crv_pth1 =  new CubicCurveTo(); // The set of curves for a
path.

    // Assemble one path.
    Path  path_n =  new Path();
    path_n.getElements().add(selected_moveTo); // Select the appropriate
start position.
    for (int j=0; j< num_cctos ; j++)
    {
      crv_pth1 = new CubicCurveTo(path_points[j][0], path_points[j][1],
path_points[j][2],
                                        path_points[j][3], path_points[j][4],
path_points[j][5]);

      path_n.getElements().add(crv_pth1);
      path_n.setStrokeWidth(Stroke_width);
      path_n.setStroke(kula);
    };

    return path_n ;
}
```

# Changing Line Color and Width for different Paths

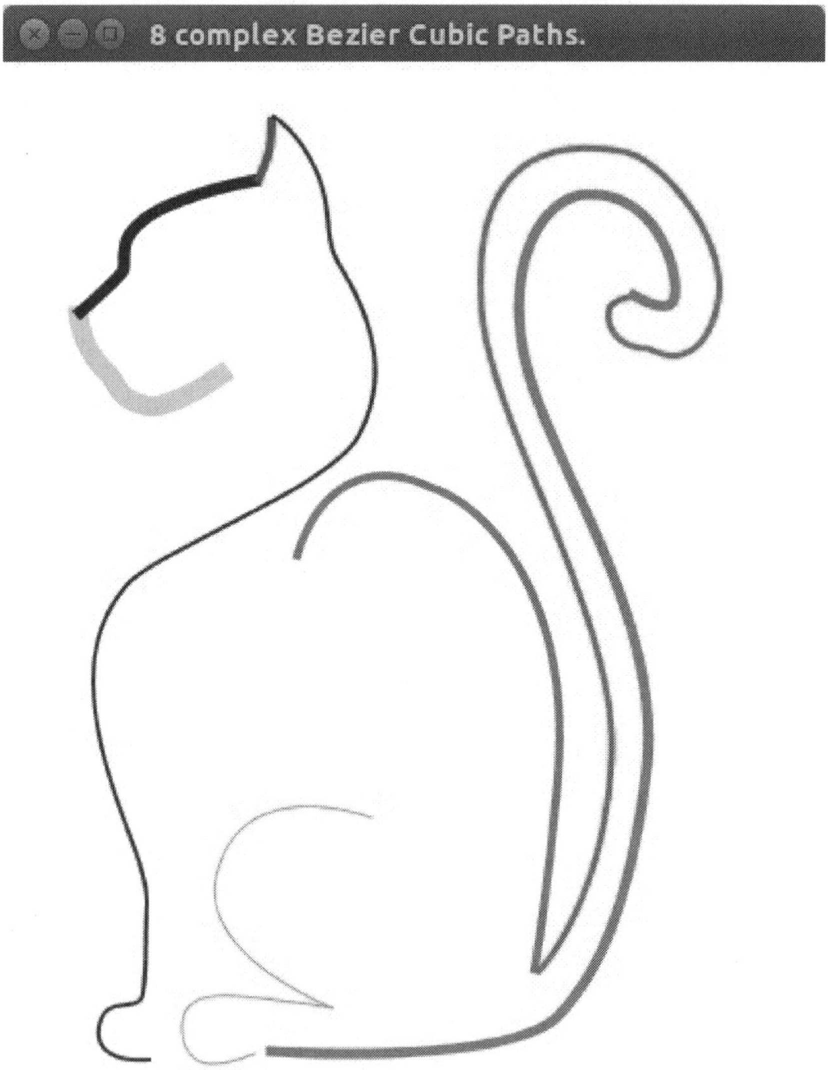


Putting this all together we can make the drawing shown here. We have control of line width and color because we made arrays for these variables and use different values via the index j of the for loop.

```
// Cubic_Cat_Draw1.java
/*
Line Properties/attribute parameters:
=====================================
path1.setStrokeWidth(4);                          // Width of the line, pixels.
path1.setStrokeLineCap(StrokeLineCap.ROUND); // Rounded ends of lines.
path1.setStroke(Color.BLUE);
    OR
path1.setStroke(Color.web("rgb(0, 0, 100%)"); // blue as an rgb percent web
value.
    OR
Color.color(0.8,      0.8,    0.8) // Range from 0.0 to 1.0
//path1.getStrokeDashArray().addAll(14d);            // Dash pattern: fill,
blank, etc
path1.getStrokeDashArray().addAll(14);              // Dash pattern: fill, blank,
etc
path1.setStrokeDashOffset(10); //Dash pattern: to shift the beginning of the
dash.

Tested on: java version "java-8-oracle"
Author: Mike Ohlson de Fine
*/

import javafx.application.Application;
import javafx.stage.Stage;
import javafx.scene.*;
import javafx.scene.paint.*;
import javafx.scene.shape.*; // Graphic primitives library, including Paths.
import java.lang.reflect.Array;

public class Cubic_Cat_Draw1 extends Application
{

   Path Points2paths(double[][] path_points, MoveTo  selected_moveTo,
double Stroke_width, Color kula)
   {
     /* Applies to : One path - the raw points that will be used to construct all
the
                    CubicCurveTos that make up the sequence of drawn
CubicCurveTo parts.
       The first position in the path is the starting MoveTo (which could be the
```

```
first vertex/point
      of the first CubicCurveTo. The "path_index" selects the correct path
      to be worked on. path_points[A][B] - "A" is the index pointing to each
CubicCurveTo section,
      "B" refers to each of the three coordinates of the cubic curves.

       The Output: An assembled path ready to be added to thw scene for
display.
     */

     int num_cctos = Array.getLength(path_points) ; // Number of
CubicCurveTos making up the path.
     CubicCurveTo crv_pth1 =  new CubicCurveTo(); // The set fo curves for a
path.

    // Assemble one path.
    Path  path_n =  new Path();
    path_n.getElements().add(selected_moveTo); // Select the appropriate
start position.
    for (int j=0; j< num_cctos ; j++)
    {
       crv_pth1 = new CubicCurveTo(path_points[j][0], path_points[j][1],
path_points[j][2],
                        path_points[j][3], path_points[j][4], path_points[j][5]);

       path_n.getElements().add(crv_pth1);
       path_n.setStrokeWidth(Stroke_width);
       path_n.setStroke(kula);
    };
    return path_n ;
   }


   public void start(Stage primaryStage)
   {
      Group rootgroup = new Group();
      Path[] rand_paths =  new Path[6];

      /*
      The raw arrays representing the eight shapes making up the cat should
      be included here.
```

```
    That is the definitions of the arrays pp1, pp2, pp3, pp4, pp5, pp6, pp7,
pp8.
    */

  // Note that for this format of declaration the keyword new" is not needed.
  MoveTo[] all_movetos = { moveTo1, moveTo2, moveTo3, moveTo4, moveTo5,

                                 moveTo6, moveTo7, moveTo8 };
  double[][][] all_pps = { pp1, pp2, pp3, pp4, pp5, pp6,  pp7, pp8 };

  Path  path1   = new Path();
  double[] lin_w = {10, 6, 4, 2, 1, 4, 3, 5 };
  Color[] kula = { Color.color(0.8, 0.8, 0.9), Color.color(0.1, 0.1, 0.1),
Color.color(0.99, 0.0, 0.0),
                     Color.color(0.0, 0.0, 0.99), Color.color(0.1, 0.9, 0.1),
Color.color(0.7, 0.4, 0.1),
                     Color.color(0.9, 0.1, 0.9), Color.color(0.1, 0.6, 0.9)  };

  for  (int j=0; j<Array.getLength(all_pps) ; j++)
  {
   path1 =  Points2paths(all_pps[j], all_movetos[j], lin_w[j], kula[j]);
   rootgroup.getChildren().addAll( path1);
  };

    Scene scene = new Scene(rootgroup, 400, 550);
    primaryStage.setTitle("8 complex Bezier Cubic Paths.");
    primaryStage.setScene(scene);
    primaryStage.show();
  }
}
```

# Using Random Distortions to make Paths more Realistic

The drawback of drawings created with computer code is that they do not have the spontaneous uncertainty that results from drawings made by the human hand. When an artist draws a line there are small deviations of thickness and curvature that give them a harm, human liveliness. We can add small random variations to our paths as well as superimpose many of these slightly imperfect curves on top of each other and result can be more pleasing to the human eye as shown here.

## The Randomizing Function

Here is the function that was used to distort the positions of the six numbers in each CubicCurveTo(…) function.

*double[][] RandomizePoints(double[][] pnt, double stdev)*
*{ /* Applies to: One path (a sequence of CubicCurveto segments).*

```
        Inputs: A 2D raw path - a collection of potential cubiccurvetos. first Dim
is the
        CubicCurveTo index, the second Dim gives access to each of six control
points in a CCTo.
        Take the 2D array of (xy) vertices, the control points of CubicCurveTos,
and add a controlled
        but random offset to each x and y.  What will be returned is a collection
of
        randomized vertices comprising a new path - slightly distorted by a
random offset to each point.
        Output: The input raw path but randomised/distorted.
      */
      Random rand1 = new Random();
      int lenn = Array.getLength(pnt) ;      // The number of CubicCurveTos in
a single path.
      double[][] pp_rand = new double[lenn][6];
      // Randomize Vertices: Every vertex gets randomized afresh here.
      for (int k=0; k<lenn; k++)  // k is the Index stepping through the
potential CubicCurves.
      {
        for  (int sxy=0; sxy<6; sxy++) // sx is the Index stepping through the 3
(x,y) vertices for each CubicCurveto.
        {
          pp_rand[k][sxy] = pnt[k][sxy]+ stdev*rand1.nextGaussian(); // x and
y are randomized independently.
        }
      }
    return pp_rand ;
  }
```

*The complete application for the randomized (more realistic) drawing is:*

```
// Cubic_Cat_Randomized_Draw1.java
/*

Random number method for Gaussian distribution:
nextGaussian(): Gives a Gaussian ("normally") distributed number with mean
value 0.0
and standard deviation 1.0

Tested on: java version "java-8-oracle"
```

```
Author: Mike Ohlson de Fine
*/

import javafx.application.Application;
import javafx.stage.Stage;
import javafx.scene.*;
import javafx.scene.paint.*;
import javafx.scene.shape.*; // Graphic primitives library.
import java.lang.reflect.Array;
import java.util.Random;

public class Cubic_Cat_Draw16 extends Application
{

   double[][] RandomizePoints(double[][] pnt, double stdev)
   { /* Applies to: One path (a sequence of CubicCurveto segments).
         Inputs: A 2D raw path - a collection of potential cubiccurvetos. first Dim
is the
         CubicCurveTo index, the second Dim gives access to each of six control
points in a CCTo.
         Take the 2D array of (xy) vertices, the control points of CubicCurveTos,
and add a controlled
         but random offset to each x and y.  What will be returned is a collection
of
         randomized vertices comprising a new path - slightly distorted by a
random offset to each point.
         Output: The input raw path but randomised/distorted.
      */
      Random rand1 = new Random();
      int lenn = Array.getLength(pnt) ;      // The number of CubicCurveTos in
a single path.
      double[][] pp_rand = new double[lenn][6];
      // Randomize Vertices: Every vertex gets randomized afresh here.
      for (int k=0; k<lenn; k++)  // k is the Index stepping through the
potential CubicCurves.
      {
        for  (int sxy=0; sxy<6; sxy++) // sx is the Index stepping through the 3
(x,y) vertices for each CubicCurveto.
         {
           pp_rand[k][sxy] = pnt[k][sxy]+ stdev*rand1.nextGaussian(); // x and
y are randomized independently.
```

```
        }
      }
     return pp_rand ;
    }


   Path Points2paths(double[][] path_points, MoveTo  selected_moveTo,
double Stroke_width, Color kula)
   {
     /* Applies to : One path - the raw points that will be used to construct all
the
                  CubicCurveTos that make up the sequence of drawn
CubicCurveTo parts.
       The Output: An assembled path ready to be added to stage for display.
     */

     int num_cctos = Array.getLength(path_points) ; // Number of
CubicCurveTos making up the path.
     CubicCurveTo crv_pth1 =  new CubicCurveTo(); // The set fo curves for a
path.

     // Assemble one path.
     Path  path_n =  new Path();
     path_n.getElements().add(selected_moveTo); // Select the appropriate
start position.
     for (int j=0; j< num_cctos ; j++)
     {
       crv_pth1 = new CubicCurveTo(path_points[j][0], path_points[j][1],
path_points[j][2],
                            path_points[j][3], path_points[j][4], path_points[j][5]);

       path_n.getElements().add(crv_pth1);
       path_n.setStrokeWidth(Stroke_width);
       path_n.setStroke(kula);
     };
     return path_n ;
   }

 public void start(Stage primaryStage)
   {
     Group rootgroup = new Group();
```

```
Path[] rand_paths =  new Path[6];

/*
The raw arrays representing the eight shapes making up the cat should
be included here.
That is the definitions of the arrays pp1, pp2, pp3, pp4, pp5, pp6, pp7,
pp8.
*/

// Note that for this format of declaration the keyword new" is not needed.
MoveTo[] all_movetos = { moveTo1, moveTo2, moveTo3, moveTo4, moveTo5,
moveTo6, moveTo7, moveTo8 };
double[][][] all_pps = { pp1, pp2, pp3, pp4, pp5, pp6,  pp7, pp8 };

double[][] pp1_b;
Path  path1   = new Path();

double[] std_dev = {0, 2, 3, 2, 1.5, 3, 1, 2.5};
double[] lin_w = {10, 1, 1, 1, 1, 1, 1, 1 };
Color[] kula = { Color.color(0.8, 0.8, 0.9), Color.color(0.1, 0.1, 0.1),
Color.color(0.99, 0.0, 0.0),
            Color.color(0.0, 0.0, 0.99),Color.color(0.1, 0.1, 0.1),
Color.color(0.1, 0.1, 0.1),
            Color.color(0.1, 0.1, 0.1), Color.color(0.1, 0.1, 0.1)   };
Path[] path_rand1 = { path1, path1, path1, path1, path1, path1, path1,
path1 };

for  (int j=0; j<Array.getLength(all_movetos) ; j++)
 {
  for (int i=0; i<8 ; i++) // 8 = number of randomized curves. Index=0 has no
distortion.
   {
    pp1_b = RandomizePoints(all_pps[j], std_dev[i]);
    path_rand1[i] =  Points2paths(pp1_b, all_movetos[j], lin_w[i], kula[i]);
    rootgroup.getChildren().addAll( path_rand1[i]);
   };
 };

Scene scene = new Scene(rootgroup, 400, 550);
primaryStage.setTitle("8 complex Bezier Cubic Paths with Randomised
Deviations.");
```

```
        primaryStage.setScene(scene);
        primaryStage.show();
    }
}
```

The drawings below were drawn using this randomization distortion

## Filling Paths with shaded color

A path is a child of the Shape class and the Shape class has methods for specifying line width, line color as well as fill color. In the example below we have filled a shape defined by a path with progressively darker shades of red. At the same time we have reduced the size of the shape using:

```
path2.setScaleX(scale_factors[k]);

path2.setScaleY(scale_factors[k]);
```

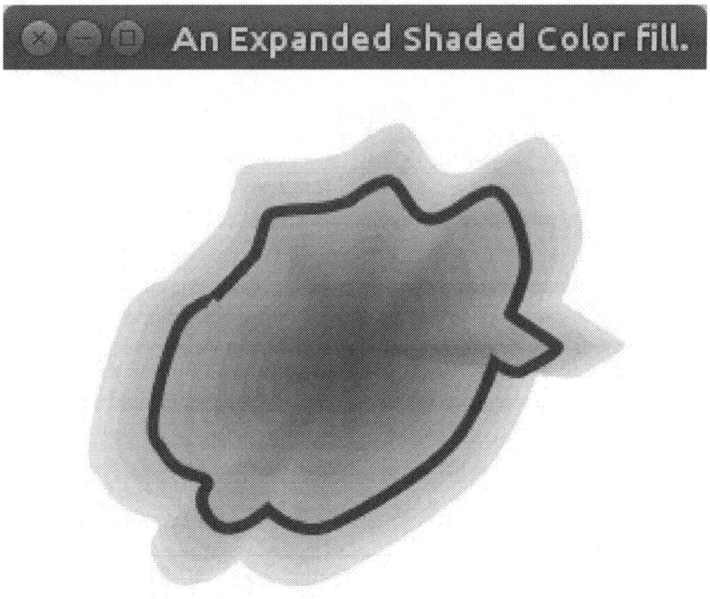


// Cubic_flower_1_wash_1.java
/*
To be used in reference to "Cubic_PolyShape_Draw8.java".

Repeated constructors creating a set of progressively different randomized cubic curves.
Random number method for Gaussian distribution:
nextGaussian(): Gives a Gaussian ("normally") distributed number with mean valye 0.0 and standard deviation 1.0

Line and Shape Properties/attribute parameters:
========================================
path1.setStrokeWidth(4); // Width of the line, pixels.
path1.setStrokeLineCap(StrokeLineCap.ROUND); // Rounded ends of lines.
path1.setStroke(Color.BLUE);
//path1.getStrokeDashArray().addAll(14d); // Dash pattern: fill, blank, etc
path1.getStrokeDashArray().addAll(14); // Dash pattern: fill, blank, etc
path1.setStrokeDashOffset(10); //Dash pattern: to shift the beginning of the dash.

```
path1.setFill(Color.PINK);   // Fill the interior of a closed shape with color.

Tested on: java version "java-8-oracle"
Author: Mike Ohlson de Fine
*/

import javafx.application.Application;
import javafx.stage.Stage;
import javafx.scene.*;
import javafx.scene.paint.*;
import javafx.scene.shape.*; // Graphic primitives library.
import java.lang.reflect.Array;
import java.util.Random;

public class Cubic_flower1_wash_1 extends Application
{

  //==========================================================
  //     Functions/Methods.
  //==========================================================

  Path Points2paths(double[][] path_points, MoveTo  selected_moveTo)
  {
      /* Applies to : One path - the raw points that will be used to construct all
the
                  CubicCurveTos that make up the sequence of drawn
CubicCurveTo parts.
      The first position in the path is the starting MoveTo (which could be the
first vertex/point
      of the first CubicCurveTo.

       The Output: An assembled path ready to be added to the JavaFX stage
for display.
      */

      int num_cctos = Array.getLength(path_points) ; // Number of
CubicCurveTos making up the path.
      CubicCurveTo crv_pth1 =  new CubicCurveTo();   // The set of curves for
a path.

      // Assemble one path.
```

```
    Path  path_n =  new Path();
    path_n.getElements().add(selected_moveTo); // Select the appropriate
start position.
    for (int j=0; j< num_cctos ; j++)
    {
      crv_pth1 = new CubicCurveTo(path_points[j][0], path_points[j][1],
path_points[j][2],
                    path_points[j][3], path_points[j][4], path_points[j][5]);

      path_n.getElements().add(crv_pth1);
      path_n.setStrokeWidth(5);
    };
  return path_n ;
  }


  public Color[] kulaInterpolate(double rr1, double gg1, double bb1,double
alfa1,
                    double rr2,  double gg2, double bb2, double alfa2,
                    int numkulas )
  {
     /* Create an interpolated sequence (array) of colors.
      Color format:  Color.color(red, green, blue, alpha) format.
      The start and end colors are respectively Color.color(rr1, gg1, bb1,
alfa1)
      and Color.color(rr2, gg2, bb2, alfa2).
     */

     double rrdelta = (rr1-rr2)/numkulas ;
     double ggdelta = (gg1-gg2)/numkulas ;
     double bbdelta = (bb1-bb2)/numkulas ;
     double rr, gg, bb , alfa;
     double rr0, gg0, bb0, alfa0;
     Color[] kulaArray = new Color[numkulas];

     for (int i=0; i<numkulas; i++ )
     {
        rr = rr1 - i*rrdelta ;
        gg = gg1 - i*ggdelta ;
        bb = bb1 - i*bbdelta ;
       kulaArray[i] = Color.color(rr, gg, bb, alfa1);
```

```
    }
  return kulaArray;
}


double[] make_scale_factors(double start_value, int num_elements)
   {
     double[] scale_factors = new double[num_elements];
     double decrement = start_value / num_elements;
     for (int i=0; i<num_elements-1; i++)
        { scale_factors[i] = start_value -= decrement ;
        }
  return scale_factors;
}

//=============================================================
//     Main Execution.
//=============================================================
public void start(Stage primaryStage)
{
   Group rootgroup = new Group();

//=============================================================
//     Variable Declarations.
//=============================================================
//flower_path1.svg
double[]  startAt1_1={214,198};
MoveTo moveTo1_1 = new MoveTo(startAt1_1[0], startAt1_1[1]);
double[][] flower1_cube1  = {{214,198 , 225.3,208.9 , 237,206.1},
{248.7,203.3 , 284.2,180.9 , 294.1,168.4},
{304.1,155.9 , 310.7,135.2 , 310.7,135.2},
{310.7,135.2 , 318.9,141.3 , 323,138.8},
{327,136.2 , 340.8,130.1 , 336.7,127.6},
{332.7,125 , 317.3,114.8 , 317.3,114.8},
{317.3,114.8 , 322.7,102.8 , 324,95.15},
{325.3,87.5 , 318.1,61.73 , 309.9,61.99},
{301.8,62.24 , 291.3,75 , 282.4,73.98},
{273.5,72.96 , 271.4,57.4 , 265.3,57.65},
{259.2,57.91 , 249,66.33 , 249,66.33},
{249,66.33 , 241.3,68.88 , 235.5,69.39},
{229.6,69.9 , 216.1,69.64 , 214,72.7},
```

```
{212,75.77 , 210.7,86.48 , 207.7,90.05},
{204.6,93.62 , 190.6,107.7 , 190.6,107.7},
{190.6,107.7 , 181.1,110.2 , 176.8,118.4},
{172.4,126.5 , 161,162.8 , 166.3,169.1},
{171.7,175.5 , 171.2,180.1 , 182.9,183.7},
{194.6,187.2 , 182.1,188.3 , 186.5,198},
{190.8,207.7 , 197.2,206.9 , 202.6,205.1},
{207.9,203.3 , 214,198 , 214,198 }};

Path  path1   = new Path();
Color kula_charcoal = Color.color(0.2, 0.2, 0.35);

double[] scale_factors = make_scale_factors(1.4, 20) ;  // Make a sequence
of decreasing factors.
//================================================================
//    Paint Color Washes.
//================================================================
int numberOfKulas = 20;
Color[] kula_flower1 = kulaInterpolate(1,0,0,1,   1,.9,.9,1,  numberOfKulas )
; // Shades of color.

for (int k=0; k<numberOfKulas; k++)
    {
        Path  path2   = new Path();
        path2 =  Points2paths(flower1_cube1, moveTo1_1);
        path2.setScaleX(scale_factors[k]);
        path2.setScaleY(scale_factors[k]);
        path2.setStroke(null);
        path2.setFill(kula_flower1[numberOfKulas-1-k]);
        path2.setTranslateX(-100);
        path2.setTranslateY(-10);
        rootgroup.getChildren().addAll( path2);
    }

//================================================================
//    Draw the Inked Outline.
//================================================================
 path1 =  Points2paths(flower1_cube1, moveTo1_1);
 path1.setFill(null);
 path1.setStroke(kula_charcoal);
 path1.setTranslateX(-100);
```

```
    path1.setTranslateY(-10);
    rootgroup.getChildren().addAll( path1);

    ////////////////////////////////////////////////////////////
     Scene scene = new Scene(rootgroup, 300, 260);
     primaryStage.setTitle("An Expanded Shaded Color fill.");
     primaryStage.setScene(scene);
     primaryStage.show();
  }
}
```

## Watercolor emulation: Pen and Wash

The final image in this chapter is a rudimentary demonstration of how to emulate a watercolor painted picture created using the Pen and Wash technique. The watercolor artist combines areas of water-paint as washes of various controlled color combined with lines drawn in waterproof ink.

Here is the basic program used to create the simulated water color which is the last image in this chapter. The code shown here the structure to reproduce pictures of almost any complexity. We have reduced it to the minimum to handle a single path.

The complete code for the entire picture is over one thousand lines long. It can be found at https://github.com , username mikeodf, folder JavaFX_Line_Shape_Color

with the title **Cubic_flower123_pen_wash_2.java**

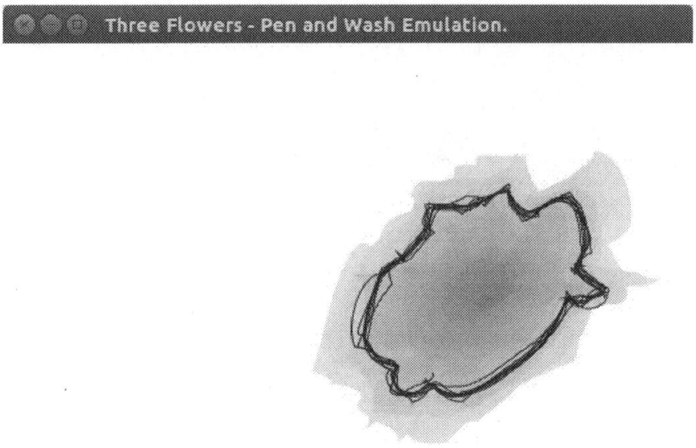


```
// Cubic_flower123_pen_wash_2.java
/*
Repeated constructors creating a set of progressively different
randomized cubic curves.
Random number method for Gaussian distribution:
nextGaussian(): Gives a Gaussian ("normally") distributed number with
mean value 0.0 and standard deviation 1.0

Tested on: java version "java-8-oracle"
Author: Mike Ohlson de Fine
*/

import javafx.application.Application;
import javafx.stage.Stage;
import javafx.scene.*;
import javafx.scene.paint.*;
import javafx.scene.shape.*; // Graphic primitives library.
import java.lang.reflect.Array;
import java.util.Random;

public class Cubic_flower123_pen_wash_2 extends Application
{
//==========================================================
//    Functions/Methods.
//==========================================================
    ////    RandomizePoints( pnt, stdev)    ////////////////
    double[][] RandomizePoints(double[][] pnt, double stdev)
    {  /* Applies to: One array of points that will become a path.
```

```
        The array of points will be transformed into a sequence of CubicCurveto
segments
         by the Points2paths method.
        Inputs: A 2D raw path - a collection of potential CubicCurvetos.
        The first index of the array is the CubicCurveTo index.
        The second index gives access to each of six control points in a CCTo.
        Randomization: Take the 2D array of (xy) vertices, the control points of
CubicCurveTos,
        and add a controlled but random offset to each x and y.  What will be
returned is a collection of
        randomized vertices comprising a new array of points - but slightly
distorted by a random offset to each point.

        Output: The input raw path but randomised/distorted.
      */
          Random rand1 = new Random();
          int lenn = Array.getLength(pnt) ;      // The number of CubicCurveTos
in a single path.
          double[][] pp_rand = new double[lenn][6];
          // Randomize Vertices: Every vertex gets randomized afresh here.
          for (int k=0; k<lenn; k++)  // k is the Index stepping through the
potential CubicCurves.
          {
            for  (int sxy=0; sxy<6; sxy++)
            // sxy is the Index stepping through the 3 (x,y) vertices for each
CubicCurveto.
            {
                pp_rand[k][sxy] = pnt[k][sxy]+ stdev*rand1.nextGaussian();
                // x and y are randomized independently.
            };
          };
       return pp_rand ;
   }


//===================================================
////    Points2paths( path_points, elected_moveTo)    ////////////////
    Path Points2paths(double[][] path_points, MoveTo  selected_moveTo)
    {
      /* Applies to : One path - the raw points that will be used to construct all
the
```

```
            CubicCurveTos that make up the sequence of drawn
CubicCurveTo parts.
      The first position in the path is the starting MoveTo (which could be the
first vertex/point
      of the first CubicCurveTo).
      The "path_index" selects the correct path to be worked on.
      path_points[A][B] - "A" is the index pointing to each CubicCurveTo
section,
      "B" refers to each of the three coordinates of the cubic curves.

      After the points have been randomized they must now be assembled into
      CubicCurveTo paths which are the output.

      The Output: An assembled path ready to be added to stage for display.
    */

        int num_cctos = Array.getLength(path_points) ; // Number of
CubicCurveTos making up the path.
        CubicCurveTo crv_pth1 =  new CubicCurveTo();   // The set fo curves
for a path.

        // Assemble one path.
        Path  path_n =  new Path();
        path_n.getElements().add(selected_moveTo);      // Select the
appropriate start position.
        for (int j=0; j< num_cctos ; j++)
        {
            crv_pth1 = new CubicCurveTo(path_points[j][0], path_points[j][1],
path_points[j][2],
                         path_points[j][3], path_points[j][4], path_points[j][5]);

            path_n.getElements().add(crv_pth1);
        };
      return path_n ;
   }


//==========================================================
////   kulaInterpolate(rr1, gg1, bb1, alfa1, rr2,  gg2, bb2, alfa2, numkulas )
   public Color[] kulaInterpolate(double rr1, double gg1, double bb1,double
alfa1,
```

```
                        double rr2,  double gg2, double bb2, double alfa2,
                        int numkulas )
   {
     /* Applies to: Six numbers in the range 0 to 1. They are the color values
for each color channel.

        This method create an interpolated sequence (array) of colors.
        The sequence that starts with one color and ends with another.
        Color format:  Color.color(red, green, blue, alpha) format.
        The start and end colors are respectively Color.color(rr1, gg1, bb1,
alfa1)
        and Color.color(rr2, gg2, bb2, alfa2).
      */

         double rrdelta = (rr1-rr2)/numkulas ;
         double ggdelta = (gg1-gg2)/numkulas ;
         double bbdelta = (bb1-bb2)/numkulas ;
         double alphadelta = (alfa1-alfa2)/numkulas ;
         double rr, gg, bb , alfa;  // Intermediate color values
         Color[] kulaArray = new Color[numkulas+1];

         for (int i=0; i<numkulas+1; i++ )
         {
            rr = rr1 - i*rrdelta ;
            gg = gg1 - i*ggdelta ;
            bb = bb1 - i*bbdelta ;
            alfa = alfa1 - i * alphadelta ;
            kulaArray[i] = Color.color(rr, gg, bb, alfa);
         };
      return kulaArray;
   }


//=====================================================================
////     make_scale_factors(start_value, num_elements)     /////////
   double[] make_scale_factors(double start_value, int num_elements)
   {
     /* Applies to: Two numbers, a double and an integer.

        This method creates a sequence of linearly decreasing scale factors
        that will be used to draw nested areas of color. Each color will be
```

```
        taken from an arry of colors created from "kulainterpolate".
        Output: An array of decreasing numbers.
       */
       double[] scale_factors = new double[num_elements];
       double decrement = start_value / num_elements;
       for (int i=0; i<num_elements-1; i++)
       { scale_factors[i] = start_value -= decrement ;
       };
        return scale_factors;
   }

//==========================================================
//     Main Execution Thread.
//==========================================================
   public void start(Stage primaryStage)
   {
      Group rootgroup = new Group();

   //==========================================================
   // SHAPES TO BE DRAWN - ORIGINALS CREATED IN INKSCAPE
   //==========================================================

    //flower_path1.svg
    double[]  startAt1_1={214,198};
    MoveTo moveTo1_1 = new MoveTo(startAt1_1[0], startAt1_1[1]);
    double[][] flower1_cube1  = {
    {214,198 , 225.3,208.9 , 237,206.1},
    {248.7,203.3 , 284.2,180.9 , 294.1,168.4},
    {304.1,155.9 , 310.7,135.2 , 310.7,135.2},
    {310.7,135.2 , 318.9,141.3 , 323,138.8},
    {327,136.2 , 340.8,130.1 , 336.7,127.6},
    {332.7,125 , 317.3,114.8 , 317.3,114.8},
    {317.3,114.8 , 322.7,102.8 , 324,95.15},
    {325.3,87.5 , 318.1,61.73 , 309.9,61.99},
    {301.8,62.24 , 291.3,75 , 282.4,73.98},
    {273.5,72.96 , 271.4,57.4 , 265.3,57.65},
    {259.2,57.91 , 249,66.33 , 249,66.33},
    {249,66.33 , 241.3,68.88 , 235.5,69.39},
    {229.6,69.9 , 216.1,69.64 , 214,72.7},
    {212,75.77 , 210.7,86.48 , 207.7,90.05},
    {204.6,93.62 , 190.6,107.7 , 190.6,107.7},
```

```
    {190.6,107.7 , 181.1,110.2 , 176.8,118.4},
    {172.4,126.5 , 161,162.8 , 166.3,169.1},
    {171.7,175.5 , 171.2,180.1 , 182.9,183.7},
    {194.6,187.2 , 182.1,188.3 , 186.5,198},
    {190.8,207.7 , 197.2,206.9 , 202.6,205.1},
    {207.9,203.3 , 214,198 , 214,198  }};

    // Flower 1 MoveTos.
    MoveTo[] all_movetos1 = { moveTo1_1 }; // These arrays can have more
elements.
    // Flower 1 CubicCurveTos.
    double[][][] all_pps1 = { flower1_cube1 }; // These arrays can have more
elements.


//================================================================
//     Variable Declarations.
//================================================================
    int x_shift = 100 ;
    int y_shift = 50 ;
    double[][] pp1_b;
    Path  path1   = new Path();
    Path[] path_rand1 = { path1, path1, path1, path1, path1, path1, path1,
path1, path1 };

    double std_dev1 = 6 ;     // Select a standard deviation.
    double[] std_dev2 = {0, 2, 3, 4, 5, 4, 3.5, 2.5};
    double[] lin_w   = {2, 2, 2, 1, 1, 1,   1,  2 };
    Color kula_charcoal = Color.color(0.1, 0.1, 0.15);

    Path[] rand_paths =  new Path[6];
    double[] scale_factors = make_scale_factors(1.4, 20) ;
//================================================================
//     Paint Color Washes - Interpolated color arrays.
//================================================================
    int numkulas = 31; // The number of colors in the series (array).
                                                    // lighter          darker
    Color[] kula_flower1 = kulaInterpolate(  1, 0.86,  .9,   1,     1,  0,  0, 1,
numkulas ) ; // reds

    // Flower 1 Color Wash.
```

```
    for (int k=0; k<20; k++)
      {
         Path  path2   = new Path();
         double[][] polycube2 = RandomizePoints(flower1_cube1, std_dev1) ;
         path2 =  Points2paths(polycube2, moveTo1_1);
         path2.setScaleX(scale_factors[k]);
        path2.setScaleY(scale_factors[k]);
         path2.setStroke(null);                   // No outline wanted.
         path2.setFill(kula_flower1[k]);
         path2.setTranslateX(x_shift);
         path2.setTranslateY(y_shift);
         rootgroup.getChildren().addAll( path2);
       }
    //vvvvvvvvvvvvvvvvvvvvvvvvvvvvvvvvvvvv
     // Many other lines may be inserted here.
    //^^^^^^^^^^^^^^^^^^^^^^^^^^^^^^^^^^^^^^^^^^^^

//============================================================
//     Draw Inklines.
//============================================================

    for  (int j=0; j<Array.getLength(all_movetos1) ; j++)
     {
       for (int i=0; i<8 ; i++) // 8 = number of randomized curves. Index=0 has
no distortion.
        {
         pp1_b = RandomizePoints(all_pps1[j], std_dev2[i]);
         path_rand1[i] =  Points2paths(pp1_b, all_movetos1[j]);
         path_rand1[i].setFill(null);
         path_rand1[i].setStroke(kula_charcoal);
         path_rand1[i].setTranslateX(x_shift);
         path_rand1[i].setTranslateY(y_shift);
         rootgroup.getChildren().addAll( path_rand1[i]);
       };
    };
   //vvvvvvvvvvvvvvvvvvvvvvvvvvvvvvvvvvvvv
     // Many other lines may be inserted here.
    //^^^^^^^^^^^^^^^^^^^^^^^^^^^^^^^^^^^^^^^^^^^^
//============================================================
//     Graphic Execution.
//============================================================
```

```
        Scene scene = new Scene(rootgroup, 500, 300);
        primaryStage.setTitle("Three Flowers - Pen and Wash Emulation.");
        primaryStage.setScene(scene);
        primaryStage.show();
    }
}
```

## Where do the Raw points for the Drawings come from?

In the next chapter we will see how the data for any drawing can be obtained using the excellent Free and Open Source drawing package “Inkscape”.

# CHAPTER 12

## SVG : SCALED VECTOR  GRAPHICS

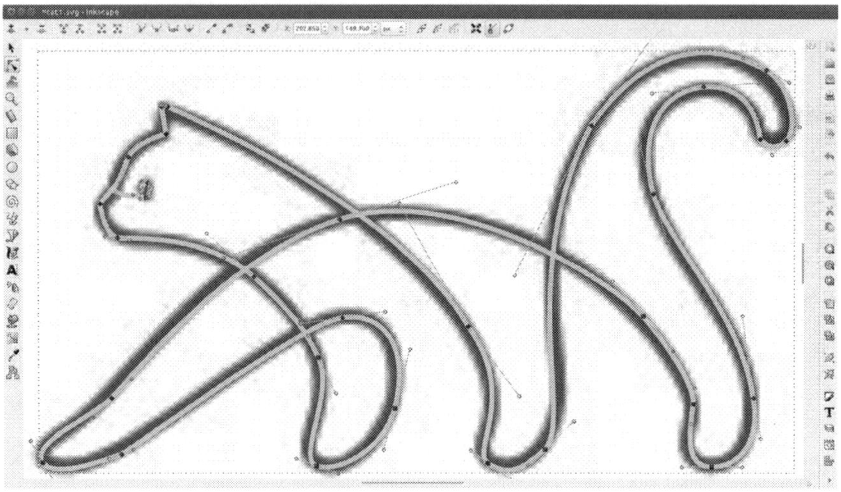

*"**Scalable Vector Graphics** (SVG) is an XML-based vector image format for two-dimensional drawings graphics with support for animation. The SVG specification is an open standarddeveloped by the World Wide Web Consortium (W3C) since 1999."* WikipediA.

*"The technobabble above tells us nothing about how truly neat and useful SVG has become." A* guy writing graphics software in Java and Python.

In this chapter we:

- Explain how to create elaborate drawings without necessarily having sophisticated artistic hand-eye skills. We use the open source vector drawing package called "Inkscape".
- We explore methods of extracting drawing data from the SVG code produced by Inkscape.
- We convert the drawings into Java code and modify the

drawings using Java commands.

## *About SVG (Scaled Vector Graphics)*

What do we mean by drawing? In the world of computer graphics there are two similar but different meanings to the word "draw" or "drawing". The first meaning refers to the act of creating pictures on a physical surface like paper using pencils, pens and brushes. The second meaning is the process of creating lines and shapes on a computer screen using graphic oriented computer code in languages like Java, Python and XML.

SVG is effectively a language for defining lines, curves and shapes as numbers and geometric operations. We do not need to know Math or Mathematics in order to use SVG as we shall see in this chapter.

### SVG is amazingly useful and widespread.

SVG images and their behaviors are defined in XML text files. This means that they can be searched, indexed, scripted, and compressed. As XML files, SVG images can be created and edited with any text editor, but are more often created with drawing software such as Inkscape, Adobe Freehand, Adobe Illustrator , Sketchup (from Google) or SVG-edit (Open Source). To compare vector drawing editors see *en.wikipedia.org/wiki/Comparison_of_vector_graphics_editors*. We have selected Inkscape because it is stable, versatile, sophisticated yet reasonably easy to use. It has excellent how-to instructions and examples available for free on the web.

All major modern web browsers—including Mozilla Firefox, Internet Explorer, Google Chrome, Opera, Safari, and Microsoft Edge—have at some degree of SVG rendering support.

SVG allows three types of graphic objects: vector graphics, raster graphics (photographic images), and text. Graphical objects, including PNG and JPEG raster images, can be grouped, styled, transformed, and composited into previously rendered objects. GIFs can be converted for animations in SVG. We do not explore animation in this book. The second book in this series will deal with animation.

## Why is SVG important to Java Graphics?

Most of the good tools for creating vector graphic drawings can export **.svg** format files. This means that an artist can make elaborate, detailed and lovely vector art and it can be imported and used in Java applications. In this chapter we explore this.

JavaFX has the **SVGPath class** that represents 2D shapes. The methods of the class are designed to decipher the character strings representing complex shapes from a typical SVG file that we can export from a drawing program like Inkscape.

## What does an exported SVG file look like?

The file begins with the four lines shown below. The important line is"**<svg**" because this declares that the lines that follow must be interpreted as SVG instructions. All the code between **<svg** … and **/svg>** is SVG code, that is instructions on drawing shapes.

```
<?xml version="1.0" encoding="UTF-8" standalone="no"?>

<!-- Created with Inkscape (http://www.inkscape.org/) -->

<svg

  xmlns:dc="http://purl.org/dc/elements/1.1/"

…

…
```

## A CubicCurveTo line.

The actual CubicCurveTo(…) points are contained in SVG instructions that look like:

d="M 63.07,165.4 C 63.07,165.4 72.97,208.5 102.5,216.9 C 138.5,227.2 163.1,201.8 163.1,201.8"

This is the description of a shape.

The six values between any two letters “C” are the same six parameters that are needed for a JavaFX CubicCurveTo instruction like:

***CubicCurveTo crv1 = new CubicCurveTo( 125,73, 127,62, 108,56 );***

For example in the SVG line above the piece C 63.07,165.4 72.97,208.5 102.5,216.9 C Should become the JavaFX instruction:

CubicCurveTo( 63.07, 165.4, 72.97, 208.5, 102.5, 216.) ;

Here are some examples of graphic primitives in SVG code. These SVG descriptions were copied from the Inkscape files saved when these shapes were drawn.

**A line**

<path ...

d="M 24.2,29.1 L 92.9,96.7"

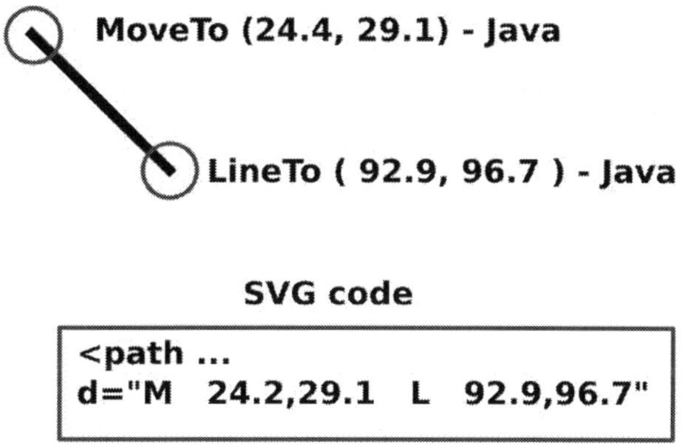

## A triangle

<path ...

d="M 82.8,58.0 L 302.9,183.8 L 82.8,323.8 Z"

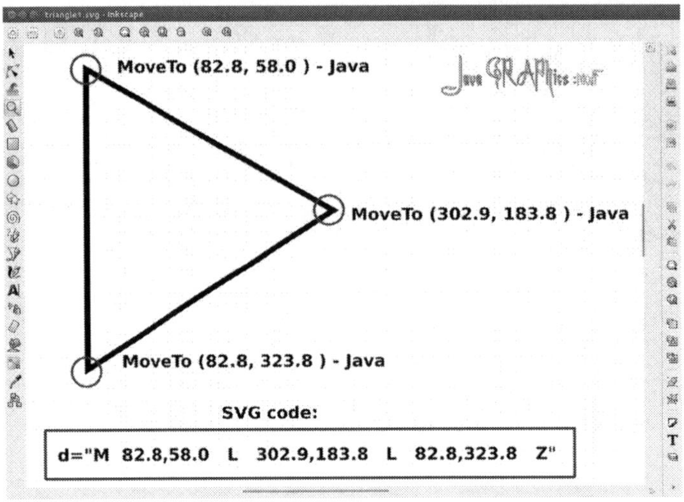


## A circle

<circle ...

cx="160"

cy="166.6"

r="137.1"

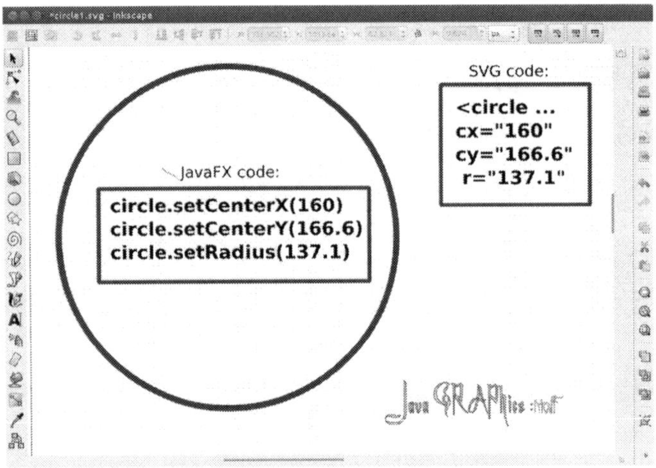

## An ellipse

<ellipse ...

cx="225.7"

cy="122.3"

rx="202.9"

ry="92.7"

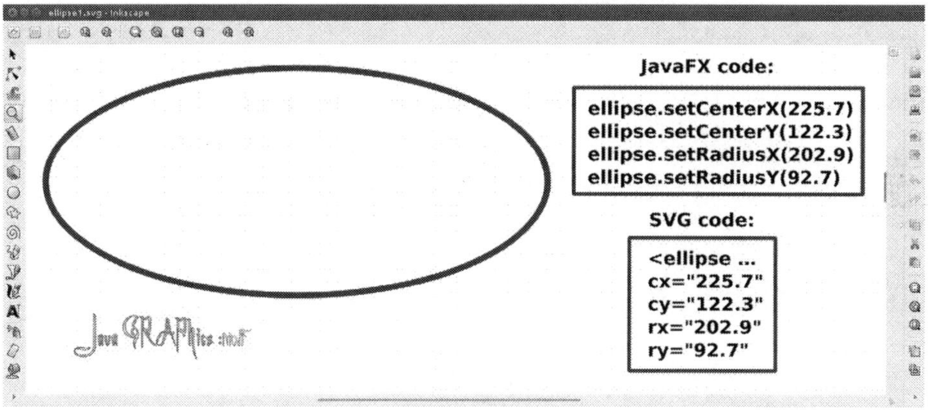

## A Quadratic Bezier Curve

<path '''

d="M 33.3,153.3   C 104,6.8   215.2,146.3   215.2,146.3"

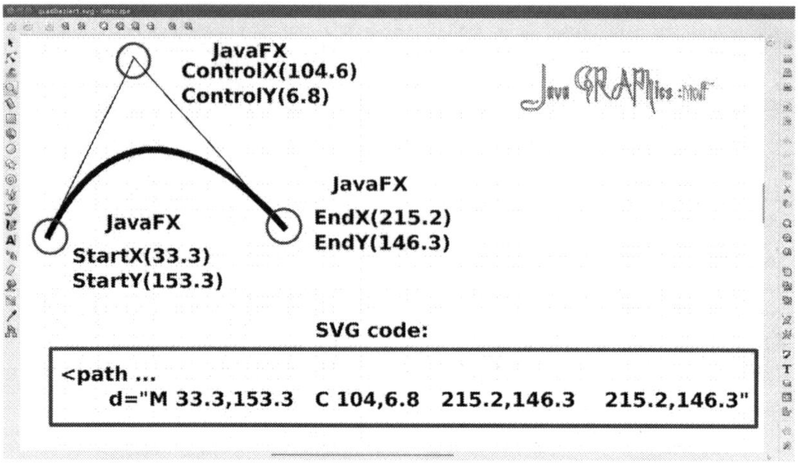


## A Cubic Bezier Curve

Cubic Bezier curves are the most important because any shape can be constructed using only Cubics, even straight line segments.

<path ...

d="M 55.7,116.6   C   55.7,116.6   90,33.8   127.1,32.3   C   164.3,30.9 200,112.4 200,112.4"

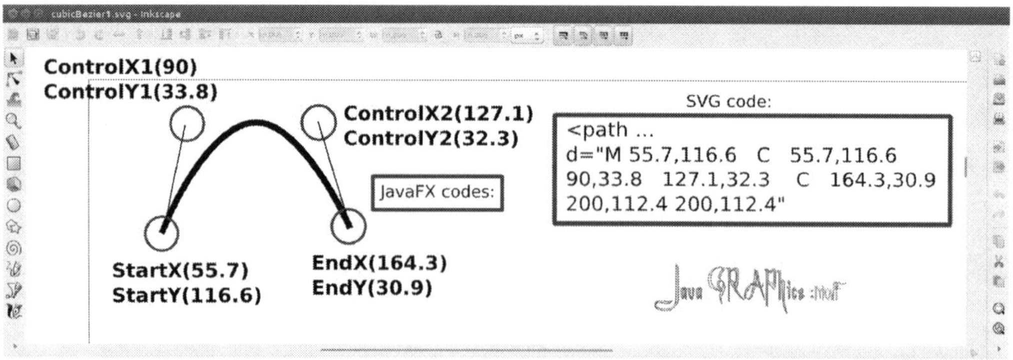

These are the valuable lines that the JavaFX SVGPath method is able to interpret as paths that can be drawn by JavaFX.

What makes SVG paths very useful is that they reproduce *smooth* Bezier curves. The

drawing of a female head at the heading of this chapter was produced by JavaFX SVGPath methods. The original vector drawing was made by tracing over the top of a JPG image using Inkscape.

## First Example

Here we use JavaFX's SVGPath class to draw a three segment line.

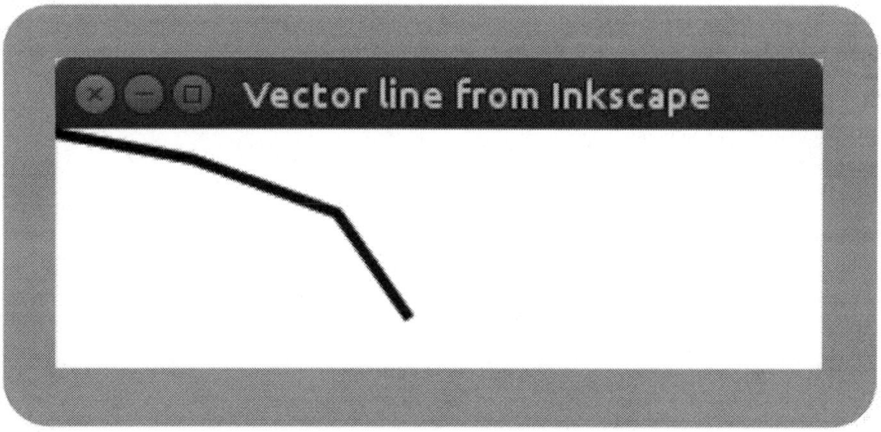


```
// SVG_InkscapeLine1.java
/*
Defines the filling rule constant for determining the interior of the path. The
value must be one of the following constants: FillRile.EVEN_ODD or
FillRule.NON_ZERO. The default value is FillRule.NON_ZERO.

Tested on: java version "java-8-oracle"
Author: Mike Ohlson de Fine
*/
import javafx.application.Application;
import javafx.scene.Group;
import javafx.scene.Scene;
import javafx.scene.shape.SVGPath;
```

```
import javafx.stage.Stage;
import javafx.scene.paint.*;

public class SVG_InkscapeLine1 extends Application {

public void start(Stage stage)
{
   final Group group = new Group();
   Scene scene = new Scene(group, 300, 330);
   stage.setScene(scene);
   stage.setTitle("Vector line from Inkscape");


  // ************************************************************
   SVGPath svg = new SVGPath();
   svg.setContent("M 0,1.804 L 53.54,11.91 L 110.1,33.12 L 137.4,72.51");
  // ************************************************************
   svg.setFill(Color.rgb(255,255,255,0.0)) ;
   svg.setStroke(Color.BLACK) ;
   svg.setStrokeWidth(4.0) ;
   group.getChildren().add(svg);
   stage.show();
  }
}
```

## How to Convert a SVG path into a JavaFX path

If we want to design games and animations in Java we will want to be able to work with JavaFX paths and polygons rather than raw SVG code. This turns out to be very simple in Inkscape. All we need to do is select “File” then “Save As...” , making sure we pick the “.fx” format. Inkscape then kindly converts the SVG instructions into JavaFX paths. It is magically convenient.

Here is the JavaFX program to produce the drawing of the cat shown below.

```
// SVG_InkscapeCat1.java
/*
A one-line cat shape.
Tested on: java version "java-8-oracle"
Author:Mike Ohlson de Fine
*/
import javafx.application.Application;
import javafx.scene.Group;
import javafx.scene.Scene;
import javafx.scene.shape.SVGPath;
import javafx.stage.Stage;
import javafx.scene.paint.*;

public class SVG_InkscapeCat1 extends Application {

 public void start(Stage stage) {
   final Group group = new Group();
   Scene scene = new Scene(group, 350, 200);
   stage.setScene(scene);
   stage.setTitle("Vector line: Inkscape");

   SVGPath svg = new SVGPath();

// Here is the single line created by InInkscape
svg.setContent("M 58.82,30.96 L 60.62,42.1 C 60.62,42.1 50.02,44.7 45.62,51.3
C 42.22,61.9 39.42,64.3 39.42,64.3 C 41.82,67.9 47.42,66.5 52.62,67.9 C
53.42,68.1 54.02,66.1 54.42,64.9 C 54.82,63.5 54.22,62.1 53.42,61.7 C
51.02,61.3 51.22,64.1 50.82,65.5 C 50.22,68.3 41.22,67.1 39.42,64.3 L
34.02,70.3 C 34.02,70.3 36.22,83.5 41.22,84.1 C 46.02,84.7 77.21,82.3
96.22,99.9 C 115.2,117.7 118.4,123.7 122.6,132.5 C 129.6,147.1 113.4,173.5
122,176.5 C 130.6,179.5 148.8,170.1 153.2,153.3 C 159.6,129.3 149.4,114.1
132.4,116.5 C 115.2,118.9 47.22,169.7 42.42,171.7 C 37.42,173.5 14.83,180.9
12.43,175.9 C 10.03,171.1 30.82,156.9 38.62,148.9 C 46.62,141.1 84.01,92.1
131.2,76.7 C 178.2,61.5 240.8,101.9 253,115.9 C 265.2,129.9 274,145.1
273.4,151.3 C 272.6,159.5 268.6,176.9 280.8,176.9 C 293.2,176.9 300.8,165.5
```

```
297.6,148.9 C 293.4,115.9 262.8,85.9 257.2,66.3 C 251.8,46.7 256.6,25.36
277.4,22.96 C 299.2,21.36 300.2,44.3 300.2,44.3 C 300.2,44.3 305,50.5
310.6,44.9 C 316,39.3 311.8,21.16 302.6,16.16 C 293.4,11.36 261.8,-4.642
232.2,38.7 C 201.6,99.3 225.2,158.5 213.4,169.7 C 206.8,176.1 199.8,181.9
190.8,175.3 C 184,170.3 203.2,148.1 183.2,120.1 C 155.2,70.3 61.02,30.96
61.02,30.96");

    svg.setFill(null) ;
    svg.setStroke(Color.BLACK) ;
    svg.setStrokeWidth(4.0) ;
    group.getChildren().add(svg);
    stage.show();
  }
}
```

## ***Where can we get Vector Drawings.***

The most direct way of obtaining vector drawings is by tracing over a .jpg or .png raster image. We import a raster image like cat1.jpg into Inkscape and trace a shape over it using Inkscape and save the .svg file where we can access it. The two tools we can use for tracing over images are the "Draw Bezier Curves and straight lines" and "Edit paths by nodes" as indicated below.

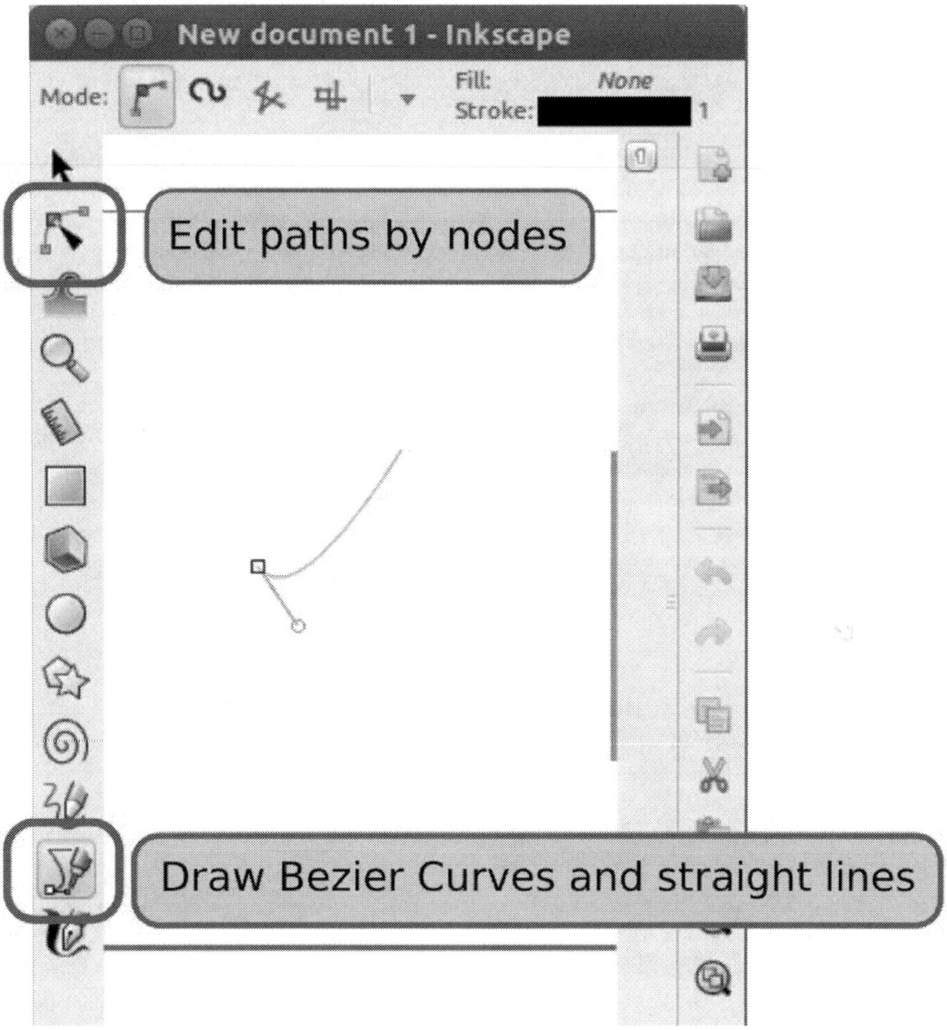


There are very clear, well written instructions on how to use these tools. Just click-open the “help” menu and select “Inkscape Manual”. This will cause the manual to download from the internet and open up inside a web browser. The Topic we should read is the “7. Paths” chapter.

The image below is an abstract image of a cat in black and white as a jpg image. The light colored lines on top are the traced Bezier curves made in Inkscape.

The faint line with circles at the end are the curvature control handles of the Bezier curves.

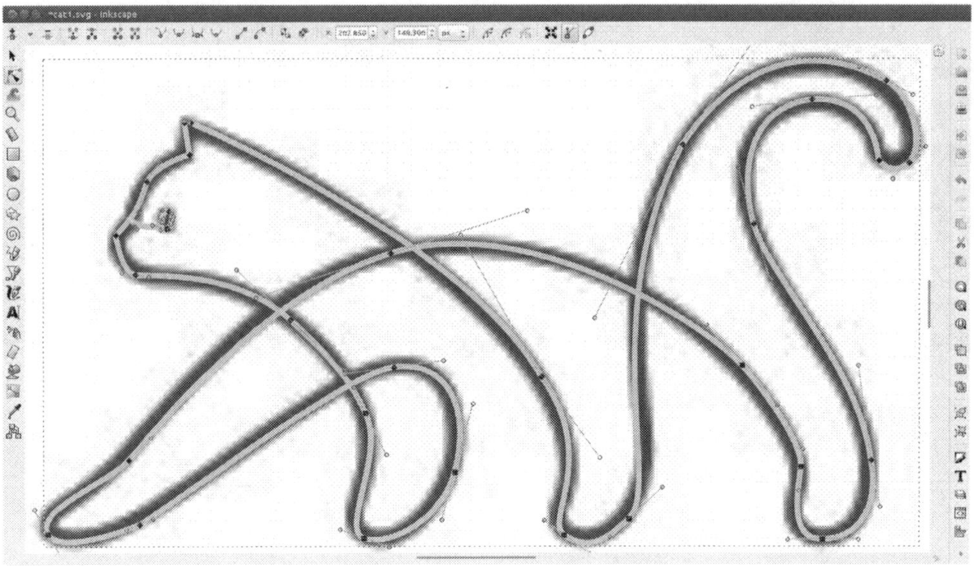

The final Java image:

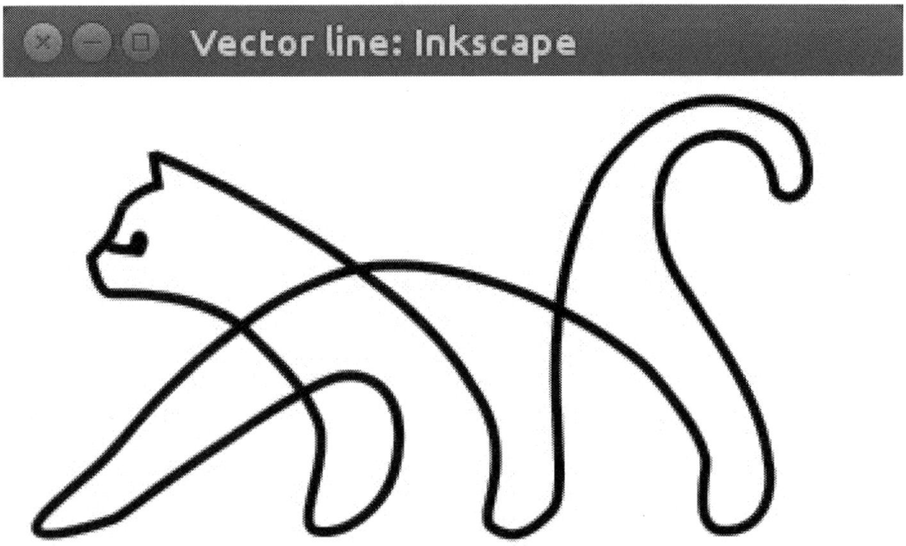

## *How to convert a SVG shape into JavaFX CubicTo paths.*

Previously we used the *SVGPath* class to convert a SVG image created in Inkscape into an image that could be exhibited from inside a JavaFX program.

The problem with this approach is that we cannot use Java instructions to adjust or manipulate individual points in the SVG file. It remains a SVG file and not a JavaFX path. As we showed in the previous chapter there is a need to be able to manipulate individual CubicCurveTo points if we want full control over our drawing style.

Therefore what we do now is to explore how to convert SVG files into collections of CubicCurveTo paths.

We start with lines drawn in Inkscape.

The saved .svg file of this drawing will contain each line in the form:
d="M 19.97,30.2 C 19.97,30.2 43.77,17.02 46.37,23.3 C 54.87,43.8 46.77,72.8 49.07,74.6 C 50.67,78.6 64.87,74.9 64.87,74.9"

d="M 63.87,19.71 C 63.87,19.71 72.97,15.82 78.37,15.43 C 86.47,14.84 93.57,17.03 93.57,17.03"

d="M 13.97,38.5 C 13.97,38.5 20.27,33.8 24.77,34.1 C 30.07,34.1 39.17,37 39.17,37"

etc. There will be 11 such lines. Using a suitable text editor like gedit we must:

- eliminate the characters between the M and the first C,
- replace the C's with },{
- add commas in the two positions occupied by space characters.
- Substitute the last character (") in each line with }; and
- place declaration headers like "double[][] gface_1 = {{" in front of each line.

We must end up with a JavaFX class containing arrays as shown below:

```
//girl_face_2.java
/* A rendering of eyes, nose and mouth

It is compiled separately as a class, to be packaged with
"CubicBezier_girlface_1.java".

Tested on: java version "java-8-oracle"
Author: Mike Ohlson de Fine
*/

public class girl_face_2
{
double[][] gface_1 = {{19.,30.,43.,17.,46.,23.},{54.,43.,46.,72.,49.,74.},
{50.,78.,64.,74.,64.,74.}};
```

```
double[][] gface_2  = {{63.,19.,72.,15.,78.,15.},{86.,14.,93.,17.,93.,17.}};

double[][] gface_3  = {{13.,38.,20.,33.,24.,34.},{30.,34.,39.,37,39.,37}};

double[][] gface_4  = {{13.,42.,21.,36.,24.,36.},{29.,36.,38.,40.,38.,40.}};

double[][] gface_5  = {{73.17,31.,81.,24.,87.,24.},{91.,25,101,31.,101,31.}};

double[][] gface_6  = {{73.,35.,76.,30.,81.,30},{89.,29.,97.,32.,97,32}};

double[][] gface_7  = {{20.,38.,20.,46.,25.,45.},{32.,45.,32.,39.,32.,39.}};

double[][] gface_8  = {{80.,31.,79.,37.,84.,37.},{90.,37.,90.,32,90.,32}};

double[][] gface_9  = {{25.,37.,23.,39.,25.,41.},{27.,42.,28.,39.,28.,39.}};
double[][] gface_10  = {{83.,31.,83.,33.,85.,33.},{86.,34.,86.,32.,86.,32.}};

double[][] gface_11  = {{46.,91.,47.,92.,50.,91.},{53.,89.,54.,87.,55.,87},
{56.,86.,57.,89.,59.,89.},{60.,89.,62.,87,64.,86.},{65.97,86.,68.,89.,70.,90.},
{71.,90.,78.,88.,78.,88.}};

double[][] gface_12  = {{50.,93.,49.,98.,53.,99},{57.,99.,59.,96.,61.,96.},
{63.,96.,62.,98.,64.,98.},{67.,98,71.,93,71.,93}};

double[][] gface_13  = {{52.,91.,57.,92,59.,92},{61.,92,67.,91.,67.,91.}};

double[][][] all_points = { gface_1,  gface_2,  gface_3,  gface_4,  gface_5,
gface_6,  gface_7,  gface_8,  gface_9,  gface_10,
 gface_11,  gface_12,  gface_13};
}
```

This can be compiled in the normal way to produce a ***girl_face_2.class*** compiled file.

## *Converting to CubicCurveTo for Display*

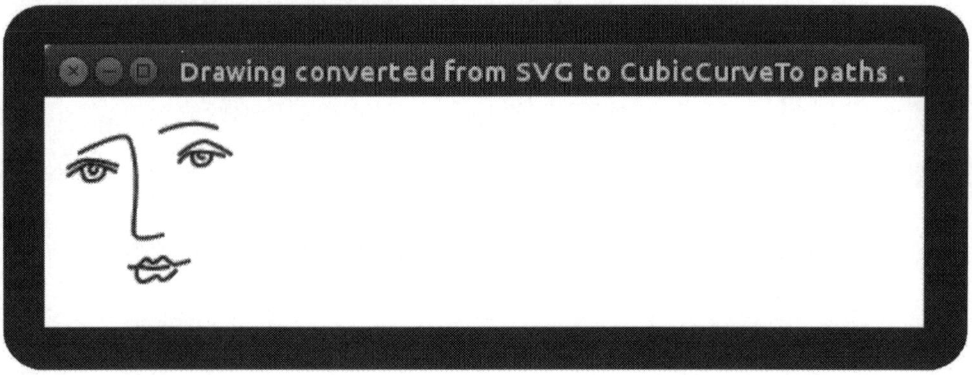


To exhibit this file we must compile and execute the following Program:

```
// CubicBezier_girlface_1.java
/*
The Collections of cubic Bezier positions is contained in "girl_face_2.java"
which has been compiled separately as a class in the same package.

The linear transforms of scaling, translation, rotation, skew,
veretical and horizontal flipping are demonstrated here.

Tested on: java version "java-8-oracle"
Author: Mike Ohlson de Fine
*/

import javafx.application.Application;
import javafx.stage.Stage;
import javafx.scene.*;
import javafx.scene.shape.*; // Graphic primitives library.
import javafx.scene.paint.*;
import java.lang.reflect.Array;
//=============================================================
public class CubicBezier_girlface_1 extends Application
{
   Path Points2paths(double[][] path_points, MoveTo  selected_moveTo,
double Stroke_width, Color kula)
   {
```

```
    /* Purpose: Convert a 2D array of Bezier points (from a SVG file) into a
JavaFX Cubic path.
            The MoveTo (start) is obtained from the
make_moveto( path_point_line0) method
            by prior arrangement.
      Applies to : One path - the raw cubic bezier points that will be used to
construct all the
               CubicCurveTos that make up the sequence of drawn
CubicCurveTo parts.
      The Output: An assembled path ready to be added to stage for display.
    */

    int num_cctos = Array.getLength(path_points) ; // Number of
CubicCurveTos making up the path.
    CubicCurveTo crv_pth1 =  new CubicCurveTo();   // The set fo curves for
a path.

    // Assemble one path.
    Path  path_n =  new Path();
    path_n.getElements().add(selected_moveTo); // Select the appropriate
start position.
    for (int j=0; j< num_cctos ; j++)
    {
      crv_pth1 = new CubicCurveTo(path_points[j][0], path_points[j][1],
path_points[j][2],
                        path_points[j][3], path_points[j][4], path_points[j][5]);

      path_n.getElements().add(crv_pth1);
      path_n.setStrokeWidth(Stroke_width);
      path_n.setStroke(kula);
    };
    return path_n ;
   }

//===========================================================
  MoveTo make_moveto(double[] path_point_line0)
    {
      double XX = path_point_line0[0] ;
      double YY = path_point_line0[1] ;
      MoveTo moveTo_out = new MoveTo(XX, YY);
      return moveTo_out ;
```

```
    }
//=================================================================

  public void start(Stage primaryStage)
  {
     girl_face_2 gface = new girl_face_2() ;  // The drawing composed of
many paths

     Group rootgroup = new Group();
     Path[] rand_paths =  new Path[6];

    Path line_path;
    double[][] cube_points;
    MoveTo moveTo1 = new MoveTo();
    int num_paths = Array.getLength(gface.all_points) ; // Number of paths.

    // Make every path visible.
    for (int i=0; i<num_paths ; i++)
    {
        // One path at a time is added to the rootgroup, root node.
        moveTo1 = make_moveto(gface.all_points[i][0]);
        line_path =  Points2paths(gface.all_points[i], moveTo1, 2,
Color.color(0.2, 0.2, 0.2));
        rootgroup.getChildren().addAll( line_path);
    }
 /
     Scene scene = new Scene(rootgroup, 900, 900);
     primaryStage.setTitle("Drawing converted from SVG to CubicCurveTo
paths .");
     primaryStage.setScene(scene);
     primaryStage.show();
  }
}
```

In chapter 20 we deal with another example like this where we explore methods of manipulating the geometry of images using Transforms.

# CHAPTER 13

## TEXT CONTROL

*"In typography, a typeface (also known as font family) is a set of one or more fonts each composed of glyphs that share common design features. Each font (size) of a typeface has a specific weight, style, condensation, width, slant, italicization, ornamentation, and designer or foundry."*

*"A glyph is an elemental symbol within an agreed set of symbols, intended to represent a readable character."* Wikipedia.

In this chapter we will cover:

- The Text class
- The fonts available on a particular computer
- How to see what the various fonts look like.
- Text alignment: center, left and right justification.
- Different font parameters.
- Transforms (scaling, rotation and shifting) on text.

Text, the written word, is simply a collection of images called typeface. There is no global standard. Different cultures have different symbols. We confine ourself to the alphabet of symbols used in the western world. The author apologizes for his limited scope because sadly he just another limited human.

Computer programming deals with the multitude of written symbols on earth with the introduction of Unicode. Unicode is an international encoding standard for

use with different languages and scripts, by which each letter, digit, or symbol is assigned a unique numeric value that applies across different platforms and programs.

The JavaFX Text class defines a node that displays a block of text.Paragraphs are separated by '\n' and the text is wrapped on paragraph boundaries.

## Constructors

**1. Text();** A basic instance of Text. The parameters can be supplied later.

2. **Text(x, y, text);** An instance positioned at the given coordinates and containing the given string of test.

3. **Text(text);** An instance containing the given string of test.

## Arrangement of text

We need to arrange text in lines and paragraphs to fit neatly into the space we provide on the display screen.

**New Lines.**

We create new lines in two cases:

1. A new line character '**\n**' in the text creates a new line causing the characters following the newline to start on the next line.

2. The Text class contains a wrappingWidth property, which is 0.0 by default. Its value is specified in pixels, not characters. If it is greater than zero, the text in each line is wrapped to at the specified pixel value.

**Line Spacing  and Alignment.**

The lineSpacing property specifies the vertical spacing in pixels between two lines. It is 0.0 by default.

The textAlignment property specifies the horizontal alignment of the text lines in the bounding box. The widest line defines the width of the bounding box. Its value has no effect in a single line Text node. Its value can be one of the constants of the textAlignment setting. The default value is *textAlignment.LEFT.* The options to choose from are LEFT, RIGHT, CENTER or JUSTIFY.

Aside from the Text class there are also Label, TextField and TextArea designed as user input mechanisms. These dealt with in chapters 18 and 19.

## A Simple Text Example:

```
// TextSimplest.java
/*
class: javafx.scene.text.Text
------------------------------------
Constructors:
1. Text(); A basic instance of Text. The parameters can be supplied later.
2. Text(x, y, text); A text instance positioned at the given coordinates and
containing the given string of text.
3. Text(text); The given string of test.

where:
x,y is the position of the start of the text.
text is the string of characters to be displayed.

Tested on: java version "java-8-oracle"
Author: Mike Ohlson de Fine
*/
import javafx.application.Application;
import javafx.scene.Scene;
import javafx.scene.text.Text;
import javafx.stage.Stage;
import javafx.scene.*;
```

```
public class TextSimplest extends Application
{
    public void start(Stage stage)
    {
        Group root = new Group();

        Text text1 = new Text(20,  10, "A Simple Display of Text");
        root.getChildren().addAll(text1);

        Scene scene = new Scene(root,300,80);
        stage.setScene(scene);
        stage.setTitle("A Simple Text Node.");
        stage.show();
    }
}
```

## What Fonts are Available on my Computer?

Most desktop and laptop computers have many, many typefaces (fonts) installed as part of any word-processor application. In addition it is easy to acquire hundreds of new fonts by downloading free one on the internet. It is useful to be able to discover what fonts are installed and then to see how they look when used.

The program below lists the fonts installed.

```
// TextListFonts1.java
/*
Display a list of all available fonts on this computer.
---------------------------------------------------

Tested on: java version "java-8-oracle"
Author: Mike Ohlson de Fine
*/
import javafx.application.Application;
import javafx.stage.Stage;
import javafx.scene.text.Font;
import java.util.List;

public class TextListFonts1 extends Application
```

```
{
  public void start(Stage stage)
  {
      List<String> familiesList = Font.getFamilies();
      System.out.println(familiesList);
     stage.show();  // Only for the convenience of exiting neatly.
  }
}
```

The output on the system terminal on one operating system particular system (Ubuntu, Linux) was:

*[Abyssinica SIL, American Brewery Rough Demo, Beautiful Every Time, Carnivalee Freakshow, Christmas Season, Circus, Colored Crayons, DK Cool Crayon, DejaVu Sans, DejaVu Sans Condensed, DejaVu Sans Light, DejaVu Sans Mono, DejaVu Serif, DejaVu Serif Condensed, Droid Arabic Kufi, Droid Arabic Naskh, Droid Naskh Shift Alt, Droid Sans, Droid Sans Arabic, Droid Sans Armenian, Droid Sans Ethiopic, Droid Sans Fallback, Droid Sans Georgian, Droid Sans Hebrew, Droid Sans Japanese, Droid Sans Mono, Droid Serif, FreeMono, FreeSans, FreeSerif, Garuda, KacstArt, KacstBook, KacstDecorative, KacstDigital, KacstFarsi, KacstLetter, KacstNaskh, KacstOffice, KacstOne, KacstPen, KacstPoster, KacstQurn, KacstScreen, KacstTitle, KacstTitleL, Kedage, Khmer OS, Khmer OS System, Kinnari, LKLUG, Laksaman, Liberation Mono, Liberation Sans, Liberation Sans Narrow, Liberation Serif, Little Lord Fontleroy NF, Lohit Bengali, Lohit Devanagari, Lohit Gujarati, Lohit Punjabi, Lohit Tamil, Loma, Lucida Bright, Lucida Sans, Lucida Sans Typewriter, Luna's Handwriting , Mallige, MathJax_AMS, MathJax_Caligraphic, MathJax_Fraktur, MathJax_Main, MathJax_Math, MathJax_SansSerif, MathJax_Script, MathJax_Size1, MathJax_Size2, MathJax_Size3, MathJax_Size4, MathJax_Typewriter, MathJax_WinChrome, MathJax_WinIE6, Meera, Monospaced, Mukti Narrow, My Hands are Holding You, NanumBarunGothic, NanumGothic, NanumMyeongjo, Norasi, OpenSymbol, Padauk, Padauk Book, Phetsarath OT, Pothana2000, Purisa, Rachana, Rekha, Romantiques, STIX, STIX Math, STIXGeneral, STIXIntegralsD, STIXIntegralsSm, STIXIntegralsUp, STIXIntegralsUpD, STIXIntegralsUpSm, STIXNonUnicode, STIXSizeFiveSym, STIXSizeFourSym, STIXSizeOneSym, STIXSizeThreeSym, STIXSizeTwoSym, STIXVariants, Saab, SansSerif, Sawasdee, Serif, Symbola, System, TakaoPGothic, Tibetan Machine Uni, Tlwg Typist, Tlwg Typo, TlwgMono, TlwgTypewriter, UNIVERSAL-COLLEGE, Ubuntu, Ubuntu Condensed, Ubuntu Light, Ubuntu Mono,*

*Umpush, Vemana2000, Victorian Parlor Vintage Alternate_free, Waree, cmex10, cmmi10, cmr10, cmsy10, esint10, eufm10, gargi, mry_KacstQurn, msam10, msbm10, rsfs10, stmary10, utkal, wasy10]*

## *How can we See the Fonts?*

Here we have selected 10 interesting looking fonts. All the fonts available on our computer could be displayed using this program. All that needs to change is the contents of the textArray.

```
// TextShowFonts2.java
/*
Inspect the appearance of fonts.
Note that a "null" font gives us a visually acceptable default font.
----------------------------------
Tested on: java version "java-8-oracle"
Author: Mike Ohlson de Fine
*/
import javafx.application.Application;
import javafx.scene.Group;
import javafx.scene.Scene;
import javafx.scene.paint.Color;
import javafx.stage.Stage;
import javafx.scene.text.Font;
import javafx.scene.text.FontPosture;
import javafx.scene.text.FontWeight;
import javafx.scene.text.Text;
```

```
public class TextShowFonts2 extends Application
{
  public void start(Stage stage)
  {
    String[] textArray = {"The Quick Brown Fox Jumps Over The Lazy
Dog","Beautiful Every Time",
                    "Abyssinica SIL","American Brewery Rough Demo",
"Carnivalee Freakshow",
                    "Christmas Season", "Circus", "DK Cool Crayon",
"MathJax_Caligraphic",
                    "Little Lord Fontleroy NF", "Victorian Parlor Vintage
Alternate_free", "null"} ;
    String font = "  font =  ";

    Group root = new Group() ;
    System.out.println("textArray.length: " + textArray.length );  // Checking
array length.

    // Because our text objects are arrays we can process large numbers of
objects compactly.
    Text[] txt = new Text[textArray.length];

    for (int i=0 ; i<(textArray.length)-1 ; i++)
    { txt[i] =  new Text(font  + textArray[i+1] + " :: " + textArray[0] );
      txt[i].setFont(Font.font(textArray[i+1], 40));
      txt[i].setY((i+1)*40);
      root.getChildren().add(txt[i]);
    } ;

    Scene scene = new Scene(root, 1000, 460);
    stage.setTitle("A display of some interesting fonts.");
    stage.setScene(scene);
    stage.show();
  }
}
```

## All the other fonts, in bite-size chunks.

Examining all the fonts available on our system is overwhelming. To break the task up into manageable parts we have resorted to programmers trick of commenting out pieces of code we do not want to execute but may want to use at a later time.

Any instructions inside the block comment symbols /*   ... * /  will be ignored by the Java compiler. So if there is a particular bunch of text we want to look at we adjust the location of the /* .. */ block comment symbols so that the chunk of code we are interested in does not appear between the block comment symbols while the rest does.

```
/ / TextShowFonts3.java
/*
Inspect the appearance of fonts.
Note that a "null" font gives us a visually acceptable default font.

Tested on: java version "java-8-oracle"
Author: Mike Ohlson de Fine
*/
import javafx.application.Application;
import javafx.scene.Group;
import javafx.scene.Scene;
import javafx.scene.paint.Color;
import javafx.stage.Stage;
import javafx.scene.text.Font;
import javafx.scene.text.FontPosture;
import javafx.scene.text.FontWeight;
import javafx.scene.text.Text;

public class TextShowFonts3 extends Application
{

  public void start(Stage stage)
  {
/*
"Abyssinica SIL","American Brewery Rough Demo","Beautiful Every
Time","Carnivalee Freakshow","Christmas Season",
"Circus","Colored Crayons","DK Cool Crayon","
DejaVu Sans","DejaVu Sans Condensed","DejaVu Sans Light","DejaVu Sans
Mono","DejaVu Serif","DejaVu Serif Condensed",
"Droid Arabic Kufi","Droid Arabic Naskh","Droid Naskh Shift Alt","Droid
Sans","Droid Sans Arabic",
"Droid Sans Armenian","Droid Sans Ethiopic","Droid Sans Fallback","Droid
Sans Georgian","Droid Sans Hebrew",
```

*"Droid Sans Japanese","Droid Sans Mono","Droid Serif",*

*"FreeMono","FreeSans","FreeSerif","Garuda","KacstArt","KacstBook","KacstDecorative",*
*"KacstDigital","KacstFarsi","KacstLetter","KacstNaskh","KacstOffice","KacstOne","KacstPen",*
*"KacstPoster","KacstQurn","KacstScreen","KacstTitle","KacstTitleL",*
*"Kedage","Khmer OS","Khmer OS System","Kinnari","LKLUG",*

*"Laksaman","Liberation Mono","Liberation Sans","Liberation Sans Narrow","Liberation Serif",*
*"Little Lord Fontleroy NF","Lohit Bengali","Lohit Devanagari","Lohit Gujarati","Lohit Punjabi","Lohit Tamil",*
*"Loma","Lucida Bright","Lucida Sans","Lucida Sans Typewriter","Luna's Handwriting ","Mallige",*

*"MathJax_AMS",*
*"MathJax_Caligraphic","MathJax_Fraktur","MathJax_Main","MathJax_Math","MathJax_SansSerif","MathJax_Script",*
*"MathJax_Size1","MathJax_Size2","MathJax_Size3","MathJax_Size4","MathJax_Typewriter","MathJax_WinChrome",*

*"MathJax_WinIE6","Meera","Monospaced","Mukti Narrow","My Hands are Holding You",*

*"NanumBarunGothic","NanumGothic",*
*"NanumMyeongjo","Norasi","OpenSymbol","Padauk","Padauk Book","Phetsarath OT","Pothana2000","Purisa","Rachana",*
*"Rekha","Romantiques","STIX","STIX Math","STIXGeneral","STIXIntegralsD","STIXIntegralsSm","STIXIntegralsUp",*
*"STIXIntegralsUpD","STIXIntegralsUpSm","STIXNonUnicode","STIXSizeFiveSym","STIXSizeFourSym","STIXSizeOneSym",*
*"STIXSizeThreeSym","STIXSizeTwoSym","STIXVariants","Saab","SansSerif","Sawasdee","Serif","Symbola","System",*

*"TakaoPGothic","Tibetan Machine Uni","Tlwg Typist","Tlwg Typo","TlwgMono","TlwgTypewriter","UNIVERSAL-COLLEGE",*
*"Ubuntu","Ubuntu Condensed","Ubuntu Light","Ubuntu Mono","Umpush","Vemana2000",*

```
"Victorian Parlor Vintage Alternate_free","Waree","
cmex10","cmmi10","cmr10","cmsy10","esint10","eufm10",
"gargi","mry_KacstQurn","msam10","msbm10","rsfs10","stmary10","utkal","w
asy10"}


    String[] textArray = {"The Quick Brown Fox Jumps Over The Lazy
Dog","Droid Arabic Kufi","Droid Arabic Naskh","Droid Naskh Shift
Alt","Droid Sans","Droid Sans Arabic",
"Droid Sans Armenian","Droid Sans Ethiopic","Droid Sans Fallback","Droid
Sans Georgian","Droid Sans Hebrew",
"Droid Sans Japanese","Droid Sans Mono","Droid Serif"} ;

    String[] textArray =
{"FreeMono","FreeSans","FreeSerif","Garuda","KacstArt","KacstBook","Kacst
Decorative",
"KacstDigital","KacstFarsi","KacstLetter","KacstNaskh","KacstOffice","Kacst
One","KacstPen",
"KacstPoster","KacstQurn","KacstScreen","KacstTitle","KacstTitleL",
"Kedage","Khmer OS","Khmer OS System","Kinnari","LKLUG"} ;
*/
    String[] textArray =
{"FreeMono","FreeSans","FreeSerif","Garuda","KacstArt","KacstBook","Kacst
Decorative",
"KacstDigital","KacstFarsi","KacstLetter","KacstNaskh","KacstOffice","Kacst
One","KacstPen",
"KacstPoster","KacstQurn","KacstScreen","KacstTitle","KacstTitleL",
"Kedage","Khmer OS","Khmer OS
System","Kinnari","LKLUG","Laksaman","Liberation Mono","Liberation
Sans","Liberation Sans Narrow","Liberation Serif",
"Little Lord Fontleroy NF","Lohit Bengali","Lohit Devanagari","Lohit
Gujarati","Lohit Punjabi","Lohit Tamil",
"Loma","Lucida Bright","Lucida Sans","Lucida Sans Typewriter","Luna's
Handwriting ","Mallige"} ;

/*
    String[] textArray = {"MathJax_AMS",
"MathJax_Caligraphic","MathJax_Fraktur","MathJax_Main","MathJax_Mat
h","MathJax_SansSerif","MathJax_Script",
"MathJax_Size1","MathJax_Size2","MathJax_Size3","MathJax_Size4","Math
Jax_Typewriter","MathJax_WinChrome",
```

```
"MathJax_WinIE6","Meera","Monospaced","Mukti Narrow","My Hands are
Holding You"} ;
/*

String[] textArray = {"NanumBarunGothic","NanumGothic",

"NanumMyeongjo","Norasi","OpenSymbol","Padauk","Padauk
Book","Phetsarath OT","Pothana2000","Purisa","Rachana",
"Rekha","Romantiques","STIX","STIX
Math","STIXGeneral","STIXIntegralsD","STIXIntegralsSm","STIXIntegralsU
p",
"STIXIntegralsUpD","STIXIntegralsUpSm","STIXNonUnicode","STIXSizeFi
veSym","STIXSizeFourSym","STIXSizeOneSym",
"STIXSizeThreeSym","STIXSizeTwoSym","STIXVariants","Saab","SansSerif
","Sawasdee","Serif","Symbola","System"} ;

String[] textArray = {"NanumBarunGothic","NanumGothic",
"NanumMyeongjo","Norasi","OpenSymbol","Padauk","Padauk
Book","Phetsarath OT","Pothana2000","Purisa","Rachana",
"Rekha","Romantiques","STIX","STIX
Math","STIXGeneral","STIXIntegralsD","STIXIntegralsSm","STIXIntegralsU
p",
"STIXIntegralsUpD","STIXIntegralsUpSm","STIXNonUnicode","STIXSizeFi
veSym","STIXSizeFourSym","STIXSizeOneSym",
"STIXSizeThreeSym","STIXSizeTwoSym","STIXVariants","Saab","SansSerif
","Sawasdee","Serif","Symbola","System"} ;


String[] textArray = {"TakaoPGothic","Tibetan Machine Uni","Tlwg
Typist","Tlwg Typo","TlwgMono","TlwgTypewriter","UNIVERSAL-
COLLEGE",
"Ubuntu","Ubuntu Condensed","Ubuntu Light","Ubuntu
Mono","Umpush","Vemana2000",
"Victorian Parlor Vintage Alternate_free","Waree","
cmex10","cmmi10","cmr10","cmsy10","esint10","eufm10",
"gargi","mry_KacstQurn","msam10","msbm10","rsfs10","stmary10","utkal","w
asy10" };
*/
    String font = "  font =  ";

    Group root = new Group() ;
```

```
    System.out.println("textArray.length: " + textArray.length );  // Checking on length of array.

    // Because our text objects are arrays we can process large numbers of objects compactly.
    Text[] txt = new Text[textArray.length];

    for (int i=0 ; i<(textArray.length)-1 ; i++)
    { txt[i] =  new Text(font  + textArray[i+1] + " :: " + textArray[0] );
      txt[i].setFont(Font.font(textArray[i+1], 20));
      txt[i].setY((i+1)*20);
      root.getChildren().add(txt[i]);
    } ;

    Scene scene = new Scene(root, 1000,900);
    stage.setTitle("A display of some interesting fonts.");
    stage.setScene(scene);
    stage.show();
  }
}
```

## Text Alignment

```
// TextAlignment1.java
/*
Arc : class: javafx.scene.text.Text
--------------------------------------
An instance of Text with given position.
Constructors:
1. Text(); A basic instance of Text. The parameters can be supplied later.
2. Text(x, y, text); An instance positioned at the given coordinates and
```

```
containing the given string of test.
3. Text(text); An instance containing the given string of test.

where:
x,y is the position of the start of the text.
text is the string of characters to be displayed.

Tested on: java version "java-8-oracle"
Author: Mike Ohlson de Fine
*/
import javafx.application.Application;
import javafx.scene.Scene;
import javafx.scene.text.Text;
import javafx.stage.Stage;
import javafx.scene.*;

public class TextAlignment1 extends Application
{
    public void start(Stage stage)
    {
        Group root = new Group();

        Text text1 = new Text(10,  20, "One");
        Text text2 = new Text(20,  30, "Two");
        Text text3 = new Text(30,  40, "Three");
        root.getChildren().addAll(text1, text2, text3);

        Scene scene = new Scene(root,300,60);
        stage.setScene(scene);
        stage.setTitle("A Simple Text Node.");
        stage.show();
    }
}
```

# Justification: Left, Right or Center

## Left Justification

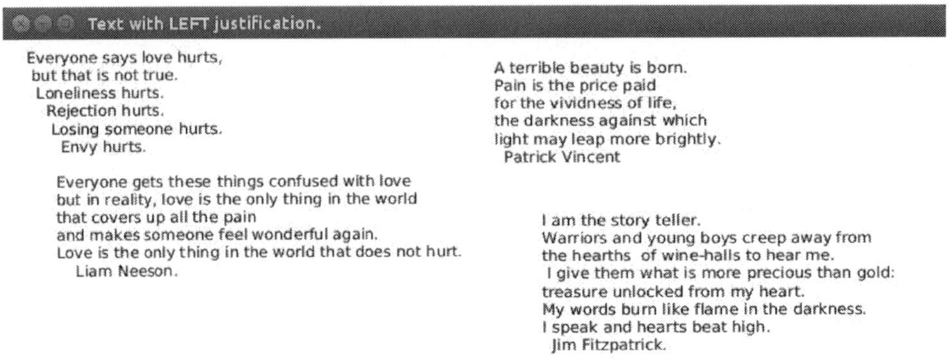


## Right Justification

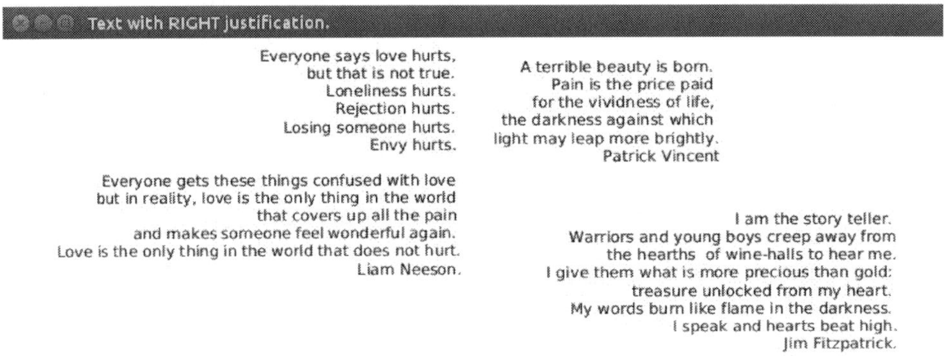


## Center Justification

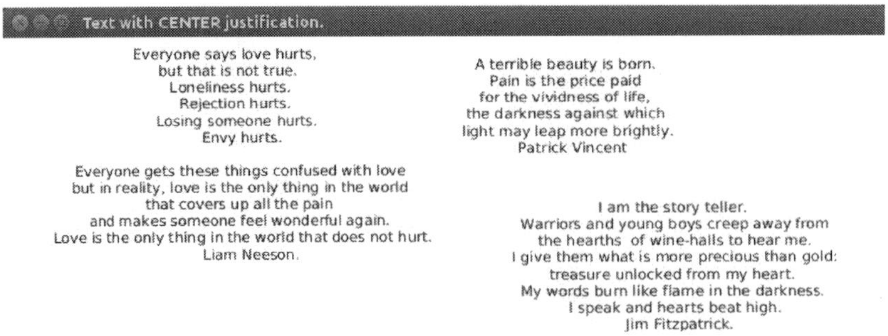

```
//TextAlignment_Left_default.java
/*
Left justification is the default.
(default = the option that is used if we do not specify anything).

Tested on: java version "java-8-oracle"
Author: Mike Ohlson de Fine
*/
import javafx.application.Application;
import javafx.scene.Scene;
import javafx.scene.text.Text;
import javafx.stage.Stage;
import javafx.scene.*;

public class TextAlignment_Left_default extends Application
{
	public void start(Stage stage)
	{
		Group root = new Group();

		Text text1 = new Text(10,  20, "Everyone says love hurts, \n but that
is not true. \n  Loneliness hurts. \n    Rejection hurts. \n      Losing someone
hurts. \n        Envy hurts. \n \n       Everyone gets these things confused with
love \n     but in reality, love is the only thing in the world \n    that covers up
all the pain \n   and makes someone feel wonderful again. \n  Love is the only
thing in the world that does not hurt.\n          Liam Neeson.");

		Text text2 = new Text(300,  30, "A terrible beauty is born. \nPain is
the price paid for the vividness of life, \nthe darkness against which light
may leap more brightly.\n  Patrick Vincent");

		Text text3 = new Text(400,  100, "I am the story teller. \nWarriors
and young boys creep away from\nthe hearths  of wine-halls to hear me.\n I
give them what is more precious than gold: \ntreasure unlocked from my
heart. \nMy words burn like flame in the darkness. \nI speak and hearts beat
high.\n  Jim Fitzpatrick.");
		root.getChildren().addAll(text1, text2, text3);

		Scene scene = new Scene(root,700,250);
		stage.setScene(scene);
```

```
        stage.setTitle("Text with default justification (LEFT).");
        stage.show();
    }
}
```

## Test the three Options

As we did near the beginning of this chapter we use the programmers trick of commenting out lines of code that we do not want to use immediately but want to preserve the option of using later. In this case we only comment out single lines using the // symbol

```
/ / TextAlignment_all.java
/*
Justification options:
LEFT, RIGHT, CENTER, JUSTIFY.
The "JUSTIFY" flag does not mean much.

Tested on: java version "java-8-oracle"
Author: Mike Ohlson de Fine
*/
import javafx.application.Application;
import javafx.scene.Scene;
import javafx.stage.Stage;
import javafx.scene.*;
import javafx.scene.text.Text;
import javafx.scene.text.TextAlignment;

public class TextAlignment_all extends Application
{
    public void start(Stage stage)
    {
        Group root = new Group();

        Text text1 = new Text(20,  20, "Everyone says love hurts, \n but that
is not true. \n  Loneliness hurts. \n    Rejection hurts. \n      Losing someone
hurts. \n       Envy hurts. \n \n       Everyone gets these things confused with
love \n       but in reality, love is the only thing in the world \n       that covers
up all the pain \n       and makes someone feel wonderful again. \n       Love is
```

```
the only thing in the world that does not hurt.\n          Liam Neeson.");
            //text1.setTextAlignment(TextAlignment.RIGHT);
            //text1.setTextAlignment(TextAlignment.LEFT);
            //text1.setTextAlignment(TextAlignment.CENTER);
            text1.setTextAlignment(TextAlignment.JUSTIFY); // Default -
identical to LEFT justification.

        Text text2 = new Text(420,  30, "A terrible beauty is born. \nPain is
the price paid \nfor the vividness of life, \nthe darkness against which
\nlight may leap more brightly.\n  Patrick Vincent");
            //text2.setTextAlignment(TextAlignment.RIGHT);
            //text2.setTextAlignment(TextAlignment.LEFT);
            //text2.setTextAlignment(TextAlignment.CENTER);
            text2.setTextAlignment(TextAlignment.JUSTIFY);// Default -
identical to LEFT justification.


        Text text3 = new Text(460,  160, "I am the story teller. \nWarriors
and young boys creep away from\nthe hearths  of wine-halls to hear me.\n I
give them what is more precious than gold: \ntreasure unlocked from my
heart. \nMy words burn like flame in the darkness. \nI speak and hearts beat
high.\n  Jim Fitzpatrick.");
            //text3.setTextAlignment(TextAlignment.RIGHT);
            //text3.setTextAlignment(TextAlignment.LEFT);
            //text3.setTextAlignment(TextAlignment.CENTER);
            text3.setTextAlignment(TextAlignment.JUSTIFY);// Default -
identical to LEFT justification.


        root.getChildren().addAll(text1, text2, text3);

        Scene scene = new Scene(root,800,300);
        stage.setScene(scene);
        stage.setTitle("Text with JUSTIFY justification.");
        stage.show();

    }
}
```

# Text Attributes: Size, stroke and fill color

```
// TextAttributes1.java
/*
The attributes are stroke color, fill color, line width (stroke), typeface and size.

Tested on: java version "java-8-oracle"
Author: Mike Ohlson de Fine
*/
import javafx.application.Application;
import javafx.scene.Group;
import javafx.scene.Scene;
import javafx.scene.paint.Color;
import javafx.stage.Stage;
import javafx.scene.text.Font;
import javafx.scene.text.FontPosture;
import javafx.scene.text.FontWeight;
import javafx.scene.text.Text;

public class TextAttributes1 extends Application
{

  public void start(Stage stage)
  {

    Text text = new Text();                //Creating a Text object.

    int type_size = 50 ;
    //Setting font to the text.
    text.setFont(Font.font("verdana", FontWeight.BOLD,
FontPosture.REGULAR, type_size));
    text.setX(30);                         // Position of the text.
    text.setY(80);
    text.setFill(Color.YELLOW);            //Setting the color of the fill.
```

```
    text.setStrokeWidth(4);                          // Outline thickness.
    text.setStroke(Color.BLUE);                      // Outline color
    text.setText("Verdana in fancy clothes");        //The actual text string.

    Group root = new Group(text);                    // The Group object to which
the text belongs.
    Scene scene = new Scene(root, 800, 800);         //The scene to for the display
of objects.

   stage.setTitle("Setting verdana font: Style, size, color, outline (width and
color).");
    stage.setScene(scene);                           //Adding the scene to the
stage.
    stage.show();                                    //Display the contents of the
stage.
  }
}
```

## Geometry Transforms on TextAlignment

As we have done previously we test various options separately by commenting out instructions that would like to experiment with later.

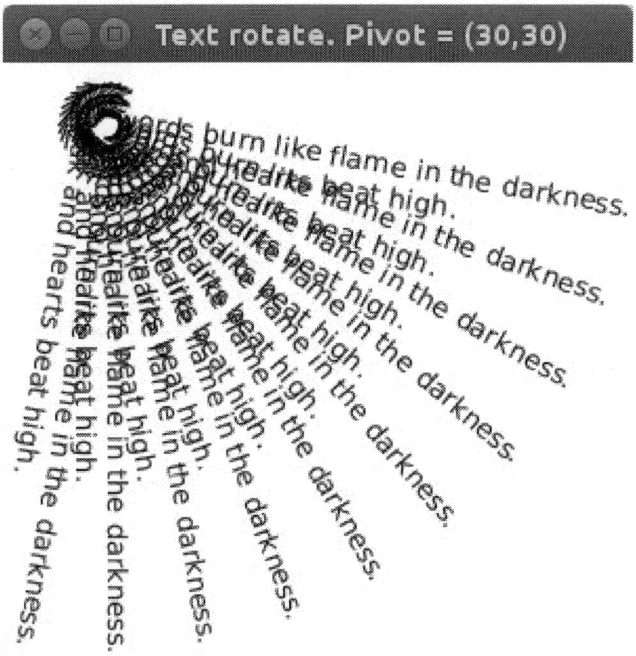

```
// TextTransform1.java
/*
Rotate(alphs, pivotX, pivotY);
Translate(x, y);
Shear(ShearX, ShearY);
Scale(ScaleX, scaleY);

Tested on: java version "java-8-oracle"
Author: Mike Ohlson de Fine
*/
import javafx.application.Application;
import javafx.scene.Scene;
import javafx.stage.Stage;
import javafx.scene.*;
import javafx.scene.text.Text;
import javafx.scene.transform.Rotate;
import javafx.scene.transform.Translate;
import javafx.scene.transform.Shear;
import javafx.scene.transform.Scale;

public class TextTransform1 extends Application

{
    public void start(Stage stage)
    {
        Group root = new Group();
         String string1 =  "My words burn.";
         Text text0 = new Text(0,10,string1);
         root.getChildren().addAll(text0);

         double alpha = 10;
         double pivotX = 100;
         double pivotY = 100;
         double scaleX = 1;
         double scaleY = 1;
         double shiftX = 10;
         double shiftY = 10;
         double shearX = 8;
         double shearY = 12;
```

```
        for (int i = 0; i<10; i++)
        {
       Text text1 = new Text(100,  10, string1);
       Text text2 = new Text(10,  10, string1);
       Text text3 = new Text(10,  10, string1);
       Text text4 = new Text(10,  10, string1);

        text1.getTransforms().add(new Rotate(alpha, pivotX, pivotY));  //
angle, pivot X, pivot Y.
        //text2.getTransforms().add(new Translate(shiftX, shiftY));  //
Shift horizontally and vertically.
        //text3.getTransforms().add(new Scale(scaleX, scaleY));  //
Change size.
        //text3.getTransforms().add(new Shear(shearX, shearY));  //
Change slant.
        alpha +=10 ;
        shiftX += 5;
        shiftY += 3;
        scaleX += 0.2;
        scaleY += 0.3;
        shearX += 1.2;
        shearY += 1.5;
        root.getChildren().addAll(text1);
        //root.getChildren().addAll(text2);
        //root.getChildren().addAll(text3);
        //root.getChildren().addAll(text4);
        }

       Scene scene = new Scene(root,600,600);
       stage.setScene(scene);
       stage.setTitle("Text Transforms: Rotate, Translate, Scale, Shear");
       stage.show();
   }
}
```

# CHAPTER 14

## IMAGE

In this chapter we will cover:

- All high definition images like photographs.
- Internet image formats like jpg, png, tiff and gif.
- Using transparency.
- Stacking images on top of each other.

**JavaFX** allows us to work with all popular digital image formats like jpg, png, and gif. But not tiff. PNG was designed to replace TIFF.

## The Image Class

The Image class deals with graphical images and is used for loading images from a specified URL or disk file. Loading am image loads the image or image stream into an area of RAM but does not display it on the screen. Displaying it on the screen is done by an ImageView method. A URL is the internet web-address of an image. A URL can also be the file address of an object on our hard drive storage disk.

Images can be resized as they are loaded (for example to reduce the amount of memory consumed by the image). The application can specify the quality of filtering used when scaling, and whether or not to preserve the original image's aspect ratio. Aspect ratio is the ratio of width to height.

All URLs supported by the URL standard can be passed to the image class constructor. If the passed string is not a valid URL, but a directory path instead, the Image is searched on the classpath in that case. Classpath is a parameter in the Java Virtual Machine or the Java compiler that specifies the location of user-defined classes and packages. The classpath is normally set up automatically when we install the Java complier. It can be altered on the command-line.

## Constructors. There are four constructors available.

**1. Image(*input_stream*)**

This constructs an Image with content loaded from the specified input stream or location. The word stream suggests that the image data we wish to use flows down a data pipe of some kind from the internet or from some local storage device like a spinning disk or memory stick. The class that handles ***input_stream*** is the *java.io.InputStream class.*

**2. Image(url, backgroundLoading)**

This constructs an Image with content loaded from the specified URL. *BackgroundLoading* is boolean flag to specify that the image should be loading in the background as a lower priority activity.

**3. Image(*input_stream*, requestedWidth, requestedHeight, preserveRatio, smooth)**

Thia will load the image and adjust its size to the desired width and height aspect ratio.

***PreserveRatio*** is a boolean flag to preserve the aspect ratio of the original image when scaling to fit the image within the bounding box provided by width and height.

If set to true, it affects the dimensions of this Image in the following way:

- •If only width is set, height is scaled to preserve the aspect ratio
- •If only height is set, width is scaled to preserve the aspect ratio
- •If both are set, they both may be scaled to get the best fit in a width by height rectangle while preserving the original aspect ratio

***smooth*** is a boolean flag which indicates whether to use a better *quality* filtering algorithm or a *faster* algorithm when scaling this image to fit within the bounding box provided by width and height. If not initialized or set to true a better *quality* filtering will be used, otherwise a faster but lesser quality filtering will be used.

**4. Image( url, requestedWidth, requestedHeight, preserveRatio, smooth, backgroundLoading)**

Construct a new Image with the specified parameters as described above.

# The ImageView Class

The ImageView is a node, similar to a group, that is used for painting (displaying) loaded images. An image is loaded with Image class and viewed with ImageView.

# Simple Viewing an Image with StackPane

```
// ShowImageSimple1.java
/*
class: javafx.scene.image.ImageView
-------------------------------------------
Constructors
1. ImageView(); Create a new image object.
2. ImageView(image); Create an image object and Identify the image to be
```

```
viewed.
3. ImageView(url); An image object and identified by its url (web address).

Tested on: java version "java-8-oracle"
Author: Mike Ohlson de Fine.
*/

import javafx.application.Application;
import javafx.scene.Scene;
import javafx.scene.image.Image;
import javafx.scene.image.ImageView;
import javafx.scene.layout.StackPane;
import javafx.stage.Stage;

public class ShowImageSimple1 extends Application
{
   public void start(Stage stage)
   {
   stage.setTitle("Load jpg Image");
   StackPane stakp = new StackPane();

   Image bird_image = new Image("mossA_200.jpg");
   ImageView imview1 = new ImageView(bird_image);
   imview1.setImage(bird_image);
  stakp.getChildren().add(imview1);

   Scene scene = new Scene(stakp);
   stage.setScene(scene);
   stage.show();
   }
}
```

## Using Transparency

When images have the normal visible rectangular background, the background of the images will obscure each other

**Gifs and Gif animations**

GIFs have a loop flag hidden inside the file which tells them to either play in a loop or not to play in a loop. It should be possible to modify the GIF file's loop property.

JavaFX does not support animated PNGs (called "APNG") which would support more than 256 colors. So the automatic image animation capabilities are limited. It is best

for the programmer to control animation using Java instructions. This will be the subject of the next book in this series.

## Image Processing and Filters

Image are stored in computer memories and hard drives as digital data. Software decoders rasterize the image data into rows of color pixels that can be seen on the computer display, on a television set or on a digital printer. The rasterized image becomes a grid of pixels, each of which has a number of bits to designate its color equal to the color depth of the device displaying it.

The image file format may store data in uncompressed, compressed, or vector formats. Throughout this book we have been using vector image formats. Once rasterized, an image becomes a grid of pixels, each of which has a number of bits to designate its color equal to the color depth of the device displaying it.

### *Image Formats: jpg, tiff, gif, png*

The PNG, JPEG, and GIF formats are most often used to display images on the Internet.

## Compression of Images

Images are usually compressed or made to occupy less memory in various ways.

A compression algorithm stores either an exact representation or an approximation of the original image in a smaller number of bytes that can be expanded back to its uncompressed form with a corresponding decompression algorithm. Images with the same number of pixels and color depth can have very different compressed file size. With some compression formats, images that are less complex may result in smaller compressed file sizes. A certain amount of detail is usually lost after compression. The original high resolution image cannot be recovered completely from the compressed image. However, graphically simple images (i.e. images with large continuous regions of a single color can be losslessly compressed into a GIF or PNG format and result in a smaller file size than a lossy JPG format.

### 1. jpg or jpeg

(Joint Photographic Experts Group) is a lossy compression method.

Nearly every digital camera can save images in the JPEG/JFIF format, which supports eight-bit grayscale images and 24-bit color images (eight bits each for red, green, and blue). JPEG applies lossy compression to images, which can result in a significant reduction of the file size. Applications can determine the degree of compression to apply. The amount of compression affects the visual quality of the result.

## 2. tiff

(Tagged Image File Format). Tiff images do not work on JavaFX. If we need to use tif format images they should first be converted into .png or .jpg images first.

The tiff format is a flexible format that normally saves eight bits or sixteen bits per color (red, green, blue) for 24-bit and 48-bit totals, respectively. The tiff structure was designed to be easily extendible, and many vendors have introduced their own proprietary special-purpose tags – with the result that no one reader handles every flavor of TIFF file. TIFFs can be lossy or lossless, depending on the technique chosen for storing the pixel data. TIFF image format is not widely supported by web browsers. TIFF remains widely accepted as a photograph file standard in the printing business. TIFF can handle device-specific color spaces, such as the CMYK defined by a particular set of printing press inks.

## 3. gif

(Graphic Interchange Format). The format supports up to 8 bit per pixel for each each of 256 different colors chosen from the24 bit RGB color space. It also allows animation. These palette limitations make the GIF format less suitable for reproducing color photographs and other images with continuous color, but it is well-suited for simpler images such as graphics or logos with solid areas of color. So it is good for line art (such as one- or two-color logos), simple drawings, animations, and basically any image that has no gradients or blends. GIF is a good format when you want to display an image with a transparent background.

## 4. png

(Portable Network Graphics) file format was created as a free, open-source alternative to GIF. The PNG file format supports eight-bit paletted images (with optional transparency for all palette colors) and 24-bit truecolor (16 million colors) or 48-bit truecolor with and without alpha channel - while GIF supports only 256 colors and a single transparent color.

Compared to JPEG, PNG excels when the image has large, uniformly colored areas. PNG is well-suited to storing images during the editing process because of its lossless compression.

PNG provides a patent-free replacement for GIF (though GIF is itself now patent-free), and can also replace many common uses of TIFF. Indexed-color, grayscale, and truecolor images are supported, plus an optional alpha channel.

## Others

The bmp file format handles graphic files within the Microsoft Windows OS. Typically, BMP files are uncompressed, and therefore large and lossless; their advantage is their simple structure and wide acceptance in Windows programs.

## Image Types that work in JavaFX

JPG, GIF and PNG images work on JavaFX. The following program demonstrates this.

```
// ShowImage_jpg_gif_png.java
/*
Displays of image format, png, jpg, gif(animated).

Tested on: java version "java-8-oracle"
Author: Mike Ohlson de Fine
*/
import javafx.application.Application;
import javafx.scene.Group;
import javafx.scene.Scene;
import javafx.scene.image.Image;
import javafx.scene.image.ImageView;
import javafx.scene.layout.HBox;
import javafx.scene.paint.Color;
import javafx.stage.Stage;

public class ShowImage_jpg_gif_png extends Application
{
    public void start(Stage stage)
    {

        Image parkrd_image = new Image("park_road_1.png");
        Image bird_image = new Image("bird_aztec_100.jpg");
        Image grommet_image = new Image("tri_grommet.gif");

        // Simple ImageView displays the image as is (no adjustment of size).
        ImageView imvw1 = new ImageView();
        imvw1.setImage(parkrd_image);

        ImageView imvw2 = new ImageView();
        imvw2.setImage(bird_image);

        ImageView imvw3 = new ImageView();
        imvw3.setImage(grommet_image);

        Group root = new Group();
        Scene scene = new Scene(root);
        scene.setFill(Color.BLACK);
        HBox box = new HBox();
        box.getChildren().add(imvw1);
```

```
    box.getChildren().add(imvw2);
    box.getChildren().add(imvw3);
    root.getChildren().add(box);

    stage.setTitle("ImageViews: a jpg, an animated gif and a png");
    stage.setWidth(50); // These values are overriden to display the Images
    stage.setHeight(50);
    stage.setScene(scene);
    stage.sizeToScene();
    stage.show();
}
}
```

# CHAPTER 15

## LAYOUT

In this chapter we deal with the following:

- Absolute Layout
- FlowPane
- TilePane
- StackPane
- GridPane
- AnchorPane
- BorderPane
- Hbox
- Vbox
- DialogPane

- TextPane

## Layout Control

Layout is the word used to describe how to arrange a collection of graphic objects on a surface. In the particular context of JavaFX layout refers to how we decide to control arrangements in our scene that is presented on a stage.

# The Layout Of All JavaFX Programs

There are three main objects that get our program onto the screen. These are three containers that fit together like boxes inside other boxes. The stage in a theater and the performances presented on the stage are a neat metaphor for getting our heads around the relationships between the parts.

- The Stage – This is the outer shell of our application and contains the entire program
- The Scene – The scene is where visible objects are shown. Think of watching a play (on a stage) and when something is happening you are watching a scene.
- When the story changes, the play goes to a new and different scene with different actors, backdrop and props. In the program, when we want to switch to another view, we can instruct the Stage to *show* a different Scene.
- The Root Pane/Container – The objects for display are arranged on a board called a pane. This pane object holds all the parts to be shown, like buttons, labels, textfields, images, shapes etc. Depending on how we want to arrange the graphic components our application, the root container can be represented by a number of JavaFX containers such as the StackPane, GridPane, BorderPane, FlowPane, and some others. GridPane,

BorderPane and FlowPane are similar because they are single sheets on which objects are positioned according to rules. The different panes have different rules and different instruction syntax.

In this chapter we will work mainly with images (pictures), labels and geometric shapes. If we want to manipulate and control images we have to do it by controlling recognized JavaFX nodes.

In the previous chapter on Images we saw how to use the Image class to identify and locate images (drawings and photographs) and then to use the ImageView class to attach our images to one of the nodes available through JavaFX.

The important ideas are:

1. Name and locate an image: *Image grasshopp = new Image("green_hopper.jpg");*

*grasshopp* is the name we specify in our program – this is the name we will use to identify the image. *"green_hopper.jpg"* is the file name of our picture in the current folder (directory) of our computer.

2. ImageView is the class that converts the image file in our computer's file system into a reserved RAM memory area that our program will use.

*ImageView imview1 = new ImageView(grasshopp);*

3. *stakp* is a recognized StackPane node, declared in *StackPane stakp = new StackPane();* We can attach our RAM image to this node called *stakp* using

stakp.getChildren().add(imview1);

4. When all these preparations have been completed then the stage is set for the scene and the curtains open for the show:

*Scene scene = new Scene(stakp);* // Make an instance of a scene.

*stage.setScene(scene);* // Place the scene on the stage.

*stage.show();* // Display the scene on the stage.

An example putting all this together in Chapter 14 is *ShowImageSimple1.java.*

*public void start(Stage stage)* // **Make a program that has a stage.**

*{*

*stage.setTitle("Load Image");*

*StackPane stakp = new StackPane();* // **Make Pane on which graphics can be displayed.**

*Image bird_image = new Image("bird_aztec_100.jpg");*

*ImageView imview1 = new ImageView(bird_image);*

*stakp.getChildren().add(imview1);* // **Place an image on the Pane**

*Scene scene = new Scene(stakp);* // **Make a scene and place the Pane in it.**

*stage.setScene(scene);* // **Place the scene on the stage**

*stage.show();* // **Make whatever is on the stage visible.**

*}*

In this chapter we explore various ways of arranging displays of multiple images.

In the first example here we have code that allows the display of an Inca bird icon using each of eleven layout classes. The idea here is to demonstrate the basic syntax

of default layouts. The lesson here is that the layout classes have a lot in common but as subsequent example will show, when many graphic nodes are to be shown then each layout class has it's own unique layout syntax.

## General Example for Eleven Different Layout Classes.

The example below is actually eleven separate examples presented all together.

We can only activate one particular line at a time. So if we want to see how a GridPane displays a single image then we must ensure there is a // symbol as the first pair of characters for each of the eleven lines except for line 4:

*GridPane rootpane = new GridPane();*

```
/ / ShowPaneBasics.java
/*
class: javafx.scene.layout.xxxPane
or javafx.scene.control.DialogPane or javafx.scene.text.TextFlow.
------------------------------------------------------------------
Constructors: Each of 11 constructors are given in the numbered tests below.
Uncomment each numbered example at a time to demonstrate the default
values for showing a simple image using the selected layout class..
Each layout type is a tool for displaying graphic notes in a particular
manner designed for programmer convenience.

Tested on: java version "java-8-oracle"
```

```
Author: Mike Ohlson de Fine.
*/

import javafx.application.Application;
import javafx.scene.Scene;
import javafx.scene.image.Image;
import javafx.scene.image.ImageView;
/* Make available the appropriate Pane class. */
import javafx.scene.layout.Pane;                    // 1.
//import javafx.scene.layout.StackPane;             // 2.
//import javafx.scene.layout.FlowPane;              // 3.
//import javafx.scene.layout.GridPane;              // 4.
//import javafx.scene.layout.BorderPane;            // 5.
//import javafx.scene.layout.AnchorPane;            // 6.
//import javafx.scene.layout.TilePane;              // 7.
//import javafx.scene.layout.VBox;                  // 8.
//import javafx.scene.layout.HBox;                  // 9.
//import javafx.scene.control.DialogPane;           // 10.
//import javafx.scene.text.TextFlow;                // 11.

import javafx.stage.Stage;

public class ShowPaneBasics extends Application
{
   public void start(Stage stage)
   {
   stage.setTitle("Load Image");
   /* Use a comment switch (//) to activate each line separately. */
   Pane rootpane = new Pane();                          // 1.
   //StackPane rootpane = new StackPane();              // 2.
   //FlowPane rootpane = new FlowPane();                // 3.
   //GridPane rootpane = new GridPane();                // 4.
   //BorderPane rootpane = new BorderPane();            // 5.
   //AnchorPane rootpane = new AnchorPane();            // 6.
   //TilePane rootpane = new TilePane();                // 7.
   //VBox rootpane = new VBox();                        // 8.
   //HBox rootpane = new HBox();                        // 9.
   //DialogPane rootpane = new DialogPane();            // 10.
   //TextFlow rootpane = new TextFlow();                // 11.

   Image bird_image = new Image("bird_aztec_100.jpg");
```

```
    ImageView imview1 = new ImageView(bird_image);

    rootpane.getChildren().add(imview1);
    Scene scene = new Scene(rootpane);
    stage.setScene(scene);
    stage.show();
    }
}
```

The children can be added and removed freely from a scene.

## *Absolute layout: Pane*

The Pane node is the basic class that is customized to create all the other layout classes. Nodes can be positioned on a Pane using absolute screen coordinates.

### Single Image Location

```
// AbsoluteImageLayout1.java
/*
A basic pane with image located using absolute coordinates.

Tested on: java version "java-8-oracle"
Author: Mike Ohlson de Fine.
```

```
*/
import javafx.application.Application;
import javafx.stage.Stage;
import javafx.scene.Scene;
import javafx.scene.layout.Pane;

import javafx.geometry.Pos;
import javafx.scene.image.Image;
import javafx.scene.image.ImageView;

public class AbsoluteImageLayout1 extends Application
{
  public void start(Stage stage)
   {
      Pane root = new Pane();

      Image frn100 = new Image("fern_100.jpg"); // Default location (0, 0).
      ImageView frn_iv1 = new ImageView(frn100);

      frn_iv1.setX(60);
      frn_iv1.setY(30);
      root.getChildren().addAll(frn_iv1);

      Scene scene = new Scene(root, 230, 180);
      stage.setTitle("Absolute layout");
      stage.setScene(scene);
      stage.show();
   }
}
```

## Multiple Image Placement

Any number of images may be added as children nodes to a root node. The most compact Java statement to achieve this is:

```
root.getChildren().addAll(frn_iv1, ham_iv1, mos_iv1, whb_iv1, bik_iv1,

                          bom_iv1, fwm_iv1, sgl_iv1);
```

Another way of getting the same result would be:

```
root.getChildren().add(frn_iv1);

root.getChildren().add( ham_iv1);

root.getChildren().add( mos_iv1);

root.getChildren().add( whb_iv1);

root.getChildren().add( bik_iv1);

root.getChildren().add( bom_iv1);

root.getChildren().add( fwm_iv1);

root.getChildren().add(  sgl_iv1);
```

```
// AbsoluteImagesLayout2.java
/*
```

```
A basic pane with images located using absolute coordinates..

Tested on: java version "java-8-oracle"
Author: Mike Ohlson de Fine.
*/
import javafx.application.Application;
import javafx.stage.Stage;
import javafx.scene.Scene;
import javafx.scene.layout.Pane;

import javafx.geometry.Pos;
import javafx.scene.paint.Color;
import javafx.scene.image.Image;
import javafx.scene.image.ImageView;

public class AbsoluteImagesLayout2 extends Application
{
  public void start(Stage stage)
   {
      Pane root = new Pane();

      Image frn100 = new Image("fern_100.jpg"); // Default location (0, 0).
      ImageView frn_iv1 = new ImageView(frn100);

      Image ham100 = new Image("hamish_100.jpg");
      ImageView ham_iv1 = new ImageView(ham100);
      ham_iv1.setX(50);
      ham_iv1.setY(30);

      Image mos100 = new Image("mossA_100.jpg");
      ImageView mos_iv1 = new ImageView(mos100);
      mos_iv1.setX(100);
      mos_iv1.setY(60);

      Image whb100 = new Image("whiteboug_100.jpg");
      ImageView whb_iv1 = new ImageView(whb100);
      whb_iv1.setX(150);
      whb_iv1.setY(90);

      Image bik50 = new Image("bike_50.jpg");
      ImageView bik_iv1 = new ImageView(bik50);
```

```
    bik_iv1.setX(250);
    bik_iv1.setY(200);

   Image bom50 = new Image("boom_50.jpg");
   ImageView bom_iv1 = new ImageView(bom50);
    bom_iv1.setX(200);
    bom_iv1.setY(250);

   Image fwm50 = new Image("fwoom_50.jpg");
   ImageView fwm_iv1 = new ImageView(fwm50);
   fwm_iv1.setX(150);
   fwm_iv1.setY(300);

   Image sgl50 = new Image("sad_girl_50.jpg");
   ImageView sgl_iv1 = new ImageView(sgl50);
   sgl_iv1.setX(100);
   sgl_iv1.setY(350);

   root.getChildren().addAll(frn_iv1, ham_iv1, mos_iv1, whb_iv1, bik_iv1,
                    bom_iv1, fwm_iv1, sgl_iv1);

   Scene scene = new Scene(root, 320, 410, Color.LIGHTBLUE);
   stage.setTitle("Absolute layout");
   stage.setScene(scene);
   stage.show();
  }

}
```

# FlowPane Control

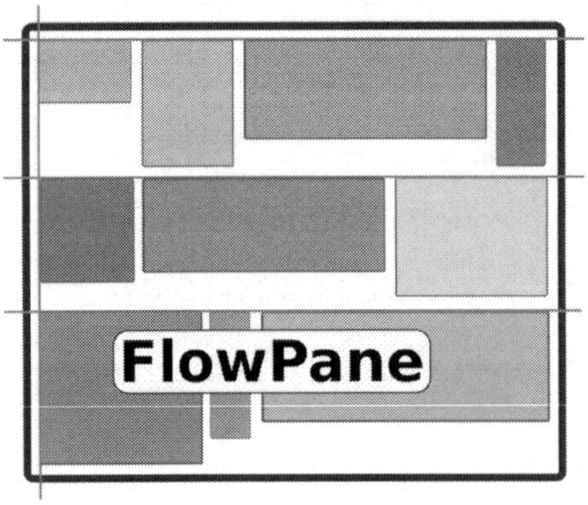

The FlowPane lays out its children nodes in a row either horizontally or vertically, one after the other, following the sequence in which the nodes are added to the scene. When the row is full then the next node to be displayed starts on the next row or column. The terminology is that the flow of node display wraps at the flowpane's boundary.

## Single node Display on a FlowPane.

*// ImageFlowPane1.java*
*/**
*Display a single image - a trivial case that is*
*simply extended to arrays of images.*

*class: javafx.scene.image.ImageView*
*class: javafx.scene.layout.FlowPane;*
*----------------------------------------*
*Constructors:*
*1. FlowPane() Creates a horizontal FlowPane layout with hgap/vgap = 0.*
*2. FlowPane(hgap, vgap) Creates a horizontal FlowPane layout with the specified hgap/vgap.*
*3. FlowPane(hgap, vgap, Node... children):Creates a horizontal FlowPane layout with the specified hgap/vgap.*
*4. FlowPane(Node... children): Creates a horizontal FlowPane layout with hgap/vgap = 0.*
*5. FlowPane(orientation): Creates a FlowPane layout with the specified orientation and hgap/vgap = 0.*
*6. FlowPane(orientation, hgap, vgap): Creates a FlowPane layout with the specified orientation and hgap/vgap.*
*7. FlowPane(orientation, hgap, vgap, Node... children): Creates a FlowPane layout with the specified orientation and hgap/vgap.*
*8. FlowPane(orientation, Node... children): Creates a FlowPane layout with the specified orientation and hgap/vgap = 0.*

```
hgap is the horizontal separation between images.

Tested on: java version "java-8-oracle"
Author: Mike Ohlson de Fine.
*/

import javafx.application.Application;
import javafx.scene.Scene;
import javafx.scene.image.Image;
import javafx.scene.image.ImageView;
import javafx.scene.layout.FlowPane;
//import javafx.geometry.Orientation; // Only need for non-default
orientation.
import javafx.stage.Stage;

public class ImageFlowPane1 extends Application
{
   public void start(Stage stage)
   {
   stage.setTitle("FlowPane: Single Horizontal flow.");
   Image drag_tsp10 = new Image("Dragon_200_133.jpg");
    FlowPane flowp = new FlowPane(); // Default Orientation.HORIZONTAL
    flowp.getChildren().add(new ImageView(drag_tsp10));

   Scene scene = new Scene(flowp);
   stage.setScene(scene);
   stage.show();
   }
}
```

## FlowPane Control of Multiple ImagesFlowPane

We will be using the following 12 images in our examples. Images of different sizes and aspect ratio (height to width ratio).

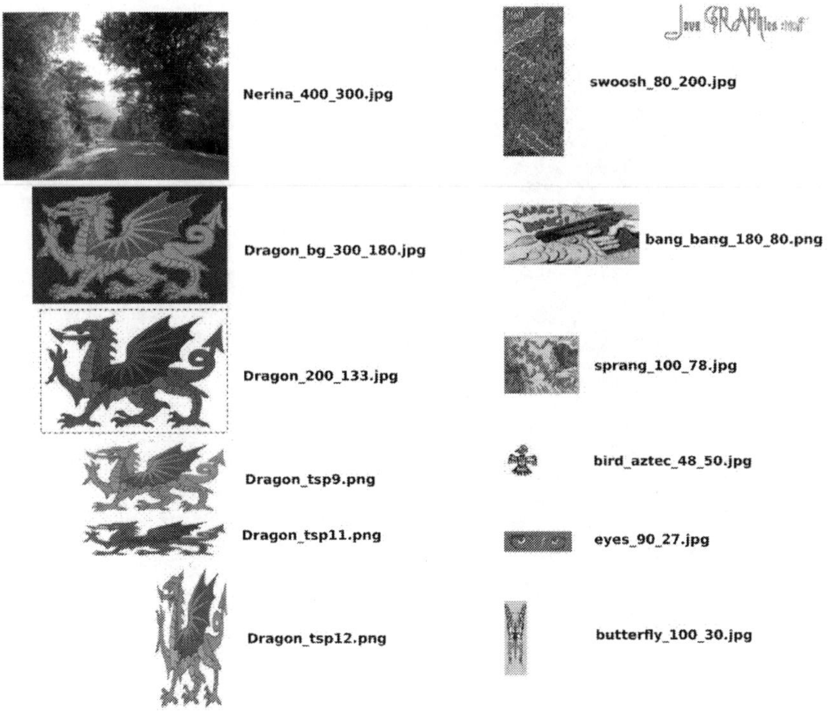


These images are a mix of png and jpg format images. The backgrounds of the png images are transparent.

Here is a FlowPane layout example that uses all 12 images and we can see that when the application has run and produced a pane with all the images on it, we can resize the viewing window (pane) and the images will flow either horizontally (the default flow direction) or vertically, but not both. As we have done in previous examples we combine two possible tests in the same program and can choose which option to compile and run by switching instructions ON or OFF using the comment symbols // at the beginning of lines we want to turn off.

The images are placed in horizontal rows. The height of each row is determined by the height of the tallest image in that row.

```
// ImagesFlowPane2.java
/*
Mixed jpg and png images.
Png images with transparent backgrounds.
Note: jpg does not support transparency

Tested on: java version "java-8-oracle"
Author: Mike Ohlson de Fine.
*/

import javafx.application.Application;
import javafx.scene.Scene;
import javafx.scene.image.Image;
```

```
import javafx.scene.image.ImageView;
import javafx.scene.layout.FlowPane;
import javafx.geometry.Orientation;
import javafx.stage.Stage;

public class ImagesFlowPane2 extends Application
{
  public void start(Stage stage)
  {
  stage.setTitle("FlowPane: Vertical flow 12 images with transparency.");

  Image drag_tsp1 = new Image("Nerina_400_300.jpg");
  Image drag_tsp2 = new Image("bang_bang_180_80.png");
  Image drag_tsp3 = new Image("swoosh_80_200.jpg");
  Image drag_tsp4 = new Image("sprang_100_78.jpg");
  Image drag_tsp5 = new Image("bird_aztec_48_50.jpg");
  Image drag_tsp6 = new Image("butterfly_100_30.jpg");
  Image drag_tsp7 = new Image("eyes_90_27.jpg");
  Image drag_tsp8 = new Image("Dragon_bg_300_180.jpg");
  Image drag_tsp9 = new Image("Dragon_tsp9.png");
  Image drag_tsp10 = new Image("Dragon_200_133.jpg");
  Image drag_tsp11 = new Image("Dragon_tsp11.png");
  Image drag_tsp12 = new Image("Dragon_tsp12.png");

   Image images[] = {drag_tsp1, drag_tsp2, drag_tsp3, drag_tsp4, drag_tsp5,
drag_tsp6,
              drag_tsp7, drag_tsp8, drag_tsp9, drag_tsp10, drag_tsp11,
drag_tsp12 };
   //FlowPane flowp = new FlowPane(); // Default
Orientation.HORIZONTAL
   FlowPane flowp = new FlowPane(Orientation.VERTICAL); // Note - The
default image flow is Horizontal.
   flowp.setVgap(10); //Gap of 10 pixels between images.
   flowp.setHgap(10);
   flowp.setPrefWrapLength(800); // preferred width = 800
   for (int i = 0; i < images.length; i++)
   {
     flowp.getChildren().add(new ImageView(images[i]));
   }

   Scene scene = new Scene(flowp);
```

```
    stage.setScene(scene);
    stage.show();
    }
}
```

The images are placed in vertical columns. The width of each row is determined by the width of the widest image in that column.

The main point to note here is that the images are automatically placed in vertical columns. The widest picture in any particular column determines the width of the column. If we re-size the height of the picture by adjusting the frame using the mouse then the images are re-flowed (adjusted) vertically to make the pictures fill in the new available space. Adjusting the horizontal width of the frame does not cause the images positions to be adjusted. As the frame is made smaller the images on the right hand side are progressively lost from the viewport.

It the image flow, orientation is changed to HORIZONTAL then the images are organized to flow into the rows. Adjusting the frame alters the number of images in the rows.

## Making Images Overlap with FlowPane

The parameter instructions:

*flowp.setVgap(10); //Gap of 10 pixels between images.*

*flowp.setHgap(10);*

Specify the spacing, in pixels, between images.

If we use negative numbers then the images will overlap by the number of pixels specified. For example if we wrote:

flowp.setVgap(-90); //Overlap of 90 pixels horizontally between images.

flowp.setHgap(-60); //Overlap of 60 pixels vertically between images.

We would get a 90 pixel overlap between columns of images and an overlap of 60 pixels between rows of images. The FlowPane display below has negative Vgaps and positive Hgaps.

## Using Transparency

When images have the normal visible rectangular background, the background of the images will obscure each other. But if the png format images have transparent regions the the previous image can show through the transparent areas as shown below. The white areas in each image was made transparent (alpha = 0.0).

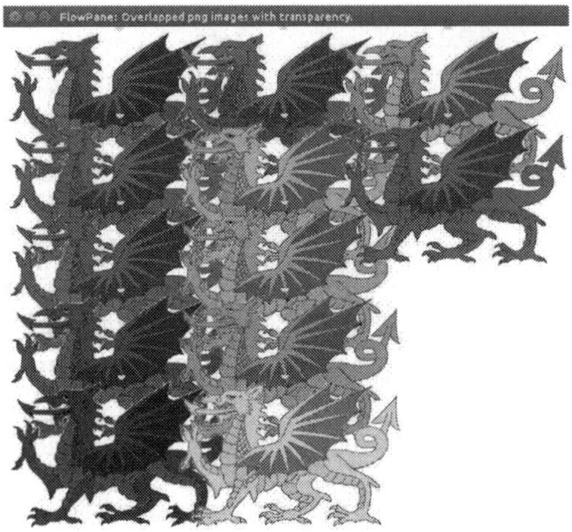

# The StackPane Class: place nodes on top of each other.

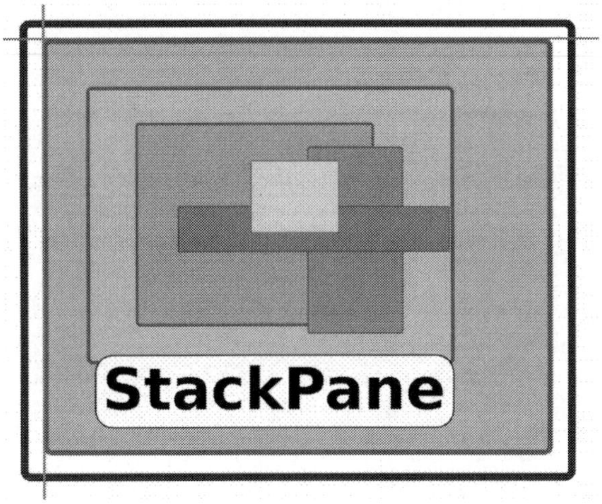


StackPanes give us a great amount of flexibility.

```
// ImageStackPane1.java
/*
Display a single image -  a trivial case that is
simply extended to arrays of images.

Tested on: java version "java-8-oracle"
Author: Mike Ohlson de Fine.
*/
import javafx.application.Application;
import javafx.scene.Scene;
import javafx.scene.image.Image;
import javafx.scene.image.ImageView;
import javafx.scene.layout.StackPane;
import javafx.stage.Stage;

public class ImageStackPane1 extends Application
{
   public void start(Stage stage)
   {
   stage.setTitle("StackPane: Single Image.");
   Image drag_tsp10 = new Image("Dragon_200_133.jpg");
```

```
    StackPane stackpane1 = new StackPane(); // Construct a StackPane root
object
    stackpane1.getChildren().add(new ImageView(drag_tsp10));

    Scene scene = new Scene(stackpane1);
    stage.setScene(scene);
    stage.show();
    }
}
```

## Stacking Multiple Images

```
// ImagesStackPane3.java
/*
Display three images in a stack.

Tested on: java version "java-8-oracle"
Author: Mike Ohlson de Fine.
*/

import javafx.application.Application;
import javafx.scene.Scene;
import javafx.scene.image.Image;
import javafx.scene.image.ImageView;
import javafx.scene.layout.StackPane;
import javafx.stage.Stage;
```

```
public class ImagesStackPane3 extends Application
{
   public void start(Stage stage)
   {
    stage.setTitle("StackPane: Three images stacked atop each other.");
    StackPane stackpane1 = new StackPane(); // Construct a StackPane root
object.

     // Three images of different sizes with transparentbackgrounds.
     Image image1 = new
Image(getClass().getResourceAsStream("Dragon_tsp1.png"));
     Image image2 = new
Image(getClass().getResourceAsStream("Dragon_small_tsp2.png"));
     Image image3 = new
Image(getClass().getResourceAsStream("Dragon_small_tsp3.png"));

      Image images[] = {image1, image2, image3 };

     for (int i = 0; i < images.length; i++)
     {
       stackpane1.getChildren().add(new ImageView(images[i]));
     }

   Scene scene = new Scene(stackpane1);
   stage.setScene(scene);
   stage.show();
   }
}
```

## GridPane

GridPane lays out its children within a flexible grid of rows and columns. If a border and/or padding is set, then its content will be laid out within those insets.

A child may be placed anywhere within the grid and may span multiple rows/columns. Children may freely overlap within rows/columns and their stacking order will be defined by the order of the gridpane's children list (0th node in back, last node in front).

# A single Image on a GridPane

```
// ImageGridPane1.java
/*
Place an image on a grid pane.

Tested on: java version "java-8-oracle"
Author: Mike Ohlson de Fine.
*/
import javafx.application.Application;
import javafx.stage.Stage;
import javafx.scene.Scene;
import javafx.scene.image.Image;
import javafx.scene.image.ImageView;
import javafx.scene.layout.GridPane;
public class ImageGridPane1 extends Application
{
  public void start(Stage stage)
  {
   stage.setTitle("GridPane: png images with transparency.");
   GridPane gridpane1 = new GridPane();// Construct a GridPane root
object

   Image image1 = new Image("Dragon_tsp1.png");
   gridpane1.getChildren().add(new ImageView(image1));

   Scene scene = new Scene(gridpane1);
   stage.setScene(scene);
   stage.show();
  }
}
```

# Multiple Images on a GridPane

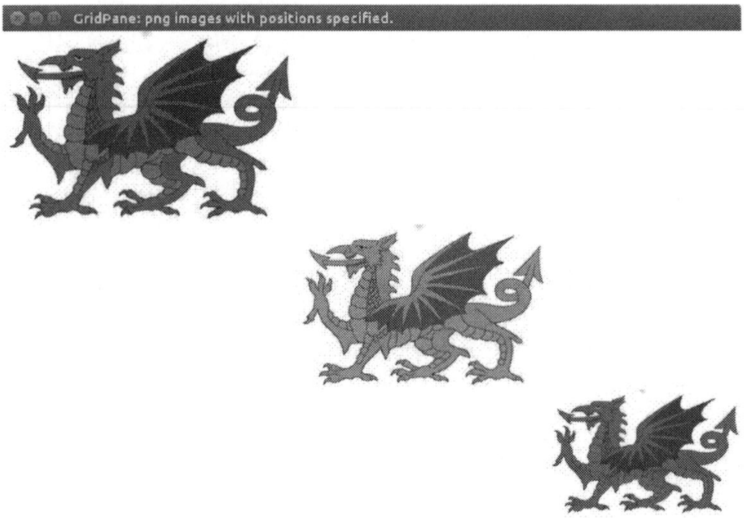


```
// ImagesGridPane3.java
/*
Place images on a grid pane.

Tested on: java version "java-8-oracle"
Author: Mike Ohlson de Fine.
*/
import javafx.application.Application;
import javafx.stage.Stage;
import javafx.scene.Scene;
import javafx.scene.image.Image;
import javafx.scene.image.ImageView;
import javafx.scene.layout.GridPane;

public class ImagesGridPane3 extends Application
{
   public void start(Stage stage)
   {
    stage.setTitle("GridPane: png images with positions specified.");
    GridPane gridpane1 = new GridPane();// Construct a GridPane root
object

    Image image1 = new Image("Dragon_tsp1.png");
    Image image2 = new Image("Dragon_small_tsp9.png");
```

```
    Image image3 = new Image("Dragon_small_tsp3.png");

    ImageView imview1 = new ImageView(image1) ;
    ImageView imview2 = new ImageView(image2) ;
    ImageView imview3 = new ImageView(image3) ;

    gridpane1.getChildren().add(imview1);
    gridpane1.getChildren().add(imview2);
    gridpane1.getChildren().add(imview3);

    // Set one row or column constraint one at a time...
    /* If grid locations are not specified then all the images are placed
      on top of each other, like a stack.
   */
    GridPane.setRowIndex(imview1, 1);
    GridPane.setColumnIndex(imview1, 2);
    GridPane.setRowIndex(imview2, 2);
    GridPane.setColumnIndex(imview2, 3);
    GridPane.setRowIndex(imview3, 3);
    GridPane.setColumnIndex(imview3, 4);

    Scene scene = new Scene(gridpane1);
    stage.setScene(scene);
    stage.show();
  }
}
```

# BorderPanes

In a border pane, the layout area is divided into five distinct areas: top, right, bottom, left, and center.

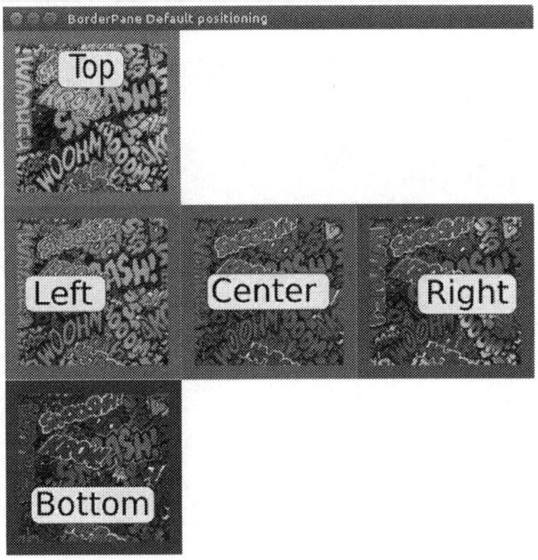


```
// BorderPaneDefault_pos1.java
/*
A border pane with 5 image nodes.

Tested on: java version "java-8-oracle"
Author: Mike Ohlson de Fine.
*/
import javafx.application.Application;
import javafx.geometry.Insets;
import javafx.geometry.Pos;
import javafx.scene.Scene;
import javafx.scene.control.Button;
import javafx.scene.layout.BorderPane;
import javafx.stage.Stage;

import javafx.scene.image.Image;
import javafx.scene.image.ImageView;

public class BorderPaneDefault_pos1 extends Application
{
 public void start(Stage primaryStage)
 {
  Image image_cent = new Image("swoosh_cent.png");
```

```
    Image image_top = new Image("swoosh_top.png");
    Image image_bot = new Image("swoosh_bot.png");
    Image image_left = new Image("swoosh_left.png");
    Image image_rite = new Image("swoosh_rite.png");

    // Create ImageView nodes that can be placed inside a BorderPane.
    ImageView imv_cent = new ImageView(image_cent) ;
    ImageView imv_top = new ImageView(image_top) ;
    ImageView imv_bot = new ImageView(image_bot) ;
    ImageView imv_left = new ImageView(image_left) ;
    ImageView imv_rite = new ImageView(image_rite) ;

    primaryStage.setTitle("BorderPane Default positioning");
    BorderPane bordp = new BorderPane();

    // Allocate each image to one of the 5 available positions in BorderPane.
    bordp.setTop(imv_top);
    bordp.setLeft(imv_left);
    bordp.setCenter(imv_cent);
    bordp.setRight(imv_rite);
    bordp.setBottom(imv_bot);

    Scene scene = new Scene(bordp, 600, 600);
    primaryStage.setScene(scene);
    primaryStage.show();
  }
}
```

# Fine Adjustment of Images Inside a BorderPane.

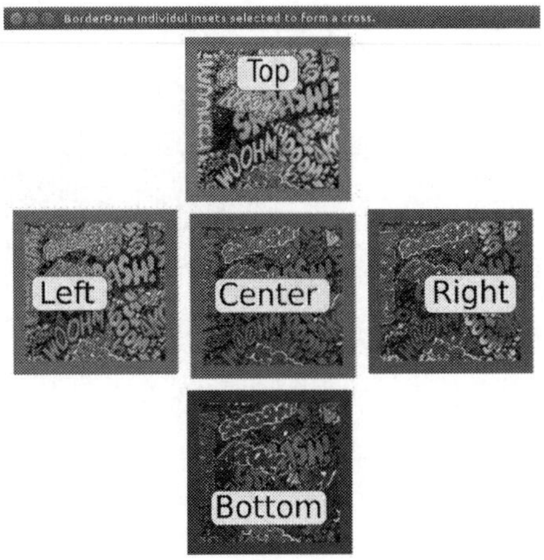

*/ / BorderPaneImageInsets2.java*
*/**
*A border pane with 5 image nodes.*
*On re-sizing the window the BorderPane layout manager tries to keep the center image (default position) in the center.*

*Pos: import javafx.geometry.Pos;*

```
Positioning a node inside its allowed area -
BOTTOM_CENTER: on the bottom vertically and on the center horizontally.
BOTTOM_LEFT:   on the bottom vertically and on the left horizontally.
BOTTOM_RIGHT:  on the bottom vertically and on the right horizontally.

CENTER:       on the center both vertically and horizontally.
CENTER_LEFT:  on the center vertically and on the left horizontally.
CENTER_RIGHT: on the center vertically and on the right horizontally.

TOP_CENTER: on the top vertically and on the center horizontally.
TOP_LEFT:   on the top vertically and on the left horizontally.
TOP_RIGHT:  on the top vertically and on the right horizontally.

Insets: javafx.geometry.Insets
A set of inside offsets for the 4 sides of a rectangular area
1. Insets(topRightBottomLeft);Constructs a new Insets instance with same
value for all four offsets.
2. Insets(top, right, bottom, left): Constructs a new Insets instance with four
different offsets.

Tested on: java version "java-8-oracle"
Author: Mike Ohlson de Fine.
*/
import javafx.application.Application;
import javafx.stage.Stage;
import javafx.scene.Scene;

import javafx.scene.layout.BorderPane;
import javafx.geometry.Insets;
import javafx.geometry.Pos;

import javafx.scene.image.Image;
import javafx.scene.image.ImageView;

public class BorderPaneImageInsets2 extends Application
{
 public void start(Stage primaryStage)
 {
  Image image_cent = new Image("swoosh_cent.png");
  Image image_top = new Image("swoosh_top.png");
  Image image_bot = new Image("swoosh_bot.png");
```

```
  Image image_left = new Image("swoosh_left.png");
  Image image_rite = new Image("swoosh_rite.png");

  ImageView imv_cent = new ImageView(image_cent) ;
  ImageView imv_top = new ImageView(image_top) ;
  ImageView imv_bot = new ImageView(image_bot) ;
  ImageView imv_left = new ImageView(image_left) ;
  ImageView imv_rite = new ImageView(image_rite) ;

   primaryStage.setTitle("BorderPane Individul Insets selected to form a
cross.");
   BorderPane bordp = new BorderPane();

   int top_edge  = 5; //  Below top edge of pane.
   int rite_edge = 5; // Inside right edge of pane.
   int bot_edge  = 5; // Above bottom edge of pane.
   int left_edge = 5;  // Inside left edge of pane.

   // Inset borders for the entire pane.
   bordp.setPadding(new Insets(top_edge, rite_edge, bot_edge, left_edge));

   // Inset adjustments for selected images relate to pane edges.
   bordp.setMargin(imv_top, new Insets(top_edge, rite_edge, bot_edge,
left_edge+210));
   bordp.setMargin(imv_bot, new Insets(top_edge, rite_edge, bot_edge,
left_edge+210));
   bordp.setMargin(imv_left, new Insets(top_edge, rite_edge, bot_edge,
left_edge));
   bordp.setMargin(imv_rite, new Insets(top_edge, rite_edge, bot_edge,
left_edge));
  bordp.setMargin(imv_cent, new Insets(top_edge, rite_edge, bot_edge,
left_edge));

   // Overall allocation of images to the 5 BorderPane general positions.
   bordp.setTop(imv_top);
   bordp.setLeft(imv_left);
   bordp.setCenter(imv_cent);
   bordp.setRight(imv_rite);
   bordp.setBottom(imv_bot);

   // Anchor positions of individual images within their local spaces.
```

```
    bordp.setAlignment(imv_top, Pos.TOP_LEFT);
    bordp.setAlignment(imv_bot, Pos.TOP_LEFT);
    bordp.setAlignment(imv_cent, Pos.TOP_LEFT);
    bordp.setAlignment(imv_left, Pos.TOP_LEFT);
    bordp.setAlignment(imv_rite, Pos.TOP_LEFT);

    Scene scene = new Scene(bordp, 650, 650);
    primaryStage.setScene(scene);
    primaryStage.show();
  }
}
```

## AnchorPane

The AnchorPane layout class allows the edges of child nodes to be anchored to an offset from the anchor pane's edges. If the anchor pane has a border and/or padding set, the offsets will be measured from the inside edge of those insets.

```
// anchorPaneImage1.java
/*
A basic pane with images located using absolute coordinates..

Tested on: java version "java-8-oracle"
Author: Mike Ohlson de Fine.
*/
import javafx.application.Application;
import javafx.scene.Scene;
import javafx.stage.Stage;
import javafx.scene.layout.AnchorPane;

import javafx.scene.image.Image;
import javafx.scene.image.ImageView;

public class anchorPaneImage1 extends Application
{
   public void start(Stage stage)
   {

      AnchorPane root = new AnchorPane();

      Image image_cent = new Image("swoosh_cent.png");
      ImageView imv_cent = new ImageView(image_cent) ;
      root.getChildren().add(imv_cent);
      root.setRightAnchor(imv_cent, 60.);

      Scene scene = new Scene(root, 320, 260);
      stage.setTitle("AnchorPane Simple");
```

```
        stage.setScene(scene);
        stage.show();
    }
}
```

## AnchorPane with Multiple Images

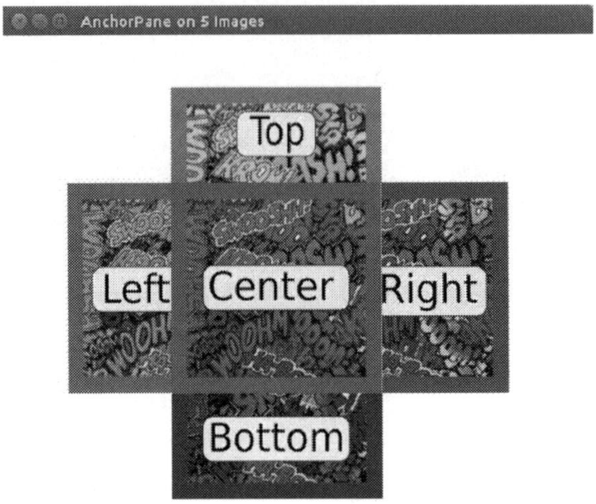


```
// anchorPaneImages2.java
/*
A basic AnchorPane with images located using absolute coordinates.
Constraint format
setTopAnchor(node, distance):       distance from the anchor pane's top inset
to the child's top edge.
setLeftAnchor(node, distance):      distance from the anchor pane's left inset
to the child's left edge.
setBottomAnchor(node, distance): distance from the anchor pane's bottom
inset to the child's bottom edge.
setRightAnchor(node, distance):  distance from the anchor pane's right inset
to the child's right edge.

Tested on: java version "java-8-oracle"
Author: Mike Ohlson de Fine.
*/

import javafx.application.Application;
```

```
import javafx.scene.Scene;
import javafx.stage.Stage;
import javafx.scene.layout.AnchorPane;

import javafx.scene.image.Image;
import javafx.scene.image.ImageView;

public class anchorPaneImages2 extends Application
{
   public void start(Stage stage)
   {
      AnchorPane root = new AnchorPane();

      Image image_cent = new Image("swoosh_cent.png");
      Image image_top  = new Image("swoosh_top.png");
      Image image_bot  = new Image("swoosh_bot.png");
      Image image_left = new Image("swoosh_left.png");
      Image image_rite = new Image("swoosh_rite.png");

      // Create ImageView nodes that can be placed inside a BorderPane.
      ImageView imv_cent = new ImageView(image_cent) ;
      ImageView imv_top  = new ImageView(image_top) ;
      ImageView imv_bot  = new ImageView(image_bot) ;
      ImageView imv_left = new ImageView(image_left) ;
      ImageView imv_rite = new ImageView(image_rite) ;

      root.getChildren().addAll(imv_left, imv_top, imv_bot, imv_rite,
imv_cent);

      root.setLeftAnchor(imv_cent, 160.);
      root.setTopAnchor(imv_cent, 140.);

      root.setLeftAnchor(imv_left, 60.);
      root.setTopAnchor(imv_left, 140.);

      root.setTopAnchor(imv_top, 50.);
      root.setLeftAnchor(imv_top, 160.);

      root.setBottomAnchor(imv_bot, 60.);
      root.setLeftAnchor(imv_bot, 160.);
```

```
        root.setLeftAnchor(imv_rite, 280.);
        root.setTopAnchor(imv_rite, 140.);

        Scene scene = new Scene(root, 560, 500);
        stage.setTitle("AnchorPane on 5 Images");
        stage.setScene(scene);
        stage.show();
    }
}
```

## Anchor Constraints

The application sets anchor constraints on each child to configure the anchors on one or more sides. If a child is anchored on opposite sides (and is resizable), the anchor pane will resize it to maintain both offsets, otherwise the anchor pane will resize it to its preferred size. If in the former case (anchored on opposite sides) and the child is not resizable, then only the top/left anchor will be honored. AnchorPane provides a static method for setting each anchor constraint.

An *anchor pane* in JavaFX is similar to a border pane - you can position nodes relative to one of the edges of the pane. But:

•An anchor pane does not divide the layout into distinct areas. Instead, every node in the layout can be tied — or *anchored* — to one or more of the four edges of the layout area. When a node is anchored to an edge, the anchor pane will position the node as close as possible to that edge after allowing for other nodes.

•A node can be anchored to more than one edge. For example, a node can be anchored to the top and right edges, which will place the node in the top-right corner of the layout.

•If a node is anchored to opposite edges (top and bottom or left and right), the node will be pulled toward both edges of the layout. This results in the node being *stretched* as the size of the layout increases.

•More than one node can be anchored to each edge. In that case, the nodes will overlap as they would in a stack pane.

The main constructors and methods of the AnchorPane class are:

**setTopAnchor(node, value)** Anchors the specified *node* to the top edge. *Value is* the offset distance from the top edge.

**setBottomAnchor(node, value)** Anchors the specified *node* to the Bottom edge. *Value is* the offset distance from the bottom edge.

s**etLeftAnchor(node, value)** Anchors the specified *node* to the left edge. *Value is* the offset distance from the left edge.

**setRightAnchor(node, value)** Anchors the specified *node* to the right edge. *Value is* the offset distance from the eight edge.

**setMinHeight( value)** Sets the minimum height of the anchor pane.

**setMinWidth( value)** Sets the minimum width of the anchor pane.

**setMaxHeight(value)** Sets the maximum height of the anchor pane.

**setPrefHeight( value)** Sets the preferred height of the anchor pane.

**setPrefWidth( value)** Sets the preferred width of the anchor pane.

**setMaxWidth( value)** Sets the maximum widtht of the anchor pane.

**setPadding( value)** Sets the minimum height of the anchor pane.

# TilePane

TilePane lays out its children in a grid of uniformly sized "tiles".

A horizontal tilepane (the default) will tile nodes in rows, wrapping at the tilepane's width. A vertical tilePane will tile nodes in columns, wrapping at the tilePane's height.

The size of each "tile" defaults to the size needed to encompass the largest preferred width and height of the tilePane's children and the tilePane will recompute the size of the tiles as needed to accommodate the largest preferred size of its children as it changes. The application may also control the size of the tiles directly by setting prefTileWidth/prefTileHeight properties to a value other than USE_COMPUTED_SIZE (the default).

The alignment property controls how the rows and columns are aligned within the bounds of the tilepane and defaults to Pos.TOP_LEFT. It is also possible to control the alignment of nodes within the individual tiles by setting tileAlignment( default is Pos.CENTER).

```
// tilePaneImage1.java
/*

Tested on: java version "java-8-oracle"
Author: Mike Ohlson de Fine.
*/
import javafx.application.Application;
import javafx.scene.Scene;
import javafx.stage.Stage;
import javafx.scene.layout.TilePane;

import javafx.scene.image.Image;
import javafx.scene.image.ImageView;

public class tilePaneImage1 extends Application
{
  public void start(Stage stage)
  {
    TilePane tilep = new TilePane();

    Image image_cent = new Image("swoosh_cent.png");
    // Create ImageView nodes that can be placed inside a TilePane.
    ImageView imv_cent = new ImageView(image_cent) ;

    tilep.getChildren().addAll(imv_cent);

    Scene scene = new Scene(tilep, 210, 210);
    stage.setTitle("TilePane on an Image.");
```

```
        stage.setScene(scene);
        stage.show();
    }
}
```

## TilePane with Multiple Images

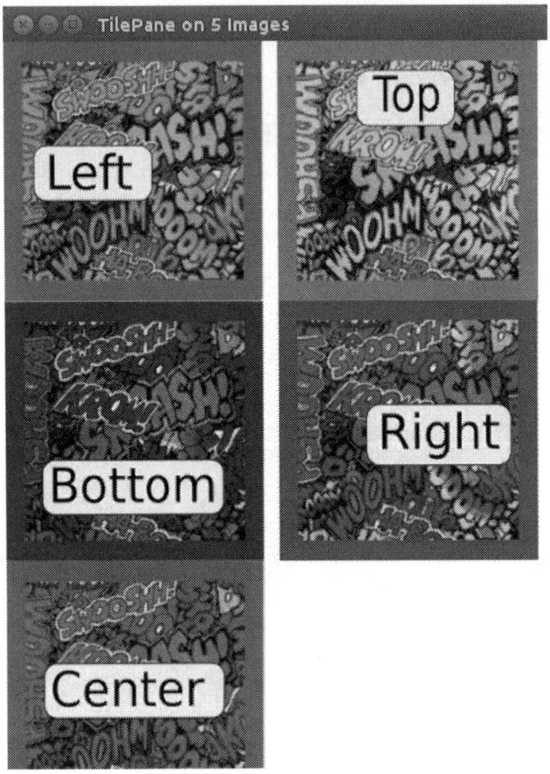


```
// tilePaneImages2.java
/*

Tested on: java version "java-8-oracle"
Author: Mike Ohlson de Fine.
*/
import javafx.application.Application;
import javafx.scene.Scene;
import javafx.stage.Stage;
import javafx.scene.layout.TilePane;

import javafx.scene.image.Image;
```

```
import javafx.scene.image.ImageView;

public class tilePaneImages2 extends Application
{
   public void start(Stage stage)
   {
      TilePane tilep = new TilePane();
      tilep.setHgap(12);

      Image image_cent = new Image("swoosh_cent.png");
      Image image_top  = new Image("swoosh_top.png");
      Image image_bot  = new Image("swoosh_bot.png");
      Image image_left = new Image("swoosh_left.png");
      Image image_rite = new Image("swoosh_rite.png");

      // Create ImageView nodes that can be placed inside a TilePane.
      ImageView imv_cent = new ImageView(image_cent) ;
      ImageView imv_top  = new ImageView(image_top) ;
      ImageView imv_bot  = new ImageView(image_bot) ;
      ImageView imv_left = new ImageView(image_left) ;
      ImageView imv_rite = new ImageView(image_rite) ;

      tilep.getChildren().addAll(imv_left, imv_top, imv_bot, imv_rite,
imv_cent);

      Scene scene = new Scene(tilep, 420, 560);
      stage.setTitle("TilePane on 5 Images");
      stage.setScene(scene);
      stage.show();
   }
}
```

# Vbox

VBox lays out its children in a single vertical column. If the VBox has a border and/or padding set, then the contents will be laid out within those insets.

VBox example:

*VBox vbox = new VBox(8); / / spacing between images = 8*

*vbox.getChildren().addAll(new Button("Cut"), new Button("Copy"), new Button("Paste"));*

VBox will resize children (if resizable) to their preferred heights and uses its fillWidth property to determine whether to resize their widths to fill its own width or keep their widths to their preferred (fillWidth defaults to true). The alignment of the content is controlled by the alignment property, which defaults to Pos.TOP_LEFT.

If a vbox is resized larger than its preferred height, by default it will keep children to their preferred heights, leaving the extra space unused. If an application wishes to have one or more children be allocated that extra space it may optionally set a vgrow constraint on the child.

## Vbox Single example.

```
// VBoxImage1.java
/*
Tested on: java version "java-8-oracle"
Author: Mike Ohlson de Fine.
*/
import javafx.application.Application;
import javafx.scene.Scene;
import javafx.stage.Stage;
import javafx.scene.layout.VBox;
import javafx.scene.image.Image;
import javafx.scene.image.ImageView;

public class VBoxImage1 extends Application
{
   public void start(Stage stage)
   {
        VBox vboxp = new VBox();
       Image image_rite = new Image("swoosh_rite.png");
       ImageView imv_rite = new ImageView(image_rite) ;

       vboxp.getChildren().add(imv_rite);

       Scene scene = new Scene(vboxp, 210, 210);
       stage.setTitle("VBox on an Image");
       stage.setScene(scene);
       stage.show();
   }
}
```

# Vbox Multiple examples

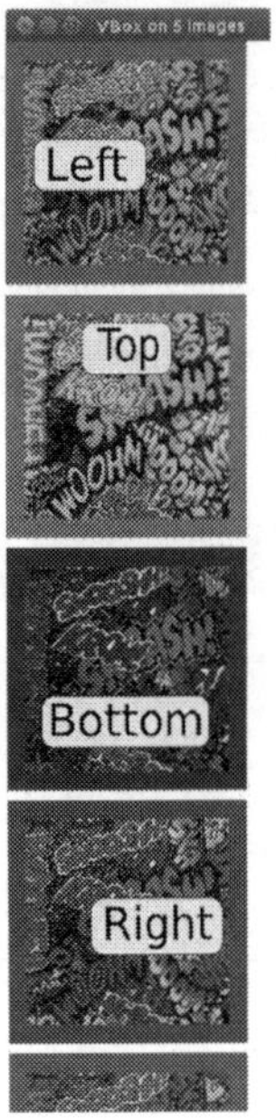


```
// VBoxImages2.java
/*
Tested on: java version "java-8-oracle"
Author: Mike Ohlson de Fine.
*/
import javafx.application.Application;
import javafx.scene.Scene;
import javafx.stage.Stage;
import javafx.scene.layout.VBox;
import javafx.scene.image.Image;
import javafx.scene.image.ImageView;

public class VBoxImages2 extends Application
{
  public void start(Stage stage)
  {
      VBox vboxp = new VBox(8); // spacing between images = 8

     Image image_cent = new Image("swoosh_cent.png");
     Image image_top  = new Image("swoosh_top.png");
     Image image_bot  = new Image("swoosh_bot.png");
     Image image_left = new Image("swoosh_left.png");
```

```
        Image image_rite = new Image("swoosh_rite.png");

        // Create ImageView nodes that can be placed inside a VBox.
        ImageView imv_cent = new ImageView(image_cent) ;
        ImageView imv_top  = new ImageView(image_top) ;
        ImageView imv_bot  = new ImageView(image_bot) ;
        ImageView imv_left = new ImageView(image_left) ;
        ImageView imv_rite = new ImageView(image_rite) ;

        vboxp.getChildren().addAll(imv_left, imv_top, imv_bot, imv_rite,
imv_cent);

        Scene scene = new Scene(vboxp, 220, 880);
        stage.setTitle("VBox on 5 Images");
        stage.setScene(scene);
        stage.show();
    }
}
```

# Hbox

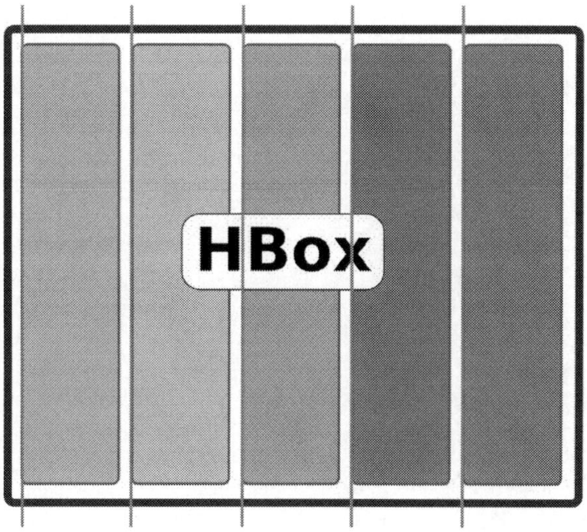


HBox lays out its children in a single horizontal column. If the HBox has a border and/or padding set, then the contents will be layed out within those insets.

HBox example:

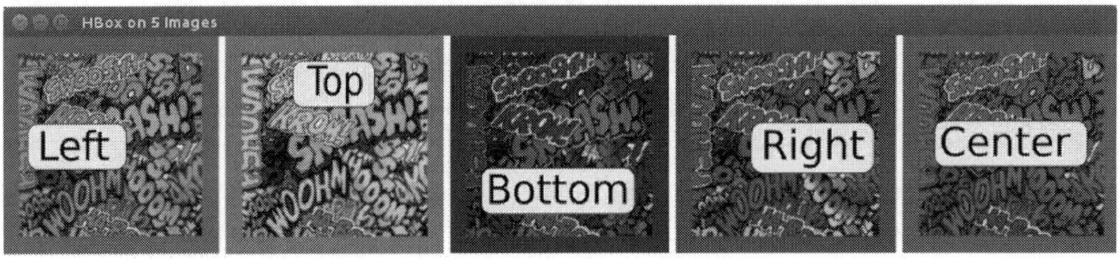


```
// HBoxImages2.java
/*

Tested on: java version "java-8-oracle"
Author: Mike Ohlson de Fine.
*/
import javafx.application.Application;
import javafx.scene.Scene;
import javafx.stage.Stage;

import javafx.scene.layout.HBox;

import javafx.scene.image.Image;
import javafx.scene.image.ImageView;

public class HBoxImages2 extends Application
{
   public void start(Stage stage)
   {
       HBox hboxp = new HBox(6); // spacing between images = 6

      Image image_cent = new Image("swoosh_cent.png");
      Image image_top  = new Image("swoosh_top.png");
      Image image_bot  = new Image("swoosh_bot.png");
      Image image_left = new Image("swoosh_left.png");
      Image image_rite = new Image("swoosh_rite.png");

      // Create ImageView nodes that can be placed inside a HBox.
      ImageView imv_cent = new ImageView(image_cent) ;
      ImageView imv_top  = new ImageView(image_top) ;
      ImageView imv_bot  = new ImageView(image_bot) ;
```

```
        ImageView imv_left = new ImageView(image_left) ;
        ImageView imv_rite = new ImageView(image_rite) ;

        hboxp.getChildren().addAll(imv_left, imv_top, imv_bot, imv_rite,
imv_cent);

        Scene scene = new Scene(hboxp, 1020, 220);
        stage.setTitle("HBox on 5 Images");
        stage.setScene(scene);
        stage.show();
    }
}
```

Instead of just using images as the nodes to be displayed we can use almost any other GUI object.

# CHAPTER 16

## VISUAL EFFECTS

*"An effect is any action that enhances the appearance of the graphics. In JavaFX, an effect is an algorithm that is applied on nodes to alter their appearance visually."*

In this chapter we will cover mainly the JavaFX Effects class:

- DropShadow
- InnerShadow
- Glow
- Bloom

- GausseanBlur
- BoxBlur
- MotionBlur
- Reflection
- Perspective
- Sepia Tone
- Lighting (point source, distant, spot light)
- Image Blending
- Color Filtering
- ColorAdjust
- DisplacementMap
- ColorInput

In JavaFX, you can set various effects to a node such as bloom, blur and glow. Each of these effects are represented by a class and all these classes are available in a package named **javafx.scene.effect.**

### Applying Effects to a Node

You can apply an effect to a node using the setEffect() method. To this method, you need to pass the object or source of the effect.

To apply an effect to a node, you need to:

- Create the node.
- Instantiate the respective class of the effect that is needed to be applied.
- Set the properties of the effect.

- Apply the effect to the node using the **setEffect()** method.

## 1. Create the Node

First of all, create the nodes in a JavaFX application by instantiating their respective classes.

For example, say we want to apply glow effect to an image in our application. Firstly, we need to create an image node. Create this image node by instantiating the Image class and set its view as shown below.

```
//Creating an image object (making an instance).
Image cat_image = new Image("Smiling Cat");

//Setting the image view
ImageView imageView = new ImageView(cat_image);

//Setting the position of the image
imageView.setX(100);
imageView.setY(70);

//setting the fit height and width of the image view
imageView.setFitHeight(200);
imageView.setFitWidth(400);

//Setting the preserve ratio of the image view
imageView.setPreserveRatio(true);
```

## 2. Instantiate the respective effect class

Instantiate the class representing the effect that is needed to be applied to the created node.
For example, to apply the glow effect, we need to instantiate the Glow class as shown below:

```
Glow glow = new Glow();
```

## 3. Setting the Properties of the Effect

After instantiating the effect class, we need to set the properties for the effect using its setter methods.

For example, to draw a 3-Dimensional box, we need to pass its width, height and depth. We can specify these values using their respective setter methods as shown below:

*//setting the level property*
*glow.setLevel(0.9);*

## 4. Add the Effect to the Node

Finally, we can apply the required effect to the node using the setEffect() method. For example, to set the glow effect to the image node, we need to pass the object of the Glow class to this method as:
*imageView.setEffect(glow);*

# The JavaFX Effects Available.

The list below gives the list of various effects (classes) provided by JavaFX. These classes exist in the package called javafx.scene.effect.

### 1. Shadow

This effect creates a duplicate of the specified node with blurry edges.

### 2. DropShadow

On applying this effect to a node, a shadow will be created behind the specified node.

### 3. InnerShadow

Here a shadow will be created inside the edges of the node.

### 4. Glow

Just like bloom, the Glow effect makes the given input image glow, making the bright pixels of the input brighter.

### 5. Bloom

On applying bloom effect, pixels in some portions of the node are made to glow.

### 6. GaussianBlur

Just like Box Blur Gaussian is an effect to blur the nodes in JavaFX.

**7. Box Blur**
The edges of the node will be made blurred or unclear, similar to seeing something out of focus. Box blur is a crude bit fast (to compute). We would use it to speed up computation when the effect has to be applied to many objects in a limited time such as when creating animations.

**8. MotionBlur**
Motion Blur is an effect to blur the nodes in JavaFX in achosen direction. This creates the impression of fast motion of the node in a particular direction. The blurring is made with a specified angle.

**9. Reflection**
On applying the reflection effect to a node in JavaFX, a reflection of it is added at the bottom of the node as if the node is above a shiney surface like a mirror, a polished floor or a wet surface.

**10. Perspective**
Distort the linear geometry to angle all vertical lines to suggest a vanishing point according the rules of artistic perspective.

**11. SepiaTone**
On applying the Sepia tone effect to an image node, it is toned with a reddish brown color reminiscent of the early days of photography.

**12. Lighting**
The lighting effect is used to simulate a light from a light source. There are different kinds of light sources:

- point sources like a light bulb in a room,
- distant light sources where the light rays are parallel,
- spot light sources that are focussed into a narrow beam.

**12 a). Light.Distant**
The light on the node appears as if it is being generated by a distant light source.
Distant Light Source – A source which is at a far distance from the node. In here, the light is attenuated in one direction from the source.

### 12 b). Light.Spot

On applying this effect to a node, a light appears as if it is being generated by a spot light. The light beam is in the shape of a cone. An object inside the cone is strongly lit.

### 12 c). Point

On applying this effect to a node, a light is simulated on it, as if it is being generated by a point light source.
Point Light Source – The light from this source attenuates in all directions from a single point. The intensity of the light gets weaker the further away the object is from the source.

### 13. Image Input

Image input effect in JavaFX just embeds an image to the JavaFX screen.

Just like Color Input effect (It is used to pass the specified colored rectangular region as input to other effect), Image Input effect is used to pass the specified image as an input to another effect.

### 14. Color Adjust

You can adjust the color of an image by applying the color adjust effect to it. This includes the adjustment of the hue, saturation, brightness and contrast on each pixel

### 15 . Color Input

Color Input Effect gives the same output as drawing a rectangle and filling it with color. Unlike other effects, if this effect is applied to any node, it displays only a rectangular box (not the node). This effect is mostly used as an input for other effects.

### 16. Blend

In general, blend means mixture of two or more different things. If we apply this blend effect, it takes the pixels of two different inputs, at the same location and it produces a combined output based on the blend mode.

### 17. Color Fitering using Blend

**18. DisplacementMap**
Displacement maps apply non-linear distortions to images.

# Dropshadows

## 1. Dropshadow 1

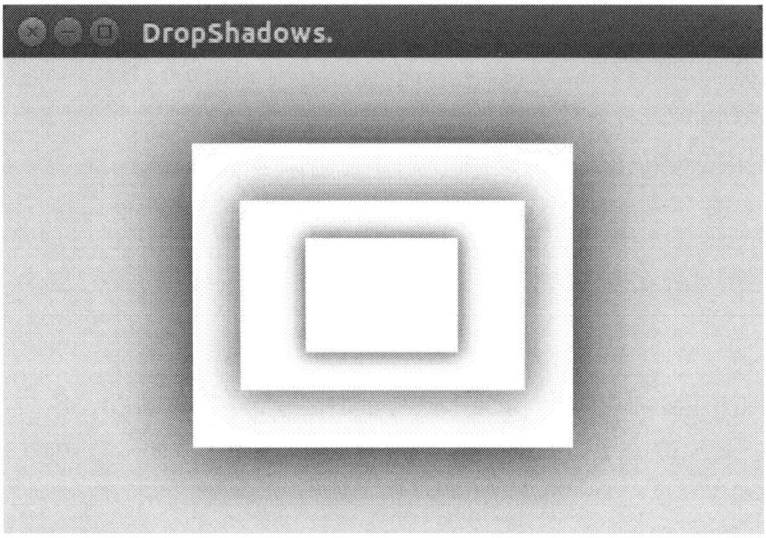


*// DropShadow1.java*
*/**
*DropShadow renders a shadow behind the object with the specified colour, radius, and offset.*

*Constructors:*
*DropShadow():A DropShadow with default parameters.*
*DropShadow(blurType,color, radius, spread, offsetX, offsetY): A DropShadow with the specified blurType, color, radius, spread, offsetX and offsetY.*
*DropShadow(radius, color):A DropShadow with the specified radius and color.*
*DropShadow(radius, offsetX, offsetY, color): A DropShadow with the specified radius, offsetX, offsetY and color.*

*Parameters:*
*blurType - the default algorithm used to blur the shadow = THREE_PASS_BOX.*
*color - the shadow Color*
*radius - the radius of the shadow blur kernel*

```
Tested on: java version "java-8-oracle"
Author: Mike Ohlson de Fine
*/

import javafx.application.Application;
import javafx.stage.Stage;
import javafx.scene.Scene;
import javafx.scene.effect.DropShadow;
import javafx.scene.layout.StackPane;
import javafx.scene.paint.Color;
import javafx.scene.shape.Rectangle;

public class DropShadow1 extends Application {

  public void start(Stage stage)
  {
     StackPane root = new StackPane();

     Rectangle rect1 = new Rectangle(0, 0, 200, 160);
     rect1.setFill(Color.WHITE);
     DropShadow dropsh1 = new DropShadow(60, Color.DARKBLUE); //
Radius, color
     rect1.setEffect(dropsh1);
     root.getChildren().add(rect1);

     Rectangle rect2 = new Rectangle(100, 0, 150, 100);
     rect2.setFill(Color.WHITE);
     DropShadow dropsh2 = new DropShadow(30, Color.BROWN);
     rect2.setEffect(dropsh2);
     root.getChildren().add(rect2);

     Rectangle rect3 = new Rectangle(200, 0, 80, 60);
     rect3.setFill(Color.WHITE);
     DropShadow dropsh3 = new DropShadow(15, Color.DARKGREEN);
     rect3.setEffect(dropsh3);
     root.getChildren().add(rect3);

    Scene scene = new Scene(root, 400, 250, Color.rgb(200, 250, 200, 1.0));

     stage.setTitle("DropShadows.");
```

```
      stage.setScene(scene);
      stage.show();
   }
}
```

# Dropshadow 2

```
// DropShadow2.java
/*
Two DropShadows applied to separate objects.

Constructors used:
1. DropShadow():A DropShadow with default parameters.
2. DropShadow(radius, offsetX, offsetY, color): A DropShadow with the
specified radius, offsetX, offsetY and color.

Parameters:
blurType - the algorithm used to blur the shadow. THREE_PASS_BOX
(default), GAUSSEAN, .
color - the shadow Color
radius - the radius of the shadow blur kernel
spread - the portion of the radius where the contribution of the source material
will be 100%
offsetX - the shadow offset in the x direction
```

```
offsetY - the shadow offset in the y direction

Tested on: java version "java-8-oracle"
Author: Mike Ohlson de Fine
*/

import javafx.application.Application;
import javafx.stage.Stage;
import javafx.scene.Scene;
import javafx.scene.effect.DropShadow;
import javafx.scene.layout.StackPane;
import javafx.scene.paint.Color;
import javafx.scene.shape.*;


public class DropShadow2 extends Application
{
   public void start(Stage stage)
   {
      StackPane root = new StackPane();

      Rectangle rect1 = new Rectangle(0, 0, 100, 100);
      rect1.setFill(Color.WHITE);

      Circle circ1 = new Circle(140, 150, 40);
      circ1.setFill(Color.rgb(250, 220, 220, 1.0));

      DropShadow dropsh1 = new DropShadow(40, Color.DARKBLUE);
      DropShadow dropsh2 = new DropShadow(25, 40, 60,
Color.DARKBLUE);

      rect1.setEffect(dropsh1);
      root.getChildren().add(rect1);

      circ1.setEffect(dropsh2);
      root.getChildren().add(circ1);

      Scene scene = new Scene(root, 300, 300, Color.rgb(200, 250, 200, 1.0));

      stage.setTitle("DropShadows.");
      stage.setScene(scene);
```

```
        stage.show();
    }
}
```

## DropShadow 3

```
//DropShadow3.java
/*
Various DropShadows applied to rectangle nodes.

Constructors used:
1. DropShadow():A DropShadow with default parameters.

Parameters:
blurType - the algorithm used to blur the shadow. THREE_PASS_BOX
(default), GAUSSEAN, .
```

```
color - the shadow Color
radius - the radius of the shadow blur kernel
spread - the portion of the radius where the contribution of the source material
will be 100%
offsetX - the shadow offset in the x direction
offsetY - the shadow offset in the y direction

Tested on: java version "java-8-oracle"
Author: Mike Ohlson de Fine
*/

import javafx.application.Application;
import javafx.stage.Stage;
import javafx.scene.Scene;
import javafx.scene.Group;
import javafx.scene.effect.DropShadow;
import javafx.scene.layout.StackPane;
import javafx.scene.paint.Color;
import javafx.scene.shape.*;

public class DropShadow3 extends Application
{
    public Rectangle createShadowedBox(double x, double y, double size,
                              double shadowWidth, double shadowHeight,
                              double offsetX, double offsetY, double radius)

     {
         Rectangle r = new Rectangle(x, y, size, size);
         r.setFill(Color.LIGHTGRAY);
         r.setStroke(Color.BLACK);
         r.setStrokeWidth(2);

         DropShadow e = new DropShadow();
         e.setWidth(shadowWidth);
         e.setHeight(shadowHeight);
         e.setOffsetX(offsetX);
         e.setOffsetY(offsetY);
         e.setRadius(radius);
         r.setEffect(e);
         return r;
      }
```

```
public void start(Stage stage)
{
    Group rootgroup = new Group() ;

    //  Memory aid for parameters: ( x,  y   size, shadW, shadH, offserX,
offsetY, radius
    Rectangle rct1 = createShadowedBox(20,  20,  60,   10,   10,   5,    5,
10);
    Rectangle rct2 = createShadowedBox(120, 20,  60,   20,   20,   10,   10,
10);
    Rectangle rct3 = createShadowedBox(230, 20,  60,   30,   30,   15,   15,
10);
    Rectangle rct4 = createShadowedBox(20,  120, 60,   20,   20,   0,    0,
10);
    Rectangle rct5 = createShadowedBox(120, 120, 60,   20,   20,   0,    10,
10);
    Rectangle rct6 = createShadowedBox(230, 120, 60,   20,   20,   10,   0,
10);
    Rectangle rct7 = createShadowedBox(20,  220, 60,   20,   20,   10,   10,
0);
    Rectangle rct8 = createShadowedBox(120, 220, 60,   20,   20,   10,   10,
20);
    Rectangle rct9 = createShadowedBox(230, 220, 60,   20,   20,   10,   10,
50);

    rootgroup.getChildren().addAll(rct1, rct2, rct3, rct4, rct5, rct6, rct7, rct8,
rct9 );
    Scene scene = new Scene(rootgroup, 340, 320, Color.rgb(200, 250, 200,
1.0));

    stage.setTitle("DropShadows Various.");
    stage.setScene(scene);
    stage.show();
  }
}
```

# 4. InnerShadow

```
// InnerShadow1.java
/*
InnerShadow .

Constructors
1. InnerShadow(radius, color)
2. InnerShadow(radius, offsetX, offsetY, color)
3. InnerShadow(blurType, color, radius, choke, offsetX, offsetY)

Parameters:
radius - the radius of the shadow blur kernel.
choke - the portion of the radius where the contribution of the source material
will be 100%.
color - the shadow Color.
offsetX - the shadow offset in the x direction.
offsetY - the shadow offset in the y direction.
blurType - the algorithm used to blur the shadow.

Tested on: java version "java-8-oracle"
Author: Mike Ohlson de Fine
*/
import javafx.application.Application;
import javafx.scene.text.Text;
import javafx.stage.Stage;
import javafx.scene.Scene;

import javafx.scene.layout.StackPane;
import javafx.scene.paint.Color;
import javafx.scene.text.Font;
import javafx.scene.text.FontWeight;
import javafx.scene.text.Text;
import javafx.scene.effect.Reflection;
import javafx.scene.effect.InnerShadow;
```

```
public class InnerShadow1 extends Application
{
   public void start(Stage stage)
   {
      StackPane root = new StackPane();

      Text text = new Text();
      text.setText("Laser-cut Carvings");
      text.setFill(Color.YELLOW);
      text.setFont(Font.font("Serif", FontWeight.BOLD, 80));

      InnerShadow innershad =  new InnerShadow(10., Color.RED);
      innershad. setOffsetX(4);
      innershad. setOffsetY(4);

      text.setEffect(innershad);

      root.getChildren().add(text);
      Scene scene = new Scene(root, 1000, 180, Color.LIGHTBLUE);
      stage.setTitle("The Inner Shadow Effect");
      stage.setScene(scene);
      stage.show();

   }
}
```

# Glow

The image below is unaltered – it has had no effect applied to it.

The next image has had the glow effect applied to it using the program *glowCat1.java*

```
// glowCat1.java
/*
Glow effect make bright pixels brighter.

Constructors:
Glow(): Glow with default parameters.
Glow(double_level): A Glow with specified intensity level of glow.
Parameters:
level - the level value, which controls the intensity of the glow effect

Tested on: java version "java-8-oracle"
Author: Mike Ohlson de Fine
*/
import javafx.application.Application;
import javafx.stage.Stage;
import javafx.scene.Scene;
import javafx.scene.effect.Effect;
import javafx.scene.effect.Glow;
import javafx.scene.Group;
import javafx.scene.image.Image;
import javafx.scene.image.ImageView;
```

```
public class glowCat1 extends Application
{
   public void start(Stage primaryStage)
   {
      primaryStage.setTitle("Glowing Bella");
      final Group rootgroup = new Group();

      ImageView viewcat = new ImageView(new Image("bella2_500.jpg"));
      final Effect glow = new Glow(5.0);
      viewcat.setEffect(glow);
      rootgroup.getChildren().add(viewcat);

      final Scene scene = new Scene(rootgroup, 500, 485);
      primaryStage.setScene(scene);
      primaryStage.show();
   }
}
```

## Bloom

The bloom effect shown below is similar to the glow effect except that the light colored areas are emphasized.

```
// bloomCat1.java
/*
Bloom effect makes bright pixels brighter.

Constructors:
Bloom(): Bloom with default parameters (Threshold = 0.3).
Bloom(double_threshold): A Bloom with specified threshold in the range 0 to
1.0
Parameters:
threshold - the level value, which controls the minimum luminosity value of
the pixels that will be made to glow.

Tested on: java version "java-8-oracle"
Author: Mike Ohlson de Fine
*/
import javafx.application.Application;
import javafx.stage.Stage;
import javafx.scene.Scene;
import javafx.scene.effect.Effect;
import javafx.scene.effect.Bloom;
import javafx.scene.Group;
import javafx.scene.image.Image;
import javafx.scene.image.ImageView;

public class bloomCat1 extends Application
{
  public void start(Stage primaryStage)
  {
    primaryStage.setTitle("Blooming Bella at 0.3");
    final Group rootgroup = new Group();

    ImageView viewcat = new ImageView(new Image("bella2_500.jpg"));
    Bloom bloom = new Bloom();
    bloom.setThreshold(0.3); // value for 0-1.0, default 0.3.
    viewcat.setEffect(bloom);
    rootgroup.getChildren().add(viewcat);

    final Scene scene = new Scene(rootgroup, 500, 485);
    primaryStage.setScene(scene);
    primaryStage.show();
  }
```

```
}
```

# SepiaTone

Here the dark-to-light range of the image has been rendered in shades of red-brown.

```
// sepiaCat1.java
/*
Sepia tones are the ranges of orange-to-brown found in antique photographs.
Bloom
Constructors:
SepiaTone(): A SepiaTone with default sepia value of 1.0.
SepiaTone(double level): A SepiaTone with the specified level between 0 and
1.0
Parameters:
level - the intensity of the effect.

Tested on: java version "java-8-oracle"
Author: Mike Ohlson de Fine
*/
import javafx.application.Application;
import javafx.stage.Stage;
import javafx.scene.Scene;
import javafx.scene.effect.Effect;
import javafx.scene.effect.SepiaTone;
```

```
import javafx.scene.Group;
import javafx.scene.image.Image;
import javafx.scene.image.ImageView;

public class sepiaCat1 extends Application
{
  public void start(Stage primaryStage)
  {
    primaryStage.setTitle("Sepia Bella at 0.8");
    final Group rootgroup = new Group();

    ImageView viewcat = new ImageView(new Image("bella2_500.jpg"));
    SepiaTone sepia = new SepiaTone();
    sepia.setLevel(0.8); // value for 0-1.0, default 1.0
    viewcat.setEffect(sepia);
    rootgroup.getChildren().add(viewcat);

    final Scene scene = new Scene(rootgroup, 500, 485);
    primaryStage.setScene(scene);
    primaryStage.show();
  }
}
```

## GausseanBlur

A Gaussian blur smears out the edges less than the central portion of any dark area.

```
// GaussianBlur1.java
/*
A GaussianBlur with the an adjustable blur radius.
Constructors:
```

```
-----------------
GaussianBlur():  A GaussianBlur with default parameters.
GaussianBlur(radius): A GaussianBlur with specified radius.

Parameters:
radius - the radius of the blur kernel

Tested on: java version "java-8-oracle"
Author: Mike Ohlson de Fine
*/
import javafx.application.Application;
import javafx.stage.Stage;
import javafx.scene.Scene;
import javafx.beans.property.DoubleProperty;
import javafx.beans.property.SimpleDoubleProperty;
import javafx.geometry.Insets;
import javafx.scene.control.Slider;
import javafx.scene.effect.GaussianBlur;
import javafx.scene.layout.VBox;
import javafx.scene.paint.Color;
import javafx.scene.text.Font;
import javafx.scene.text.Text;

public class GaussianBlur1 extends Application
{
  public void start(Stage stage)
  {

      VBox root = new VBox(30);
      root.setPadding(new Insets(20));

      DoubleProperty radius = new SimpleDoubleProperty(0);

      Text blurredText = new Text("My Eyes grow dim.");
      blurredText.setFont(Font.font(60));

      Slider slider = new Slider(1, 20, 1);
      radius.bind(slider.valueProperty());
      slider.valueProperty().addListener(event -> {
         blurredText.setEffect(new GaussianBlur(radius.get()));
      });
```

```
        root.getChildren().addAll(slider, blurredText);

        Scene scene = new Scene(root, 600, 160);
        stage.setTitle("The Gaussian Blur effect");
        stage.setScene(scene);
        stage.show();
    }
}
```

## BoxBlur

The box blur is similar to the Gaussian blur but it is less precise but can be computed faster inside the computer.

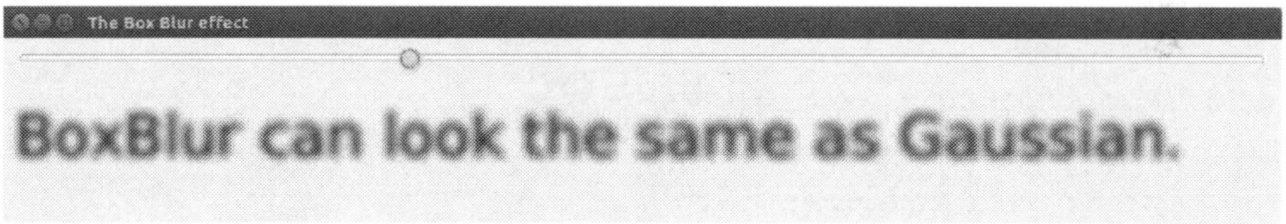


```
//BoxBlur1.java

/*
A blur effect using a simple box filter in which each pixel in the resulting
image has a value equal to the average value of its neighboring pixels
in the input image. Box blurs are used to approximate a Gaussian blur.
They are simpler and quicker to calculate provided the number of iterations is
low.
BoxBlur has separately configurable sizes in both dimensions.

Constructors:
BoxBlur(): A BoxBlur with default parameters.
BoxBlur(width, height,iterations): A BoxBlur with specified width, height and
number of iterations

Tested on: java version "java-8-oracle"
Author: Mike Ohlson de Fine
*/
import javafx.application.Application;
import javafx.stage.Stage;
```

```
import javafx.beans.property.DoubleProperty;
import javafx.beans.property.SimpleDoubleProperty;
import javafx.geometry.Insets;
import javafx.scene.Scene;
import javafx.scene.control.Slider;
import javafx.scene.layout.VBox;
import javafx.scene.paint.Color;
import javafx.scene.text.Font;
import javafx.scene.text.Text;

import javafx.scene.effect.BoxBlur;

public class BoxBlur1 extends Application
{
   public void start(Stage stage)
   {

      VBox root = new VBox(30);
      root.setPadding(new Insets(10));

      DoubleProperty radius = new SimpleDoubleProperty(0);

      Text blurredText = new Text("BoxBlur can look the same as Gaussian.");
      blurredText.setFont(Font.font(50));

      Slider slider = new Slider(1, 20, 1);
      radius.bind(slider.valueProperty());

      slider.valueProperty().addListener(event -> {
        blurredText.setEffect(new BoxBlur(radius.get(), radius.get(), 10));
      });

      root.getChildren().addAll(slider, blurredText);

      Scene scene = new Scene(root, 1100, 160, Color.BLUE);  // Color has no
effect -  VBox?

      stage.setTitle("The Box Blur effect");
      stage.setScene(scene);
      stage.show();
   }
```

```
}
```

## MotionBlur

This smears the image more in one direction than others.

```
// MotionBlur1.java

/*
A MotionBlur with the an adjustable blur radius.

Constructors:
MotionBlur():  A MotionBlur with default parameters.
MotionBlur(angle, radius): A MotionBlur with the specified angle and radius


Parameters:
radius - the radius of the blur kernel

Tested on: java version "java-8-oracle"
Author: Mike Ohlson de Fine
*/
import javafx.application.Application;
import javafx.stage.Stage;
import javafx.scene.Scene;
import javafx.beans.property.DoubleProperty;
import javafx.beans.property.SimpleDoubleProperty;
import javafx.geometry.Insets;
import javafx.scene.control.Slider;
import javafx.scene.layout.VBox;
import javafx.scene.paint.Color;
import javafx.scene.text.Font;
import javafx.scene.text.Text;
```

```
import javafx.scene.effect.MotionBlur;

public class MotionBlur1 extends Application
{
   public void start(Stage stage)

   {
      double blur_angle = 15 ;
      VBox root = new VBox(30);
      root.setPadding(new Insets(20));

      DoubleProperty radius = new SimpleDoubleProperty(0);

      Text blurredText = new Text("The Speed of the Rocket.");
      blurredText.setFont(Font.font(60));

      Slider slider = new Slider(1, 20, 1);
      radius.bind(slider.valueProperty());

      slider.valueProperty().addListener(event -> {
         blurredText.setEffect(new MotionBlur(blur_angle, radius.get()));
      });

      root.getChildren().addAll(slider, blurredText);

      Scene scene = new Scene(root, 800, 160);
      stage.setTitle("The Motion Blur effect");
      stage.setScene(scene);
      stage.show();
   }
}
```

## Reflection

This simulates reflection on a shiny surface.

```
// Reflection1.java
/*
Reflection renders a reflected copy of the input below the actual input content.

Constructors:
Reflection(): A Reflection with default parameters
public Reflection(topOffset, fraction, topOpacity, bottomOpacity): A Reflection
with the specified topOffset, fraction, topOpacity and bottomOpacity.

Parameters:
topOffset - the distance between the bottom of the input and the top of the
reflection
fraction - the fraction of the input that is visible in the reflection.
topOpacity - the opacity of the reflection at its top extreme
bottomOpacity - the opacity of the reflection at its bottom extreme

Tested on: java version "java-8-oracle"
Author: Mike Ohlson de Fine
*/

import javafx.application.Application;
import javafx.scene.Scene;
import javafx.scene.effect.Reflection;
import javafx.scene.layout.StackPane;
import javafx.scene.paint.Color;
import javafx.scene.text.Font;
import javafx.scene.text.FontWeight;
import javafx.scene.text.Text;
```

```
import javafx.stage.Stage;

public class Reflection1 extends Application
{
  public void start(Stage stage)
  {
    StackPane root = new StackPane();

    Text text = new Text();
    text.setText("Clouds Illusions Recalled");
    text.setFill(Color.BLUE);
    text.setFont(Font.font("Serif", FontWeight.BOLD, 50));

    Reflection reflect = new Reflection();
    text.setEffect(reflect);

    root.getChildren().add(text);
    Scene scene = new Scene(root, 800, 200, Color.PALEGREEN);

    stage.setTitle("The Reflection Effect");
    stage.setScene(scene);
    stage.show();
  }
}
```

## Perspective

The geometry is distorted to create the illusion of distance.

```
// Perspective1.java
/*
The PerspectiveTransform is used to provide a simulated three-dimensional
effect for otherwise two-dimensional content.
A perspective transformation is capable of mapping an arbitrary
quadrilateral into another arbitrary quadrilateral,
while preserving the straightness of lines.The parallelism of lines in the source
is not necessarily preserved in the output.

Constructor used (more available).
PerspectiveTransform(ulx, uly, urx, ury, lrx, lry, llx, lly)

Parameters:
ulx - the x coordinate of upper left corner
uly - the y coordinate of upper left corner
urx - the x coordinate of upper right corner
ury - the y coordinate of upper right corner
lrx - the x coordinate of lower right corner
lry - the y coordinate of lower right corner
llx - the x coordinate of lower left corner
lly - the y coordinate of lower left corner

Tested on: java version "java-8-oracle"
Author: Mike Ohlson de Fine
*/

import javafx.application.Application;
import javafx.stage.Stage;
import javafx.scene.Scene;
import javafx.scene.layout.Pane;
import javafx.scene.layout.StackPane;
import javafx.scene.paint.Color;
import javafx.scene.shape.Rectangle;

import javafx.scene.effect.PerspectiveTransform;

public class Perspective1 extends Application
{
   int SIZE = 50; // Size of squares on board.
```

```
  public void start(Stage stage)
  {
    StackPane root = new StackPane();
     Pane chessboard = new Pane();

     // Make a Chessboard.
     for (int row = 0; row < 8; row++)
     {
        for (int col = 0; col < 8; col++)
        {
            Rectangle rect1 = new Rectangle(col * SIZE, row*SIZE,
                              SIZE, SIZE);

           if ((col+row) % 2 == 0) { rect1.setFill(Color.WHITE); }
              else {  rect1.setFill(Color.BLACK); }

            chessboard.getChildren().add(rect1);
        }
     }

     PerspectiveTransform perspec = new PerspectiveTransform();
     perspec.setUlx(80);      // Upper-left point
     perspec.setUly(50);
     perspec.setUrx(320);     // Upper-right point
     perspec.setUry(50);
     perspec.setLlx(0);       // Lower-left point
     perspec.setLly(200);
     perspec.setLrx(400);     // Lower-right point
     perspec.setLry(200);
     chessboard.setEffect(perspec);

     root.getChildren().add(chessboard);

     Scene scene = new Scene(root, Color.BLACK);
     stage.setTitle("ChessBoard in perspective");
     stage.setScene(scene);
     stage.show();
  }
}
```

```
// Perspective2.java
/*
The PerspectiveTransform is used to provide a simulated three-dimensional
effect for otherwise two-dimensional content.
A perspective transformation is capable of mapping an arbitrary
quadrilateral into another arbitrary quadrilateral,
while preserving the straightness of lines.The parallelism of lines in the source
is not necessarily preserved in the output.

Constructor used (more available).
PerspectiveTransform(ulx, uly, urx, ury, lrx, lry, llx, lly)

Parameters:
ulx - the x coordinate of upper left corner
uly - the y coordinate of upper left corner
urx - the x coordinate of upper right corner
ury - the y coordinate of upper right corner
lrx - the x coordinate of lower right corner
lry - the y coordinate of lower right corner
llx - the x coordinate of lower left corner
lly - the y coordinate of lower left corner

Tested on: java version "java-8-oracle"
Author: Mike Ohlson de Fine
*/
import javafx.application.Application;
import javafx.stage.Stage;
```

```
import javafx.scene.Scene;
import javafx.scene.Group;
import javafx.scene.paint.Color;
import javafx.scene.image.Image;
import javafx.scene.image.ImageView;
import javafx.scene.effect.PerspectiveTransform;

public class Perspective2 extends Application
{
   public void start(Stage stage)
   {
      final Group rootgroup = new Group();
     ImageView viewcourt = new ImageView(new
Image("O_V_courtyard_500.jpg"));

      PerspectiveTransform perspec = new PerspectiveTransform();
      perspec.setUlx(90);     // Upper-left point
      perspec.setUly(10);

      perspec.setUrx(380);    // Upper-right point
      perspec.setUry(10);

      perspec.setLlx(10);     // Lower-left point
      perspec.setLly(400);

      perspec.setLrx(490);    // Lower-right point
      perspec.setLry(400);

      rootgroup.setEffect(perspec);
      rootgroup.getChildren().add(viewcourt);
;
      Scene scene = new Scene(rootgroup, 510, 410, Color.BLACK);
      stage.setTitle("Oak&Vigne in perspective");
      stage.setScene(scene);
      stage.show();
   }
}
```

# Lighting (distant, spot, point)

The three circles shown below are illuminated by a simulated spot light, a point light source and a far distant light source.

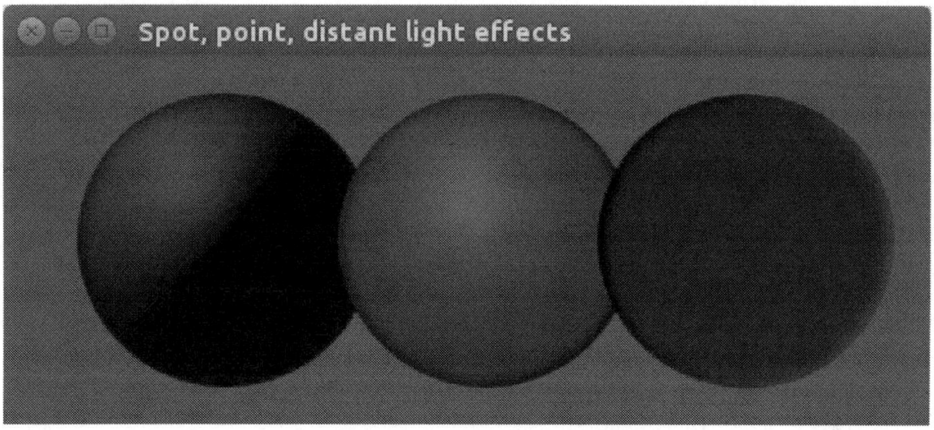


```
// Light1.java
/*
An effect that simulates a light source shining on the given content.
It is used to give flat objects a more realistic, three-dimensional appearance.

SpotLight: Parallel rays from a single source.
Point Light: Defines a point light source object. A light source that has a fixed
point in space and radiates light equally in all directions away from itself.
Distant Light: Light from very far away.

Constructors:
Lighting(): Lighting with default parameters.
Lighting(Light_light): Lighting with the specified light

Tested on: java version "java-8-oracle"
Author: Mike Ohlson de Fine
*/
import javafx.application.Application;
import javafx.stage.Stage;
import javafx.scene.Group;
import javafx.scene.Scene;
import javafx.scene.effect.Light;
import javafx.scene.effect.Light.Distant;
```

```
import javafx.scene.PointLight;
import javafx.scene.effect.Lighting;
import javafx.scene.paint.Color;
import javafx.scene.shape.Circle;

public class Lighting1 extends Application
{
  public void start(Stage stage)
  {
    Circle circle1 = new Circle(120.0, 100.0, 80.0,
Color.CORNFLOWERBLUE);
    Circle circle2 = new Circle(260.0, 100.0, 80.0,
Color.CORNFLOWERBLUE);
    Circle circle3 = new Circle(400.0, 100.0, 80.0,
Color.CORNFLOWERBLUE);

    // light1 a spot light.
    Light.Spot spotlight = new Light.Spot();
    spotlight.setColor(Color.GRAY);
    spotlight.setX(70); // Position of the light source
    spotlight.setY(55);
    spotlight.setZ(45);
    Lighting light1 = new Lighting();
    light1.setLight(spotlight);
    circle1.setEffect(light1);

    // light2 a point light source.
    Light.Point pointlight = new Light.Point();
    pointlight.setColor(Color.GRAY);
    pointlight.setX(70); // Position of the light source
    pointlight.setY(55);
    pointlight.setZ(45);
    Lighting light2 = new Lighting();
    light2.setLight(pointlight);
    circle2.setEffect(light2);

    // light3 a distant light source.
    Light.Distant distantlight = new Light.Distant();
    distantlight.setColor(Color.GRAY);
    distantlight.setAzimuth(10);   // Position of the light source
    distantlight.setElevation(15);
```

```
    Lighting light3 = new Lighting();
    light3.setLight(distantlight);
    circle3.setEffect(light3);

    Group rootgroup = new Group(circle1, circle2,circle3);
    Scene scene = new Scene(rootgroup, 500, 200, Color.GREEN);
    stage.setTitle("Spot, point, distant light effects");
    stage.setScene(scene);
    stage.show();
  }
}
```

## Lighting Sources on Text

```
// DistSpotLight1.java
/*
Looking at distant ans spot light sourves on text

SpotLight: Parallel rays from a single source.
Distant Light: Light from very far away.

Tested on: java version "java-8-oracle"
Author: Mike Ohlson de Fine
*/
import javafx.application.Application;
import javafx.stage.Stage;
import javafx.scene.Group;
import javafx.scene.Scene;
```

```
import javafx.scene.paint.Color;
import javafx.scene.shape.Rectangle;
import javafx.scene.text.*;

import javafx.scene.effect.Light;
import javafx.scene.effect.Light.Distant;
import javafx.scene.effect.Light.Spot;
import javafx.scene.effect.Lighting;

public class DistSpotLight1 extends Application
{
  public void start(Stage stage)
  {
    // DISTANT LIGHT
    Light.Distant distlight = new Light.Distant();
    distlight.setAzimuth(45.0);
    distlight.setElevation(30.0);
    Lighting Dlighting = new Lighting();
    Dlighting.setLight(distlight);
    Dlighting.setSurfaceScale(10.0);

    Text text1 = new Text();
    text1.setText("A Distant Light Source");
    text1.setFill(Color.STEELBLUE);
    text1.setFont(Font.font("null", FontWeight.BOLD, 60));
    text1.setX(80.0f);
    text1.setY(110.0f);
    text1.setTextAlignment(TextAlignment.CENTER) ;
    text1.setEffect(Dlighting);

    Rectangle rect1 = new Rectangle(40, 30, 840,120);
    rect1.setFill(Color.ALICEBLUE);
    rect1.setEffect(Dlighting);

    // SPOT LIGHT
    Light.Spot spotlight = new Light.Spot();
    spotlight.setX(650);
    spotlight.setY(100);
    spotlight.setZ(80);
    spotlight.setPointsAtX(0);
    spotlight.setPointsAtY(0);
```

```
    spotlight.setPointsAtZ(-70);
    Lighting Slighting = new Lighting();
    Slighting.setLight(spotlight);
    Slighting.setSurfaceScale(10.0);

    Text text2 = new Text();
    text2.setText("A Spot Light Source");
    text2.setFill(Color.STEELBLUE);
    text2.setFont(Font.font("null", FontWeight.BOLD, 60));
    text2.setX(80.0f);
    text2.setY(320.0f);
    text2.setTextAlignment(TextAlignment.CENTER) ;
    text2.setEffect(Slighting);

    Rectangle rect2 = new Rectangle(40, 230, 840,120);
    rect2.setFill(Color.ALICEBLUE);
    rect2.setEffect(Slighting);

    Group rootgroup = new Group(rect1, text1, rect2, text2);
    Scene scene = new Scene(rootgroup, 940, 400, Color.GREEN);
    stage.setTitle("Distant and Spot light effects");
    stage.setScene(scene);
    stage.show();
  }
}
```

## ColorAdjust (hue, saturtion, contrast)

JavaFX has a color adjust class that can adjust hue, saturation, contrast, brightness. Good image editing software like open source GIMP and some of the many Photoshop type packages are more convenient for image color adjustment.

## BlendModes

Blend is an effect that combines two images or graphic objects using one of the many predefined blend modes. A blend mode defines the manner in which the objects are mixed together.

The best way to understand this type of subtle complexity is to experiment with various choices. The program below is designed to allow us to do just that.

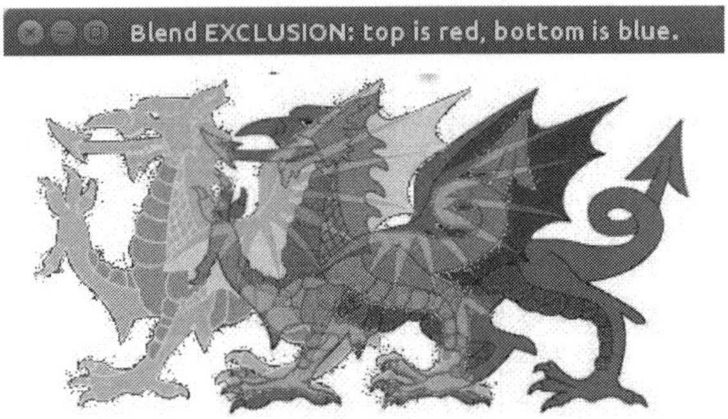


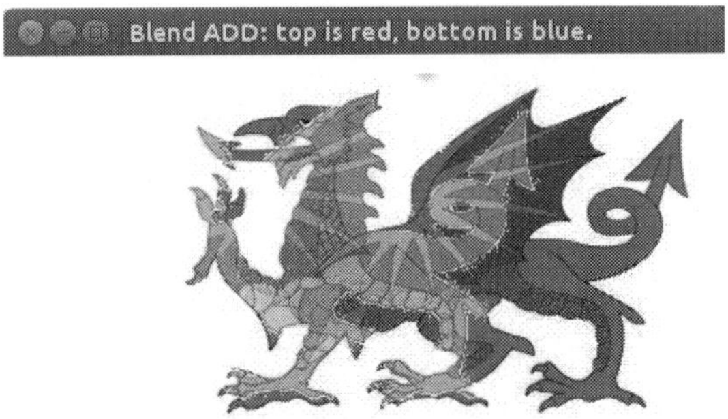


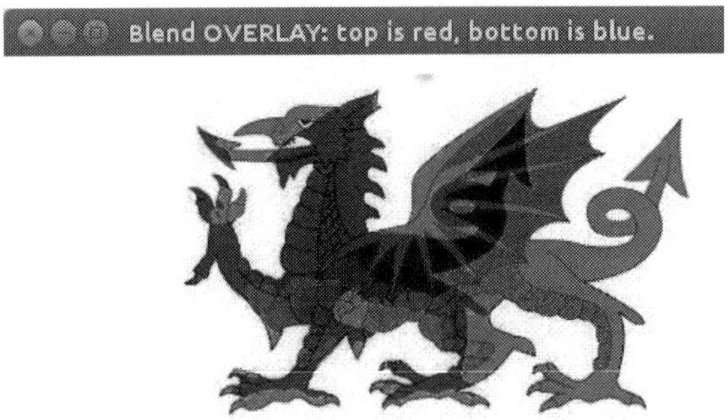

*// BlendImage1.java*
*/**
*The blend effect takes the pixels of two different inputs, does some arithmetic on each pixel*
*and produces a combined output based on the chosen blend mode.*
*Pixel for pixel each input image is blended.*

*For example, if we draw two objects; the top object covers the bottom one.*
*On applying the blend effect, the pixels of the two objects in the overlap area are combined and displayed based on the input mode.*

*Blend: class:javafx.scene.effect.Blend*
*-------------------------------------*
*Constructors*
*Blend(): A Blend with default parameters.*
*Blend(BlendMode_mode): A Blend with the specified mode.*
*Blend(BlendMode_mode, Effect_bottomInput, Effect_topInput): A Blend with the specified mode and bottom and top inputs.*

*Blend types:*
*ADD: Color values are added.*
*MULTIPLY Color values are multiplied.*
*DIFFERENCE The darker color is subtracted from the lighter one.*
*RED: Red components of the bottom are replaced by the red components of the top.*
*BLUE: Blue components of the bottom are replaced by the blue components of thetop.*
*GREEN: Green components of the bottom are replaced by the green components of thetop.*
*EXCLUSION: Color components of the two inputs are multiplied and doubled. Then they subtracted...*
*COLOR_BURN: The inverse of the bottom color is divided by the top.*
*COLOR_DODGE: The bottom input color components are divided by the inverse of the top. Thus the volor is inverted and displayed.*
*LIGHTEN:*
*DARKEN*
*SCREEN:*
*OVERLAY*
*SOFT_LIGHT*
*SRC_ATOP*
*SRC_OVER*

```
Tested on: java version "java-8-oracle"
Author: Mike Ohlson de Fine.
*/

import javafx.application.Application;
import javafx.geometry.Insets;
import javafx.scene.Group;
import javafx.scene.Scene;
import javafx.scene.effect.BlendMode;
import javafx.scene.image.Image;
import javafx.scene.image.ImageView;
import javafx.scene.layout.HBox;
import javafx.stage.Stage;

public class BlendImage1 extends Application
{
   public void start(Stage stage)
   {
      Image bottom_image = new Image("drag_blue_right_400_200.png"); //
Bottom
      Image top_image = new Image("drag_red_left_400_200.png");      // Top.

      ImageView bottom = new ImageView(bottom_image);
      ImageView top = new ImageView(top_image);
      //top.setBlendMode(BlendMode.ADD);
      //top.setBlendMode(BlendMode.MULTIPLY);
      top.setBlendMode(BlendMode.DIFFERENCE);
      //top.setBlendMode(BlendMode.RED);
      //top.setBlendMode(BlendMode.BLUE);
      //top.setBlendMode(BlendMode.GREEN);
      //top.setBlendMode(BlendMode.EXCLUSION);
      //top.setBlendMode(BlendMode.COLOR_BURN);
      //top.setBlendMode(BlendMode.COLOR_DODGE);
      //top.setBlendMode(BlendMode.LIGHTEN);
      //top.setBlendMode(BlendMode.DARKEN);
      //top.setBlendMode(BlendMode.SCREEN);
      //top.setBlendMode(BlendMode.OVERLAY);
      //top.setBlendMode(BlendMode.SOFT_LIGHT);
      //top.setBlendMode(BlendMode.SRC_ATOP);
      //top.setBlendMode(BlendMode.SRC_OVER);
```

```
        Group blend = new Group(bottom, top
        );

        HBox hbx_layout = new HBox(10);
        hbx_layout.getChildren().addAll(blend);

        hbx_layout.setPadding(new Insets(10));
        stage.setScene(new Scene(hbx_layout));
        stage.setTitle("Blend DIFFERENCE: top is red, bottom is blue.");
        stage.show();
    }
}
```

## Color Filters using BlendImage

Separate an image into its major color components: red, yellow, green, blue.

```
// BlendImageColorFilter1.java
/*
To separate an images into its primary color components.

Put the image to be filtered on the bottom and the pure color on the top (red,
green or blue)
and then use the MULTIPLY blend mode. The result will act as a pure color
filter applied
to the image.
```

```
Tested on: java version "java-8-oracle"
Author: Mike Ohlson de Fine.
*/
import javafx.application.Application;
import javafx.stage.Stage;
import javafx.scene.Group;
import javafx.scene.Scene;
import javafx.scene.effect.Blend;
import javafx.scene.effect.BlendMode;
import javafx.scene.effect.ColorInput;
import javafx.scene.paint.Color;
import javafx.scene.image.Image;
import javafx.scene.image.ImageView;

public class BlendColorFilter1 extends Application
{
  public void start(Stage stage)
  {

    Image image1 = new Image("regentB_400.png") ;
    ImageView imview1 = new ImageView(image1) ;
    Blend blend = new Blend();       //Instantiating the blend class

    // Select one four color filters: Red, Green, Blue, Yellow.
    ColorInput color_filter = new ColorInput(0, 0, 400, 400, Color.RED);    //
A rectangle of red.
    //ColorInput  color_filter = new ColorInput(0, 0, 400, 400,
Color.GREEN);  // A rectangle of green.
    //ColorInput  color_filter = new ColorInput(0, 0, 400, 400, Color.BLUE);
// A rectangle of blue.
    //ColorInput  color_filter = new ColorInput(0, 0, 400, 400,
Color.YELLOW); // A rectangle of yellow.
    blend.setTopInput( color_filter);              //setting the top input to the
blend object.

    blend.setMode(BlendMode.MULTIPLY);       // Multiply effectively filters
color.

    imview1.setEffect(blend);        //Apply the blend multiply effect to
image1.
```

```
    Group root = new Group(imview1);   //Creating a Group object

    Scene scene = new Scene(root, 400, 400);
    stage.setTitle("Blend Red filter on Nerina St.");
    stage.setScene(scene);
    stage.show();
  }
}
```

## DisplacementMaps

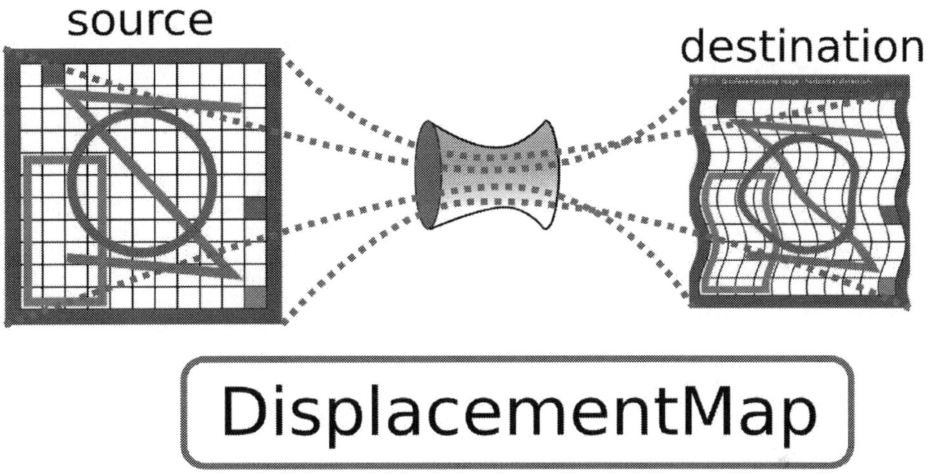


A displacement map is an effect that shifts each pixel by a distance specified by the first two bands of of the specified FloatMap. For each pixel in the output, the corresponding data from the mapData is retrieved, scaled and offset by the scale and offset attributes, scaled again by the size of the source input image and used as an offset from the destination pixel to retrieve the pixel data from the source input.

Generally speaking a mapping is the transformation of an object from one geometric space to another. The head and face shown below illustrate a mapping from a 3D geometric space to a 2D space.

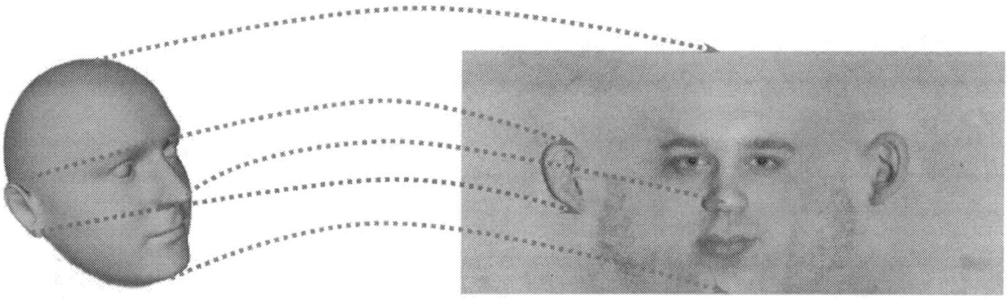

Mapping a 3D head to 2D rectangle

What is a displacement map in JavaFX? In JavaFX it is a tool for distorting the geometry of images. By distortion we mean the process of stretching parts of an image and perhaps compressing others. Additionally we may want to shift the image right or left prior to the distortion. We may want to use such techniques to create the effect of looking at parts of a picture with a magnifying glass or making thin figures look fat and fat figures look thin. In JavaFX DisplacementMaps together with FloatMaps are a way to achieve this.

The DisplacementMap looks terribly complex. However it is very versatile because we can invent almost any kind of lens effect or distortion warp we can imagine. The DisplacementMap is a kind of pixel *filter-mangler*. It takes pixels from an image one at a time and puts them into a different image. The mathematicians call this kind of space warping a mapping. Before the pixels from the source image arrive at the second image they are passed through a geometry changing mechanism of our own design. This design must be expressed in some math expressions called the FloatMap. In this chapter we will call this geometry changing mechanism the *filter-mangler* because it emphasizes the idea of distorting geometry. The Mercator projection used to draw square maps representing places on a round sphere, the Earth, is just such a mapping.

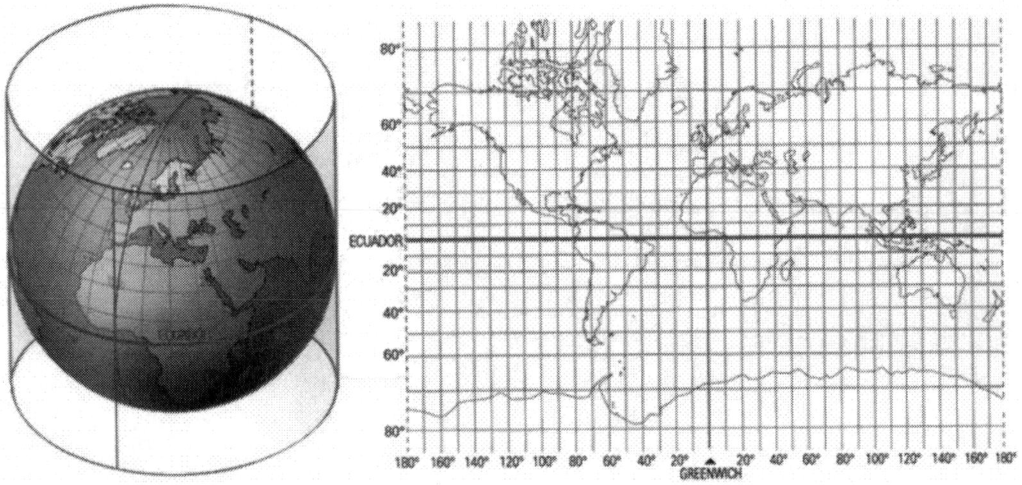


**Mercator's projection mapping: sphere to cylinder**

Pixels from one corner can be twisted and replaced near the center, some pixels can be made bigger and others smaller. The possibilities are endless, but it is tricky. We will try a series of examples that build up a general idea of how these things work.

To start off let us look at the variables that control the filter-mangler. Afterward we will explore how they operate by means of examples.

## The variables of the DisplacementMap.

**input:** The input image to the effect that we shall design.

**mapData:** Also called a FloatMap. This is the heart of the filter-mangler. It is algebra equations that determines how input pixels are mapped to output pixels.

**OffsetX:** A fixed shift horizontally that will be added to every pixel it is applied to.

**OffsetY:** A fixed shift vertically that will be added to every pixel it is applied to.

**ScaleX:** A scale or multiplication applied horizontally to pixels form the input.

**ScaleY:** A scale or multiplication applied vertically to pixels form the input.

**Wrap:** A boolean flag that signals whether or not the displacement operation should wrap around at the boundaries.

**srcWidth:** The width of the input, or source, image.

**srcHeight:** The height of the input, or source, image.

## How the Displacement Action operates

There are two equations that control how input or source pixels are mangled, one for the horizontal or x-direction and another for the vertical or y-direction.

Very simply: output[X, Y] = input[ mangled_x, mangled_y ]

In words:

Each pixel gets shifted by a distance u in the X direction and v in the Y direction specified by the first two bands of the specified FloatMap. So each pixel in the floatMap is given by a setSample() function that looks like *floatMap.setSamples(x, y, u, v);* The u and v equations can be anything we want. In some of the examples below we will use the Math.sin(…) function which creates a type of optical magnifying glass operation. This results in a distorted version of our source image sitting in memory we call the mapData. The for final display of the target image the object:

*DisplacementMap displacementMap =*

*new DisplacementMap(mapData, offsetX, offsetY, scaleX, scaleY);*

is created. That is, *f*or each pixel in the output, the corresponding data from the mapData is retrieved, scaled and offset by the scale and offset values, and then scaled again by the size of the source input image and used as an offset from the destination pixel to retrieve the pixel data from the source input.

so:

**mangled_x = x + (offsetX + scaleX * map[x, y][0]) * srcWidth**

**mangled_y= Y + (offsetY + scaleY * map[x, y][1]) * srcHeight**

here,

**map[x, y][0]** is some algebra equation (which we choose or invent) that applies to the position of the horizontal displacement, and

**map[x, y][1]** is some algebra equation (which we choose or invent) that applies to the position of the vertical displacement,

Note: For the horizontal position of a pixel in the destination image mangling algebra **map[x, y]** may use the vertical position y of the source to influence the destination position of the horizontal x pixel. In other words height location of pixels can influence width location of pixels and visa versa.

## In summary:

The pixel value at coordinates (x, y) in the output is obtained from a source pixel whose coordinates are displaced from those of the destination pixel by an amount that depends on a value obtained from a map, together with some scale factors and an offset.

## *The Effect of DisplacementMap parameters.*

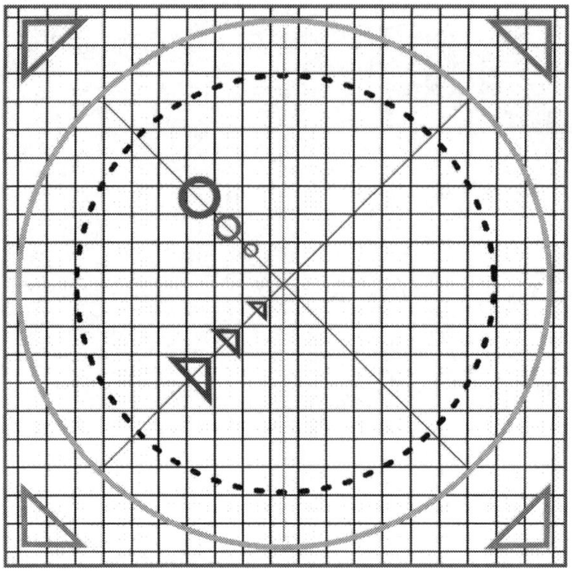

Source image: a test pattern.
Width = 500 pixels
Height = 500 pixels

## Case 1: No offset and no scaling.

**u = map[x, y][0] = u = (float) x/ srcWidth ;**

**v = map[x, y][1] = v = (float) y/ srcHeight ;**

That is the offset values are both 0 and the scale values are both 1. In this simple case,

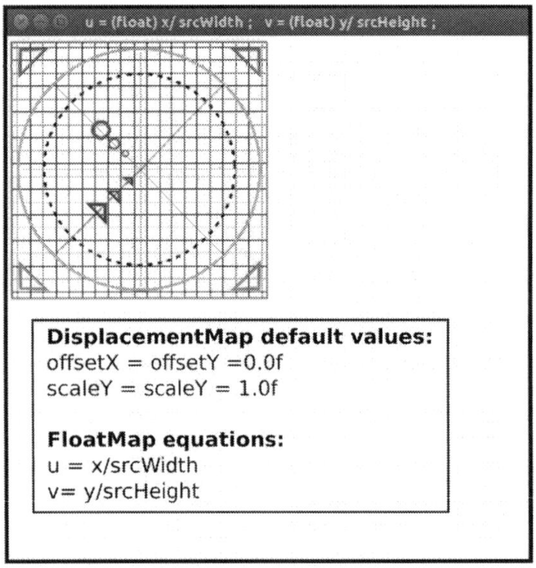

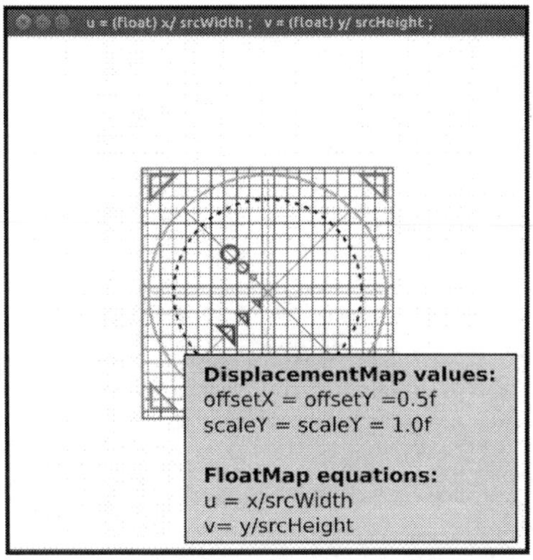


Default offsets and scale values:
OffsetX = 0
OffsetY = 0
ScaleX = 1
ScaleY = 1

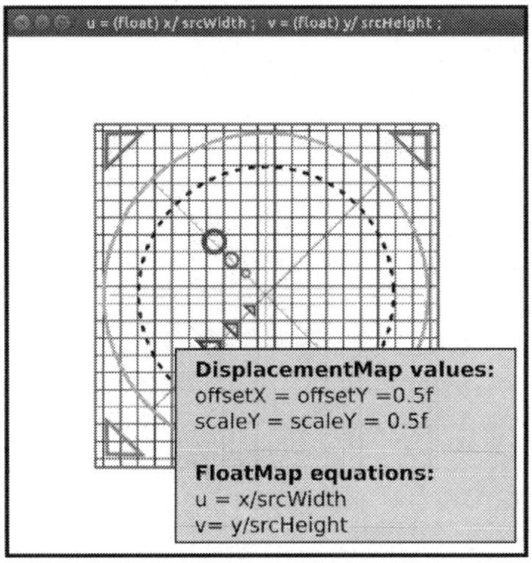


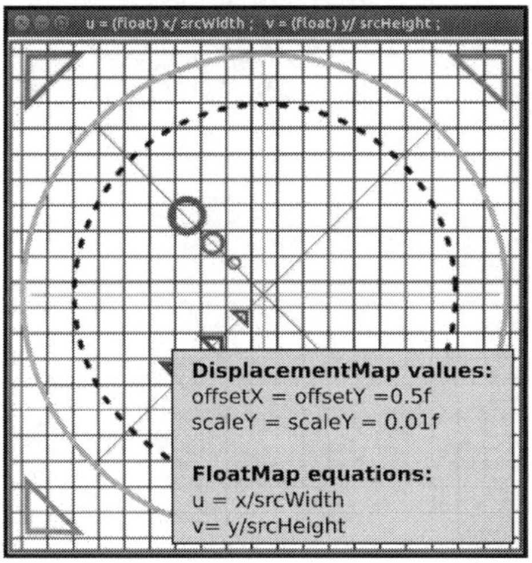

The map is a two-dimensional data structure that is indexed by the x and y coordinates of the destination point, relative to the top-left corner of the output image. Each element of this structure may contain a number of floats, which is why the class that holds these values is called a FloatMap.

TheFloatMaps that are used with a DisplacementMap must have two floats in each position, the first of which is used to control the displacement along the x-axis and the second the displacement along the y-axis.

## A Simple Example of a Basic DisplacementMap

In the example below we have four possible images to use. The first one is active in the code while the last three are non-active as they are commented out. Ant time we wish to use these we just edit out the "//" and the comment becomes an active Java instruction. The first image " *circular_target_grid_500.png"* is a special test pattern that allows us to observe what type of distortion results from the application of the DisplacementMap and it accompanying FloatMap. The FloatMap contains the algebra that distorts the geometry of the image while the DisplacementMap controls the translation and overall scaling of the distorted image.

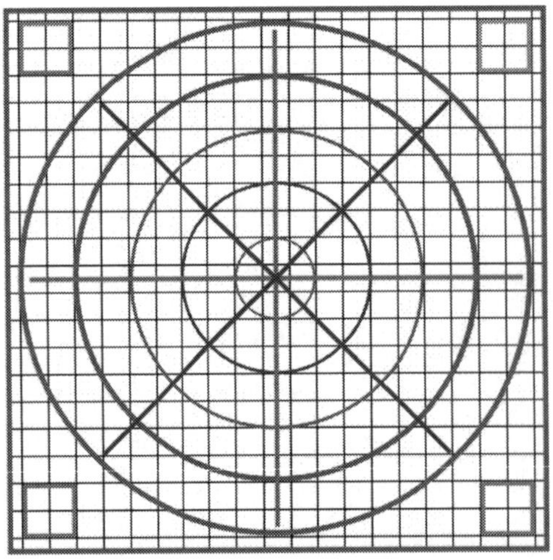

## The undistorted source Test pattern.

```
// MagnifyGlass1.java
/*
We use the sine function of trigonometry to produce a type of
magnifying optical lens that can be applied to images.
We ude the default DisplacementMap(floatMap) that has offsets of 0,
and scale factors of 1.

Tested on: java version "java-8-oracle"
Author: Mike Ohlson de Fine.
*/
import javafx.application.Application;
import javafx.stage.Stage;
import javafx.scene.Scene;

import javafx.scene.effect.DisplacementMap;
import javafx.scene.effect.Effect;
import javafx.scene.effect.FloatMap;
import javafx.scene.image.Image;
import javafx.scene.image.ImageView;
import javafx.scene.layout.StackPane;

public class MagnifyGlass1 extends Application
{
  final float sine_amplitude = 0.08f ;  // Lens Magnification factor.

  public void start(Stage primaryStage) throws Exception {
    StackPane root = new StackPane();
    root.setPrefSize(500, 500);

    ImageView view = new ImageView(new
Image("circular_target_grid_500.png"));
    //ImageView view = new ImageView(new Image("bella2_500.jpg"));
    //ImageView view = new ImageView(new Image("zoey_500.jpg"));
    //ImageView view = new ImageView(new Image("dog_500.jpg"));
    view.setEffect(createEffect(500, 500));
    root.getChildren().add(view);
```

```
        primaryStage.setTitle("DisplacementMap Magnifying Lens (ampliude:
"+sine_amplitude+").");
        Scene scene = new Scene(root);
        primaryStage.setScene(scene);
        primaryStage.show();
    }

    private Effect createEffect(int width, int height)
    {
        FloatMap floatMap = new FloatMap(width, height);

          for (int x = 0; x < width; x++)
          {
            /* The sine functions behaves similarly to a glass magnifying lens.
               The maginfication is powerful in the center and weak at the edges.
            */
            float u = (float) Math.sin(Math.PI * x / width * 2.0) * sine_amplitude;
            for (int y = 0; y < height; y++)
            {
               float v = (float) Math.sin(Math.PI * y / height * 2.0) *
sine_amplitude;
               floatMap.setSamples(x, y, u, v);
            }
          }

        DisplacementMap displacementMap = new DisplacementMap(floatMap);
        return displacementMap;
    }
}
```

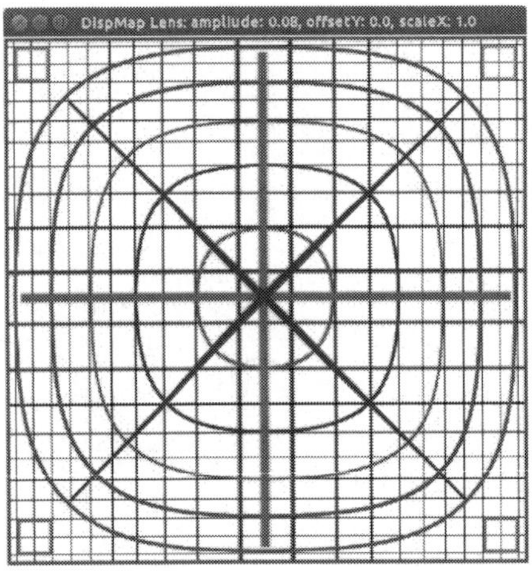


**FloatMap Lens Distortion:**
**U = Ampl*sin(b*x)**
**V = Ampl*sin(b*y)**

The line *floatMap.setSamples(x, y, u, v);* replaces each (x,y) pixel with (u,v).

Note that the FloatMap setSample() function has several overloaded variants, that is different options, of the function that we can use.

## The influence of DisplacementMap parameters.

The program below starts with:

```
public class MagnifyGlass2 extends Application

{

   final float sine_amplitude = 0.08f ; // Lens Magnification factor of FloatMapLens.

   final float offsetX = 0.0f ;        // offsetX in DisplacementMap

   final float offsetY = 0.0f ;

   final float scaleX = 1.0f ;         // Scale (multiplicaion) factor.

   final float scaleY = 0.1f ;
```

where sine_amplitude, offsetX, offsetY, scaleX, scaleY are variables whose values adjust and position the magifying lens lens.

Sine_amplitude increases the magnifying power, offsetX and offsetY shift the position of the lens in the x and y directions and scaleX and scaleY scale the resulting amplified image further, in the X and Y directions respectively.

Note that scaleX and scaleY have the effect of bringing the image closer without distorting it shape, sine_amplitude changes the shape of the image. When sine amplitude is made larger than … the image loses its identitiy and strange patterns result.

```
// MagnifyGlass2.java
/*
DisplacementMap Parameters:
input: The input (image or other array) to the effect that we shall be
designing.
mapData: Also called a FloatMap. This is the heart of the filter-mangler. It is
```

*two algebra equations, one for X and another for Y that determine how input pixels are mapped to output pixels.*
*OffsetX: A fixed shift horizontally that will be added to every pixel it is applied to.*
*OffsetY: A fixed shift vertically that will be added to every pixel it is applied to.*
*ScaleX: A scale or multiplication applied horizontally to pixels from the input.*
*ScaleY: A scale or multiplication applied vertically to pixels from the input.*
*Wrap: A boolean flag that signals whether or not the displacement operation should wrap around at the boundaries.*
*srcWidth: The width of the input image or source.*
*srcHeight: The height of the input image or source.*

*DisplacementMap Constructors:*
*1. DisplacementMap(): A DisplacementMap with the default parameters.*
*2. DisplacementMap(FloatMap_mapData): A DisplacementMap with the specified mapData.*
*3. DisplacementMap(FloatMap_mapData, offsetX, offsetY, scaleX, scaleY):*

*The parameters of the DisplacementMapare listed below:*
*mapData - the map data for this displacement effect. The distorting transform.*
*offsetX - the offset, as a proportion of the image width, by which all x coordinate offset values in the FloatMap are displaced after they are scaled*
*offsetY - the offset, as a proportion of the image width,by which all y coordinate offset values in the FloatMap are displaced after they are scaled.*
*scaleX - the scale factor by which all x coordinate offset values in the FloatMap are multiplied, or scaled up.*
*scaleY - the scale factor by which all y coordinate values in the FloatMap are multiplied, or scaled up.*

*Tested on: java version "java-8-oracle"*
*Author: Mike Ohlson de Fine.*

```
*/
import javafx.application.Application;
import javafx.stage.Stage;
import javafx.scene.Scene;
import javafx.scene.effect.DisplacementMap;
import javafx.scene.effect.Effect;
import javafx.scene.effect.FloatMap;
import javafx.scene.image.Image;
```

```
import javafx.scene.image.ImageView;
import javafx.scene.layout.StackPane;

public class MagnifyGlass2 extends Application
{
   final float sine_amplitude = 0.08f ;  // Lens Magnification factor of
FloatMapLens.
   final float offsetX = 0.0f ;          // offsetX in DisplacementMap
   final float offsetY = 0.0f ;
   final float scaleX = 1.0f ;           // Scale (multiplicaion) factor.
   final float scaleY = 0.1f ;

   public void start(Stage primaryStage) throws Exception {
      StackPane root = new StackPane();
      root.setPrefSize(500, 500);

      // Various test images, each 500 pixels wide.
      ImageView view = new ImageView(new
Image("circular_target_grid_500.png"));
      //ImageView view = new ImageView(new Image("bella2_500.jpg"));
      //ImageView view = new ImageView(new Image("zoey_500.jpg"));
      //ImageView view = new ImageView(new Image("dog_500.jpg"));
      view.setEffect(createEffect(500, 500));
      root.getChildren().add(view);

      primaryStage.setTitle("DispMap Lens: ampliude: "+sine_amplitude+",
offsetY: " + offsetY+", scaleY: "+scaleY );
      Scene scene = new Scene(root);
      primaryStage.setScene(scene);
      primaryStage.show();
   }

   private Effect createEffect(int width, int height)
   {
      // The Lens magnifiaction expressions for x and y pixel positions.
      FloatMap floatMapLens = new FloatMap(width, height);

        for (int x = 0; x < width; x++)
        {
          /* The sine functions behaves similarly to a glass magnifying lens.
             The magnification is powerful in the center and weak at the edges.
```

```
        */

        float u = (float) Math.sin(Math.PI * x / width * 2.0) * sine_amplitude;
        for (int y = 0; y < height; y++)
        {
          float v = (float) Math.sin(Math.PI * y / height * 2.0) *
sine_amplitude;
          floatMapLens.setSamples(x, y, u, v);
        }
      }

      DisplacementMap displacementMap = new
DisplacementMap(floatMapLens, offsetX, offsetY, scaleX, scaleY);
      return displacementMap;
   }
}
```

## The Wrap Variable

If we set the wrap variable of the DisplacementMap object to *true* then any portions of the image that would have been lost because they were shifted out of the visible viewing pane will be effectively wrapped around to join on the end of the image.

## The scale Variables.

The scaleX and scaleY variables are multipliers that are applied to the values from the FloatMap. If you use a scaleX value that is greater than 1, you make the offset between the source and destination pixels larger than that specified in the map. A scaleX value of 2 would double the offsets specified in the map. Similarly, if you use a value that is less than 1, the offset gets smaller. It is also possible to use a negative value, which would reverse the effect of the map.

# Using the DisplacementMap to Create a Warp

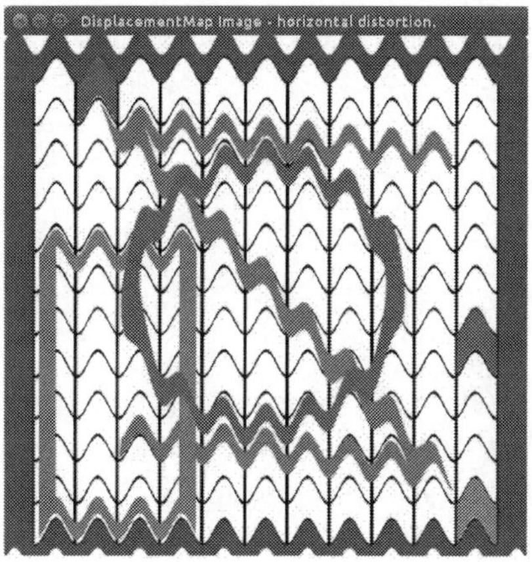


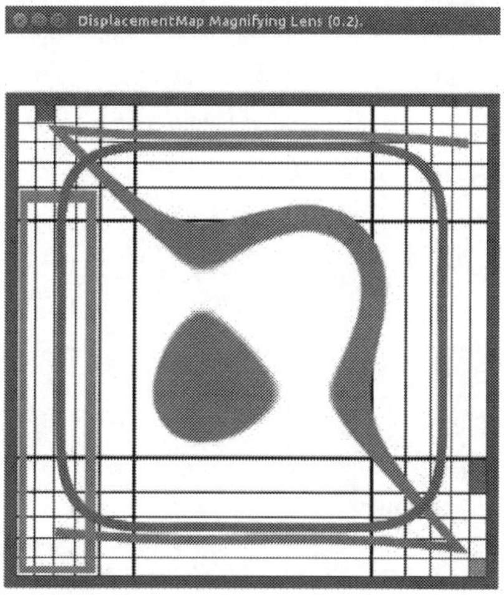


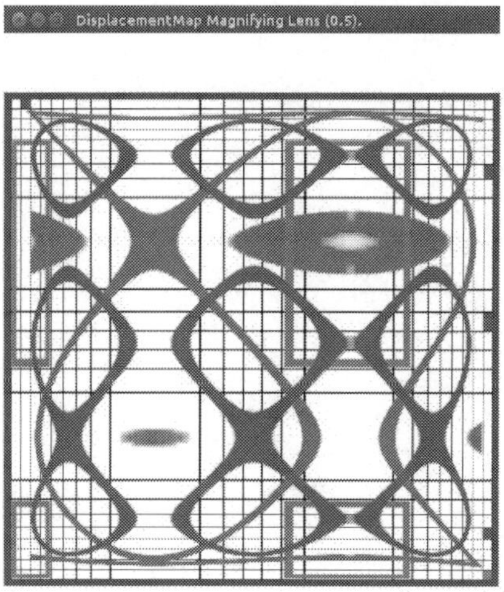

```
/ / DisplacementMap4.java
/*
DisplacementMap Parameters:
input: The input (image?) to the effect that we shall design.
mapData: Also called a FloatMap. This is the heart of the filter-mangler. It is
algebra equations that determines how input pixels are mapped to output
pixels.
OffsetX: A fixed shift horizontally that will be added to every pixel it is
applied to.
OffsetY: A fixed shift vertically that will be added to every pixel it is applied
to.
ScaleX: A scale or multiplication applied horizontally to pixels form the input.
ScaleY: A scale or multiplication applied vertically to pixels form the input.
Wrap: A boolean flag that signals whether or not the displacement operation
should wrap around at the boundaries.
srcWidth: The width of the input, or source, image.
srcHeight: The height of the input, or source, image.

DisplacementMap Constructors:
1. DisplacementMap(F): A DisplacementMap with the default parameters.
2. DisplacementMap(FloatMap_mapData): A DisplacementMap with the
specified mapData.
3. DisplacementMap(FloatMap_mapData, offsetX, offsetY, scaleX, scaleY):
A DisplacementMap with the specified parameters.
Where the parameters are:
mapData - the map data for this displacement map effect.
offsetX - the offset, in pixels, by which all x coordinate offset values in the
FloatMap are displaced after they are scaled
offsetY - the offset, in pixels, by which all y coordinate offset values in the
FloatMap are displaced after they are scaled
scaleX - the scale factor by which all x coordinate offset values in the
FloatMap are multiplied
scaleY - the scale factor by which all y coordinate values in the FloatMap are
multiplied

FloatMap Constructors:
1. FloatMap(): A FloatMap with default parameters.
2. FloatMap(width, height): A FloatMap with the specified width and height.
```

```
Further specifiable parameters:
a) setSample(x,  y, int_band, float_s): This sets the sample for a specific band
at the given (x,y) location.
The band - the band to set (must be 0, 1, 2, or 3)
s - the sample value to set
b) setSamples(x,  y, float_s0, float_s1, float_s2): This sets the sample for the
first three bands at the given (x,y) location.
c) setSamples(x,  y, float_s0, float_s1, float_s2, float_s3): This sets the sample
for the first four bands at the given (x,y) location.

Tested on: java version "java-8-oracle"
Author: Mike Ohlson de Fine.
*/
import javafx.application.Application;
import javafx.stage.Stage;
import javafx.scene.Group;
import javafx.scene.Scene;
import javafx.scene.image.Image;
import javafx.scene.image.ImageView;
import javafx.scene.effect.DisplacementMap;
import javafx.scene.effect.FloatMap;

public class DisplacementMap4 extends Application
{
  public void start(Stage primaryStage)
  {
  primaryStage.setTitle("DisplacementMap Image - anomalous horiz. and
vert. distortion.");
  Group rootgroup = new Group();
  Scene scene = new Scene(rootgroup, 600, 600);

  int w = 500;
  int h = 500;
  FloatMap map = new FloatMap();
  map.setWidth(w);
  map.setHeight(h);

  for (int i = 0; i < w; i++)
  {
    double v = (Math.sin(i / 20.0 * Math.PI + 90.) - 0.5) / 40.0; // i for
horizontal indices.
```

```
    for (int j = 0; j < h; j++)
     {
       double u = (Math.sin(j / 40.0 * Math.PI) - 0.5) / 40.0;  / / j for vertical
indices.
       map.setSamples(i, j, 0.0f, (float) u, (float) v);
     }

    DisplacementMap dismap = new DisplacementMap();
    dismap.setMapData(map);
    rootgroup.setEffect(dismap);

    Image image = new Image("source_displacement_map_500.png" );
    ImageView imv_map = new ImageView(image);
    rootgroup.getChildren().add(imv_map);

    primaryStage.setScene(scene);
    primaryStage.show();
   }
 }
}
```

# CHAPTER 17

## MOUSE CONTROL

*"A computer mouse is a hand controlled pointing device that detects two-dimensional motion relative to a surface. This motion is typically translated into the motion of a pointer on a display, which allows a smooth control of the graphical user interface."* WikipediA.

In this chapter we will cover:

- All the different input sensing of a computer input mouse.
- Event handling.
- Using event handlers.

The programs in this chapter have been made self explanatory – the comments inside the programs explain the key instructions regarding mouse event reactions.

In the next chapter we are going to explore user interfaces in some depth. User interfaces are the graphical devices on the computer screen, of a person using our Java program, that allow then to interact with our code. Images of buttons, sliders and text entry boxes are typical user interfaces or GUIs'. GUI = “Graphic User Interface”.

## A Java Event

An Event is some type of external action, usually caused by a human user. A typical event is when a graphic button on the screen is pressed by a  person using a mouse.

Thus a prerequisite of GUI design is the ability to control the mouse. A typical mouse has three main buttons on the top surface and an optical mechanism on the bottom that can measure distance and direction moved by the mouse.

In this chapter we explore the different Java commands that convert mouse actions into code instructions that we can use to make GUI actions control the action of our Java programs. On laptops the trackpad area is the direct equivalent of the mouse.

In this chapter we will use a GUI button to allow us to test button instructions. In the next chapter we will analyse button construction in detail but in this chapter we will simply  create and use simple buttons without much explanation.

## Mouse Events

The JavaFX class that has all the mouse control methods is javafx.scene.input.MouseEvent

It all starts with the operating system of our computer. The operating system is the manufactured collection of programs that are running on our computer when it is on. Microsoft Windows, Ubuntu Linux, Apple OS and Android are the most common operating systems.  As far as the operating system is concerned all events are detected all the time. Every keystroke on the keyboard, every movement of the mouse, finger stroke on a trackpad, every touch of a game joystick and every swipe of a finger on a tablet or smart-phone causes electrical signal changes at the connections of the computing chips or circuits on our computer hardware. The operating system notes these changes and has them always available to any software instruction that happens to be in control of the computer when the signal is detected.

From the point of view of our JavaFX program there can be more than one GUI icon in the same place on the computer screen. In JavaFX terminology the Graphic icons are called nodes. The nodes in the Scene can effectively lie on top of each other in layers.

When mouse event occurs, the top-most node under cursor is picked and that event is delivered to our event handling method.

The mouse (pointer's) location is available relative to several coordinate systems: x,y - relative to the origin of the MouseEvent's node, sceneX,sceneY - relative to to the origin of the Scene that contains the node, screenX,screenY - relative to origin of the screen that contains the mouse pointer.

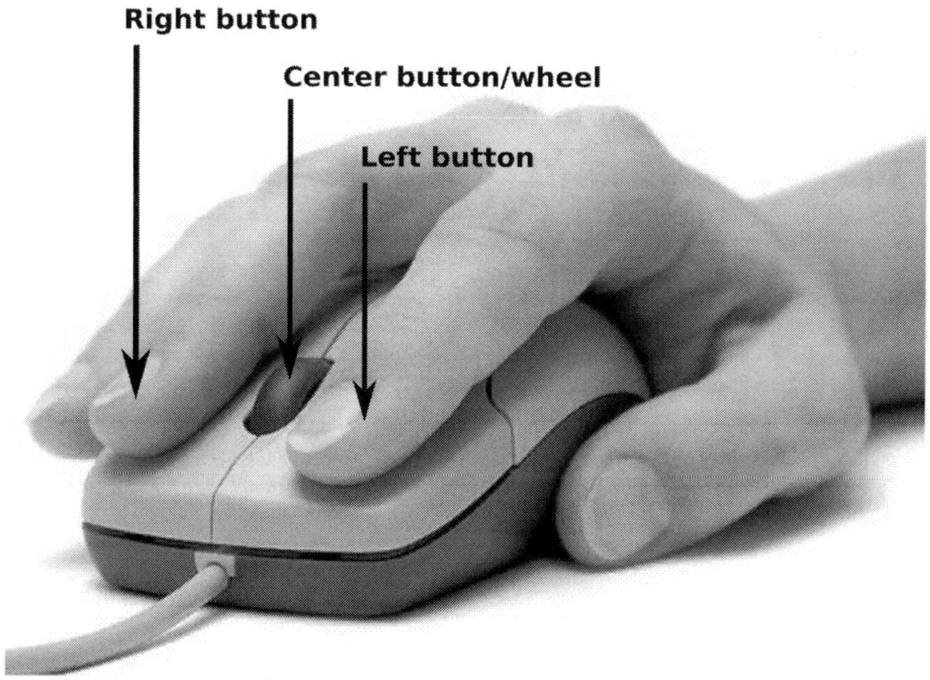

# A Simple example - pressing ANY Mouse Button

In this test, pressing any of the three mouse buttons inside the black rectangle causes the message “Mouse inside rectangle 1” to be displayed in the terminal.

```
// MouseEventSimple1.java
/*
Make a mouse event handler that reacts when a flag is raised.
The flag is called MOUSE_CLICKED. An equivalent flag
called MOUSE_PRESSED could have been used in the same way.

Class MouseEvent: javafx.scene.input.MouseEvent
------------------------------------------------
Constructor
1. A new MouseEvent event with null source and target:
MouseEvent(EventType<? extends MouseEvent> eventType, ....)

Tested on: java version "java-8-oracle"
Author: Mike Ohlson de Fine.
*/
import javafx.application.Application;
import javafx.event.EventHandler;
import javafx.scene.Group;
import javafx.scene.Scene;
import javafx.stage.Stage;
import javafx.scene.shape.*;
import javafx.scene.paint.*;
import javafx.scene.input.MouseEvent;
```

```
public class MouseEventSimple1 extends Application
{
 public void start(Stage primaryStage)
 {
  double xx, yy, width, height,;
  xx = 30 ;
  yy = 30 ;
  width = 200 ;
  height = 40 ;

  Group root = new Group();
  Scene scene = new Scene(root, 400, 150);

  Rectangle rect1 = new Rectangle();
       rect1.setX(xx);
       rect1.setY(yy);
       rect1.setWidth(width);
       rect1.setHeight(height);
       root.getChildren().add(rect1);

  // THE EVENT – in rect1a mouse button is clicked.
   // The EventType can be MOUSE-CLICKED, which is the same as
MOUSE_PRESSED..
   rect1.setOnMouseClicked(mouseHandler1);
  //rect1.setOnMousePressed(mouseHandler1); // An equivalent alternative.

  primaryStage.setTitle("A Press Event of the Mouse.");
  primaryStage.setScene(scene);
  primaryStage.show();
 }

//////////////////////////////////////////////////////////////////
//////////mouseHandler1  ///////////////////////////////////
 EventHandler<MouseEvent> mouseHandler1 = new
EventHandler<MouseEvent>()
 {
    public void handle(MouseEvent mouseEvent)
    {
      if (mouseEvent.getEventType() == MouseEvent.MOUSE_CLICKED)
      //if (mouseEvent.getEventType() ==
```

```
MouseEvent.MOUSE_PRESSED) // The alternative.
        {  System.out.println("Mouse inside rectangle 1");
        }
    }
 };
////////////////////////////////////////////////////////////////
}
```

**When Nodes Overlap**

Events on More than One Node: Depending on which rectangle the mouse cursor is inside when the mouse button is clicked, a different event handler is called to deal with the event.

This selection is determined by the instructions:

```
// Specify what flags are to be set when the mouse is clicked.

rect1.setOnMousePressed(mouseHandler1);

rect2.setOnMousePressed(mouseHandler2);
```

Note that the rectangle that was drawn last by the instruction *root.getChildren().add(rect2);*

will be on the top of the scene so that where the two rectangles overlap, only the topmost rectangle will be detected as being the originator of the event.

```
// MouseEventMultipleNodes1.java
/*
Make two mouse event handlers, one for each of two nodes (rectangles in this
example).

Tested on: java version "java-8-oracle"
Author: Mike Ohlson de Fine.
*/
import javafx.application.Application;
import javafx.stage.Stage;
import javafx.scene.Group;
import javafx.scene.Scene;
import javafx.scene.shape.*;
import javafx.scene.*;
import javafx.scene.paint.*;
import javafx.event.EventHandler;
import javafx.scene.input.MouseEvent;

public class MouseEventMultipleNodes1 extends Application {

 public void start(Stage primaryStage)
 {
  double xx1, yy1, xx2, yy2,  width, height, strokew ;
  xx1 = 30 ;
  yy1 = 30 ;
  xx2 = 100 ;
  yy2 = 100 ;
  width = 200 ;
  height = 100 ;
  strokew = 20 ;

  Group root = new Group();
  Scene scene = new Scene(root, 400, 250);

  Rectangle rect1 = new Rectangle();
        rect1.setX(xx1);
        rect1.setY(yy1);
        rect1.setWidth(width);
        rect1.setHeight(height);
        rect1.setStrokeWidth(strokew);
        rect1.setStroke( Color.BLUE);
```

```
        rect1.setFill(Color.rgb(50, 50, 150, 0.5 ));
        root.getChildren().add(rect1);

    Rectangle rect2 = new Rectangle();
        rect2.setX(xx2);
        rect2.setY(yy2);
        rect2.setWidth(width);
        rect2.setHeight(height);
        rect2.setStrokeWidth(strokew);
        rect2.setStroke(Color.RED );
        rect2.setFill(Color.rgb(150, 50, 50, 0.5 ));
        root.getChildren().add(rect2);

    // Specify what flags are to be set when the mouse is clicked.
    rect1.setOnMousePressed(mouseHandler1);
    rect2.setOnMousePressed(mouseHandler2);

    primaryStage.setTitle("Events on Overlapping Nodes.");
    primaryStage.setScene(scene);
    primaryStage.show();
  }
////////////////////////////////////////////////////////////////
////////////mouseHandler1  ///////////////////////////////////
 EventHandler<MouseEvent> mouseHandler1 = new
EventHandler<MouseEvent>()
 {
    public void handle(MouseEvent mouseEvent)
    {
      if (mouseEvent.getEventType() == MouseEvent.MOUSE_PRESSED)
      {  System.out.println("Mouse inside rectangle 1");
      }
    }
 };
////////////////////////////////////////////////////////////////
//////////// mouseHandler2  //////////////////////////////////
 EventHandler<MouseEvent> mouseHandler2 = new
EventHandler<MouseEvent>()
 {
    public void handle(MouseEvent mouseEvent)
    {
      if (mouseEvent.getEventType() == MouseEvent.MOUSE_PRESSED)
```

```
      { System.out.println("Mouse inside rectangle 2");
      }
   }
 };
}
```

## Basic Mouse Actions on a Node

In this test we detect and react mouse clicking or just the motion of the cursor across the sensitive rectangle. We do not however determine which mouse button was pressed. All the mouse buttons are treated identically.

```
// MouseEvent_TestDrive1.java
/*
Test 8 basic mouse actions:
1. Mouse button (any). Press only.
2. Release any Mouse Button.
3. Press AND followed by release, any button.
4. Once during any uninterrupted drag.
5. Continuous event generation during a drag.
6. One event when Mouse enters the target node.
7. One event when Mouse exits the target node.
8. Continuous event generation while Mouse moves across the target node.

Tested on: java version "java-8-oracle"
Author: Mike Ohlson de Fine.
*/
import javafx.application.Application;
import javafx.stage.Stage;
import javafx.scene.Group;
import javafx.scene.Scene;
import javafx.scene.shape.*;
import javafx.scene.*;
import javafx.scene.paint.*;
import javafx.event.EventHandler;
import javafx.scene.input.MouseEvent;

public class MouseEvent_TestDrive1 extends Application
{
  public void start(Stage primaryStage)
```

```
{
  double xx, yy, width, height, strokew;
  xx = 30 ;
  yy = 30 ;
  width = 300 ;
  height = 30 ;
  strokew = 4 ;

  Group root = new Group();
  Scene scene = new Scene(root, 400, 350);
  Rectangle rect1 = new Rectangle();
        rect1.setX(xx);
        rect1.setY(yy);
        rect1.setWidth(width);
        rect1.setHeight(height);
        rect1.setStrokeWidth(strokew);
        rect1.setStroke(Color.RED);
        rect1.setFill(Color.rgb(50, 50, 150, 0.5 ));
        root.getChildren().add(rect1);

   // Set various mouse flags on mouse action.
   rect1.setOnMousePressed(mouseHandler1);     // 1. Press only.
   rect1.setOnMouseReleased(mouseHandler1); // 2. Release Mouse Button.
   rect1.setOnMouseClicked(mouseHandler1);    // 3. Press AND followed by
release.
   rect1.setOnDragDetected(mouseHandler1);    // 4. Once per drag stripe.
   rect1.setOnMouseDragged(mouseHandler1); // 5. Continuous during
drag.
   rect1.setOnMouseEntered(mouseHandler1);  // 6. When Mouse enters the
target node.
   rect1.setOnMouseExited(mouseHandler1);     // 7. When Mouse exits the
target node.
   rect1.setOnMouseMoved(mouseHandler1);     // 8. While Mouse moves
across the target node.

  primaryStage.setScene(scene);
  primaryStage.show();
 }
  ////////////////////////////////////////////////////////////
  ///////////     "mouseHandler1       /////////////////////
 EventHandler<MouseEvent> mouseHandler1 = new
```

```
EventHandler<MouseEvent>()
 {
   public void handle(MouseEvent mouseEvent)
   {
       // 1. MOUSE_PRESSED -> On press only.
       if ((mouseEvent.getEventType() == MouseEvent.MOUSE_PRESSED) )
         { System.out.println("1. M Pressed: " +
MouseEvent.MOUSE_PRESSED);}

       // 2. MOUSE_RELEASED -> On Release Mouse Button.
       if ((mouseEvent.getEventType() == MouseEvent.MOUSE_RELEASED) )
         { System.out.println("2. M Released: " +
MouseEvent.MOUSE_RELEASED);}

       // 3. MOUSE_CLICKED -> Press AND followed by release.
       if ((mouseEvent.getEventType() == MouseEvent.MOUSE_CLICKED) )
         { System.out.println("3. M  Clicked: " +
MouseEvent.MOUSE_CLICKED);}

       // 4. MOUSE_DRAG_DETECTED -> Once per drag stripe.
       if ((mouseEvent.getEventType() == MouseEvent.DRAG_DETECTED) )
         { System.out.println("4. DragDetected: " +
MouseEvent.DRAG_DETECTED);}

       // 5. MOUSE_DRAGGED -> Continuous event generation during drag.
      if ((mouseEvent.getEventType() == MouseEvent.MOUSE_DRAGGED) )
        { System.out.println("5. M Dragged: " +
MouseEvent.MOUSE_DRAGGED);}

       // 6. MOUSE_ENTERED -> Once when Mouse enters the target node.
       if ( (mouseEvent.getEventType() == MouseEvent.MOUSE_ENTERED) )
         {  System.out.println("6. Node Entered: " +
MouseEvent.MOUSE_ENTERED);

       // 7. MOUSE_EXITED -> Once when Mouse exits the target node.
       if ( (mouseEvent.getEventType() == MouseEvent.MOUSE_EXITED) )
         {  System.out.println("7. Node Exited: " +
MouseEvent.MOUSE_EXITED);}

       // 8. MOUSE_MOVED -> Continuous while Mouse moves across the
target node.
```

```
        if ((mouseEvent.getEventType() == MouseEvent.MOUSE_MOVED) )
          {  System.out.println("8. M Moved: " +
MouseEvent.MOUSE_MOVED);}
    }
  };
}
```

## Which Mouse Button was Pressed?

Now we detect and react to which particular mouse button was pressed.

```
// MouseEvent_WhichButton1.java
/*
Discover which button was pressed:

1. PRIMARY -> Left side button.
2. SECONDARY -> Right side button.
3. MIDDLE -> Middle button.

Tested on: java version "java-8-oracle"
Author: Mike Ohlson de Fine.
*/
import javafx.application.Application;
import javafx.stage.Stage;
import javafx.scene.Group;
import javafx.scene.Scene;
import javafx.scene.shape.*;
import javafx.scene.paint.*;
import javafx.event.EventHandler;
import javafx.scene.input.MouseEvent;

public class MouseEvent_WhichButton1 extends Application
{
  public void start(Stage primaryStage)
  {
    Group root = new Group();
    Scene scene = new Scene(root, 400, 100);

    Rectangle rect1 = new Rectangle(30, 30, 300, 60);
```

```
    root.getChildren().add(rect1);

    // Set mouse flag when any mouse button is pushed.
    rect1.setOnMousePressed(mouseHandler1);  // 1. Press only.

   primaryStage.setTitle( "Discover Which mouse button was pressed." ) ;
   primaryStage.setScene(scene);
   primaryStage.show();

  }
    /////////////////////////////////////////////////////////////////
    ///////////       mouseHandler1        ////////////////////
  EventHandler<MouseEvent> mouseHandler1 = new
EventHandler<MouseEvent>()
  {
    public void handle(MouseEvent mouseEvent)
    {
        // 1. MOUSE_PRESSED, Which button was pressed?
        if ((mouseEvent.getEventType() == MouseEvent.MOUSE_PRESSED)  )
          { System.out.println("Which button: " +  mouseEvent.getButton()); }
    }
  };
}
```

## Where was the Mouse when Pressed?

```
// MouseEvent_GetPosition1.java
/*
Get mouse event location parameters:
getSceneX() = getX() : Relative to JavaFX scene.
getSceneY() = getY() : Relative to JavaFX scene.

getScreenX() : Relative to entire video screen.
getScreenY() : Relative to entire video screen.

Tested on: java version "java-8-oracle"
Author: Mike Ohlson de Fine.
*/
import javafx.application.Application;
import javafx.stage.Stage;
import javafx.scene.Group;
```

```
import javafx.scene.Scene;
import javafx.scene.shape.*;
import javafx.scene.*;
import javafx.scene.paint.*;
import javafx.event.EventHandler;
import javafx.scene.input.MouseEvent;

public class MouseEvent_GetPosition1 extends Application
{

 public void start(Stage primaryStage)
 {
  double xx, yy, width, height, strokew;
  xx = 100 ;
  yy = 100 ;
  width = 300 ;
  height = 200 ;
  strokew = 4 ;

  Group root = new Group();
  Scene scene = new Scene(root, 600, 400);

  Rectangle rect1 = new Rectangle();
        rect1.setX(xx);
        rect1.setY(yy);
        rect1.setWidth(width);
        rect1.setHeight(height);
        rect1.setStrokeWidth(strokew);
        rect1.setStroke(Color.RED);
        rect1.setFill(Color.rgb(50, 50, 150, 0.5 ));
        root.getChildren().add(rect1);

  // Set mouse flag on mouse action.
  rect1.setOnMousePressed(mouseHandler1);  // 1. Press only. Ignore release
or dragging

  primaryStage.setScene(scene);
  primaryStage.show();
 }

  /////////////////////////////////////////////////////////////
```

```
 ///////////       "mouseHandler1       ////////////////////
 EventHandler<MouseEvent> mouseHandler1 = new
EventHandler<MouseEvent>()
 {
  public void handle(MouseEvent mouseEvent)
  {
     // 1. MOUSE_PRESSED -> On press only.
     if ((mouseEvent.getEventType() == MouseEvent.MOUSE_PRESSED) )
       { System.out.println("1. M Pressed: " +
MouseEvent.MOUSE_PRESSED);

          System.out.println("Where X, absolute: " +
mouseEvent.getScreenX());
          System.out.println("Where Y, absolute: " +
mouseEvent.getScreenY());
          System.out.println("Where X, in scene: " +
mouseEvent.getSceneX());
          System.out.println("Where Y, in scene: " +  mouseEvent.getSceneY());
          System.out.println("Where X, relative to event source: " +
mouseEvent.getX());
          System.out.println("Where Y, relative to event source: " +
mouseEvent.getY());
       }
  }
 };
}
```

# Drawing Paths with the Mouse

Now we use path instructions that we saw in chapter 11. When the mouse is pressed a MoveTo is executed and as the the moused is dragged a continuous series of LineTo's are drawn. This sequence is stopped when the mouse button is released.

//

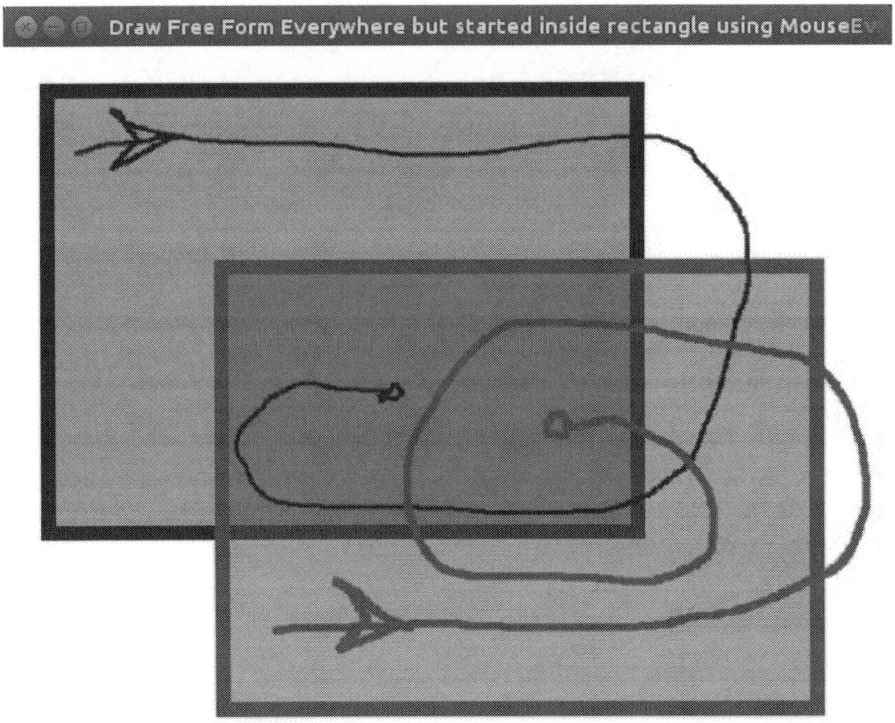


```
MouseDrawPath1.java
/*
Draw two independent paths controlled from colored rectangles.

Tested on: java version "java-8-oracle"
Author: Mike Ohlson de Fine.
*/
import javafx.application.Application;
import javafx.stage.Stage;
import javafx.scene.Group;
import javafx.scene.Scene;
import javafx.scene.shape.*;
import javafx.scene.*;
import javafx.scene.paint.*;
import javafx.event.EventHandler;
import javafx.scene.input.MouseEvent;

public class MouseDrawPath1 extends Application {

  Path path1, path2; // Declaring two Paths.
```

```
public void start(Stage primaryStage)
{
  double xx1, yy1, xx2, yy2, width, height, strokew ;
  xx1 = 30 ;
  yy1 = 30 ;
  xx2 = 150 ;
  yy2 = 150 ;
  width = 400 ;
  height = 300 ;
  strokew = 10 ;

  Group root = new Group();
  Scene scene = new Scene(root, 600, 500);

  Rectangle rect1 = new Rectangle();
       rect1.setX(xx1);
       rect1.setY(yy1);

       rect1.setWidth(width);
       rect1.setHeight(height);
       rect1.setStrokeWidth(strokew);
       rect1.setStroke(Color.BLUE );
       rect1.setFill(Color.rgb(50, 50, 150, 0.5 ));
       root.getChildren().add(rect1);

  Rectangle rect2 = new Rectangle();
       rect2.setX(xx2);
       rect2.setY(yy2);
       rect2.setWidth(width);
       rect2.setHeight(height);
       rect2.setStrokeWidth(strokew);
       rect2.setStroke(Color.RED );
       rect2.setFill(Color.rgb(150, 50, 50, 0.5 ));
       root.getChildren().add(rect2);

  // "path1" started by a mouseClick in the blue rectangle.
  path1 = new Path();
  path1.setStrokeWidth(3);
  path1.setStroke(Color.BLUE);
  root.getChildren().add(path1);
```

```
  // "path2" started by a mouseClick in the red rectangle.
  path2 = new Path();
  path2.setStrokeWidth(5);
  path2.setStroke(Color.RED);
  root.getChildren().add(path2);

  // Set Event controlled boolean flags.
  rect1.setOnMouseDragged(mouseHandler1);
  rect1.setOnMousePressed(mouseHandler1);
  rect2.setOnMouseDragged(mouseHandler2);
  rect2.setOnMousePressed(mouseHandler2);

  primaryStage.setTitle("Start inside a rectangle and Draw Free Form.");
  primaryStage.setScene(scene);
  primaryStage.show();
 }

 ////////////////////////////////////////////////////////////
 ////////////      mouseHandler1       ////////////////////
 EventHandler<MouseEvent> mouseHandler1 = new
EventHandler<MouseEvent>()
 {
  public void handle(MouseEvent mouseEvent)
  {
   if (mouseEvent.getEventType() == MouseEvent.MOUSE_PRESSED)
    {
     System.out.println("Mouse inside rectangle 1");
      path1.getElements().add(new MoveTo(mouseEvent.getX(),
mouseEvent.getY()));
    }
   else if (mouseEvent.getEventType() == MouseEvent.MOUSE_DRAGGED)
    { path1.getElements().add(new
LineTo(mouseEvent.getX(),mouseEvent.getY())); }

  }
 };

 /////////////////////////////////////////////////////////////
 ////////////      mouseHandler2       ////////////////////
 EventHandler<MouseEvent> mouseHandler2 = new
EventHandler<MouseEvent>()
```

```
 {
   public void handle(MouseEvent mouseEvent)
   {
    if (mouseEvent.getEventType() == MouseEvent.MOUSE_PRESSED)
    { System.out.println("Mouse inside rectangle 2");
      path2.getElements().add(new MoveTo(mouseEvent.getX(),
mouseEvent.getY())); }
    else if (mouseEvent.getEventType() == MouseEvent.MOUSE_DRAGGED)
      { path2.getElements().add(new LineTo(mouseEvent.getX(),
mouseEvent.getY())); }
    }
 };
}
```

## Move Objects with the MouseDrawPath

```
// MouseEventNodes1.java
/*
Explore complex responses to mouse events.
The idea is to build a framework that can be adapted for various
types of nodes.

Tested on: java version "java-8-oracle"
Author: Mike Ohlson de Fine.
*/
import javafx.application.Application;
import javafx.event.EventHandler;
import javafx.scene.Group;
import javafx.scene.Scene;
import javafx.scene.control.Button;
import javafx.scene.shape.*;
import javafx.scene.*;
import javafx.scene.paint.*;
import javafx.scene.input.MouseEvent;
import javafx.stage.Stage;

public class MouseEventNodes1 extends Application {

    Path path1, path2;
    boolean node_being_shifted = false ;  // Flag is true while node active.
```

```
    double previous_mouse_position_x, previous_mouse_position_y ;

    double xx = 30 ;       // Common parameters for rectangles.
    double yy = 30 ;
    double width = 30 ;
    double height = 30 ;
    double strokew = 4 ;
    double arcsize = 10 ;
    Rectangle rect1 = new Rectangle();  // Node 1.
    Rectangle rect2 = new Rectangle();  // Node 2.

public void start(Stage primaryStage)
{

    Group root_group = new Group();

        rect1.setX(xx);
        rect1.setY(yy);
        rect1.setWidth(width);
        rect1.setHeight(height);
        rect1.setStrokeWidth(strokew);
        rect1.setStroke(Color.BLUE);
        rect1.setFill(Color.rgb(50, 50, 150, 0.5 ));
        rect1.setArcWidth(arcsize);
        rect1.setArcHeight(arcsize);
        root_group.getChildren().add(rect1);

        rect2.setX(xx+140);
        rect2.setY(yy+height+60);
        rect2.setWidth(width+30);
        rect2.setHeight(height);
        rect2.setStrokeWidth(strokew);
        rect2.setStroke(Color.RED );
        rect2.setFill(Color.rgb(150, 50, 50, 0.5 ));
        rect2.setArcWidth(arcsize);
        rect2.setArcHeight(arcsize);
        root_group.getChildren().add(rect2);

      path1 = new Path();
      path1.setStrokeWidth(3);
      path1.setStroke(Color.BLUE);
```

```
      root_group.getChildren().add(path1);

      path2 = new Path();
      path2.setStrokeWidth(5);
      path2.setStroke(Color.RED);
      root_group.getChildren().add(path2);

   // Set various boolean flags that record the state of the mouse.
   rect1.setOnMouseDragged(mouseHandler1);
   rect1.setOnMousePressed(mouseHandler1);
   rect1.setOnMouseReleased(mouseHandler1);

   rect2.setOnMouseDragged(mouseHandler2);
   rect2.setOnMousePressed(mouseHandler2);
   rect2.setOnMouseReleased(mouseHandler2);

  Scene scene = new Scene(root_group, 400, 350);

  primaryStage.setScene(scene);
  primaryStage.setTitle( "Manipulate Nodes with the Mouse." ) ;
  primaryStage.show();
 }

 //////////////  EVENT HANDLING     ////////////////////
 ////////       mouseHandler1  - Node should follow drag path   /////
 EventHandler<MouseEvent> mouseHandler1 = new
EventHandler<MouseEvent>()
 {
  public void handle(MouseEvent mouseEvent)
  {

   ///////  Node1: MOUSE_PRESSED  Event     ////////////
   if (mouseEvent.getEventType() == MouseEvent.MOUSE_PRESSED)
   {
      if (    node_being_shifted == false )
         {
            previous_mouse_position_x = mouseEvent.getSceneX() ;
            previous_mouse_position_y = mouseEvent.getSceneY() ;
            node_being_shifted = true ;
         }
      path1.getElements().add(new MoveTo(mouseEvent.getX(),
```

```
mouseEvent.getY()));
    }

    /////////  Node1: MOUSE_DRAGGED Event    ///////////////
    else if (mouseEvent.getEventType() == MouseEvent.MOUSE_DRAGGED)
      { path1.getElements().add(new LineTo(mouseEvent.getX(),
mouseEvent.getY()));

        double mouse_movement_x = mouseEvent.getSceneX() // difference X
shifted.
                                - previous_mouse_position_x ;

        double mouse_movement_y = mouseEvent.getSceneY() // difference Y
shifted.
                                - previous_mouse_position_y ;

        previous_mouse_position_x = mouseEvent.getSceneX() ; // Update
previous position.
        previous_mouse_position_y = mouseEvent.getSceneY() ;

          rect1.setX( rect1.getX() + mouse_movement_x ) ; // Adjust node
position.
          rect1.setY( rect1.getY() + mouse_movement_y ) ;
      }
    }
  };

  ///////////////////////////////////////////////////////////
  //////     mouseHandler2 - Node2 does not follow drag path.  ///////
  EventHandler<MouseEvent> mouseHandler2 = new
EventHandler<MouseEvent>()
  {
    public void handle(MouseEvent mouseEvent)
    {
      if (mouseEvent.getEventType() == MouseEvent.MOUSE_PRESSED)
      {
        path2.getElements().add(new MoveTo(mouseEvent.getX(),
mouseEvent.getY())); }

    else if (mouseEvent.getEventType() == MouseEvent.MOUSE_DRAGGED)
      { path2.getElements().add(new LineTo(mouseEvent.getX(),
```

```
mouseEvent.getY())); }
    }
 };
  //////////////////////////////////////////////////////////////
///////////////////////////////////////////////////////////////
}
```

## MouseDragQuadCurve1.java

In Chapter 9 on Quadratic Bezier Curves we used event handlers on the mouse to see how the quadratic control points worked.

The program was **MouseDragQuadCurve1.java**. There were three separate control points and each had their own mouse event handler:

```
 /* Event handler for dragging inside circ_A - Blue */
    circ_A.setOnMouseDragged(new EventHandler<MouseEvent>()
    {
       public void handle(MouseEvent event)
       {
          circ_A.setCenterX(event.getX());
          circ_A.setCenterY(event.getY());
          line_AB.setStartX(event.getX());
          line_AB.setStartY(event.getY());
          line_CA.setEndX(event.getX());
          line_CA.setEndY(event.getY());

          quad1.setControlX(event.getX());
          quad1.setControlY(event.getY());
       }
    });

    /* Event handler for dragging inside circ_B - Red*/
    circ_B.setOnMouseDragged(new EventHandler<MouseEvent>()
    {
       public void handle(MouseEvent event)
       {
          circ_B.setCenterX(event.getX());
          circ_B.setCenterY(event.getY());
          line_BC.setStartX(event.getX());
```

```
        line_BC.setStartY(event.getY());
        line_AB.setEndX(event.getX());
        line_AB.setEndY(event.getY());

        quad1.setStartX(event.getX());
        quad1.setStartY(event.getY());
    }
});

/* Event handler for dragging inside circ_C - Violet */
circ_C.setOnMouseDragged(new EventHandler<MouseEvent>()
{
    public void handle(MouseEvent event)

    {
        circ_C.setCenterX(event.getX());
        circ_C.setCenterY(event.getY());
        line_CA.setStartX(event.getX());
        line_CA.setStartY(event.getY());
        line_BC.setEndX(event.getX());
        line_BC.setEndY(event.getY());

        quad1.setEndX(event.getX());
        quad1.setEndY(event.getY());
    }
});
```

## MouseDragCubicCurve1.java

In Chapter 10 on Cubic Bezier Curves we used event handlers on the mouse very similar to ones designed for **MouseDragQuadCurve1.java**. The the differences were that and extra node need control by the mouse and the control points needed to be connected by straight lines in a different pattern.

## Touch Enabled Screens

Smartphones and Tablets do not have computer mice but have screens that are responsive to the user's finger touches. JavaFX has a class, javafx.scene.input.TouchEvent, which contains the methods to handle events that are triggered by the movements of fingers across a touchscreen.

## Dragging gestures (events)

Generally speaking a gesture is a hand movement. In computer programming a gesture is a finger touch or swipe, which is the stroke of a finger across the screen. In addition gestures with two strokes are also catered for in generating events that can rotate and zoom graphic nodes on a screen.

JavaFX has classes and methods for handling the following events:

**Rotate:** ROTATION_STARTED, ROTATE, ROTATION_FINISHED

**Scroll:** SCROLL_STARTED, SCROLL, SCROLL_FINISHED

**Swipe:** SWIPE_LEFT, SWIPE_RIGHT, SWIPE_UP, SWIPE_DOWN

**Zoom:** ZOOM_STARTED, ZOOM, ZOOM_FINISHED

where:

**Rotate** is a two-finger turning movement where one finger moves clockwise around the other finger to rotate an object clockwise and one finger moves counterclockwise around the other finger to rotate an object counterclockwise.

**Scroll** is a sliding movement, up or down for vertical scrolling, left or right for horizontal scrolling.

**Swipe** is sweeping movement across the screen or trackpad to the right, left, up, or down. Diagonal movement is not recognized as a swipe.

**Zoom** (to make larger) is at two-finger pinching motion where fingers are brought together to zoom out and fingers are moved apart to zoom in.

The programming of touchscreens will not be explored any further in this book.

## *A Summary of Mouse Events and Parameters.*

### Events Flags

Event flags are single binary binary numbers that reflect what mouse action has just occurred.

**MOUSE_ENTERED** This event occurs when the mouse cursor enters a node without any of the mouse buttons being pressed. Even This event type is delivered only to the entered node (not to any parents).
**MOUSE_EXITED** This event occurs when mouse exits a node when none of the mouse buttons are being pressed. This event type is delivered only to the entered node (not to any parents).
**MOUSE_PRESSED** This event occurs when mouse button is pressed. All subsequent mouse events are delivered to the same node. This is because MOUSE_PRESSED activates a press-drag-release gesture.
**MOUSE_CLICKED** This event occurs when two things occur in sucession – first the mouse button is pressed AND afterward released on the same node.
Note that long drags generate CLICK events - they are delivered to the node on which the mouse was pressed.
**MOUSE_DRAGGED** This event occurs when mouse moves with any of the mouse buttons pressed. The drag ends when the button is lifted.
**MOUSE_ENTERED_TARGET** This event occurs when mouse enters a node.
This event is also delivered to *all the parents* of this entered node. This called bubbling behavior.
**MOUSE_EXITED_TARGET** This event occurs when mouse exits a node. This event is also delivered to all the parents of this entered node. This is also referred to as bubbling behavior.
**MOUSE_MOVED** This event occurs when mouse moves within a node and no buttons are pressed. If any mouse button is pressed, MOUSE_DRAGGED event occurs instead.

**MOUSE_RELEASED** This event occurs when mouse button is released.

**Mouse Parameters that can be used:**

**eventType** - The type of the event like MOUSE_PRESSED, MOUSE_DRAGGED and many others.
**X** - The x (horizontal) position of the mouse cursor By default it X is the same as screenX.
**Y** - The y (vertical) position of the mouse cursor By default it Y is the same as screenY.
**screenX** - The x coordinate relative to screen.
**screenY** - The y coordinate relative to screen.
**button** - the mouse button used, 1 primary, 2 secondary or 3 middle.
**clickCount** - number of click counts, to detect single, double or triple clicks.
**shiftDown** - true if the **shift** key is down while one of the mouse events takes place.
**controlDown** - true if **control (Ctrl)** key is down while one of the mouse events
takes place.
**altDown** - true if **alternate (Alt)** key is down while one of the mouse events takes place.
**metaDown** - true if some specified combinations of keys are pressed while a mouse event takes place. Certain old keyboards have a specific "meta" key.
**primaryButtonDown** - true if primary button ( left mouse button) was pressed.
**middleButtonDown** - true if middle button was pressed.
**secondaryButtonDown** - true if secondary button (right button) was pressed.

# Methods

**getButton()**
Which, if any, of the mouse buttons is responsible for this event.

**getClickCount()**
Returns number of mouse clicks associated with this event.

**EventType<? extends MouseEvent> getEventType()**
Gets the event type of this event.

**getSceneX**()
Returns horizontal position of the event relative to the origin of the Scene that contains the MouseEvent's source.

**getSceneY**()
Returns vertical position of the event relative to the origin of the Scene that contains the MouseEvent's source.

**getScreenX**()
Returns absolute horizontal position of the event.
**getX**()
Horizontal position of the event.

**getScreenY**()
Returns absolute vertical position of the event.
**getY**()
Vertical position of the event.

**isShiftDown**()
Is the Shift key is down on as this event takes place?

**isAltDown**()
Is the Alt key is down on as this event takes place?

**isControlDown**()
Is the Ctrl key is down on as this event takes place?

**isDragDetect**()
Determines whether this event will be followed by DRAG_DETECTED event.

**isPrimaryButtonDown**()
Returns true if primary button (button 1, usually the left) is currently pressed.

**isMiddleButtonDown**()
Returns true if middle button (button 2) is currently pressed.

**isSecondaryButtonDown**()
Returns true if secondary button (button 1, usually the right) is currently pressed.

**toString**()
Returns a string representation of this MouseEvent object.

## The Special Mouse Drag Class

Mouse Drag Events additionally have their own specialized class, javafx.scene.input.MouseDragEvent.
The constructor for the class is
**MouseDragEvent(EventType<MouseDragEvent> .....)**

The useful fields are:
**ANY** Common supertype for all mouse event types.
**MOUSE_DRAG_ENTERED** This event occurs when gesture/mouse enters a node.
**MOUSE_DRAG_ENTERED_TARGET** This event occurs when gesture/mouse enters a node.
**MOUSE_DRAG_EXITED** This event occurs when gesture/mouse exits a node.
**MOUSE_DRAG_EXITED_TARGET** This event occurs when gesture/mouse exits a node.
**MOUSE_DRAG_OVER** This event occurs when gesture/mouse moves inside a node.
**MOUSE_DETECTED** This event is delivered to a node that is identified as a source of a dragging gesture.
**MOUSE_DRAG_RELEASED** This event occurs when gesture/mouse ends (by releasing mouse button) on this node.

# CHAPTER 18

## UI USER INTERFACES – Part 1

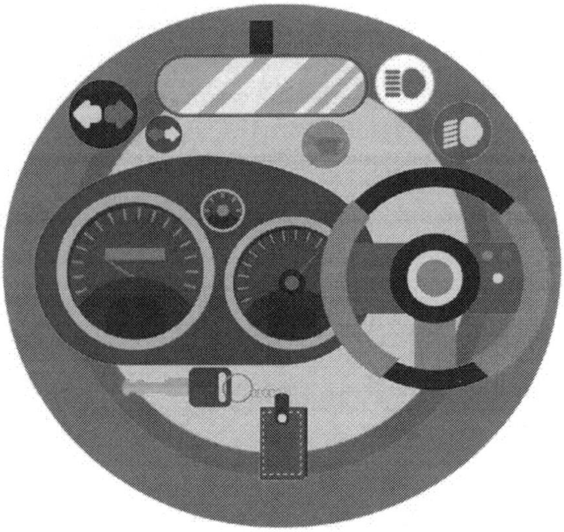

*"A graphic user interface (GUI) is a type of* ***user interface*** *that allows* ***users*** *to interact with electronic devices through* ***graphical*** *icons and visual indicators. An icon is a small picture or symbol on a computer screen that you point to and click on with a mouse to give the computer an instruction"* Wikipedia and the Cambridge Dictionary.

In this chapter we will cover:

- Button
- RadioButton
- ToggleButton
- CheckBox
- ChoiceBox
- Slider

- ProgressBar
- ProgressIndicator
- ScrollBar
- ScrollPane
- ComboBox

In the chapter after this, chapter 19, we deal with the following.

- TextField
- PasswordField
- Hyperlink
- DatePicker
- FileChooser
- Menu
- Tooltip
- Separator
- HTMLEditor
- Pagination
- ListView
- TableView
- TreeView
- Tree TableView

## User Interfaces (UI) or Graphic User Interface (GUI)

UI and GUI mean the same thing. Some UIs like labels or hints are just for displaying text and images while others like buttons and sliders are intended for changing values of the data in a program and require us to write code for Event handling.

## Label

The label is a simple way to display some text. Here the label is the child node of a group, the root node. The group is simply attached to the scene.

We can wrap the text to fit the specific space, add a graphical image, or apply visual effects by using JavaFX Label control.

```
// UILabelSimplest1.java
/*
Label : class: javafx.scene.control.Label
------------------------------------
Show Text at a specified position.
Constructors:
1. Label(); A basic instance of Text. The parameters can be supplied later.
2. Label(text); An instance positioned at the given coordinates and containing
the given string of test.
3. Label(text, graphic); An instance containing the given string of test.
where:
graphic is an image icon.
text is the string of characters to be displayed.

Tested on: java version "java-8-oracle"
```

```
Author: Mike Ohlson de Fine
*/
import javafx.application.Application;
import javafx.scene.Scene;
import javafx.scene.text.Text;
import javafx.stage.Stage;
import javafx.scene.*;

import javafx.scene.control.Label;

public class  UILabelSimplest1 extends Application
{
	public void start(Stage stage)
	{
		Group root = new Group();

		Label label1 = new Label("One");
		root.getChildren().addAll(label1);

		Scene scene = new Scene(root, 200, 40);
		stage.setScene(scene);
		stage.setTitle("A Simplest UI Label.");
		stage.show();
	}
}
```

# Buttons and ToggleButtons

A Button and a ToggleButton both trigger events when a user clicks the button using the mouse.

A ToggleButton sets or unsets the state (true or false) of an unseen software flag. Think of a "flag" as similar to a small LED light on your computer that comes on when the power is on. Its purpose is to indicate the state of the power supply.

The use of ToggleButtons is not clear or obvious as radio buttons can achieve similar objectives in a more obvious way.

The Button class extends the Label class, which can display text, an image, or both.

In the example below we have the minimal code needed to present a scene containing a button that we can press with a mouse click. The button does nothing because we have not provided an **event handler.** We explored event handlers in the previous chapter on Mouse Control.

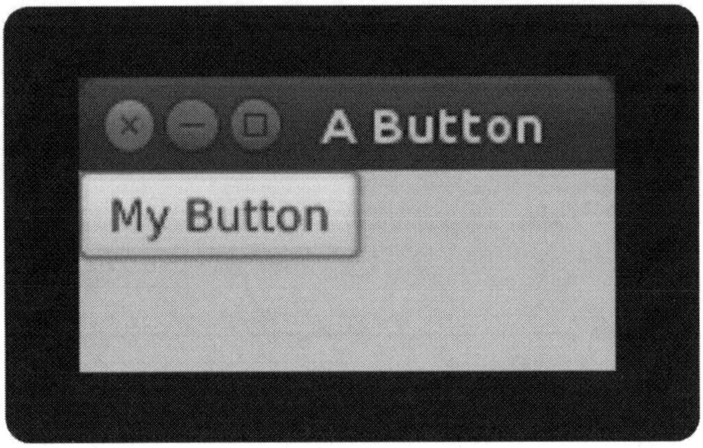


```
// ButtonSimplest.java
/*
The button in this example does nothing - it is not
connected to any action that can occur when the button is pressed.
Button: class:javafx.scene.control.Button
--------------------------------------
Constructors
1. Button( ), or
2. Button(text)
3. Button(text, imageIcon)

Tested on: java version "java-8-oracle"
Author: Mike Ohlson de Fine.
*/
import javafx.application.Application;
import javafx.scene.Group;
import javafx.scene.Scene;
import javafx.stage.Stage;
import javafx.scene.control.Button;
import javafx.scene.paint.Color;
```

```
public class ButtonSimplest extends Application {

  public void start(Stage stage) {
    Group root = new Group();
    Scene scene = new Scene(root, 160, 60, Color.PINK);

    Button button1 = new Button("My Button");
    root.getChildren().add(button1);

    stage.setTitle("A Button");
    stage.setScene(scene);
    stage.show();
  }
}
```

# Events recap

[ javafx.event.ActionEvent ]
An Event is some type of external action, usually caused by a human user.

An EventHandler is the method or function that is activated (ie. called and executed) when the event occurs. A typical event is when a graphic button on the screen is pressed by a person using a mouse. The action of clicking on a shape, dragging the shape along the screen and then releasing the button could trigger three separate types of events. The EventHandler method can be as long as we choose and perform many, many actions. Although event handling is used mostly to respond to actions like button clicks, it can also be used to respond to other types of user interactions. We can use event handling for example to write code that's executed when the user makes a selection from a combobox, moves the mouse over a label, or presses a key on the keyboard.

JavaFX events we explore in this chapter have two components:

- an event source – the device like a mouse or keyboard linked to areas on the display screen like buttons and other UI objects.

- an event handler - a software method that we write that responds to the source action.

In the example below the event source is the button named ***button1***. The event handler is the method that defines what will happen when an event occurs – in this case the event is the clicking of a mouse cursor when it is on top of the particular graphic button named button1. In the example below the event handling method is ***handle(ActionEvent e) {...}.***

## Event class Constructors

**ActionEvent();**

**ActionEvent( source_object, target_object):**

Example:

```
button1.setOnAction(new EventHandler<ActionEvent>()
    {
        public void handle(ActionEvent e)
        { System.out.println("button1 was pressed and
            this message is the resultant      action.");
        }
    }    );
```

# Button Event Handling

When a button is pushed it must DO something. We want the action to switch some kind of action on - like the flicking of a light switch in a room causes the electric light to come on. In Java the consequent action which we want should consist of a bunch of Java instructions that we place inside the special method called an event handler.

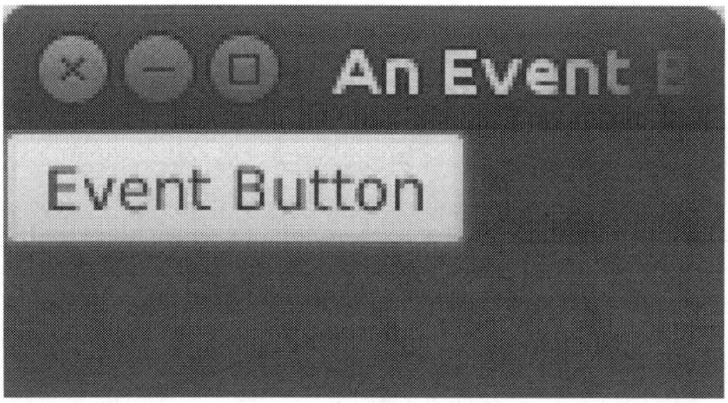


```
// ButtonEventAction1.java
/*
ActionEvent class: javafx.event.ActionEvent

-----------------------------------------
Constructors
1. ActionEvent( ); where the source and target of the event are set to
NULL_SOURCE_TARGET.
2. ActionEvent(source, target);
source - the event source which sent the event
target - the event target to associate with the event

Tested on: java version "java-8-oracle"
Author: Mike Ohlson de Fine.
*/
import javafx.application.Application;
import javafx.scene.Group;
import javafx.scene.Scene;
import javafx.stage.Stage;
import javafx.scene.control.Button;
import javafx.scene.paint.Color;

import javafx.event.ActionEvent;
import javafx.event.EventHandler;

public class ButtonEventAction1 extends Application {

  public void start(Stage stage) {
    Group root = new Group();
    Scene scene = new Scene(root, 160, 60, Color.PINK);
```

```
  Button button1 = new Button("Event Button");
  root.getChildren().add(button1);

  ////////////////////////////////////////////////////////////
  ////////// Event Handler for button1  /////////
 button1.setOnAction(new EventHandler<ActionEvent>()
     {
         public void handle(ActionEvent e)
         { System.out.println("button1 was pressed and
           this message is the resultant action.");
         }
     }     );
////////////////////////////////////////////////////////////
  stage.setTitle("An Event Button..");
  stage.setScene(scene);
  stage.show();
 }
}
```

The terminal dialog resulting from compiling and executing this program is:

```
Terminal
mike@mike-MS-7850:~$ javac ButtonEventAction1.java
mike@mike-MS-7850:~$ java ButtonEventAction1
button1 was pressed and this message is the resultant action.
```

## Multiple Event Handlers

Here we have three separate event handlers. One for each of three buttons. Now that there is more than one graphic control 'device' on our display we need to be able to arrange them across the stage/scene area in a sensible fashion. We make use of layout class objects like Hbox, Vbox and GridPanes to control the position of graphic UI objects.

```
// ThreeButtonsEventsGridPane1.java
/*
The GridPane layout class is used to arrange the buttons in a (column, row)
grid pattern.

Tested on: java version "java-8-oracle"
Author: Mike Ohlson de Fine.
*/
import javafx.application.Application;
import javafx.scene.Scene;
import javafx.scene.control.Button;
import javafx.scene.layout.GridPane;
import javafx.stage.Stage;

import javafx.event.ActionEvent;
import javafx.event.EventHandler;

public class ThreeButtonsEventsGridPane1 extends Application {

  public void start(Stage stage) {

    GridPane gridpane = new GridPane();
    Scene scene = new Scene(gridpane, 180, 100);

    Button button1    = new Button("butt. #1");
    Button button2 = new Button("butt. #2");
    Button button3    = new Button("butt. #3");
```

```
    gridpane.add(button1, 0, 0);  // button1 positioned at Column 0, Row 0
    gridpane.add(button2, 0, 1);  // button2 positioned at Column 0, Row 1
    gridpane.add(button3, 1, 1);  // button3 positioned at Column 1, Row 1

    //////////////////////////////////////////////////////////////
    /////////// Event Handlers for three Buttons   /////////

       button1.setOnAction(new EventHandler<ActionEvent>() // button1
event handler.
       {
          public void handle(ActionEvent e)
          { System.out.println("button #1 was pressed."); }
       });

       button2.setOnAction(new EventHandler<ActionEvent>() // button2
event handler.
       {
          public void handle(ActionEvent e)
          { System.out.println("button #2 was pressed"); }
       });

        button3.setOnAction(new EventHandler<ActionEvent>() // button3
event handler.
       {
          public void handle(ActionEvent e)
          { System.out.println("button #3 was pressed"); }
       });
    //////////////////////////////////////////////////////////////
    stage.setScene(scene);
    stage.show();
  }
}
```

The terminal dialog resulting from execution this program is:

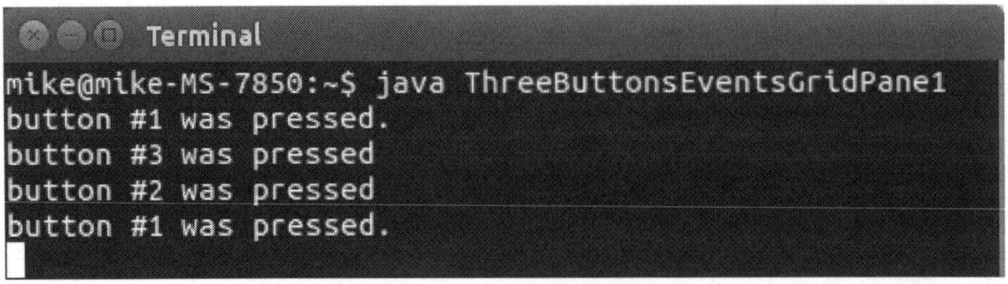

# Decorating Buttons with Images.

Good user interface design should make controls simple and obvious to use. Placing small images on buttons that help users understand what the button is for is an obvious way to improve usability.

The example here adapts the previous one and places images on each button. Instead of using the GridPane for layout arrangement we use Hbox and Vbox which are horizontal and vertical areas in which graphic objects can be placed in sequence.

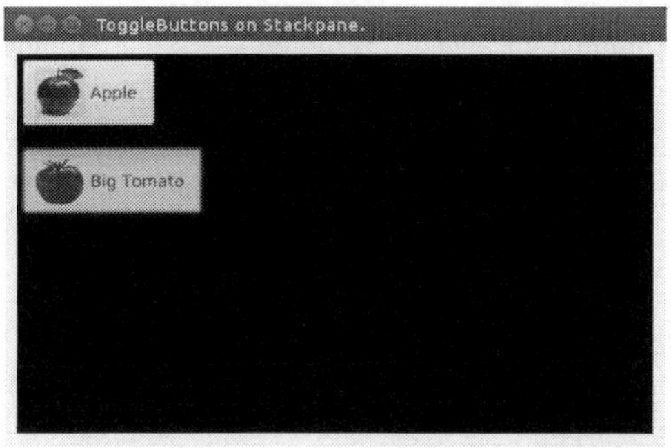

```
// ToggleButtonImages1.java
/*
Two buttons with icons (for easy identification) are used to trigger either of
two EventHandlers.
The Stackpane layout default is the Center position.
That is, all child nodes will be in the center:
"The stackpane will attempt to resize each child to fill its content area. If the
child could not be sized to fill the stackpane (either because it was not
```

```
resizable or its max size prevented it) then it will be aligned within the area
using the alignment property, which defaults to Pos.CENTER." To change
this, use for example:
StackPane.setAlignment(node_name, Pos.TOP_LEFT);

Position alignment choices:
---------------------------
BASELINE_CENTER: on the baseline vertically and on the center
horizontally.
BASELINE_LEFT:   on the baseline vertically and on the left horizontally.
BASELINE_RIGHT:  on the baseline vertically and on the right horizontally.
BOTTOM_CENTER:   on the bottom vertically and on the center horizontally.
BOTTOM_LEFT:     on the bottom vertically and on the left horizontally.
BOTTOM_RIGHT:    on the bottom vertically and on the right horizontally.
CENTER:          on the center both vertically and horizontally.
CENTER_LEFT:     on the center vertically and on the left horizontally.
CENTER_RIGHT:    on the center vertically and on the right horizontally.
TOP_CENTER:      on the top vertically and on the center horizontally.
TOP_LEFT:        on the top vertically and on the left horizontally.
TOP_RIGHT:       on the top vertically and on the right horizontally.

Tested on: java version "java-8-oracle"
Author: Mike Ohlson de Fine.
*/
import javafx.application.Application;
import javafx.scene.Scene;
import javafx.stage.Stage;
import javafx.scene.layout.StackPane;
import javafx.geometry.Insets;
import javafx.geometry.Pos;
import javafx.event.ActionEvent;
import javafx.event.EventHandler;
import javafx.scene.image.Image;
import javafx.scene.image.ImageView;
import javafx.scene.paint.*;
import javafx.scene.shape.*;

import javafx.scene.control.ToggleButton;
import javafx.scene.control.ToggleGroup;

public class ToggleButtonImages1 extends Application
```

```
{
    public void start(Stage stage)
    {
        double width =520 ;
        double height =320 ;

        StackPane stackpane1 = new StackPane();            // Construct a
StackPane root object
        Scene scene = new Scene(stackpane1, width, height); // Width, height
of pane.
        ToggleGroup grouptog1 = new ToggleGroup();         // Create a
ToggleGroup #1.

        Image apple_image = new Image("apple1.png");           // Small blue
image on a button.
        Image tomato_image = new Image("tomato1.png");         // Small blue
image on a button.
        Image apple40_image = new Image("apple_40.png");      // Large red
image.
        Image tomato40_image = new Image("tomato_40.png"); // Large red
image.
        ImageView im_v1 = new ImageView(apple_image);
        im_v1.setX(200);
        im_v1.setY(60);

        ImageView im_v2 = new ImageView(tomato_image);
        im_v2.setX(300);
        im_v2.setY(80);

        final Rectangle rect1 = new Rectangle(width - 20, height - 20);
        StackPane.setAlignment(rect1, Pos.TOP_LEFT);
        //  Gaps/borders around images.  Insets( top, right, bottom, left)
        StackPane.setMargin(rect1, new  Insets(10,   10,   10,   10));

//=============================================================
        // Create toggle button "togg_apple1" with a blue apple icon images .
        ToggleButton togg_apple1 = new ToggleButton("Apple ",
                                          new   ImageView(apple40_image));

        StackPane.setAlignment(togg_apple1, Pos.TOP_LEFT);
        togg_apple1.setTranslateX(15);
```

```
        togg_apple1.setTranslateY(15);

        // Create toggle button "togg_tomato1" with a purple tomato icon
images .
        ToggleButton togg_tomato1 = new ToggleButton("Big Tomato ",
                                        new ImageView(tomato40_image));
        StackPane.setAlignment(togg_tomato1, Pos.TOP_LEFT);
        togg_tomato1.setTranslateX(15);
        togg_tomato1.setTranslateY(85);

        // Collect the buttons in a common group.
        togg_apple1.setToggleGroup(grouptog1);
        togg_tomato1.setToggleGroup(grouptog1);
        togg_tomato1.setSelected(true);  // Make togg_tomato1 active on
startup.

        stackpane1.getChildren().add(rect1);    // Add graphic nodes onto the
pane.
        stackpane1.getChildren().add(togg_apple1);
        stackpane1.getChildren().add(togg_tomato1);  // Last node will be on
top of the pane.

//////////////////////////////////////////////////////////////////
 //======= Two Event Handlers for the ToggleButtons   =============

     togg_apple1.setOnAction(new EventHandler<ActionEvent>() // Event
Handler No. 1
      {   // Display the apple and make the rectangle violet.
          public void handle(ActionEvent e)
          { System.out.println("ToggleButton #1 Apple");
            rect1.setFill(Color.VIOLET);
            stackpane1.getChildren().remove(im_v2); // Remove the tomato.
            stackpane1.getChildren().add(im_v1);     // Show the apple.
          }
      });

      togg_tomato1.setOnAction(new EventHandler<ActionEvent>()  // Event
Handler No. 2
      {   // Display the tomato and make the rectangle blue.
          public void handle(ActionEvent e)
          { System.out.println("ToggleButton #2 Tomato");
```

```
            rect1.setFill(Color.BLUE);
            stackpane1.getChildren().remove(im_v1); // Remove the apple.
            stackpane1.getChildren().add(im_v2);     // Show the tomato
          }
      });
      //=========================================================
    stage.setScene(scene);
    stage.setTitle("ToggleButtons on Stackpane.");
    stage.show();
  }
}
```

# Arrange Buttons in Columns (Vbox) or Rows (Hbox)

```
// VBoxButtonGraphics1.java or HBoxButtonGraphics1.java
/*
Displays an image on vertically arranged buttons.

HBox lays out its children in a single horizontal row.
VBox lays out its children in a single vertical column.

The horizontal alternative is available by swapping the roles of vbox and hbox
instances,
by converting between commented and uncommented lines of code.

Tested on: java version "java-8-oracle"
Author: Mike Ohlson de Fine
*/
import javafx.application.Application;
import javafx.event.ActionEvent;
import javafx.event.EventHandler;
import javafx.scene.Group;
import javafx.scene.Scene;
import javafx.scene.*;
import javafx.scene.control.Button;
import javafx.scene.control.ToggleButton;
import javafx.scene.layout.VBox;
import javafx.scene.layout.HBox;
import javafx.stage.Stage;

import javafx.scene.image.Image;
import javafx.scene.image.ImageView;

public class VBoxToggleButtonGraphics1 extends Application
{
  public void start(Stage stage)

   {

      VBox vbox = new VBox();
      Scene scene = new Scene(vbox);

      HBox hbox = new HBox();
      //Scene scene = new Scene(hbox);
     Image birdy_image = new
```

```
Image(getClass().getResourceAsStream("bird_aztec_100.jpg"));
        Image butterfly_image = new Image("butterfly_100.jpeg");
        Image redpaint_image = new Image("red_paint_100.jpg");

        Button button1 = new Button("Press");
        button1.setGraphic(new ImageView(birdy_image)); // This places the
image on the button.

        Button button2 = new Button("Push");
        button2.setGraphic(new ImageView(butterfly_image));

        Button button3 = new Button("splash");
        button3.setGraphic(new ImageView(redpaint_image));

        vbox.getChildren().add(button1); // Comment-out for HBox option.
        vbox.getChildren().add(button2); // Comment-out for HBox option.
        vbox.getChildren().add(button3); // Comment-out for HBox option.
        vbox.setSpacing(10); // Vertical spacing between graphic objects.
Comment-out for HBox.
        /*
        hbox.getChildren().add(button1); // Comment-out for VBox option.
        hbox.getChildren().add(button2); // Comment-out for VBox option.
        hbox.getChildren().add(button3); // Comment-out for VBox option.
        */
        ////////////////////////////////////////////////////////////
        ///// Event Handlers for three image decorated buttons //////
        button1.setOnAction(new EventHandler<ActionEvent>()
        {
                                public void handle(ActionEvent e)
                                { System.out.println("The birdy button was pressed");
}
        });

        button2.setOnAction(new EventHandler<ActionEvent>()
        {
                                public void handle(ActionEvent e)
                                { System.out.println("The butterfly button was
nudged"); }
        });

        button3.setOnAction(new EventHandler<ActionEvent>()
```

```
    {
                    public void handle(ActionEvent e)
                    { System.out.println("The red paint was splashed"); }
    });
    ////////////////////////////////////////////////////
    stage.setScene(scene);
    stage.setTitle("Vertical (VBox) Decorated Buttons, Events");
    stage.show();
  }
}
```

## A Point to Note: How to switch code on and off.

For any programmer who is actively developing code the ability to switch instructions on and off, without deleting them, is very useful. You may be modifying some existing code to serve a different function or you may be testing the value of a variable. We would like to introduce and test our modifications in reversible stages. If we introduce some new code it is a good idea to keep the old code in place and just make it inactive by turning each line into a comment. This means that if the new, modified instructions do not work we can easily comment-out the new instructions and re-activate the older, trusted, instructions.

In the program above we have used the */* commented-out block of instructions */* method of neutralizing a block of code. What works just as well is to place // (backslashes) in front of each line we wish to neutralize.

# RadioButton

Old tape recordes used to have a row of buttons, each for a different function like record, rewind, play, eject tape etc. Only one function could be on/active at a time. So when you pushed one down all the others would go off. The radio buttons are usually grouped together to let user to do a single selection. That is, the user of the application can only choose one item in the radio button list.

Typically more than one choice is offered and the user can only select one of them. For example, when choosing shoe size we normally select one size among the list. A radio button is either selected or deselected.

# ToggleButton

A toggle button has two states: selected (on) or not selected (off). When we push a toggle to the “on” state it stays on until it gets pushed a second time.

We can combine two or more toggle buttons into a group and allow user to select only one button or none.

Although a Toggle Button looks similar to a standard Button it is different in behavior. A standard Button is a "command" button which calls a function when clicked. A ToggleButton on the other hand simply sets the state of a boolean flag, the *selected* flag. Selected = ***true*** state is set if the button has been clicked. If the button is clicked a second time the flag becomes ***false***.

ToggleButton can also be placed in groups that link them in behavior. When in a group, only one ToggleButton at a time within that group can be selected. To put two ToggleButtons in the same group, simply assign them both the same value for ToggleGroup. By default, a ToggleButton is not in a group.

Note however that unlike RadioButtons, ToggleButtons in a ToggleGroup do not attempt to force at least one selected ToggleButton in the group to be selected=true. This means that if a ToggleButton happens to be selected, clicking on it will cause it to become unselected. With RadioButton, clicking on the selected button in the group will have no effect.

## Constructors

1. **ToggleButton( );** Creates a toggle button with an empty string for its label.

2. **ToggleButton(text);** Creates a toggle button with the specified text as its label.

3. **ToggleButton(text, graphic);** Creates a toggle button with the specified text and icon for its label.

**Methods**

**setToggleGroup(group);** To set a toggle group to a toggle button.

**setSelected(true);** Is used to preselect a toggle button.

**setUserData("text1");** To set a value of a toggle button.

**GetUserData();** It return the value of the toggle button.

## A Single ToggleButton

The way the toggle buttons is displayed on the screen is slightly different in an attempt to make the state visible. The "on" state is slightly darker than the "off" state but the effect is visually weak.

```
// ToggleButtonSimplest.java
/*
ToggleButton: class:javafx.scene.control.ToggleButton
--------------------------------------
```

```
Constructors
1. ToggleButton( ), or
2. ToggleButton(text)
3. ToggleButton(text, graphic)

Tested on: java version "java-8-oracle"
Author: Mike Ohlson de Fine.
*/
import javafx.application.Application;
import javafx.scene.Group;
import javafx.scene.Scene;
import javafx.stage.Stage;
import javafx.scene.control.ToggleButton;
import javafx.scene.paint.Color;
//import javafx.scene.image.ImageView ;
//import javafx.scene.image.Image ;
public class ToggleButtonSimplest1 extends Application {

  public void start(Stage stage) {
    Group root = new Group();
    Scene scene = new Scene(root, 160, 60, Color.GREEN);

    ToggleButton radButton1 = new ToggleButton("A Toggle Button");
    root.getChildren().add(radButton1);

    stage.setTitle("A Toggle Button");
    stage.setScene(scene);
    stage.show();
  }
}
```

## Grouped and Decorated ToggleButtons

```
// ToggleButtonGroup1.java
/*
Demonstrate how to make toggle groups.
No event handlers have been provided for this simplified demonstration.

ToggleButton: class:javafx.scene.control.ToggleButton
-------------------------------------
Constructor used for this example:
ToggleButton(text, graphic);

Tested on: java version "java-8-oracle"
Author: Mike Ohlson de Fine.
*/
import javafx.application.Application;
import javafx.scene.Scene;
import javafx.scene.layout.HBox;
import javafx.stage.Stage;
import javafx.scene.image.Image;
import javafx.scene.image.ImageView;
import javafx.scene.control.ToggleButton;
import javafx.scene.control.ToggleGroup;

public class ToggleButtonGroup1 extends Application
{
  public void start(Stage stage)
  {
     stage.setTitle("Toggle Buttons Grouped");
     HBox root = new HBox();                    // Use Hbox layout
     ToggleGroup grouptog = new ToggleGroup(); //Create a ToggleGroup

      Image birdy_image = new Image("bird_aztec_100.jpg");
      Image butterfly_image = new Image("butterfly_100.jpeg");
      Image redpaint_image = new Image("red_paint_100.jpg");

     // Create the toggle buttons with icon images.
```

```
    ToggleButton togbutt1 = new ToggleButton("#1:Yes ", new
ImageView(birdy_image));
    ToggleButton togbutt2 = new ToggleButton("#2: No ", new
ImageView(butterfly_image));
    ToggleButton togbutt3 = new ToggleButton("#3: No ", new
ImageView(redpaint_image));

    // Make the toggle buttons belong to grouptog.
    togbutt1.setToggleGroup(grouptog);
    togbutt2.setToggleGroup(grouptog);
    togbutt3.setToggleGroup(grouptog);

    //Set value to togbutt1 and togbutt2 but not togbutt3.
    togbutt1.setUserData("butt1 user data: togbutt1 is unselected (default
value) out the blocks.");
    togbutt2.setUserData("butt2 user data: togbutt1 is selected to begin
with.");

    //Verify the data values by printing the user values of togbutt1 ,togbutt2.
and togbutt3.
    System.out.println(togbutt1.getUserData());
    System.out.println(togbutt2.getUserData());
    System.out.println(togbutt3.getUserData());

    //pre-select togbutt2 button.
    togbutt2.setSelected(true);

    //Add all children to Hbox layout (root).
    root.getChildren().addAll(togbutt1, togbutt2, togbutt3);

    Scene scene = new Scene(root, 400, 120);
    stage.setScene(scene);
    stage.show();
 }
}
```

# CheckBoxes, RadioButtons, ChoiceBoxes

## Checkbox

The check box allows users to do multiple selections. This contrasts with a radio button which only allows one choice from a group. For example, when ordering pizza we can add more than one topping. The radio button or the toggle button are for single choice or no choice.

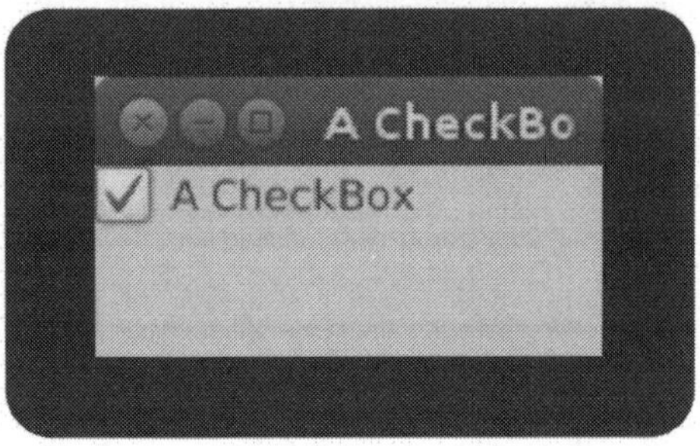


```
// CheckBoxSimplest.java
/*
CheckBox: class:javafx.scene.control.CheckBox
--------------------------------------
Constructors
1. CheckBox( ), or
2. CheckBox(text)

Tested on: java version "java-8-oracle"
Author: Mike Ohlson de Fine.
*/
import javafx.application.Application;
import javafx.scene.Group;
import javafx.scene.Scene;
import javafx.stage.Stage;
import javafx.scene.control.CheckBox;
import javafx.scene.paint.Color;

public class CheckBoxSimplest extends Application {

 public void start(Stage stage) {
   Group root = new Group();
   Scene scene = new Scene(root, 160, 60, Color.PINK);

   CheckBox checkBx1 = new CheckBox("A CheckBox");
   root.getChildren().add(checkBx1);

   stage.setTitle("A single CheckBox");
```

```
    stage.setScene(scene);
    stage.show();
  }
}
```

## Multiple CheckBoxes

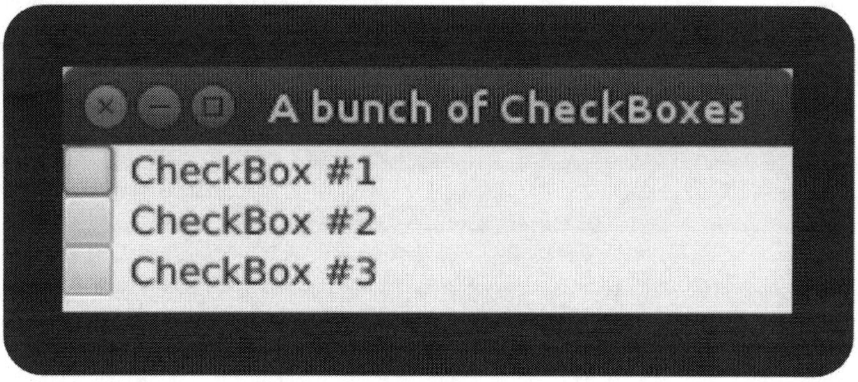


```
// CheckBoxesGroup1.java
/*
CheckBox: class:javafx.scene.control.CheckBox
--------------------------------------
Constructors
1. CheckBox( ), or
2. CheckBox(text)

Tested on: java version "java-8-oracle"
Author: Mike Ohlson de Fine.
*/
import javafx.application.Application;
import javafx.scene.Scene;
import javafx.stage.Stage;
import javafx.scene.control.CheckBox;
import javafx.scene.paint.Color;
import javafx.scene.layout.VBox;

public class CheckBoxesGroup1 extends Application {

  public void start(Stage stage) {
```

```
    VBox vbox = new VBox();    // Use Vbox layout
    Scene scene = new Scene(vbox, 260, 60, Color.PINK);


    CheckBox checkBx1 = new CheckBox("CheckBox #1");
    CheckBox checkBx2 = new CheckBox("CheckBox #2");
    CheckBox checkBx3 = new CheckBox("CheckBox #3");

    vbox.getChildren().addAll(checkBx1, checkBx2, checkBx3 );

    stage.setTitle("A bunch of CheckBoxes");
    stage.setScene(scene);
    stage.show();
  }
}
```

## ChoiceBox

A ChoiceBox allows the user to quickly select between a few options. The ChoiceBox is used for presenting the user with a relatively small set of predefined choices from which they may choose. The ChoiceBox, when "showing", will display to the user these choices and allow them to pick exactly one choice. When not showing, the current choice is displayed.

By default, the ChoiceBox has no item selected unless otherwise specified.

The configuration of the ChoiceBox is order independent. You may either specify the items and then the selected item, or you may specify the selected item and then the sub-items. Either way will function correctly.

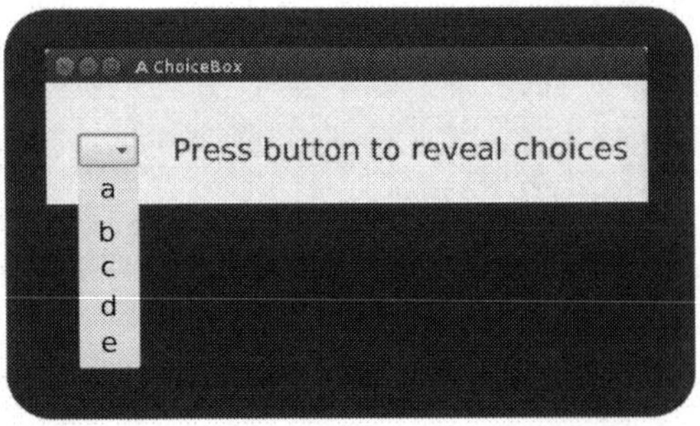

```
// ChoiceBoxSimple1.java
/*
The default Choicebox properties.
Note: Aside from mouse control, the arrow keys on the keyboard can cycle
through the choices,
and the enter key can select a choice.

Constructors
ChoiceBox(ObservableList<T> items)

Tested on: java version "java-8-oracle"
Author: Mike Ohlson de Fine.
*/
import javafx.application.Application;
import javafx.scene.Scene;
import javafx.stage.Stage;

import javafx.beans.value.ChangeListener;
import javafx.beans.value.ObservableValue;
import javafx.collections.FXCollections;
import javafx.geometry.Insets;
import javafx.geometry.Pos;

import javafx.scene.control.ChoiceBox;
import javafx.scene.control.Label;
import javafx.scene.layout.HBox;


public class ChoiceBoxSimple1 extends Application {

  public void start(Stage stage) {

    HBox hbox = new HBox();
    Scene scene = new Scene(hbox, 500, 100 );

    Label label = new Label("Press button to reveal choices");
    label.setStyle("-fx-font: 25 arial;");
    label.setLayoutX(40);

    String[] greetings = new String[] { "A", "B", "C", "D", "E" };
```

```
    ChoiceBox<String> choicebx = new ChoiceBox<String>(
      FXCollections.observableArrayList("a", "b", "c", "d", "e"));

    choicebx.getSelectionModel().selectedIndexProperty()
      .addListener(new ChangeListener<Number>() {
        public void changed(ObservableValue obsvalue, Number value, Number
new_value) {
          label.setText(greetings[new_value.intValue()]);
        }
      });

    hbox.getChildren().addAll(choicebx, label);
    hbox.setSpacing(30);
    hbox.setAlignment(Pos.CENTER);
    hbox.setPadding(new Insets(10, 0, 0, 10));

    stage.setScene(scene);
    stage.setTitle("ChoiceBoxes");
    stage.show();

  }
}
```

# RadioButtons

RadioButtons create a series of items where only one item out of a group can be selected. RadioButtons are a specialized type of toggle button. When a RadioButton is pressed and released an ActionEvent is triggered. Our application should perform some action based on this event by implementing an Eventhandler which we need to write.

**Grouped RadioButtons:** Only one RadioButton can be selected when placed in a ToggleGroup. Clicking on an already selected RadioButton will have no effect. A RadioButton that is not in a ToggleGroup can be selected and unselected. By default a RadioButton is not in a ToggleGroup. Calling ToggleGroup.getSelectedToggle() will return the RadioButton that has been selected.

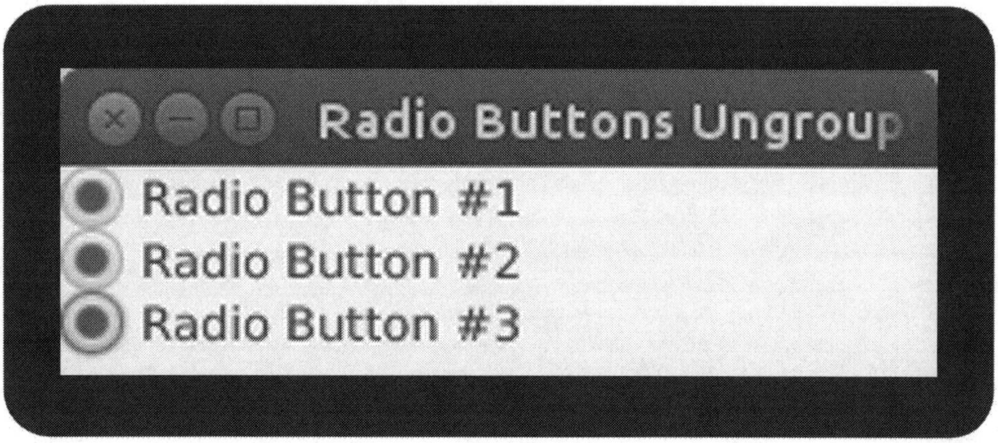


```
// RadioButtonsUngrouped.java
/*
RadioButton: class:javafx.scene.control.RadioButton
--------------------------------------
When ungrouped in a ToggleGroup, each button can be switched on or off
independently of the other buttons it is displayed with.
Once placed in a group then they are linked such that only one
may be selected.

Constructors
1. RadioButton( ), or
2. RadioButton(text)

Tested on: java version "java-8-oracle"
Author: Mike Ohlson de Fine.
*/
import javafx.application.Application;
import javafx.scene.Scene;
import javafx.stage.Stage;
import javafx.scene.control.RadioButton;
import javafx.scene.paint.Color;
import javafx.scene.layout.VBox;

public class RadioButtonsUngrouped extends Application
{

  public void start(Stage stage)
  {
```

```
    VBox vbox = new VBox();     // Use Vbox layout
    Scene scene = new Scene(vbox, 250, 60, Color.PALEGREEN);

    RadioButton radButton1 = new RadioButton("Radio Button #1");
    vbox.getChildren().add(radButton1);

    RadioButton radButton2 = new RadioButton("Radio Button #2");
    vbox.getChildren().add(radButton2);

    RadioButton radButton3 = new RadioButton("Radio Button #3");
    vbox.getChildren().add(radButton3);

    stage.setTitle("Radio Buttons Ungrouped");
    stage.setScene(scene);
    stage.show();
  }
}
```

## ToggleGrouped RadioButtons

Only one RadioButton can be selected when placed in a ToggleGroup. Clicking on a RadioButton that has already been selected will have no effect.

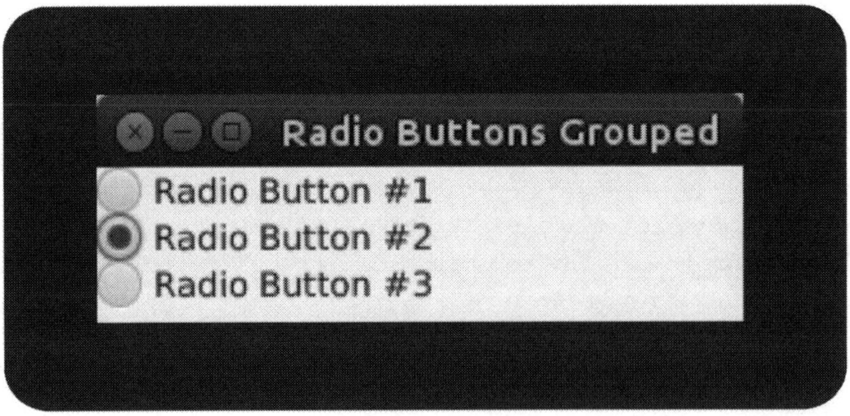


```
// RadioButtonsToggleGrouped1.java
/*
RadioButton: class:javafx.scene.control.RadioButton
-------------------------------------
```

```
When grouped in a ToggleGroup, each button is dependent on the state of the
other buttons in the same group.
Only one may be on. Selecting a particular button
will switch off whichever other button was on.

Tested on: java version "java-8-oracle"
Author: Mike Ohlson de Fine.
*/
import javafx.application.Application;
import javafx.scene.Scene;
import javafx.stage.Stage;
import javafx.scene.control.RadioButton;
import javafx.scene.control.ToggleGroup;
import javafx.scene.paint.Color;
import javafx.scene.layout.VBox;

public class RadioButtonsToggleGrouped1 extends Application
{
 public void start(Stage stage)
 {
  VBox vbox = new VBox();    // Use Vbox layout.
  Scene scene = new Scene(vbox, 250, 60, Color.PALEGREEN);

  // All three buttons will become members of this group "togGroup".
  ToggleGroup togGroup = new ToggleGroup();

  RadioButton radButton1 = new RadioButton("Radio Button #1");
  radButton1.setToggleGroup(togGroup); // First member of togGroup.
  vbox.getChildren().add(radButton1);

  RadioButton radButton2 = new RadioButton("Radio Button #2");
  radButton2.setToggleGroup(togGroup); // Second member of togGroup.
  vbox.getChildren().add(radButton2);

  RadioButton radButton3 = new RadioButton("Radio Button #3");
  radButton3.setToggleGroup(togGroup); // Third member of togGroup.
  vbox.getChildren().add(radButton3);

  stage.setTitle("Radio Buttons Grouped");
  stage.setScene(scene);
  stage.show();
```

```
  }
}
```

# Sliders

The Slider is a graphic device for entering numbers into a Java program. Sliders can display and interact with a range of numeric values.

The Slider Control is used to display a continuous or discrete range of valid numeric choices and allow the user to interact with the control. It is typically represented visually as having a "track" and a "knob" or "thumb" which is dragged within the track. The Slider can optionally show tick marks and labels indicating the different slider position values.

The three fundamental variables of the slider are **min**, **max**, and **value**. The value should always be a number between min and max. min defaults to 0, and max defaults to 100.

On the track we can choose to include tick marks and labels that indicate numeric values of the range.

## Simplest Slider

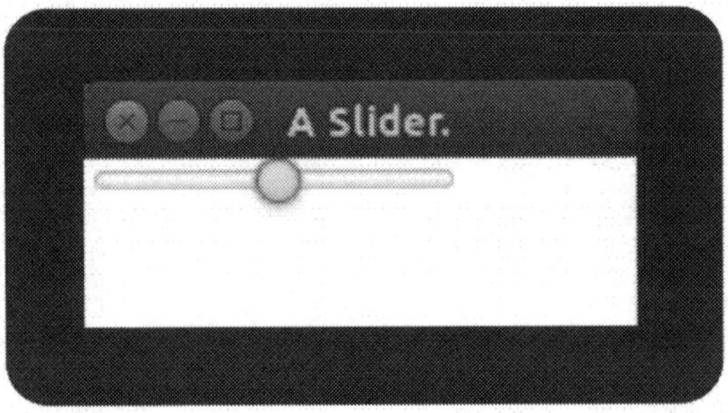


```
// SliderSimplest.java
/*
The Slider is a graphic device for entering numbers into a java program.
Class slider: javafx.scene.control.Slider
----------------------------------------
```

```
Constructors:
Slider();
Slider( min,  max,  initial_value) - max-min =  range.

Tested on: java version "java-8-oracle"
Author: Mike Ohlson de Fine.
*/
import javafx.application.Application;
import javafx.scene.Group;
import javafx.scene.Scene;
import javafx.scene.control.Slider;
import javafx.stage.Stage;

public class SliderSimplest extends Application
{

   public void start(Stage stage)
   {
      Group root = new Group();
      Scene scene = new Scene(root, 200, 60);
      stage.setScene(scene);
      stage.setTitle("A Slider.");

      Slider slider = new Slider(0, 1, 0.5);
      root.getChildren().add(slider);

      stage.show();
   }
}
```

# Quantitative Slider: Position IN and Slider Value OUT

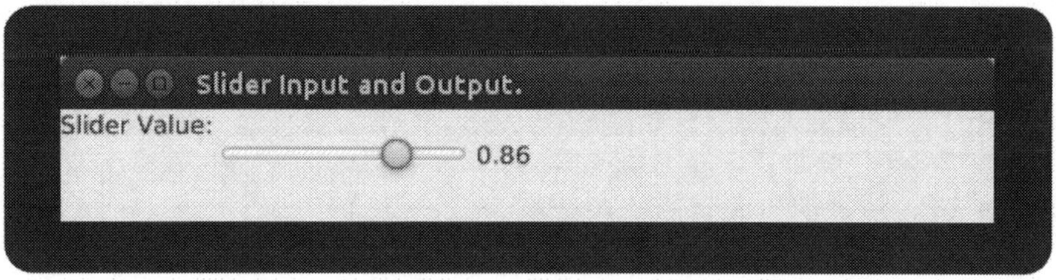

```
// SliderValue1.java
/*
Sliders don't have ActionEvents. Instead they have a number
called valueProperty that contains the current value of the slider.
Slider class: javafx.scene.control.Slider
-----------------------------------------
Constructors
Slider(): A default Slider instance.
Slider(min, max, value): A Slider control with the specified slider min, max
and initial value value.

Tested on: java version "java-8-oracle"
Author: Mike Ohlson de Fine.
*/
import javafx.application.Application;
import javafx.beans.value.ChangeListener;
import javafx.beans.value.ObservableValue;
import javafx.stage.Stage;
import javafx.scene.Group;
import javafx.scene.Scene;
import javafx.scene.control.Label;
import javafx.scene.control.Slider;
import javafx.scene.layout.GridPane;

public class SliderValue1 extends Application
{

   final Slider slidebar = new Slider (0.5, 1, 1); //Slider(min, max, initial
value)
   final Label sliderCaption = new Label("Slider Value:");
   final Label sliderValue = new Label( Double.toString(slidebar.getValue()));

   public void start(Stage stage)
   {
      Group root = new Group();
      Scene scene = new Scene(root, 500, 60);
      stage.setScene(scene);
      stage.setTitle("Slider Input and Output.");

      GridPane grid = new GridPane();
```

```
        scene.setRoot(grid);
        ///////////////////////////////////////////////////////////////
        // Listener type Event handler.
        slidebar.valueProperty().addListener(new ChangeListener<Number>()
        {
          public void changed(ObservableValue<? extends Number> ov,
                      Number old_val, Number new_val)
          {
               sliderValue.setText(String.format("%.2f", new_val));
          }
        });
        ///////////////////////////////////////////////////////////////
        grid.getChildren().add(sliderCaption);

        GridPane.setConstraints(slidebar, 1, 3); // The slider INPUT.
        grid.getChildren().add(slidebar);

        GridPane.setConstraints(sliderValue, 2, 3); // Slider Value OUTPUT.
        grid.getChildren().add(sliderValue);

        stage.show();
    }
}
```

# ProgressIndicator (Circular)

```
// ProgressIndicator1.java
/*
A circular control which is used for indicating progress, either indeterminate
(ie. going on and on ) or some finite value of a variable. Often used for
representing progress of background Tasks.
```

```
Class ProgressIndicatorr: javafx.scene.control.ProgressIndicator
----------------------------------------
Constructors:
ProgressIndicator(): A new indeterminate ProgressIndicator.
ProgressIndicator(progress_value): A new ProgressIndicator with the given
progress value.

Tested on: java version "java-8-oracle"
Author: Mike Ohlson de Fine.
*/
import javafx.application.Application;
import javafx.geometry.Insets;
import javafx.scene.Scene;
import javafx.stage.Stage;
import javafx.scene.control.ProgressIndicator;
import javafx.scene.layout.FlowPane;

public class ProgressIndicator1 extends Application
{
   public void start(Stage stage)
   {
      ProgressIndicator progressIndicator = new ProgressIndicator();
      FlowPane root = new FlowPane();
      root.getChildren().addAll( progressIndicator);

      Scene scene = new Scene(root, 300, 70);
      stage.setTitle("ProgressIndicator / Throbber. ");
      stage.setScene(scene);
      stage.show();
   }
}
```

# ProgressBar (Horizontal Gauge)

```
// ProgressBar1.java
/*
An alternative to the ProgressIndicator which is represented as a horizontal
bar.
It indicates progress, either infinite or indeterminate (ie. going on and on
forever)
or bar whose length represents the value of some variable.
Often used for representing progress of background Tasks.

Class ProgressBar: avafx.scene.control.ProgressBar
----------------------------------------
Constructors:
ProgressBar(): A new indeterminate ProgressIndicator.
ProgressBar(progress_value): A new ProgressIndicator with the given progress
value.

Tested on: java version "java-8-oracle"
Author: Mike Ohlson de Fine.
*/
import javafx.application.Application;
import javafx.stage.Stage;
import javafx.scene.Scene;
import javafx.scene.control.ProgressBar;
import javafx.scene.layout.FlowPane;
```

```
public class ProgressBar1 extends Application
{
   public void start(Stage stage)
   {
      ProgressBar progressBar = new ProgressBar();
      // or  ProgressBar progressBar = new ProgressBar(double value);
      FlowPane root = new FlowPane();
      root.getChildren().addAll(progressBar);

      Scene scene = new Scene(root, 180, 40);
      stage.setTitle("ProgressBar ");
      stage.setScene(scene);
      stage.show();
   }
}
```

# ScrollBar Simplest – Horizontal

A ScrollBar is either a horizontal or vertical bar with increment and decrement buttons and a "thumb" or slider which the user can move using the mouse cursor. Typically a scrollbar is not used alone but used for building up more complicated controls . The channel sensitivity/volume controls on a studio sound production console use vertical scrollbar type controls.

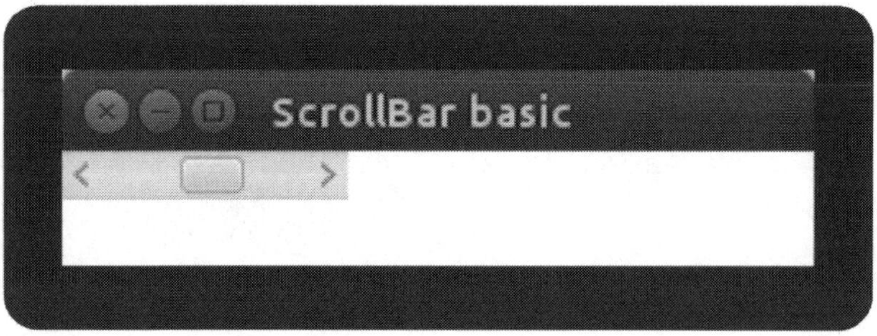


```
// ScrollBarSimplest1.java
/*
Either a horizontal or vertical bar with increment and decrement buttons and
a "thumb" with which the user can interact. Typically not used alone but used
for building up more complicated controls such as the ScrollPane and
```

```
ListView.

Class ScrollBar: avafx.scene.control.ProgressBar
-----------------------------------------
Constructors:
ScrollBar(): A new horizontal ScrollBar (ie getOrientation() ==
Orientation.HORIZONTAL)

Tested on: java version "java-8-oracle"
Author: Mike Ohlson de Fine.
*/
import javafx.application.Application;
import javafx.geometry.Orientation;
import javafx.scene.Group;
import javafx.scene.Scene;
import javafx.scene.control.ScrollBar;
import javafx.stage.Stage;

public class ScrollBarSimplest1 extends Application {

   public void start(Stage stage) {
      Group root = new Group();
      Scene scene = new Scene(root, 260, 40);
      stage.setScene(scene);

      ScrollBar s1 = new ScrollBar();

      root.getChildren().add(s1);
      stage.setTitle("ScrollBar basic");
      stage.show();
   }
}
```

## ScrollBar Vertical

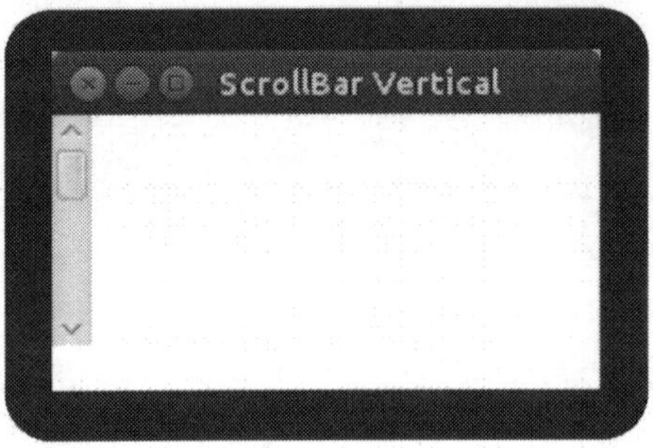


```
// ScrollBarVertical1.java
/*
To change to vertical: scrollbar1.setOrientation(Orientation.VERTICAL);

Tested on: java version "java-8-oracle"
Author: Mike Ohlson de Fine.
*/
import javafx.application.Application;
import javafx.stage.Stage;
import javafx.scene.Group;
import javafx.scene.Scene;
import javafx.scene.control.ScrollBar;
import javafx.geometry.Orientation;

public class ScrollBarVertical1 extends Application
{
  public void start(Stage stage)
  {
    Group root = new Group();
    Scene scene = new Scene(root, 240, 120);
    stage.setScene(scene);

    ScrollBar scrollvert1 = new ScrollBar();
    scrollvert1.setOrientation(Orientation.VERTICAL);

    root.getChildren().add(scrollvert1);
    stage.setTitle("ScrollBar Vertical");
    stage.show();
  }
}
```

# ScrollBar Event Handling

In the example below we have an event handler

```
  skrolb1.valueProperty().addListener((ObservableValue<? extends Number>
ov,
        Number old_val, Number new_val) ->
    {
            System.out.println(new_val.doubleValue());
            sliderValue.setText(String.format("%.2f", new_val));
    });
```

The skrollbar object is the scroll bar and whenever the position of its slider-handle is changed an event is generated. The list on numbers captured in the terminal as shown below are the positions of the slider as it is moved using the mouse.

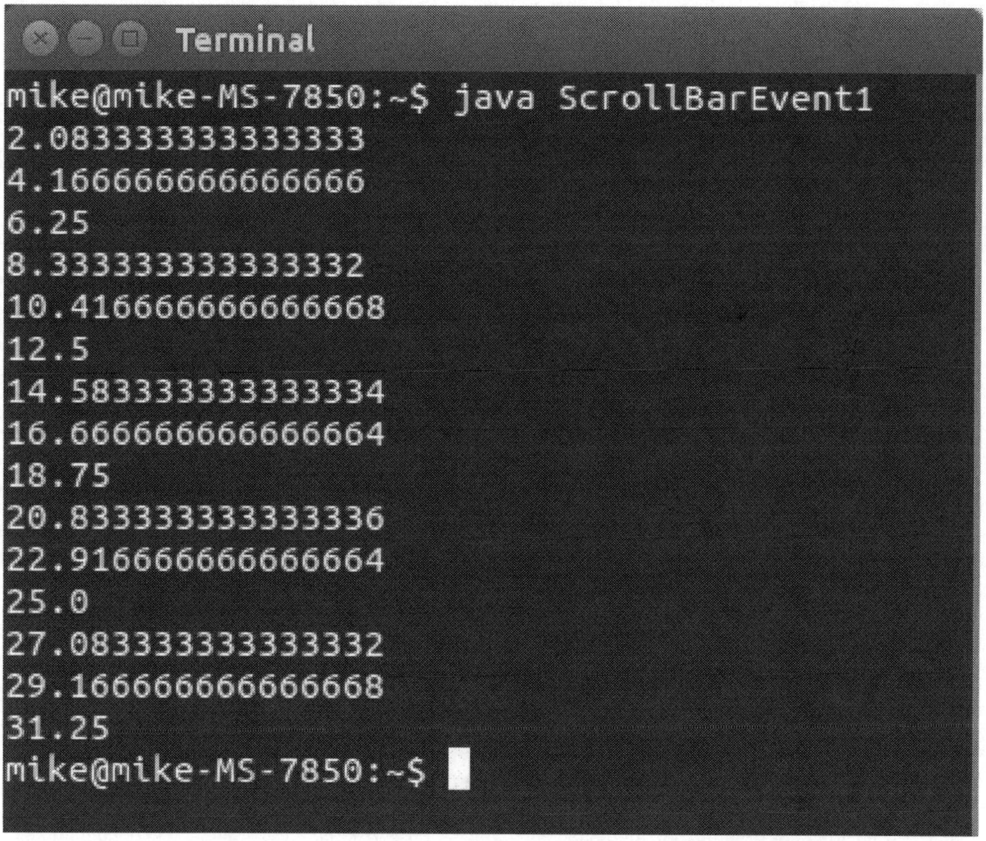

```
// ScrollBarEvent1.java
/*
Event Handling for Scrollbar

Tested on: java version "java-8-oracle"
Author: Mike Ohlson de Fine.
*/
import javafx.application.Application;
import javafx.beans.value.ObservableValue;
import javafx.stage.Stage;
import javafx.scene.Group;
import javafx.scene.Scene;
import javafx.scene.control.Label;
import javafx.scene.control.ScrollBar;
import javafx.scene.layout.GridPane;

public class ScrollBarEvent1 extends Application
{
   public void start(Stage stage)
   {
      Group gruproot = new Group();
      Scene scene = new Scene(gruproot, 500, 200);
      stage.setScene(scene);

      ScrollBar skrolb1 = new ScrollBar();
      Label sliderValue = new Label( Double.toString(skrolb1.getValue()));
      GridPane grid = new GridPane();
      scene.setRoot(grid);
      ///////////////////////////////////////////////////////
      /////////   EventHandler for  //////////
      skrolb1.valueProperty().addListener((ObservableValue<? extends
Number> ov,
         Number old_val, Number new_val) ->
      {
```

```
            System.out.println(new_val.doubleValue());
            sliderValue.setText(String.format("%.2f", new_val));
        });
        //////////////////////////////////////////////////////
        GridPane.setConstraints(skrolb1, 1, 3); // The slider.
        grid.getChildren().add(skrolb1);

        GridPane.setConstraints(sliderValue, 2, 3);
        grid.getChildren().add(sliderValue);

        stage.show();
    }
}
```

# ScrollPane

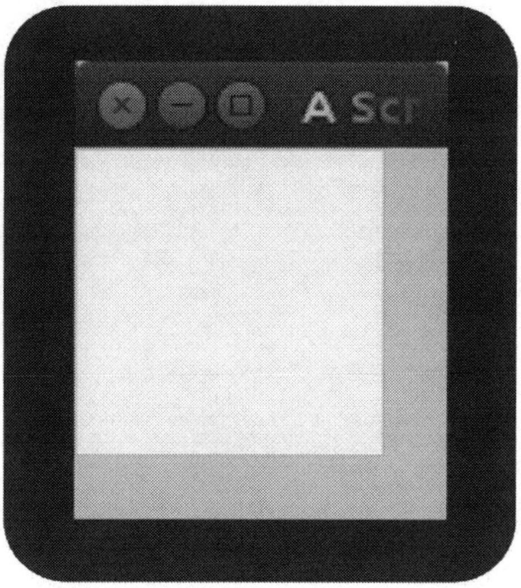


```
// ScrollPaneSimplest1.java
/*
A Control that provides a scrolled, clipped viewport of its contents. It allows
the user to scroll the content around either directly (panning) or by using
scroll bars. The ScrollPane allows specification of the scroll bar policy, which
determines when scroll bars are displayed: always, never, or only when they
are needed.
ScrollPane: class:javafx.scene.control.ScrollPane
-------------------------------------
```

```
Constructor
1. ScrollPane(): A new ScrollPane.
ScrollPane(Node_content): A new ScrollPane.

Tested on: java version "java-8-oracle"
Author: Mike Ohlson de Fine.
*/
import javafx.application.Application;
import javafx.scene.Group;
import javafx.scene.Scene;
import javafx.stage.Stage;
import javafx.scene.control.ScrollPane;
import javafx.scene.paint.Color;

public class ScrollPaneSimplest1 extends Application
{
  public void start(Stage stage)
  {
    Group root = new Group();
    Scene scene = new Scene(root, 120, 120, Color.PINK);
    ScrollPane scrollPane = new ScrollPane();
    root.getChildren().add(scrollPane);
    stage.setTitle("A ScrollPane");
    stage.setScene(scene);
    stage.show();
  }
}
```

## ScrollPane with Images

```
//ScrollPaneImages1.java
/*
Tested on: java version "java-8-oracle"
Author: Mike Ohlson de Fine
*/
import javafx.application.Application;
import javafx.stage.Stage;
import javafx.scene.Scene;
import javafx.scene.control.ScrollPane;
import javafx.scene.image.Image;
import javafx.scene.image.ImageView;
import javafx.scene.layout.VBox;

public class ScrollPaneImages1 extends Application
{
   final ScrollPane skrolp = new ScrollPane();
   final Image[] images = new Image[5];
   final ImageView[] imv_pics = new ImageView[5];
   final VBox vwbox = new VBox();
   final String [] imageNames = {"apple1.jpg", "Dragon_small_2.jpg",
```

```
"fern_100.jpg", "hamish_100.jpg", "mossA_100.jpg"};

    public void start(Stage stage)
    {
        VBox box = new VBox();
        box.getChildren().addAll(skrolp);

        for (int i = 0; i < 5; i++)
        {
            images[i] = new Image(imageNames[i]);

            imv_pics[i] = new ImageView(images[i]);
            imv_pics[i].setFitWidth(100);
            imv_pics[i].setPreserveRatio(true);
            vwbox.getChildren().add(imv_pics[i]);
        }

        skrolp.setContent(vwbox);
        Scene scene = new Scene(box, 180, 180);
        stage.setScene(scene);
        stage.setTitle("Scroll Pane");
        stage.show();
    }
}
```

# CHAPTER 19

## UI USER INTERFACES – Part 2

In this chapter we will cover:

- TextField
- TextArea
- PasswordField
- Hyperlink
- DatePicker
- ColorPicker
- FileChooser
- Menu
- Tooltip

- Combobox
- ListView
- TreeView
- Separator
- HTMLEditor
- Pagination
- TableView
- Tree TableView

## User Interfaces (UI) or Graphic User Interface (GUI)

The topics in this chapter do not have direct relevance to the drawing and graphic design approach focus of the rest of the book. However they are classes that are part of the JavaFX design.

Aside from TextField we introduce very basic examples with the objective of giving you, dear reader, one example of each topic on which to build up your understanding. The official JavaFX documentation on these topics is often perfunctory, opaque and without simple illustrative examples. Examples given on tutorial websites are often excessively long and complicated and worse still give rise to multiple errors and warnings. The process of learning from bad documentation is very frustrating.

No examples on the topics of HTMLEditor, Separator or Pagination have been given. They are more the area of web design than graphics. The two topics of TableView and TreeView are problematic and no simple, clear and error free examples of their usage have been found. They appear to be JavaFX design orphans – unsupported perhaps.

## TextField: The Input Text to an Application

The TextField is for a user to enter a single line of text input. The text will be unformatted text – the font type and size are not selectable. For multi-line input the **TextArea** control must be used. Additionally, if you want a form of rich-text editing, there is also the HTMLEditor control.

TextField can show prompt text to the user when there is no text already in the TextField. This is handy way of informing the user what is expected in the text field.

If we need to enter more than a single line of text then a separate class the TextArea should be used. This is dealt with further on.

```
// TextFieldSimplest.java
/*
The default Textfield properties.
Constructors:
TextField()
TextField(line of text)

Tested on: java version "java-8-oracle"
Author: Mike Ohlson de Fine.
*/
import javafx.application.Application;
import javafx.geometry.Insets;
import javafx.scene.Group;
import javafx.scene.Scene;
```

```
import javafx.scene.control.Label;
import javafx.scene.control.TextField;
import javafx.scene.layout.GridPane;
import javafx.stage.Stage;

public class TextFieldSimplest extends Application {

 public void start(Stage stage) {
   Scene scene = new Scene(new Group(), 450, 250);

   TextField prompt = new TextField ("Enter your name here") ;

   GridPane grid = new GridPane();
   grid.setVgap(4);
   grid.setHgap(10);
   grid.setPadding(new Insets(5, 5, 5, 5));
   grid.add(new Label("Name: "), 0, 0);
   grid.add(prompt, 1, 0);

   Group root = (Group) scene.getRoot();
   root.getChildren().add(grid);
   stage.setScene(scene);
   stage.show();
 }
}
```

## TextField in and Terminal out.

When the “Enter-key” is pressed causes an event is initiated on the textField. The getText() method returns the line of text that was found in the textfield.

The event handler method is:

```
 // Event Handler for "Enter-key"

      textFieldEntry.setOnAction(action ->

            {

               System.out.println(textFieldEntry.getText());
```

```
            }          );
```

So the complete application to take whatever is typed into the textfield and output it to the system terminal is:

```
// TextFieldEnterKey.java
/*
The default Textfield properties. Type the line of text into the
textfield provided, the hit ENTER. The ENTER key automatically
triggers a"TextField" event.

Constructors:
TextField()
TextField(initial line of text)

Tested on: java version "java-8-oracle"
Author: Mike Ohlson de Fine.
*/

import javafx.application.Application;
import javafx.scene.Scene;
import javafx.scene.control.TextField;
import javafx.scene.layout.HBox;
import javafx.stage.Stage;

public class TextFieldEnterKey extends Application {

  public void start(Stage primaryStage)
  {
    primaryStage.setTitle("TextField Input");

    TextField textFieldEntry = new TextField();

    // Event Handler for "Enter-key"
    textFieldEntry.setOnAction(action ->
          {
             System.out.println(textFieldEntry.getText());
          }     );

    HBox hbox = new HBox(textFieldEntry);
```

```
        Scene scene = new Scene(hbox, 200, 100);
        primaryStage.setScene(scene);
        primaryStage.show();

    }
}
```

## Typical TextField input for user data entry

In a typical application a pane be presented to the user with a text field that waits for user data entry. The data would be assigned to a variable and then displayed visibly for verification.

```
// TextFieldEntry2variable.java
/*
The Textfield starts off with a user prompt message.
Once a line of text has been entered and the "Enter" key pressed the value of a
new string variable called "entered_text" will be assigned
to be whatever text was typed into the text field.

Constructors:
TextField()
TextField(initial line of text)

Tested on: java version "java-8-oracle"
Author: Mike Ohlson de Fine.
*/
import javafx.application.Application;
import javafx.scene.Scene;

import javafx.scene.control.TextField;
import javafx.scene.layout.HBox;
import javafx.stage.Stage;

public class TextFieldEnterKey2variable extends Application {
    public void start(Stage primaryStage)
    {
        primaryStage.setTitle("TextField Input");
        TextField textFieldEntry = new TextField("Enter your name here");

        // Event Handler for "Enter-key"
```

```
        textFieldEntry.setOnAction(action ->
            {
                String entered_text = new String(textFieldEntry.getText());
                System.out.println(entered_text);
            }       );

        HBox hbox = new HBox(textFieldEntry);
        Scene scene = new Scene(hbox, 200, 100);
        primaryStage.setScene(scene);
        primaryStage.show();

    }
}
```

## Other Event Triggers

Hitting the "Enter" key is not the only way to trigger the execution of an event handler that will return the contents of the textfield. We could just as easily have used a button to trigger the event handler as shown below.

```
// ButtonTriggeredTextFieldEntry.java
/*
The Textfield captured triggered by Button event.

Tested on: java version "java-8-oracle"
Author: Mike Ohlson de Fine.
*/
import javafx.application.Application;
import javafx.scene.Scene;
import javafx.scene.control.Button;
import javafx.scene.control.TextField;
import javafx.scene.layout.HBox;
import javafx.stage.Stage;


public class ButtonTriggeredTextFieldEntry extends Application {
```

```
  public void start(Stage stage)
   {

      TextField textFieldContents = new TextField("Enter your name here");

      Button button = new Button("Click to transfer text");

      // Button event handler.
      button.setOnAction(action -> {
         System.out.println(textFieldContents.getText());
      });

      HBox hbox = new HBox(textFieldContents, button);

      stage.setTitle("Button triggered input");
      Scene scene = new Scene(hbox, 200, 100);
      stage.setScene(scene);
      stage.show();
   }
}
```

## TextArea for multi-line input.

TextArea is for text input that allows a user to enter multiple lines of plain text. This means that the enter key will not trigger the event handler. For rich-text editing, there is the HTMLEditor control.

TextArea allows us to show prompt text to the user when there is no text already in the TextArea. This is a useful way of informing the user about what is expected in the text area.

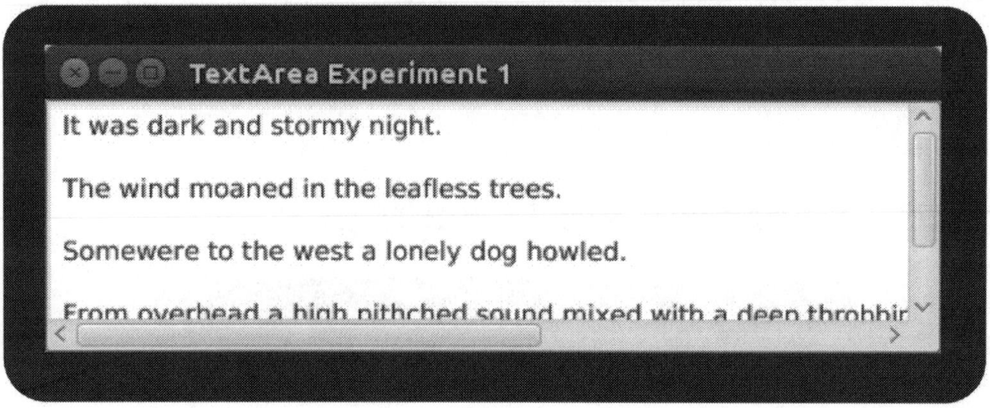


```
// TextAreaSimple.java
/*
The TextArea allows the user to type in multiple lines of text.
In other words the "Enter" key does signal the end of the entry.
It just causes a new line character to be become part of the text.

Constructors:
TextArea()
TextArea(initial prompt text)

Tested on: java version "java-8-oracle"
Author: Mike Ohlson de Fine.
*/
import javafx.application.Application;
import javafx.scene.Scene;
import javafx.scene.control.TextArea;
import javafx.scene.layout.VBox;
import javafx.stage.Stage;

public class TextAreaSimple extends Application
{
   public void start(Stage stage)
   {
      TextArea textArea1 = new TextArea();

      VBox vbox = new VBox(textArea1);

      stage.setTitle("TextArea Example");
      Scene scene = new Scene(vbox, 200, 100);
```

```
        stage.setScene(scene);
        stage.show();
    }
}
```

# Button Triggered TextArea Input

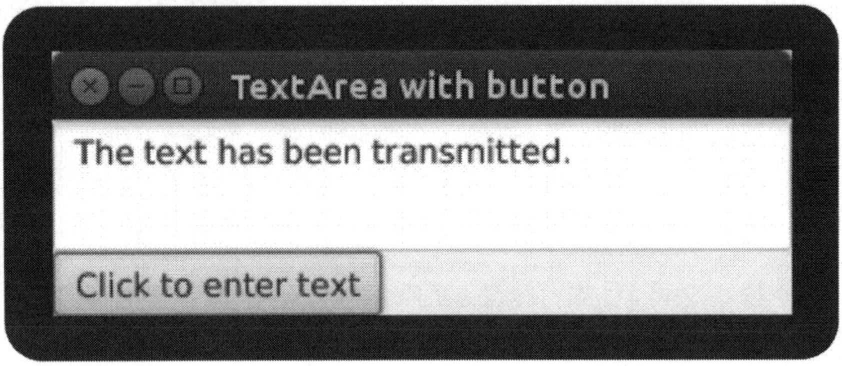


```
// TextAreaButtonEvent.java
/*
The TextArea allows the user to type in multiple lines of text.
In other words the "Enter" key does signal the end of the entry.
It just causes a new line character to be become part of the text.

Constructors:
TextArea()
TextArea(initial prompt text)

Tested on: java version "java-8-oracle"
Author: Mike Ohlson de Fine.
*/
import javafx.application.Application;
import javafx.scene.Scene;
import javafx.scene.control.Button;
import javafx.scene.control.TextArea;
import javafx.scene.layout.VBox;
import javafx.stage.Stage;

public class TextAreaButtonEvent extends Application
{
  public void start(Stage primaryStage) throws Exception {
      primaryStage.setTitle("TextArea with button");
```

```
        TextArea textarea2 = new TextArea("Type in your story and then click the
button");

        Button button = new Button("Click to enter text");
        button.setMinWidth(50);

        // Event handler
        button.setOnAction(action -> {
          System.out.println(textarea2.getText());
          textarea2.setText("The text has been transmitted.");
        });

        VBox vbox = new VBox(textarea2, button);

        Scene scene = new Scene(vbox, 300, 100);
        primaryStage.setScene(scene);
        primaryStage.show();
    }
}
```

## Discover which Fonts (Typefaces) are on our Computer

Here is a short program that will list all the fonts that are installed on our computer.

```
// FontsAlphabetical1.java
/*
Alphabetic list of fonts available on this computer.

Tested on: java version "java-8-oracle"
Author: Mike Ohlson de Fine
*/

import javafx.application.Application;
import javafx.stage.Stage;
import javafx.scene.text.Font;
import java.util.List;

public class FontsAlphabetical1 extends Application
```

```
{
  public void start(final Stage stage)
  {
    stage.setTitle("Text Fonts available, alphabetical");

    List<String> familiesList = Font.getFamilies();

        for(int i=0;i<familiesList.size();i++)
         {
              System.out.println(familiesList.get(i));
        }

    stage.show();
  }
}
```

In chapter 13 we have programs that allow us to see what thc various fonts actually look like.

## PasswordField

The PasswordField is for password input. The characters typed by a user are hidden by displaying an echo string of small circles.

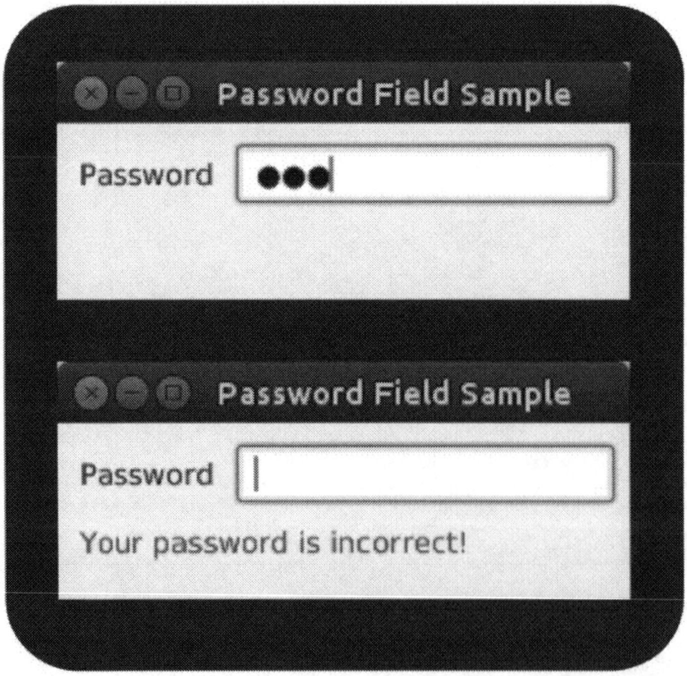

```
// PasswordFieldSimplest.java
/*
A keyboard entered password is compared with a password embedded in the
code.
Note that this is a very weak way to do passwords.

Constructor:
PasswordField()

Tested on: java version "java-8-oracle"
Author: Mike Ohlson de Fine.
*/
import javafx.application.Application;
import javafx.event.ActionEvent;
import javafx.event.EventHandler;
import javafx.scene.Group;
import javafx.scene.Scene;
import javafx.scene.control.Label;
import javafx.scene.control.PasswordField;
import javafx.scene.layout.HBox;
import javafx.scene.layout.VBox;
import javafx.scene.paint.Color;
import javafx.stage.Stage;
public class PasswordFieldSimplest extends Application
{
 final Label message = new Label("");

 public void start(Stage stage)
 {
  Group root = new Group();
  VBox vb = new VBox();
  HBox hb = new HBox();

  Label label = new Label("Password");
  final PasswordField pb = new PasswordField();

  // Event handler.
  pb.setOnAction(new EventHandler<ActionEvent>()
  {
```

```
    public void handle(ActionEvent e)
    {
      if (!pb.getText().equals("abcd")) // "abcd" is the password.
      {
        message.setText("Your password is incorrect!");
        message.setTextFill(Color.web("red"));
      } else
        {
        message.setText("Your password has been confirmed");
        message.setTextFill(Color.web("black"));
        }
      pb.setText("");
    }
  });
  hb.getChildren().addAll(label, pb);
  vb.getChildren().addAll(hb, message);

  Scene scene = new Scene(root, 260, 80);
  stage.setScene(scene);
  stage.setTitle("Password Field Demonstration");
  scene.setRoot(vb);
  stage.show();
 }
}
```

# Hyperlink

The Hyperlink class represents the hyper links similar to the anchor links on the web pages in JavaFX.
An HTML-like label which can be a graphic and/or text can respond to rollovers and clicks from the mouse. When a hyperlink is clicked/pressed a flag called ***isVisited()*** becomes true and this flag can be made use of to make some choice or initiate action. A Hyperlink behaves just like a button - when a hyperlink is pressed and released an ActionEvent is triggered, and your application can perform some action based on this event.

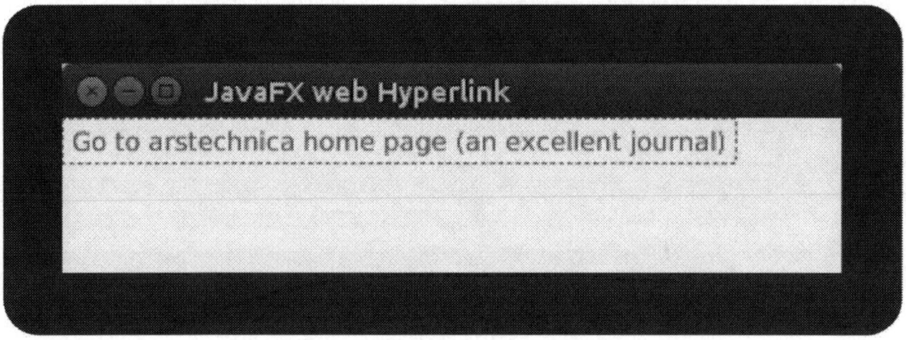


```
// HyperlinkSimplest.java
/*
Go to an Internet address.

Tested on: java version "java-8-oracle"
Author: Mike Ohlson de Fine.
*/
import javafx.application.Application;
import javafx.event.ActionEvent;
import javafx.event.EventHandler;
import javafx.scene.Scene;
import javafx.scene.control.Hyperlink;
import javafx.scene.layout.FlowPane;
import javafx.stage.Stage;

public class Hyperlink1 extends Application
{
   public void start(Stage stage) {

      Hyperlink hyperlink = new Hyperlink("Go to arstechnica home page (an
excellent journal)");

      // Event handler.
      hyperlink.setOnAction(new EventHandler<ActionEvent>() {
         public void handle(ActionEvent event) {
            getHostServices().showDocument("https://arstechnica.com/"); //
Internet address.
         }
      });
```

```
        FlowPane root = new FlowPane();

        root.getChildren().addAll(hyperlink);

        Scene scene = new Scene(root, 400, 80);
        stage.setTitle("JavaFX web Hyperlink");
        stage.setScene(scene);
        stage.show();
    }
}
```

## DatePicker

The DatePicker control allows the user to enter a date as text or to select a date from a calendar popup. The calendar is based on either the standard ISO-8601 chronology or any of the other chronology classes defined in the java.time.chrono package.

The value property represents the currently selected LocalDate. An initial date can be set via the constructor or by calling ***setValue()***. The default value is null.

**The DatePicker control consists of a combo box with a date field and a date chooser.**

```
// DatePickerSimplest.java
/*
Allows the user to enter a date as text or to select a date from a calendar
popup.
Note: Aside from mouse control that the arrow keys on the keyboard
can also be used to select choices.

Constructor:
public DatePicker()

Tested on: java version "java-8-oracle"
Author: Mike Ohlson de Fine.
*/
import javafx.application.Application;
import javafx.scene.Scene;

import javafx.scene.control.DatePicker;
import javafx.scene.layout.VBox;
import javafx.stage.Stage;

public class DatePickerSimplest extends Application {

 public void start(Stage stage)
 {
  VBox vbox = new VBox(20);

  DatePicker seeDatePicker = new DatePicker();

  vbox.getChildren().add(seeDatePicker);

  Scene scene = new Scene(vbox, 260, 80);
  stage.setScene(scene);
  stage.show();
 }
}
```

# ColorPicker

The color picker control enables users to select a color from the available range, or to set an additional color by specifying an RGB or HSB combination.

JavaFX ColorPicker control has the color chooser, color palette, and custom color dialog window.

```
// ColorPicker1.java
/*
Enables users to select a color from a graphical pallette.

Tested on: java version "java-8-oracle"
Author: Mike Ohlson de Fine.
*/
import javafx.application.Application;
import javafx.event.ActionEvent;
import javafx.scene.Scene;
import javafx.scene.control.ColorPicker;
import javafx.scene.layout.HBox;
import javafx.scene.paint.Color;
import javafx.scene.text.Text;
import javafx.stage.Stage;

public class ColorPicker1 extends Application {

  public void start(Stage stage)
  {

    HBox hbox = new HBox(20);

    ColorPicker colorPicker = new ColorPicker();
    colorPicker.setValue(Color.RED);

    Text text = new Text("Color picker:");
    text.setFill(colorPicker.getValue());

    // Event handler.
    colorPicker.setOnAction((ActionEvent t) -> {
        text.setFill(colorPicker.getValue());
    });

    hbox.getChildren().addAll(colorPicker, text);
    Scene scene = new Scene(hbox, 260, 80);
    stage.setScene(scene);
    stage.show();
```

```
  }
}
```

# FileChooser

The FileChooser allows users to navigate the file system and choose a file or a folder.

A FileChooser can be used to invoke file open dialogs for:

- selecting single file (showOpenDialog),
- multiple files (showOpenMultipleDialog),
- file save dialogs (showSaveDialog).

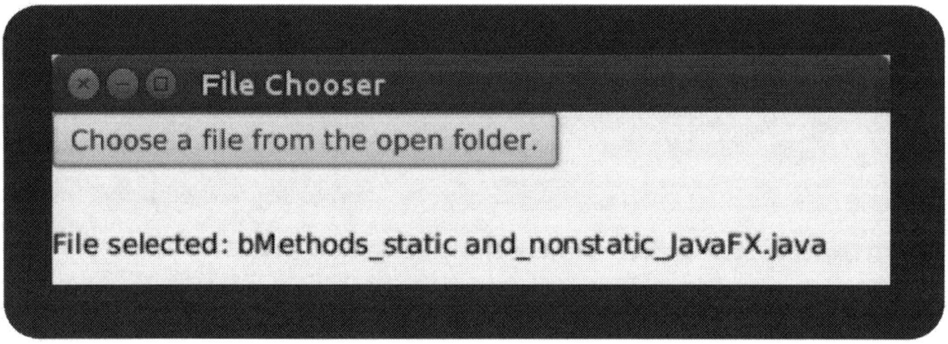


```
// SelectFileChooser1.java
/*
Open a folder and select a file.

Tested on: java version "java-8-oracle"
Author: Mike Ohlson de Fine.
*/
import javafx.application.Application;
import javafx.stage.Stage;
import javafx.stage.FileChooser;
import javafx.scene.Scene;
import javafx.scene.layout.VBox;
import javafx.scene.layout.HBox;
```

```
import javafx.scene.text.Text;
import javafx.scene.control.Button;

import javafx.event.ActionEvent;
import javafx.event.EventHandler;
import java.io.File;

public class SelectFileChooser1 extends Application
{
    private Text actionStatus;

    public void start(Stage stage)
    {
        Button button1 = new Button("Choose a file from the open folder.");
        button1.setOnAction(new SingleFcButtonListener());
        HBox buttonHb1 = new HBox(10);
        buttonHb1.getChildren().addAll(button1);

        actionStatus = new Text(); // Status message: file selected.

        VBox vbox = new VBox(30);
        vbox.getChildren().addAll(buttonHb1, actionStatus);

        Scene scene = new Scene(vbox, 300, 100);
        stage.setTitle("File Chooser");
        stage.setScene(scene);
        stage.show();
    }

    private class SingleFcButtonListener implements
EventHandler<ActionEvent>
    {
        public void handle(ActionEvent e)
        {
            showSingleFileChooser();
        }
    }

    private void showSingleFileChooser()
    {
        FileChooser fileChooser = new FileChooser();
```

```
            File selectedFile = fileChooser.showOpenDialog(null);

            if (selectedFile != null)
             {
                 actionStatus.setText("File selected: " + selectedFile.getName());
            }
            else
             {
                 actionStatus.setText("File selection cancelled.");
            }
        }
}
```

## Menu

Menus are a standard way for desktop applications to select options. Menus and menu items can have key combinations to select options, known as keyboard shortcuts.

A popup menu of actionable items is displayed to the user only upon request. When a menu is visible, in most use cases, the user can select one menu item before the menu goes back to its hidden state. Thus the menu is a good place to put important functionality that does not necessarily need to be visible at all times to the user.

Menus are typically placed in a MenuBar, or as a sub-menu of another Menu.

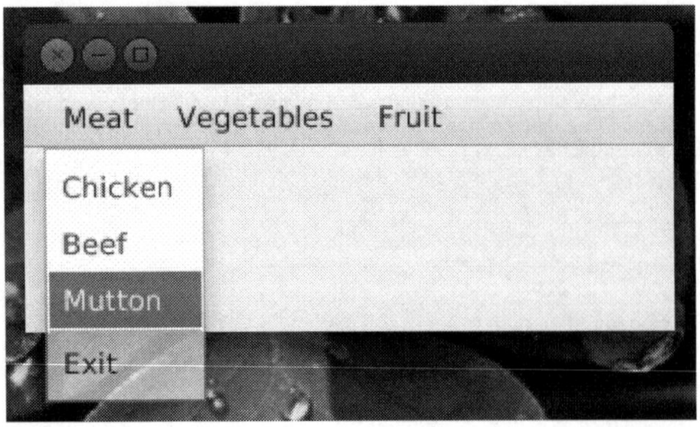

```
// MenuSimple.java
/*
The default menu.
Note that the arrow keys on the keyboard toggle the choices.

Constructors:
1. Menu( text)
Constructs a Menu and sets the display text with the specified text.

2. Menu(text, Node graphic)
Constructs a Menu and sets the display text with the specified text and sets the
graphic Node to the given node.

3. Menu( text, Node graphic, MenuItem... items)

Constructs a Menu and sets the display text with the specified text, the
graphic Node to the given node,
 and inserts the given items into the items list.

Tested on: java version "java-8-oracle"
Author: Mike Ohlson de Fine.
*/
import javafx.application.Application;
import javafx.application.Platform;
import javafx.stage.Stage;
import javafx.scene.Scene;

import javafx.scene.control.CheckMenuItem;
import javafx.scene.control.Menu;
import javafx.scene.control.MenuBar;
import javafx.scene.control.MenuItem;
import javafx.scene.control.RadioMenuItem;
import javafx.scene.control.SeparatorMenuItem;
import javafx.scene.control.ToggleGroup;
import javafx.scene.layout.BorderPane;

public class MenuSimple extends Application
{

  public void start(Stage primaryStage)
```

```
{
  BorderPane root_pane = new BorderPane();
  Scene scene = new Scene(root_pane, 300, 250);

  MenuBar menuBar = new MenuBar();
  menuBar.prefWidthProperty().bind(primaryStage.widthProperty());
  root_pane.setTop(menuBar);

  // 1. Meat menu - Chicken, Beef, Mutton or go away.
  Menu MeatMenu = new Menu("Meat");
  MenuItem menuItem1 = new MenuItem("Chicken");
  MenuItem menuItem2 = new MenuItem("Beef");
  MenuItem menuItem3 = new MenuItem("Mutton");
  MenuItem exitMenuItem = new MenuItem("Exit");
  exitMenuItem.setOnAction(actionEvent -> Platform.exit());

  MeatMenu.getItems().addAll(menuItem1, menuItem2, menuItem3,
                    new SeparatorMenuItem(), exitMenuItem);

  // 2. Vegetable menu - Potatoes, Cabbage.
  Menu VeggieMenu = new Menu("Vegetables");
  CheckMenuItem PotatoesItem = new CheckMenuItem("Vegetables");
  PotatoesItem.setSelected(true);
  VeggieMenu.getItems().add(PotatoesItem);

  CheckMenuItem CabbageItem = new CheckMenuItem("Cabbage");
  CabbageItem.setSelected(true);
  VeggieMenu.getItems().add(CabbageItem);

  Menu FruitMenu = new Menu("Fruit");
  ToggleGroup tGroup = new ToggleGroup();
  RadioMenuItem ApplesItem = new RadioMenuItem("Apples");
  ApplesItem.setToggleGroup(tGroup);

  RadioMenuItem OrangesItem = new RadioMenuItem("Oranges");
  OrangesItem.setToggleGroup(tGroup);
  OrangesItem.setSelected(true);

  FruitMenu.getItems().addAll(ApplesItem, OrangesItem,
    new SeparatorMenuItem());
```

```
    Menu RecipeMenu = new Menu("Recipes");
    RecipeMenu.getItems().addAll(
        new CheckMenuItem("Stewed Apple"),
        new CheckMenuItem("Orange Cocktail"),
        new CheckMenuItem("Apple-Orange Surprise"));

    FruitMenu.getItems().add(RecipeMenu);

    menuBar.getMenus().addAll(MeatMenu, VeggieMenu, FruitMenu);

    primaryStage.setScene(scene);
    primaryStage.show();
  }
}
```

# Tooltip

The tooltip appears when that control is hovered over by the mouse cursor.

The tooltip is used to display additional information or hints about the UI control.

The Tooltip has two different states: activated and showing. There is some delay between activated and shown states.

```
// ToolTip1.java
/*
Demonstrate the tool tip display on hovering.

Tested on: java version "java-8-oracle"
Author: Mike Ohlson de Fine
```

```
*/
import javafx.application.Application;
import javafx.scene.Group;
import javafx.scene.Scene;
import javafx.stage.Stage;

import javafx.scene.layout.HBox;  // Root node.
import javafx.scene.text.Font;
import javafx.scene.control.Button;
import javafx.scene.control.Tooltip;

public class ToolTip1 extends Application
{

public void start(Stage stage) {

        Button button = new Button();
        button.setText("Hover over me!");
        Tooltip tt = new Tooltip();
        tt.setText("This message appears when the pointer hovers over the
button");
        tt.setStyle("-fx-font: normal bold 24 Langdon; "
         + "-fx-base: #AE3522; "
         + "-fx-text-fill: orange;");

         button.setTooltip(tt);

        // Nominate the root node and make it a performer on the stage/scene.
        HBox hbox_root = new HBox();                    //   Construct/instantiate
the container.
        Scene scene = new Scene(hbox_root,1100, 200);   //  Make the container
the root node.
        hbox_root.getChildren().add(button);            // Give the root node a
child to show.

        // Lights, camera, action.
        stage.setTitle("Tooltip show.");
        stage.setScene(scene);
        stage.show();
    }
 }
```

# Separator

The Separator class represents a horizontal or vertical separator line. It divides elements and does not produce any action.

We can style, apply visual effects, and animate a separator.

By default, the separator is horizontal. We can change its orientation by using the setOrientation method.

The visual appearance of this separator can be controlled via CSS. A horizontal separator occupies the full horizontal space allocated to it (less padding), and a vertical separator occupies the full vertical space allocated to it (less padding). The *halignment* (horizontal alignment) and *valignment* (vertical alignment) properties determine how the separator is positioned in the other dimension, for example, how a horizontal separator is positioned vertically within its allocated space.

The separator is horizontal (i.e. *isVertical() == false*) by default.

# ComboBox

A ComboBox allows users to choose one of several options. Users can scroll to the drop down list. The ComboBox can be editable and uneditable.

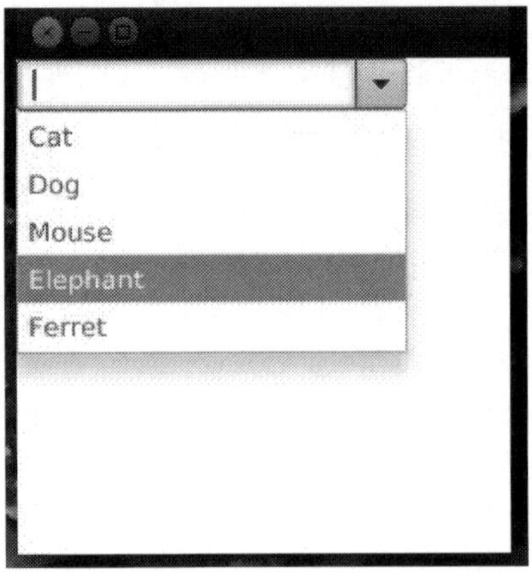


```
// ComboBoxSimplest.java
/*
The default menu.
Note that the arrow keys on the keyboard toggle the choices.
Constructor
ComboBox(ObservableList<T> items)
Creates a default ComboBox instance with the provided items list and a
default selection model.

Tested on: java version "java-8-oracle"
Author: Mike Ohlson de Fine.
*/
import javafx.application.Application;
import javafx.scene.Group;
import javafx.scene.Scene;
import javafx.scene.control.ComboBox;
import javafx.stage.Stage;
public class ComboBoxSimplest extends Application
{
  public void start(Stage stage)
  {
    Scene scene = new Scene(new Group(), 250, 250);

    ComboBox<String> myComboBox = new ComboBox<String>();
    myComboBox.getItems().addAll("Cat","Dog","Mouse","Elephant","Ferret");
    myComboBox.setEditable(true);

    Group root = (Group) scene.getRoot();
```

```
    root.getChildren().add(myComboBox);
    stage.setScene(scene);
    stage.show();

  }
}
```

# ListView

The ListView class allows us to display a scrollable list of items.
A ListView displays a horizontal or vertical list of items from which the user may select. A ListView is able to have its generic type set to represent the type of data in the backing model. Doing this has the benefit of making various methods in the ListView, as well as the supporting classes (mentioned below), type-safe. In addition, making use of the generic supports substantially simplifies development of applications making use of ListView, as all modern IDEs are able to auto-complete far more successfully with the additional type information.

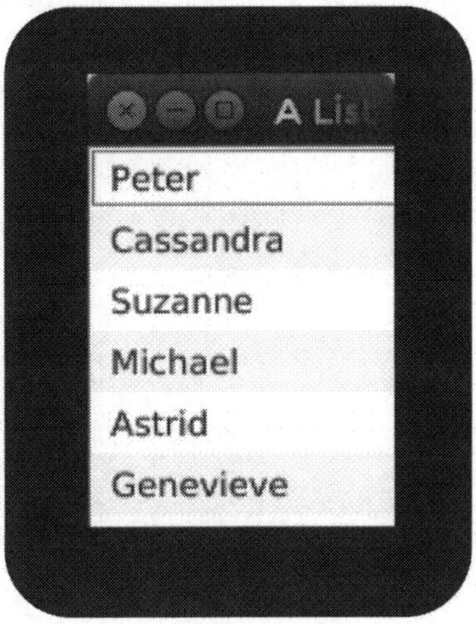


```
// ListViewSimple1.java
/*
A scrollable list of items.

Constructors
1. ListView()
1. ListView(listItems)
```

```
Tested on: java version "java-8-oracle"
Author: Mike Ohlson de Fine.
*/
import javafx.application.Application;
import javafx.scene.Group;
import javafx.scene.Scene;
import javafx.stage.Stage;
import javafx.scene.control.ListView ;
import javafx.scene.paint.Color;
import javafx.collections.FXCollections;
import javafx.collections.ObservableList;

public class ListViewSimple1 extends Application {

  public void start(Stage stage) {
    Group root_group = new Group();
    Scene scene = new Scene(root_group, 120, 150);
    ObservableList<String> names = FXCollections.observableArrayList(
        "Peter", "Cassandra", "Suzanne", "Michael", "Astrid", "Genevieve",
"Candace");
     ListView<String> listView = new ListView<String>(names);
    root_group.getChildren().add(listView);

    stage.setTitle("A ListView");
    stage.setScene(scene);
    stage.show();
  }
}
```

## TreeView

The TreeView UI control provides us a way to present tree structures. A tree has a root node which contains all the hierarchical values. The TreeView control provides a view onto a tree root. By using a TreeView, it is possible to drill down into the children of a TreeItem, recursively until a TreeItem has no more children (that is, it is a *leaf* node in the tree). In TreeView it is only necessary to specify the root node.

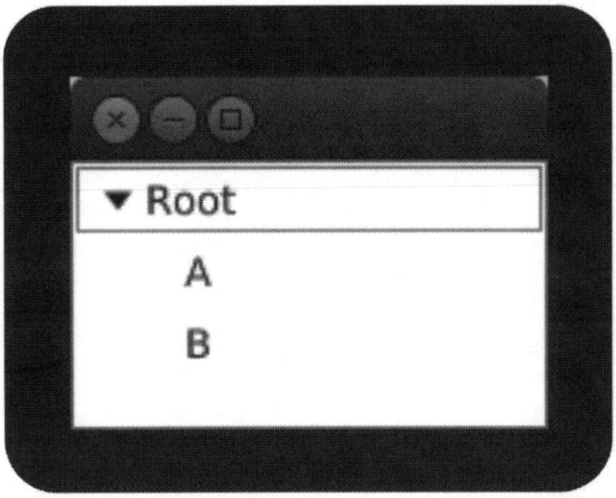


```
// TreeViewSimple.java
/*
Note that the arrow keys on the keyboard toggle the choices.
Constructor
TreeView(TreeItem<T> root)
Creates a TreeView with the provided root node.

Tested on: java version "java-8-oracle"
Author: Mike Ohlson de Fine.
*/
import javafx.application.Application;
import javafx.scene.Scene;
import javafx.stage.Stage;

import javafx.scene.control.TreeItem;
import javafx.scene.control.TreeView;

import javafx.scene.layout.StackPane;

public class TreeViewSimple extends Application {

  public void start(Stage primaryStage)
  {
     TreeItem<String> rootItem = new TreeItem<>("Root");
    rootItem.setExpanded(true);
```

```
    TreeItem<String> item = new TreeItem<>("A");
    rootItem.getChildren().add(item);

    item = new TreeItem<>("B");
    rootItem.getChildren().add(item);

    TreeView<String> tree = new TreeView<>(rootItem);
    StackPane root = new StackPane();
    root.getChildren().add(tree);
    primaryStage.setScene(new Scene(root, 300, 250));
    primaryStage.show();
  }
}
```

## HTMLEditor

The HTMLEditor control is a rich text editor that provides control over text properties like colors, fonts, lists, alignment.

## Pagination

The pagination control is used to navigate through multiple pages. Blogs use pagination control for a web pages. In the bottom of a blog page we can always see a rectangle area which as a list of number to indicate the page index and a next/previous button to link to next/previous pages.

In touch devices, a pagination control can be used to browse through single pages of an article or to navigate between screens.

### TableView

The use of TableView is problematic and not recommended at this time.

The table classes ought to sort data in columns and to resize columns when necessary.

The TableView control is designed to visualize an unlimited number of rows of data, broken out into columns.

## TreeTableView

The use of TreeTableView is problematic and not recommended at this time.

JavaFX TreeTableView presents an hierarchy of data in table columns.

The TreeTableView control is designed to visualize an unlimited number of rows of data, broken out into columns.

# CHAPTER 20

## GEOMETRY TRANSFORMS

*"Transform: to change in composition or structure; to change the outward form or appearance; to change in character or condition"* Mirriam-Webster dictionary.

*" Transmogrify: to change or alter greatly and often with grotesque or humorous effect"*

In this chapter we will cover how to draw:

- Rotation
- Scaling
- Translation
- Shearing
- Flipping, horizontal and vertical

- Combinations of Transforms

Transformation means changing the shape of a graphic object. We can have various types of transformations such as Translation, Scaling Up or Down, Rotation, Shearing and Combinations of any or all of these. The very important thing to know at this early stage is that order or sequence of transform operations is critical. The rotation of an object followed by a translation will have a completely different result from the same translation followed by the same rotation.

Linear Algebra and Matrix Theory are a very important branch of mathematics in computer graphics. Fortunately we do not need to know any math to use them and in this chapter we plan to keep the methods of transforming shapes free of any necessity to know any of the math.

With vector graphics it is relatively easy to construct code that achieves rotation, scaling, translation ans shearing. Rotation always requires more thought and planning than the other transforms because when we rotate a shape we have to decide what point we are going to rotate around. That is before we apply rotation to any single point we must know where the center of rotation will be.

Without using the transformations provided in the javafx.scene.transform class library we also develop the transform methods using basic Java instruction (*bare metal*). This would have use if we needed to selectively transform only parts of an image such as when altering the expressions on characters faces without altering the outlines of the faces.

Are 2D and 3D Transforms Similar?

Yes indeed they are. This will be handled in the third book of this series.

# *The JavaFX Transform Classes*

Standard graphic objects from JavaFX like ellipses, rectangles, polygons and paths can be rotated, scaled, translated and sheared using transform methods contained in the **javafx.scene.transform** library. The JavaFX classes for Transforms are:

javafx.scene.transform.Rotate,
javafx.scene.transform.Scale,
javafx.scene.transform.Translate,
javafx.scene.transform.Shear,

The methods available to perform transforms are :

**rotate(angle, pivotX, pivotY)**
Rotate the object by angle degrees around a pivot point at **pivotX, pivotY**

**translate( move_x, move_y)**
Translate the object by **move_x** horizontally, **move_y** vertically).

**scale( scale_x, scale_y)**
Scale the object by multipliers **scale_x** in the horizontal direction and **scale_**y in the vertical direction .

**scale( scale_x, scale_y, pivotX, pivotY)**
Scale the object about the given pivot point.

**shear( shear_x, shear_y)**
Shear the object by **shear_x** in the horizontal and **shear_y** in the vertical.

**shear( shear_x, shear_y, pivotX, pivotY)**
Shear the object by **shear_x** and **shear_y** about the given pivot point.

# Translation

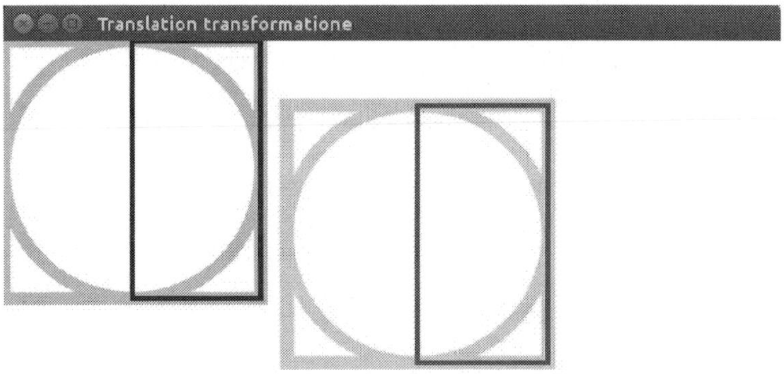


```
// Translation1.java
/*
translate( move_x, move_y):
Translate the object by move_x horizontally, move_y vertically).

Tested on: java version "java-8-oracle"
Author: Mike Ohlson de Fine.
*/

import javafx.application.Application;
import javafx.stage.Stage;
import javafx.scene.Group;
import javafx.scene.Scene;
import javafx.scene.paint.Color;
import javafx.scene.shape.Circle;
import javafx.scene.shape.Rectangle;
import javafx.scene.transform.Translate; // Translation class.

public class Translation1 extends Application {
  public void start(Stage stage) {

//*****************************************************************
    // Shapes used. Three are unchanged.
    Circle circle1 = new Circle(100, 100, 100); // Circle1, unchanged.
     circle1.setStrokeWidth(10);
     circle1.setStroke(Color.SKYBLUE);
     circle1.setFill(null);
    Rectangle rect1 = new Rectangle(0, 0, 200, 200);  // Rectangle1,
```

```
unchanged.
      rect1.setStrokeWidth(10);
      rect1.setStroke(Color.SKYBLUE);
      rect1.setFill(null);

    Rectangle rect2 = new Rectangle(100, 0, 100, 200);  // Rectangle2,
unchanged.
      rect2.setStrokeWidth(4);
      rect2.setStroke(Color.BLUE);
      rect2.setFill(null);

    // Shapes used. Three are transformed.
    Rectangle rect3 = new Rectangle(0, 0, 200, 200);  // Rectangle3,
transformed.
      rect3.setStrokeWidth(10);
      rect3.setStroke(Color.PALEGREEN);
      rect3.setFill(null);

    Rectangle rect4 = new Rectangle(100, 0, 100, 200);  // Rectangle3,
transformed.
      rect4.setStrokeWidth(4);
      rect4.setStroke(Color.GREEN);
      rect4.setFill(null);

    Circle circle2 = new Circle(100, 100, 100); // Circle2, transformed.
      circle2.setStrokeWidth(10);
      circle2.setStroke(Color.PALEGREEN);
      circle2.setFill(null);

//**********************************************************************
      // Construction/instantiation to enable translation to take place
      Translate translate = new Translate();

      //Translation: Setting the X,Y coordinates.
      translate.setX(220);
      translate.setY(120);

      //Executing the translation on circle2, rect3,  rect4
      circle2.getTransforms().addAll(translate);
      rect3.getTransforms().addAll(translate);
      rect4.getTransforms().addAll(translate);
```

```
    Group root = new Group(circle1,circle2, rect1, rect2, rect3, rect4);
    Scene scene = new Scene(root, 460, 370);
    stage.setTitle("Translation transformation");
    stage.setScene(scene);
    stage.show();
  }
}
```

# Rotation

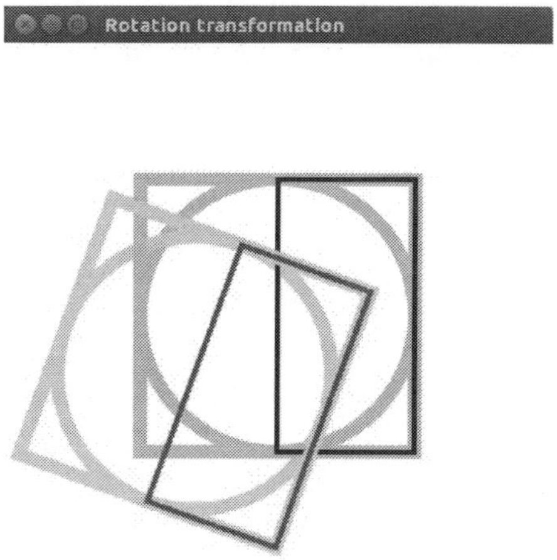


```
// Rotation1.java
/*
rotate(angle, pivotX, pivotY):
Rotate the object by angle in degrees around a pivot point at  pivotX, pivotY

Tested on: java version "java-8-oracle"
Author: Mike Ohlson de Fine.
*/

import javafx.application.Application;
import javafx.stage.Stage;
import javafx.scene.Group;
import javafx.scene.Scene;
import javafx.scene.paint.Color;
import javafx.scene.shape.Circle;
import javafx.scene.shape.Rectangle;
```

```
import javafx.scene.transform.Rotate; // Rotation class.

public class Rotation1 extends Application {

 public void start(Stage stage) {

   //************************************************************************
   // Shapes used. Three are unchanged.
   Circle circle1 = new Circle(200, 200, 100); // Circle1.
    circle1.setStrokeWidth(10);
    circle1.setStroke(Color.SKYBLUE);
    circle1.setFill(null);

   Rectangle rect1 = new Rectangle(100, 100, 200, 200);  // Rectangle1.
    rect1.setStrokeWidth(10);
    rect1.setStroke(Color.SKYBLUE);
    rect1.setFill(null);

   Rectangle rect2 = new Rectangle(200, 100, 100, 200);  // Rectangle2.
    rect2.setStrokeWidth(4);
    rect2.setStroke(Color.BLUE);
    rect2.setFill(null);

   // Shapes used. Three will be transformed.
   Circle circle2 = new Circle(200, 200, 100); // Circle2.
    circle2.setStrokeWidth(10);
    circle2.setStroke(Color.PALEGREEN);
    circle2.setFill(null);

   Rectangle rect3 = new Rectangle(100, 100, 200, 200);  // Rectangle3.
    rect3.setStrokeWidth(10);
    rect3.setStroke(Color.PALEGREEN);
    rect3.setFill(null);

   Rectangle rect4 = new Rectangle(200, 100, 100, 200);  // Rectangle3.
    rect4.setStrokeWidth(4);
    rect4.setStroke(Color.GREEN);
    rect4.setFill(null);


 //************************************************************************
```

```
    Rotate rotate = new Rotate();          // Rotate.

    //Rotation: Setting the angle and pivot X,Y coordinates.
    rotate.setAngle(20);
    rotate.setPivotX(50);
    rotate.setPivotY(50);

    //Adding rotation to circle2, rect3,  rect4
    circle2.getTransforms().addAll(rotate);
    rect3.getTransforms().addAll(rotate);
    rect4.getTransforms().addAll(rotate);

    Group root = new Group(circle1,circle2, rect1, rect2, rect3, rect4);
    Scene scene = new Scene(root, 400, 420);
    stage.setTitle("Rotation transformation");
    stage.setScene(scene);
    stage.show();
  }
}
```

# Scaling

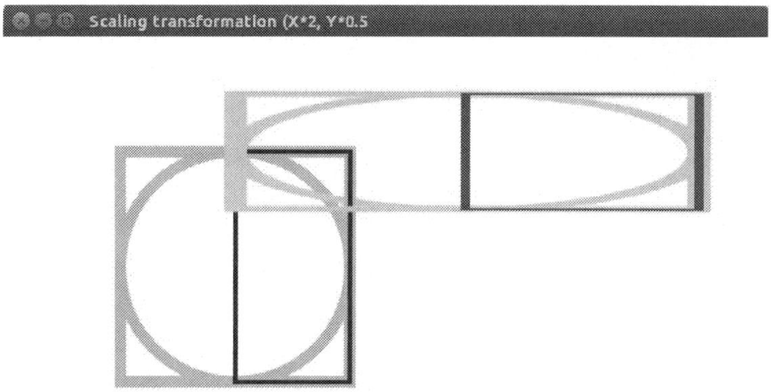


```
// Scaling1.java
/*
scale( scale_x, scale_y):
Scale the object by multipliers scale_x in the horizontal direction and  scale_y
in the vertical direction  .

scale( scale_x,  scale_y, pivotX, pivotY):
```

```
Scale the object about the given pivot point.

Tested on: java version "java-8-oracle"
Author: Mike Ohlson de Fine.
*/

import javafx.application.Application;
import javafx.stage.Stage;
import javafx.scene.Group;
import javafx.scene.Scene;
import javafx.scene.paint.Color;
import javafx.scene.shape.Circle;
import javafx.scene.shape.Rectangle;
import javafx.scene.transform.Scale;

public class Scaling1 extends Application {

  public void start(Stage stage) {

    //*************************************************************
    // Shapes used. Three are unchanged.
    Circle circle1 = new Circle(200, 200, 100); // Circle1.
      circle1.setStrokeWidth(10);
      circle1.setStroke(Color.SKYBLUE);
      circle1.setFill(null);

    Rectangle rect1 = new Rectangle(100, 100, 200, 200);  // Rectangle1.
      rect1.setStrokeWidth(10);

      rect1.setStroke(Color.SKYBLUE);
      rect1.setFill(null);

    Rectangle rect2 = new Rectangle(200, 100, 100, 200);  // Rectangle2.
      rect2.setStrokeWidth(4);
      rect2.setStroke(Color.BLUE);
      rect2.setFill(null);

    // Shapes used. Three will be transformed.
    Circle circle2 = new Circle(200, 200, 100); // Circle2.
      circle2.setStrokeWidth(10);
      circle2.setStroke(Color.PALEGREEN);
```

```
    circle2.setFill(null);

   Rectangle rect3 = new Rectangle(100, 100, 200, 200);  // Rectangle3.
    rect3.setStrokeWidth(10);
    rect3.setStroke(Color.PALEGREEN);
    rect3.setFill(null);

   Rectangle rect4 = new Rectangle(200, 100, 100, 200);  // Rectangle3.
    rect4.setStrokeWidth(4);
    rect4.setStroke(Color.GREEN);
    rect4.setFill(null);

   //*********************************************************************
    // Construction/instantiation to enable scaling to take place
    Scale scale = new Scale();

    //Scale: Setting the horizontal and vertical amplification.
    scale.setX(2);
    scale.setY(0.5);
    scale.setPivotX(0);
    scale.setPivotY(0);

    //Adding scaling to circle2, rect3,  rect4
    circle2.getTransforms().addAll(scale);
    rect3.getTransforms().addAll(scale);
    rect4.getTransforms().addAll(scale);

    Group root = new Group(circle1,circle2, rect1, rect2, rect3, rect4);
    Scene scene = new Scene(root, 660, 380);
    stage.setTitle("Scaling transformation (X*2, Y*0.5");
    stage.setScene(scene);
    stage.show();
  }
}
```

# Shear

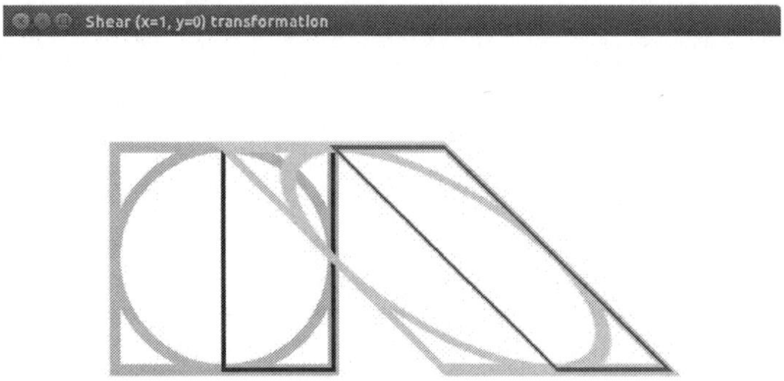


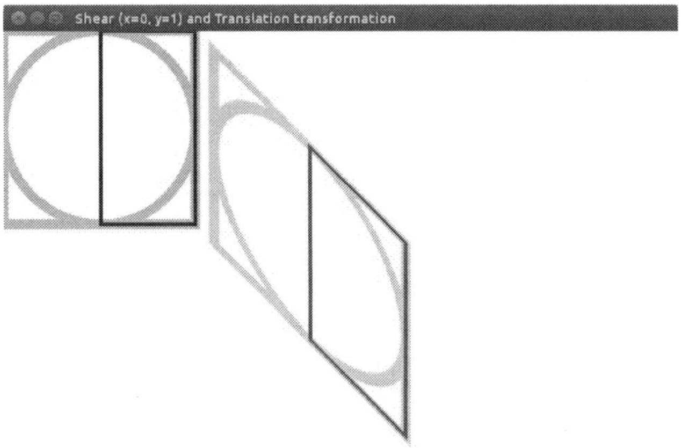


```
// Shear1.java
/*
shear( shear_x,  shear_y):
Shear the object by shear_x  in the horizontal and shear_y  in the vertical.

shear( shear_x,  shear_y,  pivotX,  pivotY):
Shear the object by shear_x   and shear_y   about the given pivot point.

Tested on: java version "java-8-oracle"
Author: Mike Ohlson de Fine.
*/

import javafx.application.Application;
import javafx.stage.Stage;
```

```
import javafx.scene.Group;
import javafx.scene.Scene;
import javafx.scene.paint.Color;
import javafx.scene.shape.Circle;
import javafx.scene.shape.Rectangle;
import javafx.scene.transform.Shear; // Shear class

public class Shear1 extends Application {

  public void start(Stage stage) {

    //*************************************************************
    // Shapes used. Three are unchanged.

    Circle circle1 = new Circle(200, 200, 100); // Circle1.
      circle1.setStrokeWidth(10);
      circle1.setStroke(Color.SKYBLUE);
      circle1.setFill(null);

    Rectangle rect1 = new Rectangle(100, 100, 200, 200);  // Rectangle1.
      rect1.setStrokeWidth(10);
      rect1.setStroke(Color.SKYBLUE);
      rect1.setFill(null);

    Rectangle rect2 = new Rectangle(200, 100, 100, 200);  // Rectangle2.
      rect2.setStrokeWidth(4);
      rect2.setStroke(Color.BLUE);
      rect2.setFill(null);

    // Shapes used. Three will be transformed.
    Circle circle2 = new Circle(200, 200, 100); // Circle2.
      circle2.setStrokeWidth(10);
      circle2.setStroke(Color.PALEGREEN);
      circle2.setFill(null);

    Rectangle rect3 = new Rectangle(100, 100, 200, 200);  // Rectangle3.
      rect3.setStrokeWidth(10);
      rect3.setStroke(Color.PALEGREEN);
      rect3.setFill(null);

    Rectangle rect4 = new Rectangle(200, 100, 100, 200);  // Rectangle3.
```

```
        rect4.setStrokeWidth(4);
        rect4.setStroke(Color.GREEN);
        rect4.setFill(null);

    //*************************************************************************
        // Construction/instantiation to enable shear to take place
        Shear shear = new Shear();

        //Shear: Setting the horizontal and vertical shear distortion.
        shear.setX(1.0);
        shear.setY(0.0);
        shear.setPivotX(0);
        shear.setPivotY(0);

        //Adding shear to circle2, rect3,  rect4
        circle2.getTransforms().addAll(shear);
        rect3.getTransforms().addAll(shear);
        rect4.getTransforms().addAll(shear);


        Group root = new Group(circle1,circle2, rect1, rect2, rect3, rect4);
        Scene scene = new Scene(root, 700, 400);
        stage.setTitle("Shear (x=1, y=0) transformation");
        stage.setScene(scene);
        stage.show();
    }
}
```

# Combined Transforms

## Rotation first then Translation

```
// RotationTranslation1.java
/*
First rotate the objects, then translate them

Tested on: java version "java-8-oracle"
Author: Mike Ohlson de Fine.
*/

import javafx.application.Application;
```

```
import javafx.stage.Stage;
import javafx.scene.Group;
import javafx.scene.Scene;
import javafx.scene.paint.Color;
import javafx.scene.shape.Circle;
import javafx.scene.shape.Rectangle;
import javafx.scene.transform.Translate; // Translation class.
import javafx.scene.transform.Rotate;     // Rotation class.

public class RotationTranslation1 extends Application {

  public void start(Stage stage) {

    //*****************************************************************
    // Shapes used. Three are unchanged.
    Circle circle1 = new Circle(100, 100, 100); // Circle1, unchanged.
      circle1.setStrokeWidth(10);
      circle1.setStroke(Color.SKYBLUE);
      circle1.setFill(null);

    Rectangle rect1 = new Rectangle(0, 0, 200, 200);  // Rectangle1,
unchanged.
      rect1.setStrokeWidth(10);
      rect1.setStroke(Color.SKYBLUE);
      rect1.setFill(null);

    Rectangle rect2 = new Rectangle(100, 0, 100, 200);  // Rectangle2,
unchanged.
      rect2.setStrokeWidth(4);
      rect2.setStroke(Color.BLUE);
      rect2.setFill(null);

    // Shapes used. Three are transformed.
    Rectangle rect3 = new Rectangle(0, 0, 200, 200);  // Rectangle3,
transformed.
      rect3.setStrokeWidth(10);
      rect3.setStroke(Color.PALEGREEN);
      rect3.setFill(null);

    Rectangle rect4 = new Rectangle(100, 0, 100, 200);  // Rectangle3,
transformed.
```

```
rect4.setStrokeWidth(4);
 rect4.setStroke(Color.GREEN);
 rect4.setFill(null);

Circle circle2 = new Circle(100, 100, 100); // Circle2, transformed.
 circle2.setStrokeWidth(10);
 circle2.setStroke(Color.PALEGREEN);
 circle2.setFill(null);
//*****************************************************************
 // Construction/instantiation to enable translation to take place
 Translate translate = new Translate();
 Rotate rotate = new Rotate();

 //Translation set up (not execution): Set the X,Y coordinates.
 translate.setX(220);
 translate.setY(120);

 //Rotation: set up (not execution): Set the angle of rotation.
 rotate.setAngle(40);

 /* SEQUENCE OF TRANSFORM EXECUTION:
   first rotate then  transate.
   The actual execution of the transform occurs when the
   instruction "nodeN.getTransforms().addAll(rotate);"
   is executed.
 */

//FIRST: Execute rotation to circle2, rect3,  rect4
 circle2.getTransforms().addAll(rotate);
 rect3.getTransforms().addAll(rotate);
 rect4.getTransforms().addAll(rotate);
 //SECOND: Executing the translation on circle2, rect3,  rect4
 circle2.getTransforms().addAll(translate);
 rect3.getTransforms().addAll(translate);
 rect4.getTransforms().addAll(translate);

 Group root = new Group(circle1,circle2, rect1, rect2, rect3, rect4);
 Scene scene = new Scene(root, 460, 460);
 stage.setTitle("Rotation followed by Translation transformation");
 stage.setScene(scene);
```

```
    stage.show();
  }
}
```

## Translation first then Rotation

```
// TranslationRotation1.java
/*
First transate the objects, then rotate them

Tested on: java version "java-8-oracle"
Author: Mike Ohlson de Fine.
*/

import javafx.application.Application;
import javafx.stage.Stage;
import javafx.scene.Group;
import javafx.scene.Scene;
import javafx.scene.paint.Color;
import javafx.scene.shape.Circle;
import javafx.scene.shape.Rectangle;
import javafx.scene.transform.Translate; // Translation class.
import javafx.scene.transform.Rotate;      // Rotation class.

public class RotationTranslation1 extends Application {

  public void start(Stage stage) {

    //***********************************************************
    // Shapes used. Three are unchanged.
    Circle circle1 = new Circle(100, 100, 100); // Circle1, unchanged.
     circle1.setStrokeWidth(10);
     circle1.setStroke(Color.SKYBLUE);
     circle1.setFill(null);

    Rectangle rect1 = new Rectangle(0, 0, 200, 200);  // Rectangle1,
unchanged.
     rect1.setStrokeWidth(10);
```

```
    rect1.setStroke(Color.SKYBLUE);
    rect1.setFill(null);

  Rectangle rect2 = new Rectangle(100, 0, 100, 200);  // Rectangle2,
unchanged.
    rect2.setStrokeWidth(4);
    rect2.setStroke(Color.BLUE);
    rect2.setFill(null);

  // Shapes used. Three are transformed.
  Rectangle rect3 = new Rectangle(0, 0, 200, 200);  // Rectangle3,
transformed.
    rect3.setStrokeWidth(10);
    rect3.setStroke(Color.PALEGREEN);
    rect3.setFill(null);

  Rectangle rect4 = new Rectangle(100, 0, 100, 200);  // Rectangle3,
transformed.
    rect4.setStrokeWidth(4);
    rect4.setStroke(Color.GREEN);
    rect4.setFill(null);

  Circle circle2 = new Circle(100, 100, 100); // Circle2, transformed.
    circle2.setStrokeWidth(10);
    circle2.setStroke(Color.PALEGREEN);
    circle2.setFill(null);
  //***********************************************************
    // Construction/instantiation to enable translation to take place

   Translate translate = new Translate();
   Rotate rotate = new Rotate();

    //Translation set up (not execution): Set the X,Y coordinates.
   translate.setX(220);
   translate.setY(120);

    //Rotation: set up (not execution): Set the angle of rotation.
   rotate.setAngle(40);
```

```
    /* SEQUENCE OF TRANSFORM EXECUTION:
      first translate then rotate.
      The actual execution of the transform occurs when the
      instruction "nodeN.getTransforms().addAll(rotate);"
      is executed.
    */

    //FIRST: Executing the translation on circle2, rect3,  rect4
    circle2.getTransforms().addAll(translate);
    rect3.getTransforms().addAll(translate);
    rect4.getTransforms().addAll(translate);
    //SECOND: Execute rotation to circle2, rect3,  rect4
    circle2.getTransforms().addAll(rotate);
    rect3.getTransforms().addAll(rotate);
    rect4.getTransforms().addAll(rotate);


    Group root = new Group(circle1,circle2, rect1, rect2, rect3, rect4);
    Scene scene = new Scene(root, 460, 460);
    stage.setTitle("Translation followed by Translation
transformation");
    stage.setScene(scene);
    stage.show();
  }
}
```

## Using ALTERNATIVE Methods to perform transforms.(Bare-metal, from scratch, code)

If we need to have greater control over portions of drawings then we need to be able to apply different transformations to separate portions of a complex drawing.

It is not excessively difficult to perform transforms on arrays of coordinated such as those resulting from the creation of complex drawings using a Scaled Vector Graphics tool like Inkscape as was explored in chapter 12.

The problem with large intricate drawings is that the lists of coordinates defining each position and curve in the drawing, become large and unwieldy. The transform methods and the large data lists should be kept separate. We will separate the data (coordinates) and the methods for manipulating the resulting drawings into separate classes in the same way as was done at the end of chapter 4.

The code shown below was created without reference to any Java transform libraries.

Is is presented mainly as an illustration of how very complex graphical structures can be conveniently and code-efficiently manipulated as lists of coordinates.

The complete "Le Chat Noir" drawing is a collection of 42 cubic Bezier paths. The whole drawing is handled as a three dimensional array:

```
double[][][] all_pps = { chat_cube1, chat_cube1b,
chat_cube2, chat_cube3, chat_cube4,
chat_cube5,chat_cube6, chat_cube7, chat_cube8,
chat_cube9,chat_cube10, chat_cube11, chat_cube12,
chat_cube13,chat_cube14, chat_cube15, chat_cube16,
chat_cube17,chat_cube18, chat_cube19, chat_cube20,
chat_cube21,chat_cube22, chat_cube23, chat_cube24,
chat_cube25,chat_cube26, chat_cube27, chat_cube28,
chat_cube29,chat_cube30, chat_cube31, chat_cube32,
chat_cube33,chat_cube34, chat_cube35, chat_cube36,
chat_cube37,chat_cube38, chat_cube39, chat_cube40,
chat_cube41
 };
```

Where each element such as *chat_cube1* is a two dimensional array like:

*double[][] chat_cube1 = {{47.71,35.65, 48.16,34.5, 49.93,33.79}, {51.7,33.08,53.08,33.4,54.94,32.27}, .... ,{47.59,35.49,47.71,35.65,47.71,35.65}};*

The start of each cubic Bezier path is defined as a MoveTo(...) path element and is extracted from the first (x,y) coordinates of the first CubicTo(...) element of each path using the the method *make_moveto(...)* shown below:

```
MoveTo make_moveto(double[] path_point_line0)
      { /* Purpose: Construct the appropriate MoveTo object from the first
Bezier point
          (from a SVG file) for assembly into a JavaFX Cubic path using
Points2paths(...).

        Applies to : One path - the raw cubic bezier points that will be used to
construct
                    all the CubicCurveTos that make up the sequence of drawn
CubicCurveTo parts.
        The Output: The starting position MoveTo for a path.
        */
        double XX = path_point_line0[0] ;
        double YY = path_point_line0[1] ;
        MoveTo moveTo_out = new MoveTo(XX, YY);
        return moveTo_out ;
      }
```

The transform methods are given below.

# Scaling Alt (enlarging or shrinking)

```
double[][] Scale_big_small(double[][] path_points, double scaleX, double
scaleY)
  {
    /* Purpose: Scale (increase / decrease) the size of a shape.
      Applies to : One path - the raw points preceding CubicCurveTos that
               make up the sequence of drawn CubicCurveTo parts.
      The Output: A scaled path.
      Note. The array "pts_temp" is necessary to sever the link to cnd.all_pps.
          The logical reason is not clear but empirically is has been found
          to be necessary.
    */

    int num_cctos = Array.getLength(path_points) ; // Number of
CubicCurveTos making up the path.
    double[][] pts_temp =  new double[num_cctos][6];
   for (int j=0; j< num_cctos ; j++)
   {
      pts_temp[j][0] = path_points[j][0]*scaleX;
      pts_temp[j][1] = path_points[j][1]*scaleY;
      pts_temp[j][2] = path_points[j][2]*scaleX;
      pts_temp[j][3] = path_points[j][3]*scaleY;
      pts_temp[j][4] = path_points[j][4]*scaleX;
      pts_temp[j][5] = path_points[j][5]*scaleY;
   };
   return pts_temp ;
  }
```

# Translation Alt (shifting)

```
double[][] Shift_translate(double[][] path_points,double shiftX, double shiftY)
  {
    /* Purpose: Translate a shape by the amount (shiftX, shiftY).
      Applies to : One path - the raw points preceding CubicCurveTos that
               make up the sequence of drawn CubicCurveTo parts.
      The Output: A shifted path.
    */
```

```
    int num_cctos = Array.getLength(path_points) ; / / Number of
CubicCurveTos making up the path.

   for (int j=0; j< num_cctos ; j++)
   {
      path_points[j][0] = path_points[j][0] + shiftX ;
      path_points[j][1] = path_points[j][1] + shiftY ;
      path_points[j][2] = path_points[j][2] + shiftX ;
      path_points[j][3] = path_points[j][3] + shiftY ;
      path_points[j][4] = path_points[j][4] + shiftX ;
      path_points[j][5] = path_points[j][5] + shiftY ;
   };
   return path_points ;
  }
```

# Rotation Alt

```
double[][] Rotate_aboutXY(double[][] path_points,  double centerX, double
centerY, double alphadeg)
  {
    /* Purpose: Rotate a raw path precursor about a selected center of
rotation.
        Applies to : One path - the raw points preceding CubicCurveTos
```

```
            that make up the sequence of drawn CubicCurveTo parts.
   The Output: A path rotationally transformed around (centerX, centerY).
 */

 int num_cctos = Array.getLength(path_points) ; // Number of
CubicCurveTos making up the path.

 double hypotenuse ;
 double X1, Y1, X2, Y2, X3, Y3;
 double alpharad = alphadeg*Math.PI/180.;
 double current_angl ; // Polar coordinate angle relative to center of
rotation.

 for (int j=0; j< num_cctos ;j++)
 {
    // Note: Java angles must be in radians.
    X1 = (path_points[j][0] - centerX) ;
    Y1 = (path_points[j][1] - centerY) ;
    current_angl = Math.atan2(Y1,X1);
    current_angl =  alpharad + current_angl ;
    hypotenuse =Math.sqrt(X1*X1 + Y1*Y1 ) ;
    path_points[j][0] = centerX + hypotenuse * Math.cos(current_angl)  ;
    path_points[j][1] = centerY + hypotenuse * Math.sin(current_angl)  ;

    X2 = (path_points[j][2] - centerX) ;
    Y2 = (path_points[j][3] - centerY) ;
    current_angl = Math.atan2(Y2,X2);
    current_angl =  alpharad +current_angl ;
    hypotenuse =Math.sqrt(X2*X2 + Y2*Y2 ) ;
    path_points[j][2] = centerX + hypotenuse * Math.cos(current_angl)  ;
    path_points[j][3] = centerY + hypotenuse * Math.sin(current_angl)  ;

    X3 = (path_points[j][4] - centerX) ;
    Y3 = (path_points[j][5] - centerY) ;
    current_angl = Math.atan2(Y3,X3);
    current_angl =  alpharad +current_angl ;
    hypotenuse =Math.sqrt(X3*X3 + Y3*Y3 ) ;
    path_points[j][4] = centerX + hypotenuse * Math.cos(current_angl)  ;
    path_points[j][5] = centerY + hypotenuse * Math.sin(current_angl)  ;

 };
```

```
   return path_points ;
  }
```

# Shearing Alt

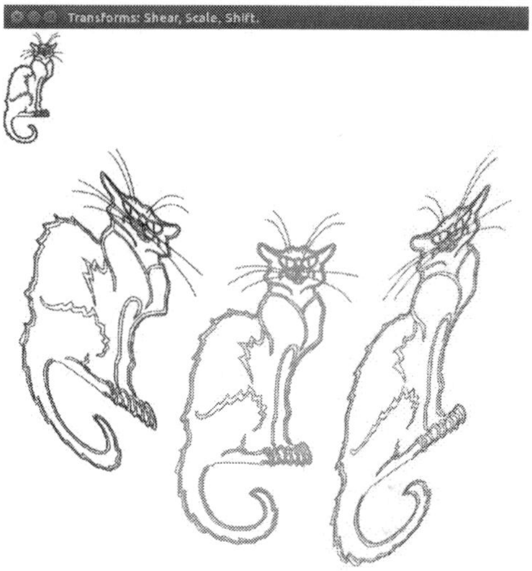


```
double[][] Shear_XY(double[][] path_points,double[] minmaxspan, double
shearX, double shearY)
  {
   /* Purpose: Shear or skew distort a shape.
     Applies to : One path - the raw points preceding CubicCurveTos that
                make up the sequence of drawn CubicCurveTo parts.
     The Output: A skewed path.
   */
   double minx = minmaxspan[0] ;
   double maxx = minmaxspan[1] ;
   double spanx = minmaxspan[2] ;
   double miny = minmaxspan[3] ;
   double maxy = minmaxspan[4] ;
   double spany = minmaxspan[5] ;

  {
     int num_cctos = Array.getLength(path_points) ; // Number of
CubicCurveTos making up the path.

     for (int j=0; j< num_cctos ; j++)
     {
```

```
            path_points[j][0] = path_points[j][0] + shearX * (path_points[j][1]-
miny) / spany ;
            path_points[j][1] = path_points[j][1] + shearY * (path_points[j][0]-
minx) / spanx ;

            path_points[j][2] = path_points[j][2] + shearX * (path_points[j][3]-
miny) / spany ;
            path_points[j][3] = path_points[j][3] + shearY * (path_points[j][2]-
minx) / spanx ;

            path_points[j][4] = path_points[j][4] + shearX * (path_points[j][5]-
miny) / spany ;
            path_points[j][5] = path_points[j][5] + shearY * (path_points[j][4]-
minx) / spanx ;

        };
    }
    return path_points ;
   }
```

When applying shear to a complex collection of lines it is vital to apply exactly the correct amount of shear to each path. To do this there is a need to get the coordinates of the bounding box of the entire drawing. The bounding box that box into which the drawing will fit exactly. The method which achieves this is:

```
double[] get_national_min_max_span(double[][][] all_path_points)
   {      /*  Purpose: Obtain the minimum and maximum coordinate positions,
width and height
                 of the raw precursor of a cubic path.
          Applies to : One path - the raw points preceding CubicCurveTos that
make up
                    the sequence of drawn CubicCurveTo parts.
          The Output: The center of the bounding box of the shape.
     */

     double minX = 0.;
     double maxX = 0.;
     double minY = 0.;
     double maxY = 0.;
```

```
    int num_paths = Array.getLength(all_path_points) ; // Number of paths
for the entire drawing.

    for (int i=0; i< num_paths ; i++)
    {
      int num_cctos = Array.getLength(all_path_points[i]) ; // Number of
CubicCurveTos making a particular path Selected by index i.
      for (int j=0; j< num_cctos ; j++)
      {
        // We inspect X at index [4] and Y at [5] doing max and min extration
on each point to
        //   discover the bounding box for the figure.
        minX = Math.min(minX, all_path_points[i][j][4])  ;
        maxX = Math.max(maxX, all_path_points[i][j][4])  ;

        minY = Math.min(minY, all_path_points[i][j][5])  ;
        maxY = Math.max(maxY, all_path_points[i][j][5])  ;
      };
    };
    double spanX = maxX - minX ; // The width.
    double spanY = maxY - minY ; // The height.
    double[] minmaxspanXY =  { minX, maxX, spanX, minY,  maxY , spanY} ;
    return minmaxspanXY;
  }
```

# Flip Horizontal Alt

```
double[][] Flip_Horizontal(double[][] path_points, double flipX)
  {
    /* Purpose: Flip horizontally a set of curves about the center of the figure.
      Applies to : One path - the raw points preceding CubicCurveTos that
                make up the sequence of drawn CubicCurveTo parts.
      The Output: A horizontal flip of all points about the centroid.
    */
    int num_cctos = Array.getLength(path_points) ; // Number of
CubicCurveTos making up the path.

   for (int j=0; j< num_cctos ; j++)
   {
      path_points[j][0] = 2*flipX - path_points[j][0] ;
      path_points[j][1] = path_points[j][1]  ;
      path_points[j][2] = 2*flipX - path_points[j][2] ;
      path_points[j][3] = path_points[j][3]  ;
      path_points[j][4] = 2*flipX - path_points[j][4] ;  ;
      path_points[j][5] = path_points[j][5]  ;
   };
   return path_points ;
  }
```

# Flip Vertical Alt

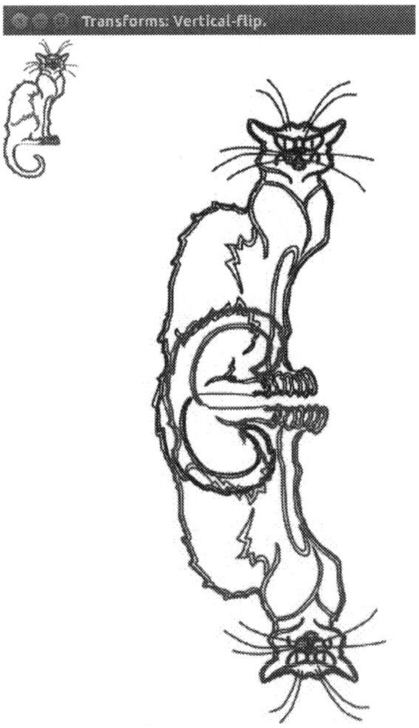

```
double[][] Flip_Vertical(double[][] path_points, double flipY)
  {

    /* Purpose: Flip vertically a set of curves (upside down) about the center of
the figure.
       Applies to : One path - the raw points preceding CubicCurveTos that
                  make up the sequence of drawn CubicCurveTo parts.
       The Output: A Vertical flip of all points about the centroid.
    */
    int num_cctos = Array.getLength(path_points) ; // Number of
CubicCurveTos making up the path.

   for (int j=0; j< num_cctos ;j++)
   {
      path_points[j][0] = path_points[j][0]  ;
      path_points[j][1] =  2*flipY - path_points[j][1]  ;
      path_points[j][2] = path_points[j][2]  ;
      path_points[j][3] = 2*flipY - path_points[j][3]  ;
      path_points[j][4] = path_points[j][4]  ;
      path_points[j][5] =  2*flipY - path_points[j][5]  ;

   };
   return path_points ;
  }
```

## Assembly Instructions

Assembling these transform functions into an application and testing each in turn we could have:

```
// CubicBezier_chatnoir_transforms_1.java
/*
The Collections of cubic Bezier positions is contained in "chat_noir_dwg.java"
which has been compiled separately as a class in the same package.

The linear transforms of scaling, translation, rotation, skew,
veretical and horizontal flipping are demonstrated here.

Tested on: java version "java-8-oracle"
Author: Mike Ohlson de Fine
```

```
*/

import javafx.application.Application;
import javafx.stage.Stage;
import javafx.scene.*;
import javafx.scene.paint.*;
import javafx.scene.shape.*; // Graphic primitives library.
import java.lang.reflect.Array;
import java.lang.Math;

//+++++++++++++++++++++++++++++++++++++++++++++++++++++++++
public class CubicBezier_chatnoir_transforms_1 extends Application

{
   chat_noir_dwg cnd = new chat_noir_dwg() ; // Instantiate drawing from
"chat_noir_dwg.class".

   Path Points2paths(double[][] path_points, MoveTo  selected_moveTo,
double Stroke_width, Color kula)
   {...}
//=======================================================
   double[][] Scale_big_small(double[][] path_points, double scaleX, double
scaleY)
   {...}
//=======================================================
   double[][] Shift_translate(double[][] path_points,double shiftX, double
shiftY)
   { ...}
//=======================================================
   double[][] Shear_XY(double[][] path_points,double[] minmaxspan, double
shearX, double shearY)
   { ...}
//=======================================================
   double[][] Flip_Horizontal(double[][] path_points, double flipX)
   {...}
//=======================================================
   double[][] Flip_Vertical(double[][] path_points, double flipY)
   {... }
//=======================================================
   double[][] Rotate_aboutXY(double[][] path_points,  double centerX, double
centerY, double alphadeg)
```

```
   {...}
//===========================================================
  double[] get_national_min_max_span(double[][][] all_path_points)
   {...}
//===========================================================
  MoveTo make_moveto(double[] path_point_line0)
     { ...}
//===========================================================
   // Main executuion.
   public void start(Stage primaryStage)
   {
      Group rootgroup = new Group();

     chat_noir_dwg cnd = new chat_noir_dwg() ;
     Path line_path;
     double[][] cube_points;
     MoveTo moveTo1 = new MoveTo();

     int num_paths = Array.getLength(cnd.all_pps) ; // Number of paths.

     /* Test drive each method.
       Blocks of stand alone code are commented out.
       Remove "/*" and "*/" block-comment instructions to test a
       particular block.
     */

     // No Transform applied.
     for (int i=0; i<num_paths ; i++)
     {
         // Draw the Unmodified before any transforms are applied.
         moveTo1 = make_moveto(cnd.all_pps[i][0]);
         line_path =  Points2paths(cnd.all_pps[i], moveTo1, 1, Color.color(0.2,
0.2, 0.2)); // Charcoal
         //rootgroup.getChildren().addAll( line_path);
     }

      // Enlarge and shift.
     for (int j=0; j<num_paths ; j++)
     {
         // Enlarge transform (scaling).
     cube_points = Scale_big_small(cnd.all_pps[j], 3, 3); // Scaled up by 3
```

```
    cube_points = Shift_translate(cube_points, 140, 30);

    moveTo1 = make_moveto(cube_points[0]);
    line_path =  Points2paths(cube_points, moveTo1, 2, Color.color(0.0, 0.0,
0.6)); // Blue
    rootgroup.getChildren().addAll( line_path);
   }

   /*
   // Rotate and shift.
   for (int j=0; j<num_paths ; j++)
   {
        // Enlarge  and rotate transforms.
    cube_points = Scale_big_small(cnd.all_pps[j], 4, 4); // Scaled up by 4.
    cube_points = Rotate_aboutXY(cube_points,  50, 50, 15.); // rotate by 15
degrees.
    cube_points = Shift_translate(cube_points, 300, 50);

    moveTo1 = make_moveto(cube_points[0]);
    line_path =  Points2paths(cube_points, moveTo1, 1, Color.color(0.6, 0.0,
0.0)); // Red
    rootgroup.getChildren().addAll( line_path);
   }
   */

   /*
   // Get the bounding box and spans of the entire drawing.
   // minmaxspanXY =  { minX, maxX, spanX, minY,  maxY , spanY} ;
   double[] minmaxspan = get_national_min_max_span( cnd.all_pps);
   double minx  = minmaxspan[0] ;
   double maxx  = minmaxspan[1] ;
   double spanx = minmaxspan[2] ;
   double miny  = minmaxspan[3] ;
   double maxy  = minmaxspan[4] ;
   double spany = minmaxspan[5] ;

   // For reassurance.
   System.out.println("minX: "+minmaxspan[0]);
   System.out.println("maxX: "+minmaxspan[1]);
   System.out.println("spanX: "+minmaxspan[2]);
   System.out.println("minY: "+minmaxspan[3]);
```

```
    System.out.println("maxY: "+minmaxspan[4]);
    System.out.println("spanY: "+minmaxspan[5]);

    double centerX = (minx + maxx)/2. ;
    double centerY = (miny + maxy)/2. ;


    // Shear-right horizontal and shift.
    for (int j=0; j<num_paths ; j++)
    {
     cube_points = Scale_big_small(cnd.all_pps[j], 3, 3); // Scaled up by 3.
     cube_points = Shear_XY(cube_points, minmaxspan, -100., 0.);// Negative
-> shear right.
     cube_points = Shift_translate(cube_points, 500, 50);
     moveTo1 = make_moveto(cube_points[0]);
     line_path = Points2paths(cube_points, moveTo1, 1, Color.color(0.0, 0.6,
0.0));// Green
     rootgroup.getChildren().addAll( line_path);
    }
    */

    /*
    // Shear-left horizontal and shift.
    for (int j=0; j<num_paths ; j++)
    {
     cube_points = Scale_big_small(cnd.all_pps[j], 3, 3); // Scaled up by 3..
     cube_points = Shear_XY(cube_points, minmaxspan, 100., 0.);// Positive
-> shear right.
     cube_points = Shift_translate(cube_points, 50, 50);
     moveTo1 = make_moveto(cube_points[0]);
     line_path = Points2paths(cube_points, moveTo1, 1, Color.color(0.0, 0.0,
0.6)); // Blue
     rootgroup.getChildren().addAll( line_path);
    }
    */

    /*
    // Shear-right vertical and shift.
    for (int j=0; j<num_paths ; j++)
    {
     cube_points = Scale_big_small(cnd.all_pps[j], 3, 3); // Scaled up by 3.
```

```
    cube_points = Shear_XY(cube_points, minmaxspan, 0., -50.); // Negative
-> shear right-up.
    cube_points = Shift_translate(cube_points, 380, 260);
    moveTo1 = make_moveto(cube_points[0]);
    line_path = Points2paths(cube_points, moveTo1, 1, Color.color(0.0, 0.6,
0.0)); // Green
    rootgroup.getChildren().addAll( line_path);
   }
   */

   /*
   // Shear-left vertical and shift.
   for (int j=0; j<num_paths ; j++)
   {
    cube_points = Scale_big_small(cnd.all_pps[j], 3, 3); // Scaled up by 3.
    cube_points = Shear_XY(cube_points, minmaxspan, 0., 50.); // Positive
-> shear right-down.
    cube_points = Shift_translate(cube_points, 20, 50);
    moveTo1 = make_moveto(cube_points[0]);
    line_path = Points2paths(cube_points, moveTo1, 1, Color.color(0.0, 0.0,
0.6)); // Blue
    rootgroup.getChildren().addAll( line_path);
   }
    */


   /*
   // Flip vertical.
   for (int j=0; j<num_paths ; j++)
   {
    cube_points = Scale_big_small(cnd.all_pps[j], 3, 3); // Scaled up by  3.
    cube_points = Flip_Vertical(cube_points, centerY);
    cube_points = Shift_translate(cube_points, 150, 520);
    moveTo1 = make_moveto(cube_points[0]);
    line_path = Points2paths(cube_points, moveTo1, 2, Color.color(0.6, 0.0,
0.0)); // Blue
    rootgroup.getChildren().addAll( line_path);
   }
   */
   // Flip horizontal.
   for (int j=0; j<num_paths ; j++)
```

```
    {
     cube_points = Scale_big_small(cnd.all_pps[j], 3, 3); // Scaled up by 3.
     cube_points = Flip_Horizontal(cube_points, centerY);
     cube_points = Shift_translate(cube_points, 150, 30);
     moveTo1 = make_moveto(cube_points[0]);
     line_path =  Points2paths(cube_points, moveTo1, 2, Color.color(0.6, 0.0, 
0.0));// Red
     rootgroup.getChildren().addAll( line_path);
    }

      Scene scene = new Scene(rootgroup, 900, 900);
      primaryStage.setTitle("Transforms: Rotation, scaling and shift.");
      primaryStage.setScene(scene);
      primaryStage.show();
  }
}
```

# The END,

of this book but not the series.

*This is the first book in a planned series on Java Graphics for Games. The source code for the Java programs used in this book are freely available at GitHub at https://github.com under the username mikeodf. The programs are contained in suitably named folders. The folder for this book is **JavaFX_Line_Shape_Color**. The code is open source – take it and use it. Derive an income from it if you wish. Do not stop others doing the same. You may not copyright it. Acknowledge the source if you are honest and ethical.*

*Criticism and suggestions for improvements will be welcomed at mike.ohlsondefine@gmail.com*

*The titles in the series will be:*

*Java Graphics for Games 1: JavaFX Line, Shape and Color.*

*Java Graphics for Games 2: JavaFX Animation.*

*Java Graphics for Games 3: JavaFX Working In 3 Dimensions.*

*Java Graphics for Games 4: JavaFX Game Elements.*

# ABOUT THE AUTHOR

Mike Ohlson de Fine is a graduate Electrical Engineer specializing in industrial process measurement and control. He has a Diploma in Electronics and Instrumentation from Technikon Witwatersrand, an Electrical Engineering degree from the University of Cape Town, and a Masters in Automatic Control from Rand Afrikaans University (now re-named the University of Johannesburg). He has worked for mining and mineral extraction companies for the last 30 years. His first encounter with computers was learning Fortran 4 using punched cards on an IBM 360 as an undergraduate. Since then he has experimented with Pascal, Forth, Intel 8080 Assembler, MS Basic, C, C++, Python and Java. As a working engineer solving industrial process control problems he needed tools that facilitated the understanding and solution of these problems using simulations and computer models of real processes. Modern Computer Games are simulations and the tools that build games can also be used create meaningful engineering simulations.  He is now an author of books on Java and Python programming for simulation in games and engineering processes. He is an advocate of Free and Open Source software. He relaxes by hiking the foothills of the lovely Rivierzonderend mountains in a little village where he lives.

# Alphabetical Index

Made in United States
Orlando, FL
04 November 2026

90202663R00337